BAROQUE

First operas	**1600**	Shakespeare, *Hamlet*
Weelkes, *As Vesta Was . . .*	**1601**	Kepler, astronomy
Carissimi, b.	**1605**	Tsar Boris Godunov, d.
Monteverdi, *Orfeo*	**1607**	Jamestown founded
Praetorius collected hymns	**1610**	King James Bible
Gabrieli, *Canzona*	**1615**	
	1620	Pilgrims at Plymouth Rock
Lully, b.	**1632**	John Locke, b.
Venice public opera house	**1637**	
Monteverdi, *Poppea*	**1642**	Gabrieli, d.
	1643	Louis XIV King of France
Charpentier, b.	**1645**	
Corelli, b.	**1653**	
A. Scarlatti, b.	**1660**	
	1667	Milton, *Paradise Lost*
Couperin, b.	**1668**	
Rameau, b.	**1683**	Peace treaty with Indians
D. Scarlatti, b.	**1685**	Edict of Nantes revoked
Purcell, *Dido and Aeneas*	**1689**	
Pachelbel, *Canon in D*	**c.1690**	
Bach, *Toccata in D Minor*	**1705**	
Gluck, b.; C.P.E. Bach, b.	**1714**	Fahrenheit thermometer
Handel, *Water Music*	**1717**	
	1719	Pompeii rediscovered
Bach, *Brandenburg Concertos*	**1721**	
Telemann "No" to St. Thomas's	**1723**	
Handel, *Julius Caesar*	**1724**	
Vivaldi, *Four Seasons*	**1725**	
	1726	Swift, *Gulliver's Travels*
John Gay, *Beggar's Opera*	**1728**	
Bach, *St. Matthew Passion*	**1729**	
Bach, *Cantata No. 140*	**1731**	
J. C. Bach, b.	**1735**	Hogarth, *A Rake's Progress*
Handel, *Messiah*	**1742**	
William Billings, b.	**1746**	
Bach, *B-Minor Mass* assembled	**1749**	
Handel, *Royal Fireworks*	**1749**	

CLASSIC

Haydn, *Symphony No. 1*	**1759**	Voltaire, *Candide*
Mozart (age 8), *Symphony No. 1*	**1764**	Winckelmann, Art history
	c.1770	Factory system
Burney, Music History	**1776**	American Independence
Mozart, Last three symphonies	**1788**	
	1789	French Revolution
Mozart, *Piano Concerto, No. 27*	**1791**	*Bill of Rights*
Mozart, *Magic Flute*	**1791**	
Haydn, *Symphony No. 94*	**1791**	
Rossini, b.	**1792**	
	1793	Eli Whitney, cotton gin
Haydn, *Quartet in C* (Emperor)	**1797**	
Donizetti, b.	**1797**	
Haydn, *The Creation*	**1798**	
Beethoven, *Sonata* (Pathétique)	**1799**	Rosetta Stone
Bellini, b.	**1801**	
	1804	Napoleon crowned Emperor
Beethoven, *Symphony No. 5*	**1808**	Goethe, *Faust,* Part I
Schubert, *Erlkönig*	**1815**	Battle of Waterloo
Schubert, *Die Forelle*	**1817**	Erie Canal begun
Gounod, b.	**1818**	Karl Marx, b.
Franck, b.	**1822**	Congress of Vienna
Beethoven, *Symphony No. 9*	**1824**	
Bruckner, b.	**1824**	Lord Byron, d.

Continued

Guided Listening

Guided Listening
A Textbook for Music Appreciation

Eleanor Ray Hammer
Los Angeles Valley College

Malcolm S. Cole
University of California at Los Angeles

 Wm. C. Brown Publishers

Book Team

Editor *Meredith M. Morgan*
Production Editor *Diane Clemens*
Visuals/Design Freelance Specialist *Barbara J. Hodgson*
Photo Editor *Carrie Burger*
Visuals Processor *Andréa Lopez-Meyer*
Visuals/Design Consultant *Marilyn A. Phelps*

Wm. C. Brown Publishers

President *G. Franklin Lewis*
Vice President, Publisher *Thomas E. Doran*
Vice President, Operations and Production *Beverly Kolz*
National Sales Manager *Virginia S. Moffat*
Group Sales Manager *Eric Ziegler*
Executive Editor *Edgar J. Laube*
Director of Marketing *Kathy Law Laube*
Marketing Manager *Kathleen Nietzke*
Managing Editor, Production *Colleen A. Yonda*
Manager of Visuals and Design *Faye M. Schilling*
Production Editorial Manager *Julie A. Kennedy*
Production Editorial Manager *Ann Fuerste*
Publishing Services Manager *Karen J. Slaght*

WCB Group

President and Chief Executive Officer *Mark C. Falb*
Chairman of the Board *Wm. C. Brown*

Cover image © Comstock Incorporated

Design interior and cover by Benoit & Associates

Copyeditor Nikki S. Herbst

The credits section for this book begins on page 493, and is considered
an extension of the copyright page.

Printed in the United States of America by Wm. C. Brown Publishers,
2460 Kerper Boulevard, Dubuque, IA 52001

10 9 8 7 6 5 4 3 2 1

Contents

PART ONE
Fundamental Elements

PART THREE
The Renaissance

PART FOUR
The Baroque

PART FIVE
The Classic Period

PART SIX
The Romantic Period

PART SEVEN
The Twentieth Century

Listening Guides
and Recordings

Listening guide numbers appear in parentheses. Roman numerals indicate movements of complete works. Page references locate the first page of listening guide. CD track numbers are given in brackets. Minute-second timings follow performers' names. A single letter (a-r) refers to Courtesy lines at end.

CONTENTS   **xv**

Preface

This book is planned as a textbook for a college-level course that might bear the title "Music Appreciation" or a more up-to-date label such as "Introduction to Music."

We assume that the duration of the course is less than a full year, whether one semester or two quarters, and that it is designed for the *general* student, not the music major. No prior formal training in music is expected, though a willingness to listen repeatedly to selections studied in class is essential.

When instructors of this course were polled about their primary goal for the class, a majority of those responding stressed music *listening* rather than music *history*. Nonetheless, they preferred to organize the course around style periods treated in chronological order and to include a reasonably generous amount of historical and biographical information. In so doing, they have posed an engrossing challenge for themselves and us: how does one involve students in active listening to a wide range of music in styles that are probably new to them while showing them how a broader context of style-related matters can enhance their listening experiences?

Because we have found that students need help in learning to listen, detailed listening guides are provided as a means of *studying* musical works, as opposed to "sampling" them—or daydreaming while they are played. The guides are descriptions of "what to listen for," to borrow a phrase from the venerable American composer Aaron Copland, whose book *What to Listen for in Music* first appeared in 1939 (reprinted 1988).

Almost every textbook provides either general descriptions or brief outlines—and sometimes both—for the musical works that the authors suggest for study. Our guides put all the information about a work in one place. Most of the guides have been tested in classroom use as they evolved over a twenty-year period. After the instructor plays a work in class, identifying its various sections as they are described in a guide, the average student can follow that guide independently in study of a work outside of class. Ideally, students will purchase their own recording package for repeated listening at their convenience. Many institutions provide listening equipment as part of their library or media center.

Our listening guides stress qualities of sound, for example, tone color changes and silence, that are easy to hear yet often overlooked by writers on music. The guide describing the *Prelude to Carmen* in Chapter 2 is typical of those for instrumental music. Guides for vocal music are structured around the words or the libretto. Minute and second timings, in parentheses, are accurate for the specific performance found in the accompanying recording package.

C

How this Book is Organized

At all levels, we have stressed clarity of organization. Indeed, this preface displays the **A, B, C,** style of outlining we prefer. This technique facilitates references to particular elements of a chapter, as does the division into many relatively short chapters. Most chapters concentrate on one composer because we have found students are more interested in composers as people than they are in abstract ideas such as "Baroque Instrumental Music."

Part One contains brief introductions to those fundamental matters—the characteristics of sound and the elements of music that are traditionally covered at the outset of the course. This is done to establish a basic vocabulary for discussing music. The explanations in Part One are brief, because most of the topics will return in the remaining chapters, which are organized chronologically. Accordingly, instrumental families are merely outlined in this preliminary section; fuller descriptions of the individual instruments accompany their later appearance in the discussions of particular style periods. For example, while the English horn is listed as a member of the orchestra, more information about it is not needed until we reach the Romantic period.

Three kinds of musical examples illustrate the topics covered in Part One: familiar songs (at least we hope that they are familiar, and if not, that they are simple enough to become part of a student's background easily), relevant passages from the *Prelude to Carmen,* and selections drawn from individual chapters of Parts Two through Seven. These are identified in each chapter and set off from the main body of the text. The topics are complete without them, but if "examples" are played, an instructor can give a more complete introduction to what will be covered in the class.

Parts Two through Seven are devoted to historical style periods, from the Middle Ages through the twentieth century, partly because a chrono*logical* organization is "logical," and partly because it is becoming a standard practice to perform older music in "authentic" styles, a topic we cover in Chapter 9. This book, it must be stressed, is not a music history text, which must present a balanced view of all periods. Because today's concert repertoire consists largely of music composed between 1700 and the present, we allot more space to that era than to earlier times. By intentionally omitting a number of topics that are essential for music history students, we can focus more intensely on subjects vital for the aspiring general listener. (Our Instructor's Manual gives suggestions for covering many of these omitted areas, if the instructor so wishes.)

In preliminary chapters to each style period, we sketch the historical background and review the characteristics of sound and the elements of music that formed the core of Part One as they apply to the particular era under discussion. These preliminary chapters furnish reference materials for the entire part they introduce. For each composer chapter, a capsule biography precedes a section in which one particular aspect of the composer's life is highlighted. Admittedly, some of these topics reflect familiar stereotypes—for example, the "surprises" in the music of Haydn—but they should help the student picture these composers as individuals. Then comes the musical portion, beginning with the composer's best-known works, or "greatest hits," such as Brahms's *Lullaby* and Mendelssohn's *Wedding March*. We have found that most students enjoy hearing familiar music, although they could not previously identify the title or composer, because bits of "classical" music appear so frequently in television commercials and in film scores. Typically, the chapter concludes with one or more of that composer's works analyzed in listening guides for study.

Each chapter begins with a "preview" that summarizes its contents in a few sentences. Pronunciation helps are given. Musical terms appear in **bold face** when they are first discussed and defined. The entries in the Glossary/Index were planned to serve as reminders of meanings. If the brief definition found there proves insufficient, the page references should guide further study.

D

The Need for Technical Terms and Notation

Like any field, music has technical terms that must be learned, though our list is as short as we could make it. Some musical terms are potentially confusing because these words appear also in ordinary language, as is the case with "harmony," "orchestrate," "low key," and "crescendo," among others. Such terms receive explanations of their double meanings. The inclusion of music notation sometimes concerns students without musical training. The notation in this book, however, most often shows but a single melody line. It is there to be *followed* as a means of directing attention to a specific musical situation. That is a much simpler task than *reading* it—turning it into sound—as a musician does. Research studies have shown that seeing the musical notation for a melody helps students remember it, even though they do not "read" music.

E

The Music and Composers Represented Here

A number of works, such as Mozart's *Symphony No. 40 in G Minor,* K. 550, or Beethoven's *Symphony No. 5,* are described in this book and in almost every similar text. They are like Shakespeare's *Hamlet:* everyone should know something about these masterpieces in order to be "culturally literate." A similar consensus exists about a limited number of composers, such as the "three B's"—Bach, Beethoven, and Brahms—who must be represented. Regarding the years before 1700 and the twentieth century, no such consensus is likely. Consequently, in these areas we have attempted to present a cross-section that is both representative and, considering length of pieces and availability of scores and recordings, practical. Women's role in music receives attention with inclusion of an electronic piece by Beverly Grigsby and references to the careers of other women composers.

A broad coverage of performing media, genres, and musical forms can be seen in the eighty-five compositions (counting separate movements and individual pieces) that are described in listening guides. One factor influencing their selection was the desire to offer opportunities for comparisons—for example, two songs by Schubert, two movements of a Tchaikovsky symphony. In such pairings, the similarities and the differences are readily apparent. Another factor was the urge to include pieces currently available in new forms of technology, such as videocassettes (particularly valuable in the case of opera), compact discs with video elements, and interactive videodiscs.

Obviously, because textbook space and classroom time are always limited, many areas of music simply had to be omitted along with many composers. Just as no instructor ever really gets "done" in this kind of course, so is its textbook destined to remain incomplete. For further study, we recommend standard references, such as the *Harvard Concise Dictionary of Music,* edited by Don Michael Randel (Harvard University Press, 1978); *The New Harvard Dictionary of Music,* edited by Don Michael Randel (Harvard University Press, 1986); *The New College Encyclopedia of Music,* edited by J. A. Westrup and Frank L. I. Harrison (Norton, 1981); the *Norton/Grove Concise Encyclopedia of Music,* edited by Stanley Sadie (Macmillan, 1988); or the twenty-volume *New Grove Dictionary of Music and Musicians,* edited by Stanley Sadie (Macmillan, 1980).

F

Supplementary Materials Available

A recording package (six compact discs or cassettes) is available from the publishers, containing all the selections described in listening guides. Within the severe limits imposed by contractual agreements, the choice of performers covers a wide range. Some represent a traditional approach; others incorporate the most recent ideas of "authentic" performance. The Instructor's Manual contains a bank of almost 600 test questions available through the Wm. C. Brown TestPak program, expanded content for each chapter except those of Part One for which an outline summary is given, suggested outlines for courses of varying lengths, recommended sources of video materials, and other teaching aids, such as a concert report form.

Acknowledgments

Since 1964, Dr. Hammer's music appreciation students at Los Angeles Valley College have contributed vitally to this book as their successes—and failures—in following the listening guides have governed the many revisions these guides have undergone. Thanks are due to the following for translations, editorial tasks, reading of the manuscripts, advice in suggesting recordings, and preparation of the musical examples: Dennis Bade, Nicole Baker, Joy Baratta, Lee Cronbach, Dr. Robert Fowells, Ed Grossman, F. David Hammer, Steven A. Hammer, Robert Hirsch, Dr. Lorraine Eckhardt Kimball, Prof. Raymond Knapp, the late Robert J. La-Fontaine, the late Dr. Esther Landon, Giselle Schmitz, Melvin Smokler, and Dr. Dan Stehman.

The contributions of prepublication reviewers were substantial. They are:

Zoe Ann Abrahamson
   Buena Vista–Mason City
Richard P. Birkemeier
   California State University–Long Beach
David Eiseman
   Oregon State University
Kenneth Keaton
   Palm Beach Community College
William L. Kellogg
   University of Southern Colorado
Charles S. Larkowski
   Wright State University
Richard J. Perkins
   Anoka-Ramsey Community College
Edwin Schatkowski
   University of PA-Kutztown
Charles Schwartz
   East Carolina State University
Patrick J. Setzer
   Drexel University
William Shepherd
   University of Northern Iowa
Rory M. Thompson
   Louisiana Tech University

Fundamental Elements

LISTENING VERSUS HEARING 1

PREVIEW Learning to appreciate music is dependent upon the ability to listen attentively. Surrounded as we are by music that is designed to be only heard, not listened to, you may need guidance in learning this skill—guidance your class should provide.

You may already "appreciate" music, or you may resemble the legendary American president who claimed to recognize two tunes: one was "Yankee Doodle" and the other wasn't. People vary in their ability to get something out of any art, or out of a sporting event, for that matter. Typically, what they get out of an experience depends a great deal on what they bring to it.

A

We just used the word "appreciate." It involves value. When people buy real estate, they assume that it will appreciate, or become more valuable. (They are resigned to the fact that automobiles depreciate!) One who "appreciates" music values it highly.

Learning to Appreciate Music

Imagine, for example, a couple at a symphony concert. He is an experienced concert-goer. She, on the other hand, has never attended such an event before, although she doesn't want that fact to be obvious. The sight of a stage-full of musicians playing together in amazing synchronization impresses her greatly, and she enjoys the beautiful sounds. When the orchestra comes to its first obvious stop, she is all set to clap vigorously, but she is saved from doing so because no one else does. She wonders to herself why the symphony goes on and on for so long. She steals a glance at the program, at the people in the next row. . . . When the symphony finally does end, some fifty minutes or so later, she realizes with a start that her mind has been a thousand miles away, planning her next vacation.

He, however, is in no danger of clapping prematurely and has no trouble keeping his mind on the music. He owns several recordings of the Mahler symphony that's on the program, all nearly worn out—something that can't happen

This boys' choir takes advantage of the opportunities for informal concerts that today's shopping malls offer. (Photograph © Claire Rydell.)

to the compact discs recently added to his audio equipment. In fact, he knows the symphony so well that he feels as if he is making music along with the players—or better yet, as if he could be up there conducting it. A glorious sense of being immersed in sound overwhelms him. He is sorry when the symphony is over.

There can be little doubt about which of these two people appreciates music more. He gets more out of it than she does, because he is a more experienced listener. Of course people differ in their basic ability to listen to music, but everyone can improve in the art of attentive listening.

B

Learning to Listen

As our inexperienced concert-goer discovered, a special kind of listening is required to appreciate some kinds of music. Listening in an attentive, concentrated, focused way seems difficult for many, perhaps because of some twentieth-century developments. Music surrounds us in elevators, at the dentist's office, perhaps at work, and it is music that is designed *not* to be listened to. Indeed, an industry has grown up to supply "Muzak," a trademarked term for "background" music. So we become conditioned to hear in general, not to listen in particular.

Another conditioning process has gone on in almost everyone's mind. From a lifetime of absorbing music as a background for motion pictures and television programs, we have learned to associate music with dramatic scenes. We know that something terrible is going to happen to our heroine even before the action on the

Since 1920, when the first commercial broadcasting station was established, radio has made worldwide transmission of music possible.

screen makes it obvious—the background music suddenly begins to sound ominous. As a result of this association, we often do the reverse—we imagine a scene when we hear ominous-sounding music. One imaginary scene follows another as we hear music, and pretty soon we are not listening at all.

How ironic it is that the very technology that has enabled everyone to experience music almost at will, a blessing inconceivable to previous generations, has made the "background music syndrome" possible. The more music there is to hear, the less we seem to listen.

As a nonmusical example of attentive listening, imagine the following. Someone has just told you that he would disclose the secret of becoming a millionaire. Despite your doubts, you would listen—very carefully. So his voice begins to recite, slowly and monotonously, "two, four, six, eight, ten, twelve, fourteen, sixteen, eighteen, twenty, twenty-one. . . ." You should react at this point. Twenty-one is not right. If you were merely *hearing* the drone of his voice, it would make no difference. But you were *listening,* just as you would if someone had said: "Repeat after me." You were probably *internalizing* the numbers, echoing inside your head what the speaker was saying aloud. You were *anticipating* what number was coming next. And you were *surprised* when the number was wrong. These three factors also apply to music listening.

Experienced listeners hum melodies in their heads—not aloud, we hope, if others are nearby. They react to rhythms with some muscular movements—even quiet foot-tapping; they feel tensions induced by the harmonies. They anticipate what the music will do next; they sense when a section is coming to a close. Surprises occur when the music deviates somewhat from what they expected, because

Degas' Father Listening to Lorenzo Pagans Playing the Guitar is one of the many music-related works by Hilaire-Germain-Edgar Degas (1834–1917), a French painter we will encounter later. In this oil painting (c. 1870), Degas's aging father, an enthusiastic performer himself, intently listens to the younger man singing as he accompanies himself. (Oil on Canvas, 81.6 × 65.2 cm. Courtesy, Museum of Fine Arts, Boston. Bequest of John T. Spaulding.)

music is strikingly less predictable than is counting by two's. But music has tendencies. How the tendencies are fulfilled, and how the deviations from the expected occur, account for much that is vital, and valuable, in music.

At this point you might well wonder: What about all of us inexperienced listeners? Fortunately, most people have heard enough music to have acquired some of the expectations already. Still, if the style of a particular piece is completely new to you, you may feel as lost as if you were hearing numbers recited in Greek. You might need help. So we can state the rationale for the music appreciation class and this book: to introduce you to a variety of works in differing musical styles, and as you study these works, to guide your listening in specific ways so that you too take on the expectations of an experienced listener. Since a significant part of these expectations involves knowledge of style periods, composers, musical forms, and other matters, such topics also form a part of our study.

2 FOLLOWING A LISTENING GUIDE

PREVIEW In this chapter, we present a listening guide typical of those to be found in later portions of this book, explain how it is designed, and outline some of the many considerations involved in describing music.

To introduce our listening guides, we invite you to try the following experiment. First, listen to the *Prelude* from Georges Bizet's opera *Carmen* without reading anything about it in advance. (If you are familiar with it, pretend you are not.) See if you can monitor what goes on in your head as you listen.

If you are at all typical, your "unguided" listening was probably accompanied by imaginative fantasies along these lines: as the music began you could "see" happy people, perhaps at a parade. You might have experienced a flash of recognition in the middle of this piece as a familiar tune appeared. After a pause and an abrupt change of mood, something seemed threatening and sad. Oddly enough, the "sad" music stopped abruptly, without having reached a satisfactory conclusion.

We do not say that there is anything wrong with such listening, but there is much more to hear in this music and much to learn from it. Listen again, following this brief outline-form description:

1. Orchestra begins loudly.
2. Orchestra repeats item 1.
3. Quieter moment occurs; then music gets louder.
4. Orchestra repeats item 1.
5. Brief interlude; much softer; familiar melody played.
6. Familiar melody repeats; louder.
7. Item 1 returns as before; emphatic ending.
8. After pause, soft, ominous-sounding music begins.

To "study" this music, read first the demonstration listening guide that describes it and then see if you can follow the guide as you listen. You will probably

Georges Bizet.

encounter ideas and terms that you do not understand—after all, this is only Chapter 2. If we were studying *Carmen* in the context of its period (the Romantic era), it would be much later in the course and you would have learned the new ideas presented in the guide. Indeed, students often find that in the process of guided listening they absorb almost without effort many of the musical concepts described. With each playing, you should be aware of more and more detail in the music.

A Demonstration Guide

The French composer Georges Bizet [pronounced bee-ZAY] (1838–75) wrote several operas, of which *Carmen,* first performed in 1875, is the best-known. American opera companies alone mounted nineteen productions of it in the 1988–89 season, which gives an idea of its popularity. Its short prelude falls into three sections, each built from themes that occur later in the opera. The marchlike music of the prelude's beginning later accompanies a procession to the bullfight arena. (Although Bizet never set foot in Spain, he made effective use of Spanish elements in this work.) A second section presents the melody sung by the character Escamillo, the "Toreador." The prelude concludes with an extensive development of a motive that is associated throughout the opera with the heroine, Carmen. Because she foresees the tragic fate that will eventually overtake her, commentators label these five notes the "Fate" motive.

Bizet: *Prelude to Carmen* (3:35) ①

CD1
1   ml Cymbals crash as the full orchestra begins *fortissimo,* with quickly
        moving notes. The high pitches of the melody (ex. 2.1) help the
1   listener picture a festive event, and the steady duple meter is
        marchlike.

Allegro Giocoso

Example 2.1

(0:16)
2   The music of item 1 is repeated, exactly.

2

Carmen is portrayed in the opera as a free spirit, always on the lookout for a new man to conquer. The gritty realism of Bizet's setting is reflected in the stage design and costume for Carmen herself in this production. (Courtesy of San Francisco Opera, Bill Acheson, photographer.)

(0:31)

3a   m17   A new melody, softer in volume and with an emphasis on woodwinds and strings, provides a brief interruption. The softer percussion section contributes to a more relaxed effect, although the tempo remains constant.

3

(0:39)

3b   m25   A sudden change in dynamics marks the start of this portion. A crescendo prepares for a return of the opening music.

(0:49)

4   m35   Once again the music of item 1 is repeated, demonstrating a
              common musical form: AABA.

[4]

(1:04)

5a   m51   Soft chords come from the trumpets and trombones, forming a tiny
              interlude. The chords continue as the accompaniment for what

[5]   follows.

(1:08)

5b   m55   Strings in unison play the familiar Toreador song (ex. 2.2) softly, in
              a legato style. As in item 3a, while the music may seem slower, it
              really continues in the same tempo. An ascending scale passage in
              strings and woodwinds leads into the next section.

Example 2.2

p

(1:31)

6   m79   Again the Toreador song sounds, now an octave higher and with
              winds added; louder, it is no longer legato but staccato. A brief

[6]   return to the soft, legato style is followed by a crescendo that
              emphasizes a transition back to the original mood.

(1:54)

7   m101   The music of item 1 returns once more. Increased activity in the
              percussion and a fanfarelike call in the brass make for a definite

[7]   cadence.

(2:14)   *Andante Moderato*

8a   m120   Though a pause might fool the listener, the Prelude is not over.
              Violins and violas play a minor chord, employing the device of

[8]   tremolo (quick, back-and-forth bow strokes). This tension-producing
              technique continues throughout as an accompaniment to the five-note
              Fate motive (ex. 2.3) played by a combination of instruments, with
              cellos the most prominent. Its downward-moving line and minor key
              hint at the tragedy to come. After each of the first two statements of
              the Fate motive, heavy timpani strokes on beats two and three (the

Example 2.3

meter is now in three) increase the tension. A tiny rest follows the third playing of the Fate motive.

(2:45)

8b   m131   The Fate motive resumes, again three times, in the style of item 8a, but here beginning at higher pitch levels.

(3:10)

8c   m139   More appearances of the Fate motive occur, rising ever higher in pitch and loudness. This passage ends abruptly, with an unresolved chord. In an opera performance, the curtain rises on Act I at this point, thus justifying the unusual ending of the prelude in dramatic terms. In a concert performance, this would seem quite surprising. When the *Carmen Suite* is performed, other selections from the opera follow immediately after the prelude.

B

The Rationale for Listening Guides

Listening to music is a little like going on a journey. The first time we make the trip, we gain only a general impression of the territory. With repeated visits, details come into focus because landmarks emerge to divide the journey into recognizable segments. With each landmark comes a sense of arrival, but also the need to proceed on.

In music too, there are points of arrival that become the most obvious and important landmarks. Those are described in our listening guides. Less attention is necessarily given to what happens in between the landmarks, since it is quite impossible to describe everything in a piece. Travelers often consult maps to guide them on the journey, but no one would say that studying a map is a substitute for taking that trip. Similarly, reading a description of music is no substitute for listening to it.

Your "guided" listening to the *Prelude to Carmen* should have revealed a number of things that you might not have noticed otherwise. In so doing it necessarily employed some vocabulary that you need to learn—terms that deal with characteristics of sound: *pitch* (high, low, ascending, octave), *dynamics* (loud, *fortissimo,* soft, crescendo), and *tone color* (orchestra, cymbals, woodwinds, tremolo, strings, cello, timpani, percussion). Other terms refer to basic elements of music: *rhythm* (duple and triple meter, allegro, andante), *melody* (scale, motive, song), and *harmony* (chords, minor, unresolved cadence). There are general terms to describe how tones are performed, whether connected or separated (legato, staccato), and labels to designate the *form* created by repetition and contrast (AABA). Some terms are specific to a particular type of piece—here, opera and prelude. These will all be explained in the remaining pages of this book.

Guides for instrumental music include measure numbers (for example, m1, m17), something we define in our discussion of rhythm. Measure numbers are needed by anyone who wishes to verify the information by looking in the composer's score. **Score** means several things in music. As a general term, it refers to the written music that musicians must learn to read as they learn to perform. The individual parts that members of an orchestra play from are printed in a "full score," lined up one under another. The conductor works from this, and such scores are available in libraries. The measure numbers also serve as a very rough estimate of the amount of time that will elapse between items on that guide. Item numbers (for example, 1a, 1b) can be cited by an instructor to let the class know "where we are" in a piece at any given moment. Or, by raising hands when the music arrives at a particular item, the students can show that they are following the guide. These item numbers can also facilitate class discussion of a work, or allow the individual student studying the piece to note problem places.

C

Describing music in even the most minimal terms makes a philosophical statement. You cannot describe something without revealing what you think about the object in question. So what is music, anyway? A twentieth-century composer, Edgard Varèse (1883–1965) called his own music "**organized sound**" and referred to himself as "a worker in rhythms, frequencies, and intensities." At a minimum, *music consists of sounds organized in time.* But is that all it is?

Some claim that music is a language—the "universal language of mankind," wrote the American poet Henry Wadsworth Longfellow—a language that communicates emotion in some way that has not yet been explained adequately. Many assert that music is descriptive, or representational, that it tells stories. Such music is called **programmatic.** Smetana's *Moldau* and Vivaldi's *Four Seasons* are examples. Accordingly, you can expect that what is written about these works will include a consideration of the nonmusical references that their composers authorized, starting with the given titles. In contrast, many prefer to regard music as a "pure" or **absolute** art, free of overt connections to nonmusical ideas. "Sonatas" and "symphonies" are examples of absolute music. A discussion of such a work is likely to center upon its "themes" and the ways that these themes are organized.

Philosophers have been trying for more than two thousand years to explain the enigma of music. A Romantic composer, Robert Schumann, wrote that while the other arts are based on nature, "Music is a poor orphan whose father and

Describing Music

A conductor follows a full score showing all the instrumental parts, one under another, as in this opening page of the score for Beethoven's *Symphony No. 5.*

Allegro con brio. ♩ = 108.

2 Flutes

2 Oboes

2 Clarinets in B-flat

2 Bassoons

2 French horns

2 Trumpets

2 Timpani in C and G

Violin I

Violin II

Viola

Cello

Double bass

mother no one can name." And the twentieth-century poet W. H. Auden (1907–73) eloquently conveyed a similar thought in his sonnet *The Composer:*

> All the others translate: the painter sketches
> A visible world to love or reject;
> Rummaging into his living, the poet fetches
> The images out that hurt and connect,
> From Life to Art by painstaking adaption,
> Relying on us to cover the rift;
> Only your notes are pure contraption,
> Only your song is an absolute gift.*

Most of us who write about music are neither poets nor philosophers. Having been conditioned by our musical training, we tend to use a special vocabulary that leans heavily on the ways music is organized. Our descriptions contain technical, or at least fairly objective, terms. Even though words like "agitated" or "serene" may appear, the words are metaphors: the "agitation" is not real. Everyone agrees that music packs a genuine emotional power. Talking about that emotional dimension, without seeming sentimental, is difficult to do. Consequently, most musical descriptions you will read in program notes—and textbooks, including this one—may seem cool and academic. Words can guide your listening, but they cannot explain the mystery of music. While the prosaic-sounding phrase "Violins play the theme" is objectively true, it is hardly complete. It necessarily leaves out many important dimensions because words can only hint at the nature of music.

Although we cannot give you a final, unequivocal "answer" to the "what is music" question, the search for it is stimulating. Students interested in exploring this challenging area could begin with the entry "Aesthetics" in the *New Harvard Dictionary of Music,* where the philosophical issues of this field are outlined.

*Reprinted by permission of Faber and Faber Ltd. from COLLECTED POEMS by W. H. Auden.

3 SOUND, THE PHYSICAL BASIS OF MUSIC

PREVIEW Music is an art dependent on sound. Sound can be discussed in a scientific manner. Its four characteristics—pitch, dynamics, tone color, and duration—are explained in terms of their physical basis and related to the ways music is notated.

Sound, the physical basis of music, can be measured objectively and is the foundation for the science of acoustics. All sounds result from vibrating objects. Musical tones are created by *regular vibrations*. Although we usually call *irregular* vibrations **noise,** noise has a place in music. A cymbal crash is certainly noisy, yet it enhances the excitement that the *Prelude to Carmen* generates in its opening moments.

At least three secondary qualities of sound affect music, though they are often overlooked.

1. For instance, the acoustical surroundings in which music is performed contribute varying degrees of *reverberation*. In a concert hall, the one or two seconds required for a loud sound to die away, or "decay," adds a "warmth" to the music. Performers usually complain that a hall with little or no reverberation has "dry acoustics." This condition results when carpeting, upholstered seats, certain types of wall treatments, and the audience itself absorb too much of the sound. In contrast, a large stone cathedral may have as much as six seconds of reverberation. Here, individual tones overlap and mingle as they are sustained by the reflected sounds. Choral and organ music benefit from this quality, which seems appropriate to the church environment; other types of music may become unacceptably blurred.

2. *Spatial relationships,* that is, how the performers are seated in relation to each other and to the audience, can be a consideration also. Some twentieth-century composers have wanted performers to surround the audience. Trumpets playing offstage form a part of many orchestral scores.

3. In addition, we assume that music exists against a background of *silence,* yet outside of a sound laboratory silence is not absolute. Many extraneous noises intrude that we ignore—or try to. "Rests," periods of silence or pauses written into the music, are described later as a part of duration.

In Part One, set off from the main body of text and identified with the graphic symbol   , are some suggested listening experiences that illustrate the topic just covered. These are pieces covered later as part of a composer's chapter, where detailed study is appropriate. At this point, only a brief sampling is in order. Bach's *Toccata in D Minor* ㉗ contains several pauses in its first few moments. Depending upon where they were recorded, most performances will demonstrate varying amounts of reverberation. Gabrieli's *Canzona on the Ninth Tone* ⑭ was written for two separate quartets of instruments, each playing in different areas of St. Mark's church, Venice.

Any individual musical note exhibits four basic qualities: (1) *pitch,* (2) *dynamics* or volume, (3) *tone color* or tone quality, and (4) *duration.* Although they operate simultaneously in music, we shall temporarily isolate each. We describe each of these primary characteristics of sound in two ways: (1) its physical basis, and (2) its representation in the score.

A

Pitch depends upon the *speed* or the *frequency of vibrations.* The number of vibrations per second of any given tone is often identified with the term **Hertz.** Anyone buying high-fidelity sound equipment has seen the abbreviation, **Hz.** For example, the lowest piano key has a frequency of 27.5 Hz; the highest key has a frequency of over 4000 Hz. The human ear can hear up to 20,000 Hz. We almost automatically feel that fast vibrations produce high pitches and slow vibrations low pitches. The piano is useful for demonstrating pitch concepts. Play its keys from left to right and a span of pitches results from low to high. Examining the piano strings will reveal long, heavy strings on the left and short, thin ones on the right. (See example 3.2 for a diagram of the piano keyboard.)

Pitch

Pitch offers tremendous potential for emotional messages in music. In the *Prelude to Carmen,* the marchlike music owes much of its high spirits to the high pitches of its melody, while the dark, ominous mood of the Fate motive is in part due to its descending pitch line.

Individual pitches have *letter names*—just the first seven letters of the alphabet, repeated over and over. One particular pitch, the **A** that vibrates **440** times a second, is a universally accepted standard in Western music. The lowest key on the piano happens to be an A (assuming a full-size, eighty-eight key piano). To find the 440 A, count up to the fifth A, the one near the manufacturer's label. This is the pitch to which performers tune their instruments. Other individual pitches are occasionally named, especially in referring to singers or trumpet players who might have the ability to "hit a high C."

The arrangement of the black and white keys of the piano forms a pattern which occurs seven times in all. (To see this, ignore the three lowest keys.) If you play any two keys with the same letter name, you will discover that one almost duplicates the other, blending so well that they sound like one tone. The **interval** or distance between these two keys is measured by counting all the letter names involved—A, B, C, D, E, F, G, A. Consequently we say that from one A to the next A (or whatever key we have chosen to demonstrate this effect) is the interval of an **octave.** ("Octave" comes from the Latin word meaning "eight.")

The ancient Greeks explained the octave phenomenon after their discovery that a string half as long as another one will sound an octave higher, if all other factors are constant. When men and women sing the same melody together, they usually sing an octave apart because men's voices are lower. The song "Somewhere Over the Rainbow" begins with an octave leap on the word "somewhere."

Counting both black and white piano keys, the octave is divided into twelve **half-steps,** the distance from any piano key to the next adjacent key. Although the octave is a universal phenomenon, some non-Western musical cultures choose to divide it into more than twelve intervals. Intervals smaller than a half-step are sometimes called **microtones.** As we shall see, many instruments can produce these smaller intervals, but of course the piano cannot.

Keyboard instruments produce pitches in separate and distinct steps. Built upon this principle, our musical notation system ignores the possibility of any gradual shifts in pitch and tends to suggest that pitches in all music move as separately as they must do on the piano. This is not so; indeed, many sound sources can move up and down the pitch spectrum like a siren—although we hope the result is more pleasant. The voice, trombone, and string instruments can glide or slide from one pitch to another, with performers deciding how obvious to the listener they wish to make these connections.

A slight undulation or wavering of pitch on one specific note creates **vibrato.** String players produce it by making back-and-forth motions with their left hand and lower arm. Vibrato is possible on some other types of instruments as well.

Pitch notation relates to its sound in a graphic, visual way. A somewhat egg-shaped symbol is placed on a **staff** (plural staves), a set of five horizontal lines. If these symbols are placed higher on the staff, they indicate a series of ascending pitches, if lower, they indicate descending pitches. For examples, see the staff in example 3.1. The notation is always read from left to right. Notes may be placed (1) on the lines, (2) in the spaces between the lines, and (3) on, or between, short segments of lines added above or below the basic five-line staff. These segments are called ledger lines, sometimes spelled "leger."

Example 3.1

"Allow me to introduce you to my staff."..

The span of available pitches is far too big to fit upon a five-line staff, so a **clef,** a special symbol placed at the beginning of every staff, identifies the specific pitch range covered by that staff. The diagram (ex. 3.2) shows only the central part of a piano keyboard in relationship to the two most important clefs.

The **treble clef,** the symbol on the upper staff, covers the right-hand half of the piano keyboard, from middle C (the fourth C) upwards. Most of our musical examples are in treble clef, since melodies tend to appear in the higher range. (Its symbol circles around G, the second line, and for that reason the treble clef is also called the "G clef.") The **bass clef** [pronounced BASE] (also called the "F clef" because the symbol's two dots highlight F, the second line from the top) appears on the lower staff and covers the left-hand half of the piano. When both clefs are needed, as in keyboard music, the two staves are linked together as shown, producing a **grand staff.**

Example 3.2

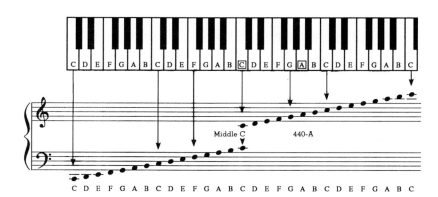

Only the white keys have letter names. The black keys are named in relationship to the white keys, using the words **sharp** or **flat.** For instance, the black key between C and D may be called C-sharp (higher than C) or D-flat (lower than D), depending upon some musical complexities that need not concern us. The term **accidentals** is applied to sharps and flats because they sometimes appear irregularly, not consistently. In spite of the word "accidentals," there is nothing accidental about them: musicians write them on purpose. The sharp, which looks much like the number symbol #, raises a given pitch a half-step. The flat, which slightly resembles the lowercase letter b, lowers a pitch by a half-step. **Natural signs,** which look something like a sharp minus some of its protruding lines, function in music to cancel earlier accidentals. Examples of these signs appear in the *Prelude to Carmen* listening guide in item 8a.

B

Dynamics

Loudness or softness in music is known as **dynamics.** Because these effects give a sensation of relative fullness, the word **volume** also applies, as in the "volume" control knob on a radio. (Be careful not to confuse the words "low and high," which describe pitch, with "low and high" volume.) Differences in dynamics result from the amount of force employed by the vibrating medium. The harder a piano string is struck, for example, the wider is the arc in which it moves and the louder it sounds. The performing media differ greatly in their control of dynamics. A singer or violinist, for example, can swell or decrease a single note at will—an impossibility for the pianist, whose tones can only get softer until they die away.

Differences in dynamic levels can be measured scientifically in decibels (abbreviated db). The very softest violin tone is about twenty-five db, while an orchestra at its loudest measures about 100 db. Your eardrums are in danger at 125 db.

Even though this scientific measuring system is available, musicians are seldom concerned with it. They refer to dynamics in relative terms only; one tone is louder or softer than another but by how much no one can say for certain. Practical reasons dictate why dynamics in music must remain a relative matter. The size of the performing space, its furnishings, and the audience all have an effect upon the perceived loudness level. Also, the total possible decibel count is variable. A loud flute note would not be as loud, objectively, as a loud note on the trumpet. Another factor involves present-day recording technology, which makes it possible for the listener, not to mention the recording engineer, to alter dynamics with a turn of a dial.

Directions for dynamics appear in musical notation in the form of Italian terms. When composers first began to indicate such directions, Italians dominated music composition. Two words are basic: *piano* (soft) and *forte* (loud). When joined, they give a name to the **pianoforte.** When it was first invented, this keyboard instrument was unique in its ability to control both soft and loud volume through the amount of pressure the player gave the keys. Today we usually shorten the name to the familiar "piano." In this book, *piano* (in italics, as a foreign term) refers to soft and piano (in Roman type) means the instrument. **Mezzo,** meaning middle or half, specifies a moderate value for any term. The Italian suffix "*-issimo*" indicates a superlative form, thus intensifying a term's meaning. Following is a list of these terms with their abbreviations, arranged in order from softest to loudest:

pp	*pianissimo*	very soft
p	*piano*	soft
mp	*mezzo piano*	moderately soft
mf	*mezzo forte*	moderately loud
f	*forte*	loud
ff	*fortissimo*	very loud

In the past century, composers began to call for enormous dynamic extremes, asking for "ppp" or "pppp" and "fff" or "ffff." Since dynamic levels in music are only relative anyway, such refinement might appear excessive. A gradual change in dynamics can be indicated by these abbreviations, words, or symbols:

cresc.	*crescendo*	gradually louder	
decresc.	*decrescendo*	gradually softer	
dim.	*diminuendo*	gradually softer	

These symbols relate in a graphic way to the dynamic change, for the crescendo sign shows a gradual opening up, while the decrescendo sign shows a closing down.

In the *Prelude to Carmen,* a crescendo contributes to the growing tension of the ending portion. Incidentally, the word "crescendo" seems to carry an additional, nonmusical meaning. Lovers are swept off their feet in "a growing crescendo of passion," or so claim the writers of light fiction.

Changes in both pitch levels and dynamics are obvious in the opening section of *Also sprach Zarathustra* ⑥⁴ , an orchestral work by Richard Strauss. It begins, pp, on a tone so low in pitch and so soft it is almost inaudible and gets louder as more instruments enter on higher pitches. Particularly effective is the crescendo at the end of this section.

C

The quality of a note produced on one instrument or human voice differs from the same pitch produced on another instrument or voice. This difference is called **tone color,** the third fundamental property of a musical tone. The French

Tone Color

term *timbre* [pronounced TAM-bre] means the same thing as tone color. The physical basis for this difference stems from a peculiarity of vibrating materials: they vibrate as a whole, producing the basic pitch, the **fundamental tone,** and at the same time they vibrate in segments, according to mathematical ratios. For example, a vibrating string sixty inches long is also vibrating in halves, in two thirty-inch segments. Each of the segments produces a faint but audible sound, one octave higher than the fundamental pitch. The string is also vibrating in three twenty-inch segments, four fifteen-inch segments, five twelve-inch segments, and so on, each division producing a higher tone. These partial tones are called overtones or harmonics.

The actual number and relative strengths of the overtones differ greatly in musical media. For example, the flute, lacking almost all the overtones except the first, emits a "pure" sound. In contrast, the intensity of the oboe derives from its rich complex of overtones. The blend of overtones with the fundamental creates the different tone colors. People vary in ability to hear the higher overtones; consequently some aspects of tone color fall quite literally on "deaf ears."

Another characteristic of tone color is often overlooked: the particular sound created at the beginning of a note. For instance, fingers on piano keys and bows on strings create a certain amount of noise that may help in identifying some instruments.

Usually composers indicate tone color in notation by specifying the particular performing media desired and, for many works, by giving a piece its title. Certain understandings have grown up around some of these titles, however. Musicians may refer to "quartets," not bothering to say "string quartets."

Not only are certain instruments or certain types of voices wanted: directives tell the performers to alter the tone color at specific points. String players, for example, can pluck the strings instead of using their bows, which is an effect called **pizzicato.**

The resources of tone color have grown amazingly throughout music history. With the increase in the number of performing media there also developed a greater interest in tone color as a vital part of music. We think it advisable, therefore, to discuss specific instruments and performing groups in connection with the historical period during which they first flourished. In order to prepare the student to understand the tone colors heard in examples of music that might be sampled in class at this time, we furnish only a brief, general outline of the categories of voices and instruments, listing them in order from high to low.

The four major *vocal categories* are: women's voices, **soprano** (high) and **alto** or **contralto** (low), and men's voices, **tenor** (high) and **bass** (low). **Mezzo-soprano** (you should remember "mezzo" from the discussion of dynamics) denotes a mid-range female voice, and **baritone** the mid-range male voice. In our culture, we expect "classical music" to be performed by highly trained voices, which have a distinctive quality not found in the untrained voice and almost always have a wider pitch span, perhaps of two octaves or more, and greater dynamic range.

A men's singing group has long been a fixture of college life. The Men's Glee Club of UCLA is rehearsing.

No fixed number of singers is needed to form a **chorus** or a **choir.** In some choral organizations, boys and men sing the parts that otherwise would go to women's voices. With its added dimension of text, vocal music constantly challenges the singer to make the words intelligible to the listener.

Some of the terms that define voices apply to instruments as well, for example, the "alto flute" and the "tenor saxophone." People also make analogies such as "the soprano of the brass section is the trumpet." Or the string section may be called the "string choir."

Two solos from *Rigoletto,* by Verdi, demonstrate high voices. *Caro nome* (55) calls for a very high soprano voice, and *La donna è mobile* (56) features the tenor. *Ave Maria* (12), by Victoria, is sung by an unaccompanied choir, while the *Hallelujah* chorus (24) from Handel's *Messiah* is accompanied by instruments.

Instrumental categories reflect the materials that instruments are made of and the ways these materials create sound. Traditional categorization assembles **families of instruments,** often with a limitation to those families found in the modern

String instruments.

symphony orchestra. The concept of "family" is useful, especially when you remember that in some human families the members resemble each other and in
some they differ greatly. Furthermore, later on we will refer to the "ancestors" of
some modern-day instruments.

1. The **string family** of the orchestra consists of the violin, viola, cello [pro-
nounced CHEL-lo], and bass. Although differing greatly in size, the string family
members look alike. They are usually played with a bow, or as an English come-
dienne inelegantly puts it, horsehair is scraped across catgut. (Her joke is spoiled
by the knowledge that metal strings have replaced gut strings on the instruments
of most players today.) Having a similar sound, the string family members blend
together well. In expressive capability, string instruments approach the human voice.
In order to soften and slightly alter the tone color, players can attach a mute, a
device in the shape of a little clamp, to the bridge, which is that part of the instrument over which the strings pass.

Some string instruments, among them the guitar, the Japanese koto, and the Indian sitar, require no bow; they are plucked. Though the harp has strings—which are plucked—and is commonly found in the orchestra, we will not place it in the string family since it is not played with a bow.

2. The **woodwind family** consists of instruments that are made of wood. (Why the flute is an exception is explained later.) There are four principal instruments, each with a related instrument or "cousin," given here in parentheses: flute (piccolo), oboe (English horn), clarinet (bass clarinet), and bassoon (contrabassoon). This is a heterogeneous family. Its members neither look nor sound alike. Not surprisingly, they do not blend together very readily. They differ in the specific ways in which a column of air is set in motion: whether by the player's lips (flute), one vibrating reed (clarinet), or the vibration of two reeds bound together, as in the **double reed** instruments (oboe and bassoon). Many people associate the woodwinds with nature and the out-of-doors.

3. The **brass family** of the orchestra includes as its four principal instruments the trumpet, trombone, French horn (musicians usually say just "horn," but to avoid confusion, we will say "French horn"), and tuba. Like the strings, it is a homogeneous family. All the instruments are made of brass, although they differ

The wind quintet is composed of the four major woodwind instruments, plus a French horn. Most listeners are surprised at how well this brass instrument blends with the woodwinds. The Mladi quintet is shown here in rehearsal. (Photograph © Claire Rydell.)

Brass instruments.

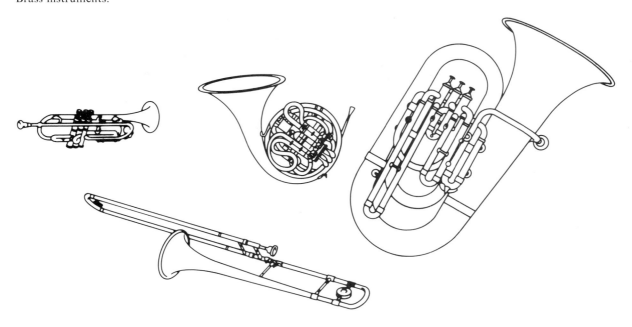

in several important details of construction and are obviously unlike in appearance. In this group the player's lips vibrate or "buzz" into a mouthpiece to set an air column in motion. Some brass instruments, such as the cornet and the sousaphone, belong in a marching band rather than in the orchestra. The history of brass instruments links them to the military, to hunting, and to royal ceremony. When played at full strength, they can drown out the rest of the orchestra.

4. The **percussion family** instruments produce their sound by being struck or shaken. In the drums, a membrane (today made of plastic) stretched over a frame vibrates when struck. Bells or cymbals, on the other hand, vibrate as a whole. The traditional categorization for percussion instruments divides them into two groups: those which produce a *definite* pitch and those which produce an *indefinite* pitch. For example, the timpani (kettledrums) are tuned to definite pitches and the player's music shows specific pitches to play. In contrast, the bass drum player's notation gives rhythm symbols only, because that instrument's pitch is indefinite.

5. Instruments with **keyboards,** such as piano, organ, and harpsichord, are grouped together. Despite the common denominator of a keyboard, they are quite unlike in the ways they produce sound and consequently almost defy classification—at least, there is no single family for them. They can be heard as solo instruments or in accompanying roles.

6. New in this century are the **electronic** instruments, or **electrophones.** The Hammond organ, the electric piano, and the amplified guitar resemble their older, acoustic "parents," while the synthesizer is truly a new product. Its extremely complex technology enables it to imitate traditional tone colors as well as create new sounds, as we shall see in discussing twentieth-century developments.

The first four of these groups are represented in the *Prelude to Carmen,* which utilizes a symphony orchestra, a performing body we study in connection with the Classic period. In this piece, although the majority of the instruments play most of the time, it is not hard to pick out individual lines and associate them with orchestral families.

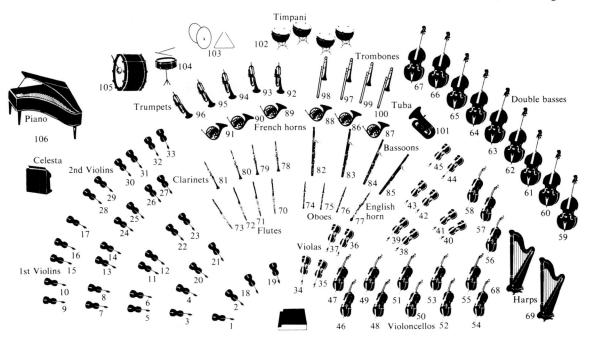

The third movement of Tchaikovsky's *Symphony No. 4* ⑥⓪ provides an exceptionally clear example of the string, woodwind, and brass families, because the degree to which each section plays alone is unusual. The contrast of keyboard instruments can be heard by listening to Joplin's *The Entertainer,* ⑦⑦ for piano; Bach's *Toccata in D Minor* ㉗ , for organ; and Bach's *Brandenburg Concerto No. 5* ㉕ , first movement, in which the harpsichord has a prominent role, sharing the spotlight with a solo violin and flute and supported by a small group of strings.

A "wind ensemble" or more simply, a "band," is composed of instruments from the woodwind, brass, and percussion families. For some concert situations, string basses are added. (Photograph © Claire Rydell.)

Duration

The length of time that a note or a period of silence lasts is its **duration.** The possible duration of a sound depends to a large extent upon the physical characteristics of the performing medium involved and also upon the skills of the performer. Obviously, sounds created by the human breath must terminate when the player runs out of air. String instrument players can manipulate their up-and-down bow motions so skillfully that they create the illusion of infinitely sustained tones. The tones of a piano eventually die away; plucked string instrument sounds die quickly. Only the organ and today's electronic instruments can go on forever—or at least as long as the electric power holds out. Composers know these limitations and calculate their desired effects accordingly.

Earlier, we saw that noteheads represent pitches on the musical staff. Commonly added to those noteheads are additional graphic features, which instruct the musician how long to hold any given note in relation to other notes. While this system assumes an absolute quantity for pitch—the 440 A is expected to vibrate that many times a second—the notation of duration is only relative. However long we happen to sustain a whole note (the egg-shaped symbol) in any given situation, a half note (the egg-shaped symbol with an added vertical line) will take half as long; a quarter note (the half note filled in) will take just a quarter of that time, and so on. Because silence is also a part of music, notation includes **rests,** which are periods of time when no sound takes place—at least on purpose. A chart (ex. 3.3) shows the most commonly used notes and rests. You can see that the "blacker" the note, the shorter it is; the "whiter" the note, the longer it is.

Example 3.3

Rests:	Notes:	Value:	Equal in time to:
▬	𝅝	whole	
▬	𝅗𝅥	half	$\frac{1}{2}$ of 𝅝
𝄽	♩	quarter	$\frac{1}{4}$ of 𝅝 or $\frac{1}{2}$ of 𝅗𝅥
𝄾	♪	eighth	$\frac{1}{8}$ of 𝅝 or $\frac{1}{2}$ of ♩
𝄿	𝅘𝅥𝅯	sixteenth	$\frac{1}{16}$ of 𝅝 or $\frac{1}{2}$ of ♪

Actually the system goes all the way to 128th notes by adding more curves to the note stems. These curving lines are called flags, rather appropriately—they do look somewhat like flags billowing gently in a slight breeze. Another way to print groups of flagged notes is to join them with heavy horizontal lines, called beams, making them easier to read. A dot, placed just to the right of the affected note, extends the note's duration by 50 percent. A dotted half note lasts as long as a half-note plus a quarter. A tie—a short, slightly curved line—connects two notes of the same pitch and means that the two notes are performed as if they were one continuous note lasting as long as the sum of the combined durations. Flags, beams, a dot, dotted notes, and the tie symbol make up example 3.4.

Example 3.4

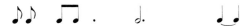

flags; beams; dot; dotted half note, tied notes

A few other musical terms affect duration. If each note is detached, separated, or shortened in value, the performer is probably playing **staccato.** Shortening a note by half its value is a conventional rule for staccato. Staccato in modern notation is notated with a dot placed over or under a note and should not be confused with the duration-extending kind of dot.

The opposite effect, **legato,** or a smooth, unbroken connection of notes, is often taken for granted. A long, curved line written above or below the affected notes will show that legato has been specified. We saw (and heard) the contrast of staccato and legato in the "Toreador Song" portion of the *Prelude to Carmen.*

Pitch, dynamics, and tone color are isolated for discussion in the preliminary chapters that will introduce each style period in Parts Two through Seven. Duration is not, because it is inseparable in music from rhythm, our next topic of discussion.

Credit: Richard Anderson.

a bass bass

4 MUSICAL ELEMENTS: RHYTHM

PREVIEW Sounds are organized in order to create music. Each of the five basic elements of music will be studied in a separate chapter, starting with the most fundamental element: rhythm. Rhythm is a product of duration and accents, resulting in these rhythmic concepts: beat and meter; rhythm patterns; tempo and tempo terms; and syncopation.

Sound, though essential, is still only raw material, as the minimal definition of music as "sounds organized in time" suggests. The passage of time marks the fundamental distinction between sound and music. It takes but a split second to recognize a trumpet tone, for example, or to identify a pitch as high or low. A melody, however, cannot be recognized as such until at least a couple of seconds have elapsed. Indeed, the passing of time creates a fundamental distinction between experiencing music and some other arts. While we can take in a painting at a single glance, we can only listen to music one moment at a time. We can go back to that painting and look as long as we wish, or reread a passage in a book that puzzles us, but there is no instant replay in music—at least not in live performance. We must trust our musical memories to establish the relationship between what just happened in the music and what is now happening; otherwise, we are only hearing the sound and not really listening to the music.

Because time is so important, we must show how it underlies the five elements of music: (1) *rhythm,* (2) *melody,* (3) *harmony,* (4) *texture,* and (5) *form.* Each is discussed separately, although in music they usually occur simultaneously. With some practice it is possible to isolate an element for study, just as you can examine a painting for its color or analyze a poem for its rhyme scheme.

The words commonly associated with **rhythm** show how close is the connection between it and time. We speak of "keeping time" to the music as we tap our foot or nod our head. If a performer's rhythm seems unconvincing, people say that his or her "timing" is wrong. In a general sense, rhythm is a *catch-all term for everything in music related to time.*

When we tap our foot as we listen, we are reacting to the **beat** of music, the basic pulse that forms a backdrop to everything else. The word should remind us of our ever-present heartbeat, telling us that rhythm is a physical thing, not just an intellectual matter. Of course, the musical beat is not as simple as the regular thump-thump of our hearts. Musical beats can be much faster or slower than our heartbeat; they can be heavily marked, as in most rock music, or so subtle that they are barely felt. It is incorrect to say that a piece has rhythm. All music has rhythm because all music exists in time. By this phrase, people probably mean that a piece has a strongly marked, regular beat.

Our minds tend to organize regular sounds into groups. Thus we say that a clock says "tick-tock" even though it more likely sounds a plain "tick-tick." "Tick-tock" is more interesting. Similarly, your eye gets lost in a long line of dots, as in the following: . . . . but making every other dot darker will give you more to look at, the visual equivalent of "tick-tock": . . . .

In like fashion, our minds organize a series of beats into groups, even if all the beats are equally stressed. Usually some beats really do receive more stress than others. The simplest way of creating that stress is to make some beats louder. The organization of stressed and unstressed beats into regular, repeated patterns creates **meter.** A march needs a meter of two, or **duple meter,** to fit its LEFT-right LEFT-right movement. We count ONE-two ONE-two, accenting the ONE without noticing it.

We literally measure time by arranging the notes in **measures,** each measure containing the same number of beats and consequently taking the same amount of elapsed time. For an example, think of the familiar "Twinkle, Twinkle, Little Star." The rhythm notation for its first seven notes is shown here with short vertical lines called **bar lines** dividing up the music into measures (ex. 4.1). Measures themselves are often referred to as **bars.**

Example 4.1

By long-standing tradition, the first note of each measure receives a certain stress or accent. Just how much stress is given depends upon factors beyond the scope of this introduction. The division into measures is not arbitrary; here it fits the natural stresses of the words. You are not likely to say "twin-KLE, twin-KLE, lit-TLE st-AR."

The meter is shown by the **time signature** placed at the beginning of a piece. This is a set of two numbers, for example, the 2 and the 4 shown in example 4.1. That number is not a fraction, although writers on music sometimes employ this style: 2/4. The upper number, 2, indicates duple meter; the lower number, 4, refers

to the kind of note that equals one beat. In this example, it is the quarter note. If an eighth note gets the beat, the lower number will be an 8; if a half note, the number will be a 2, and so on. The top number, indicating the meter, is the important one for our purpose in studying musical examples.

We met **triple meter,** ONE-two-three, ONE-two-three, in the ending portion of the *Prelude to Carmen,* although the meter in that part was less obvious than the duple meter of the march that began this piece. The patriotic song "America," often called "My country, 'tis of Thee" (ex. 4.2), is in triple meter. Waltzes, such as the well-known "Blue Danube Waltz," are as fundamentally linked to triple meter as marches are to duple.

Example 4.2

Music is commonly written in **quadruple meter**—so often, in fact, that another name for 4/4 meter is **common time.** The letter *C* frequently appears instead of the numbers 4/4 to indicate this meter, for historical reasons having nothing to do with the coincidence of "common" beginning with a letter C. You will probably not be able to feel any difference between two measures of duple (ONE-two ONE-two) and one measure of quadruple (ONE-two-THREE-four), since THREE almost always receives a secondary stress. Consequently, we shall make no distinction between them.

Quintuple meter is rare, though it has a famous example in popular music: "Take Five" as performed by the Dave Brubeck Quartet. It turns out to be a combination of three and two: ONE-two-three FOUR-five. The reverse combination is also possible: ONE-two-THREE-four-five.

A meter of six, **sextuple meter,** ONE-two-three-FOUR-five-six, offers two possible perceptions. In a slow tempo, as in "Silent Night," sextuple meter will feel like two measures of triple meter. Here again we shall ignore the distinction and discuss a slow sextuple meter as if it were triple. When sextuple meter is fast enough that only the ONE and the FOUR are felt by the listener, it will seem like duple. It is also likely that two listeners will react differently, one feeling the fast triple meter and the other the slower duple. So in a larger sense, most meters are in two or in three.

Composers can elect to change meter within a selection. At the opposite pole stands **nonmetrical** music, usually vocal, with the stresses created by word accents, which vary, as in prose.

Both the first and second movements of Vivaldi's *Winter (Four Seasons)* ⑱ ⑲ , a work featuring string instruments, are in a clearly-marked duple meter. Our medieval dance example, *Estampie* ⑨ , played by two instruments, one much like a flute and the other an ancestor of the cello, is in a fast triple meter. The second movement of Mozart's *Symphony No. 40* ㉟ (for orchestra), a slow sextuple meter that feels like triple, forms a contrast to Smetana's *Moldau* ㊳ , (also for orchestra) which begins in a sextuple meter that is fast enough to seem like duple. Some Renaissance choral music, for example, Palestrina's *Benedictus* ⑪ , is performed with such subtlety that you may not feel any meter, though it is present. Our example of Gregorian chant, *Alleluia, Dies sanctificatus* ② , is nonmetrical.

B

The regularity of the beats forms a kind of background. Superimposed on it are foreground **rhythm patterns,** made up of combinations of longer and shorter notes plus accents and rests. Such patterns often serve as unifying factors in music. For example, in the song "America," the rhythmic pattern of the first two measures (shown earlier in ex. 4.2) occurs four times in all in this short song.

Rhythm Patterns: Even and Uneven

Rhythm patterns can become associated with certain geographical areas. Thus the tango rhythm (the first four notes are shown in ex. 4.3) evokes Spain for many people, though Argentina is the true home of the tango. It is no accident that in the musical *My Fair Lady,* the composer Frederick Loewe fits a tango rhythm to the words "The Rain in Spain Stays Mainly in the Plain." In a much different context, add a whole note to that tango pattern, perform it using the pitches C, D, E-flat, C, F-sharp, and the "Dragnet" theme (second part, ex. 4.3) results.

Example 4.3

Two commonly found rhythm patterns offer a striking contrast. *Evenly spaced* durations, as in most of the "Twinkle, Twinkle" song (shown earlier in ex. 4.1), provide a relaxed effect. Most of the notes in this song are quarter notes, all the same length. Much more active is an *unevenly spaced* pattern of long-short-long-short. No special name designates the evenly spaced pattern; the unevenly spaced pattern is called a **dotted rhythm.** Dots, as explained earlier, lengthen the duration of a note by 50 percent. Each dotted note is followed by a much shorter one. The dots that follow every other note not only give the pattern its name but help you to identify it visually. A familiar example is the "Battle Hymn of the Republic" (ex. 4.4), whose text begins: "Mine eyes have seen the glory of the coming of the Lord." The first half of this song is filled with dotted rhythms, interrupted with evenly spaced notes on the words "His truth is marching on."

Example 4.4

The second movement of Haydn's *Symphony No. 94* �33 begins with evenly spaced notes in a pattern identical to that of "Twinkle, Twinkle." After its slow beginning, *Montagues and Capulets* �73, a section of Prokofiev's ballet suite for orchestra, *Romeo and Juliet,* is full of dotted rhythms.

C

Tempo and Tempo Terms

The speed of the beats determines the **tempo** of a piece. This is independent of the speed of individual notes. Composers can specify an exact tempo by making use of metronome marks, which are a combination of the letters "MM" and a

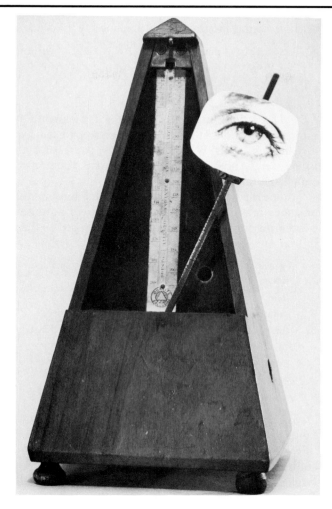

Indestructible Object (*or Object to be Destroyed*) is the provocative title of this 1964 work by the artist Man Ray (1890–1976). Preexisting objects assembled in new ways is one aspect of modern art. (Replica of 1923 original. Metronome with cutout photograph of eye on pendulum, 8 7/8″ × 4 3/8″ × 4 5/8″ Collection, The Museum of Modern Art, New York. James Thrall Soby Fund.)

number, indicating how many beats should occur per minute. The traditional metronome is pyramidlike in shape and emits a metallic, tick-tock sound. Even though this device for objective measurement of tempo has existed since about 1812, musicians prefer the more subjective description communicated by Italian tempo terms. Besides tempo, these terms traditionally imply a certain general character for the music as well.

The listener needs to know some of these terms because they constantly appear as titles. Large musical works, such as symphonies, sonatas, and concertos, customarily contain three or four separate, more-or-less independent **movements.** The tempo term for each movement serves to identify it. That is why you see tempo indications like "andante" or "allegro" on concert programs and on record jackets. A piano recital program might include the following entry:

Sonata in C-sharp Minor, Op. 27, No. 2   Ludwig van Beethoven
    Adagio
    Allegretto
    Presto agitato

This sonata, one better known by its nickname "Moonlight," consists of three movements. The first is very slow, the second somewhat faster, and the last very fast and "agitated." When the performer pauses after the first movement, the sonata is not over. (And it is *not* time to applaud! The proper place for applause is at the end of the third, and last, movement.)

The following list includes the most important tempo terms with translations, arranged in order from slow to fast. Writers on music do not always agree on the exact order for these terms; this listing is based on the entry "Performance marks" in the *New Harvard Dictionary of Music.*

1.	**grave**	[GRAH-vay], very slow, serious
2.	**largo**	broad
3.	**lento**	slow
4.	**adagio**	[a-DAGH-ee-o], slow; at ease
5.	**andante**	literally, walking, going; moderately slow
6.	**moderato**	moderate
7.	**allegro**	literally, cheerful; fast
8.	**vivace**	[vee-VAH-cheh], lively
9.	**presto**	very fast

Certain suffixes can modify the meanings of a few of these basic words. The "plus value" suffix, or "**-issimo**," intensifies meanings as it did for *fortissimo.* "**Prestissimo**" means very, very fast. At the opposite pole are two "minus value" suffixes, "**-ino**" and "**-etto,**" which take away from the value of the word. Thus **larghetto** is not quite as slow as largo, and **allegretto** is not quite as fast as allegro. But **andantino** confused no less a master than Beethoven, who wrote a letter indicating that he was not sure whether andantino was faster, or slower, than andante. Of course it depends upon whether walking is considered a fast or slow activity. If you have just had a meal of Italian pasta you might be inclined to walk slowly as you take your after-dinner stroll. Today andantino means a tempo slightly quicker than andante. Since none of these terms has a fixed meaning, there is some overlap among them and room for considerable variation in interpretation.

Other Italian words serve to qualify these terms, as in molto (very), assai (much), and non troppo (not too much). You encountered allegro giocoso (fast, humorous) in the discussion of the *Prelude to Carmen.* Sometimes it is safe to guess at the meanings of terms—con espressione (with expression) is a good example. For terms not listed in the Glossary/Index, you may want to consult a music dictionary.

Modifications of tempo are mandated by the words **accelerando** (speed up) and **ritardando** (slow down). **A tempo** is a directive to resume the original tempo after a change. Even though tempo terms may seem to demand a clockworklike precision from musicians, that is not generally the rule. In fact, an absolutely rigid, mechanical tempo is unmusical in any case.

Despite the fact that Italian terms are standard and understood worldwide (in this sense at least, music is indeed an international language), you will encounter terms in other languages as well, such as German or French—and now and then, even English! As a nationalistic gesture, composers sometimes pointedly reject Italian words in favor of their own native languages.

Many works that we shall study, such as the symphonies by Beethoven, Brahms, Mozart, and Tchaikovsky, the string quartet by Haydn, the piano sonata by Beethoven, and the concertos by Mendelssohn and Mozart, offer examples of tempo terms functioning as movement titles.

D

Syncopation is usually defined as an accent that occurs on normally weak beats or between beats; in other words, in an unexpected place. For example, count out loud a repeated pattern of ONE-two-THREE-four, while clapping hands on beats two and four. The expected place to clap is on beats one and three. Anything that renders the weak beats prominent, such as an accent, a longer tone, or a higher tone, results in syncopation. Although we tend to associate syncopation with jazz or folk music styles, it is found widely in many types of music. A simple example appears in the familiar song "Old Folks at Home," perhaps better known by its opening words: "Way down upon the Swanee River." The second syllable of "river" comes between beats three and four, a normally weak position. Added emphasis is given this syllable because it is higher in pitch than most other tones in the phrase (ex. 4.5).

Syncopation

Example 4.5

Familiar to most people is the piano rag by Scott Joplin, *The Entertainer* ⑦. From start to finish, it provides many examples of syncopation in the right-hand melody.

MUSICAL ELEMENTS: MELODY 5

PREVIEW Pitch and rhythm combine to create melody. In our discussion, we shall address the following groups of melody-related topics: scale, major, minor, tonality, and key; tune, motive, theme, and sequence; and melodic motion and range.

Melody means a *series of individual tones that can be perceived as an entity*. Just as the words of a sentence collectively make sense, the notes of a melody seem to hang together: one note leads to the next until a conclusion is reached. Thousands of melodies are all fashioned from the same basic ingredients: pitch and rhythm.

A

Melodies are closely connected with **scales;** in fact, some melodies simply move up and down the scale. A collection of pitches *arranged in consecutive order from low to high or high to low* makes a scale. Latin syllables identify the tones of the ascending scale: *do, re, mi, fa, sol, la, ti,* and another *dô,* an octave higher than the first. Note that the higher "*do*" is printed here with a caret mark to distinguish it from the lower "*do.*" This convention will be observed whenever confusion could arise about which octave is meant. [These syllables are pronounced: doh, ray, mee, fah, so, lah, tee.]

Scale, Major, Minor, Tonality, Key

To demonstrate a scale on the piano, play the white keys from any C to the next C on its right: C,D,E,F,G,A,B,C. "Scale" comes from the Italian "scala," a word that means "ladder." We even talk about the "steps of a scale." Just as a ladder rests upon the ground or the floor, the scale rests on its beginning tone, *do.*

A well-known Christmas song begins by moving downward through all eight tones of the scale. Incidentally, this song illustrates how rhythm transforms a downward-moving scale into a melody. If you play C,B,A,G,F,E,D,C evenly, with the same amount of time for each tone, you have played a simple scale. Play those same tones in the rhythm shown here and the result is "Joy to the World" (ex. 5.1).

Example 5.1

If you look closely at the notation for this song, you can see that the notes appear alternately on spaces and lines. That pattern of space-line-space-line is a clear indication of movement along the scale—up or down.

In our Western musical system, scales are constructed from a series of **whole-steps** and **half-steps.** As defined in Chapter 3, half-steps are the *intervals between any two immediately adjacent piano keys.* In each octave there exist two sets of white keys that are placed right next to each other with no black key in between them. Half-steps also occur between any black key and its neighboring white key.

Whole-steps are made up of two half-steps. The pattern for the C scale—all white keys, from one C to the next C—contains two half-steps. If you match the *do-re-mi-fa-sol-la-ti-dô* pattern to this scale, you will discover that the half-steps fall between the third and fourth notes (*mi-fa,* or E-F) and between the seventh and eighth notes (*ti-dô,* or B-C). All other intervals in this scale are whole-steps. This pattern of half- and whole-steps makes up the **major scale.** The melodies mentioned so far—and most familiar songs for that matter—are built on major scales.

Next in importance to the major scale is the **minor scale.** The opening portions of two well-known songs provide good examples of minor: a Christmas carol, "We Three Kings," and the Russian "Volga Boat Song" (ex. 5.2).

Example 5.2

In a minor scale, the third tone is one half-step lower than in a major scale. In comparing the first five tones of the C major scale (C,D,E,F,G) and the C minor scale (C,D, E-flat,F,G), we find only one different tone, E-flat. (On the piano, E-flat is the black key on the right in a group of two black keys.) "Minor" is potentially a confusing topic because the sixth and seventh tones are also one half-step lower, compared to a major scale, in some but not all varieties of minor scales. We need not be overly concerned with this complication. The essential thing to remember is the lowering of that third scale tone. While it may seem like a very small thing, it creates an amazing difference in emotional effect, a matter for further consideration in studying harmony.

A word of Greek origin, **diatonic,** designates an unaltered seven-note scale. A diatonic scale contrasts with the **chromatic** scale, which needs the twelve tones that are found in playing all the piano keys, black and white, in one octave. "Chromatic" comes from "chroma," the Greek word for color. A few familiar melodies are based on a portion of the chromatic scale. One example is the Irving Berlin song "White Christmas," which begins: E,F,E,D-sharp,E,F,F-sharp,G. A more extended chromatic scale provides the foundation for the "Habanera" (ex. 5.3), sung early in the opera by the sultry heroine of *Carmen*. Something about its downward chromatic line seems appropriate to her seductive intent.

Example 5.3

Other scales exist, among them the modal, pentatonic, and whole-tone. We shall postpone discussion of them until they are needed. Our Western concentration on major and minor has dulled our ears to the many other exotic possibilities available worldwide.

The most important note in any scale is the starting (and ending) note, *do,* referred to as the **keynote** or **tonic.** All other notes are dependent upon it to varying degrees, with *ti* being the most dependent of all. Stopping a scale on *ti* will create an almost physical need to finish the scale—something like waiting for the proverbial other shoe to drop. That dependency upon a tonic note and the relationships of all the scale tones to that tonic is known as **tonality.** Whether it is based on some "laws of nature" or on cultural conditioning, it is found worldwide, although the details of producing tonality vary greatly. As if to reinforce tonality, most familiar melodies end on *do.*

When we identify one particular pitch as the tonic, we have identified the **key** of a melody. For example, "Joy to the World" has C as *do* and is based on the C scale. We say that it is in the key of C, or in the tonality of C. Since there are twelve pitches in the octave, any of them can serve as the tonic for a key. To locate another scale, start on a G, for example, and play all the white keys from one G to the next. Everything will sound fine until you reach F. By trial and error, you can find that the black key immediately to the right of F (F-sharp, the lowest of a group of three black keys) produces the sound needed. In musical terms, you have discovered the G scale and with it, the key of G. Half-steps occur just as they do in the C scale, between the third and fourth scale tones (B and C) and between the seventh and eighth scale tones (F-sharp and G).

You might very well wonder why other keys are needed at all. For an answer, consider "America," which could very well be sung in the key of C, beginning C,C,D,B. Many singers find this pitch range too low; they prefer to start higher, in the key of G, as here (ex. 5.4), with the beginning notes of G,G,A,F-sharp.

Example 5.4

DENNIS THE MENACE

"DO YOU KNOW THE PORKY PIG THEME FROM LOONY TOONS?"

If you examine the music for "America," you may be surprised to find no sharp symbol in front of F, its fourth note. Clearly, a piece in the key of G would need so many F-sharps that it would be tedious to write in the symbol for each one. To simplify the musician's task, a system of **key signatures** has developed: that is, the necessary sharps or flats are marked at the beginning of each staff. From that point on, the performer must remember them. The key signature identifies *do*. For "America" in the key of G, a single sharp (on the highest line, F) is indicated at the very beginning of the staff.

Perhaps it is unfortunate that the word "key" has two meanings: the white or black keys that the fingers play on the piano, and the musical relationships between the sounds we have described. The familiar expression "low-key," referring to a pattern of restrained behavior has nothing to do with music. "Off-key" in ordinary language refers to a performance in which the pitches were badly mangled.

The key is often part of the title of a work. In titles quoted in this book, Chopin's *Etude in G-flat,* for instance, you can assume that the piece is in major if the key is not followed by the word "minor," as in Mendelssohn's *Violin Concerto in E Minor.*

Plate 1 Musical instruments have always provided inspiration for artists. David Adickes created this whimsical sculpture, which stands in front of an office building in downtown Houston.

Plate 2 The German artist Mathias Grünewald (c. 1480–1528) is best known for the *Isenheim Altarpiece*. Part of its middle portion shows an "Angel Concert," with angels playing string instruments only somewhat like those on earth.

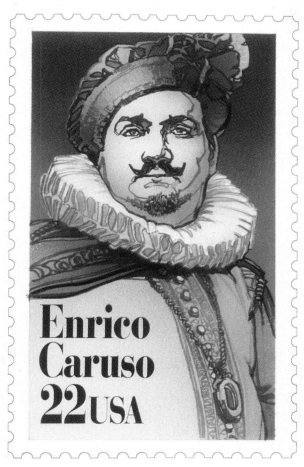

Plate 3 Italian-born tenor Enrico Caruso (1873–1921) made opera known to millions of Americans. The postal service issued this stamp in 1987, showing Caruso in costume for his role as the Duke in *Rigoletto,* an opera we study. (Copyright 1986 U.S. Postal Service)

Plate 4 Drums have many nonmusical associations, as this stamp makes clear. (U.S. Postal Service)

Plate 5 Henri Matisse (1869–1954) was famous for his love of, and innovative uses of, color. *The Piano Lesson,* 1916, shows the artist's son at the piano. Notice the metronome, which dominates the lower right-hand corner of the painting—perhaps as a hint that the metronome also dominates the child's performance. (Oil on canvas, 8'1/2" × 6'11 3/4". Collection, The Museum of Modern Art, New York. Mrs. Simon Guggenheim Fund.)→

Plate 6 Italian-born Arturo Toscanini (1867–1957) was a dynamic conductor. He dominated the field for decades, as this postage stamp of 1989 reminds us. (Copyright 1989 U.S. Postal Service)

Plate 7   Though the symbols for Gregorian notation are very old, this example shows the latest (1979) printing, from the Graduale Triplex. The markings in red below the notes show even older symbols (they are called neumes) from one manuscript, while the ones in black above the notes represent those in still another source.

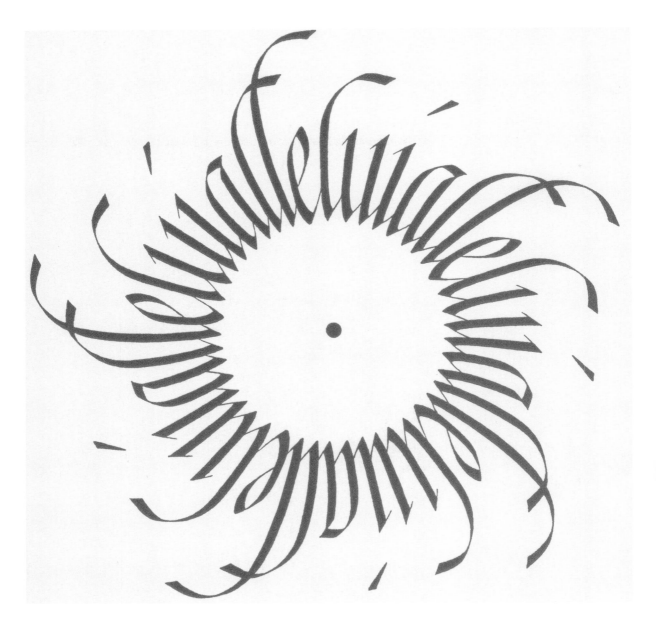

Plate 8 A contemporary designer, Michael Podesta, demonstrates that calligraphy can be a fine art. He forms the word "alleluia" into a circle, itself a symbol.

B

Tune, Motive, Theme, and Sequence

It is difficult to make real distinctions among tune, motive, and theme. It is probably safe to say that **tunes** are singable, easily remembered by the average listener. Sometimes people think of tunes as exclusively folk songs, perhaps on the order of "Yankee Doodle." Yet when the "theme" or main melody from the last movement of Beethoven's *Symphony No. 9* is given a new set of words and put into a hymnal for church congregations to sing, it is called a **hymn tune.** Hymn tunes have names, distinct from the words to which they might be sung. Beethoven's melody (ex. 5.5) is labeled "Hymn to Joy."

Example 5.5

It is not necessary for a melody to be tuneful: there are great melodies about which this cannot be said.

Motives are short melodic ideas, perhaps only three or four notes—five in Carmen's Fate motive. Unlike a tune, which is complete in itself, a motive functions as a building block for something longer. **Themes** are longer than motives. Indeed, they often result from a combination of motives. They serve as a basis for extended works such as symphonies or sonatas. Frequently a theme undergoes considerable change, even fragmentation, as it recurs, yet it somehow maintains its identity. Themes may be quite melodic, even tuneful—but not always—so there is no specific quality that marks a theme *as* a theme.

Beethoven furnishes a memorable example of a motive with the famous, attention-getting motive that begins his *Symphony No. 5* ㊶: short-short-short-long. By varying and combining statements of that motive, he built the main theme of the symphony's first movement. A similar process is at work in the first movement of Mozart's *Symphony No. 40* ㉞, where a three-note motive underlies the main theme. For a more "tuneful" theme, listen to the beginning of Section VII of *Appalachian Spring* (75) by Copland. This music is based upon an American folk song, played here by the clarinet.

Often, but by no means always, melodies contain **sequences,** in which a particular group of notes is restated at a higher or a lower pitch level. (Do not confuse this term with "a sequence of events" in nonmusical language.) Sequences add continuity to a melody. Two or three restatements are about the limit for a successful sequence—at least, most composers seem to have adopted this restriction. "America" furnishes a simple example. The pitch relationships for the phrase "Land where my fathers died" are duplicated a step lower for the succeeding phrase, "Land of the pilgrims' pride" (ex. 5.6).

Example 5.6

C

Melodic Motion and Range

To describe melodies, musicians, borrowing terms from the field of art, talk about the "contour" or the "line" of a melody. We shall sum up these ideas as melodic motion. Indeed, we are strongly conditioned to the idea that pitches will move. Simply staying on a single pitch for any extended time is tension-provoking—we wait for some change to take place. To change that initial pitch, only three things are possible: repeat the first note; move to a higher note; move to a lower note. In moving up or down, the possibilities are twofold: selecting adjacent notes of the scale or selecting more distant notes.

Moving along the scale is called **conjunct** (stepwise or scalewise) motion. Moving to nonadjacent notes is called **disjunct** (skipping or leaping) motion. These two kinds of motion produce quite different emotional reactions. A conjunct melody sounds smooth and relaxed, a disjunct melody angular and active. To compare the two types of motion, listen to two national melodies. "America" (shown earlier in ex. 5.4) moves almost exclusively up and down the tones of the scale, while "The Star Spangled Banner" (ex. 5.7) does far more skipping.

Example 5.7

Notice how the notation shows this contrast: line-space-line in "America" and line-line-line in "The Star Spangled Banner."

The **range** of a melody refers to the span of pitches from its lowest tone to its highest. Some children's songs, such as "Mary Had a Little Lamb," (ex. 5.8) cover only five tones, from *do* to *sol*.

Example 5.8

Simple songs that almost everyone can sing have a range of an octave or less. A range exceeding an octave practically guarantees that a melody will seem difficult for the average person. Indeed, that has been the unhappy fate of "The Star Spangled Banner," with its octave-and-a-half range. Melodies designed for instruments often cover a larger range, simply because instruments have bigger ranges than do voices.

Most melodies represent a combination of disjunct and conjunct motion. Schubert's *Die Forelle* ㊸ begins in a disjunct fashion but soon turns to a downward scale passage. The entire song spans less than an octave in range.

A line drawing based on a melody can show its up-and-down movement, with lengths of lines corresponding to durations of notes. See if you can associate these diagrams with the familiar songs they represent: "Joy to the World," "Mary Had a Little Lamb," "Ode to Joy," "The Star Spangled Banner," "Volga Boat Song," "We Three Kings."

A

B

C

D

E

F

6 MUSICAL ELEMENTS: HARMONY

PREVIEW   Harmony is the element that most distinguishes Western music from that of other cultures. We take it for granted that a melody will be accompanied by some kind of harmony. Much of our harmony discussion expands upon some terms already encountered in the melody chapter, covering these groups of basic concepts: intervals, chords, and triads; consonance and dissonance; major and minor; and harmonic progressions and tonality.

The simplest kind of harmony, the drone of a bagpipe, can be heard in many parts of the world, but most people associate the instrument with Scotland.

A

Unlike melody, which results from a series of *consecutive* pitches, **harmony** is based upon the sounding of *simultaneous* tones. Music notation places all notes that are to be sounded at the same time in a vertical relationship, one note above or below another, while consecutive tones appear horizontally from left to right.

The simplest harmony is demonstrated by a bagpipe, which can play a melody simultaneously with the accompaniment of a **drone,** which is a long, sustained note. But while many musical cultures are satisfied with such a limited diet, the beauty of Western music's highly developed harmony is unique in the world. For the average reader, harmony is a more complicated subject than rhythm or melody, which seem more obvious. (Perhaps we should add that the familiar phrase "living together in harmony" has nothing to do with music!)

Intervals, Chords, and Triads

We first met the word interval in connection with the octave, which is produced by two piano keys with the same letter name. Although only two tones are necessary to create an octave, its name reflects the fact that eight letters are involved, counting from the bottom up and including the top tone, as for example C,D, E,F,G,A,B,C. All intervals get their names by a similar process. A melodic interval is the distance between two tones sounded consecutively. A harmonic interval is the distance between two tones sounded simultaneously.

Some intervals, such as the third (for example, C and E) and the sixth (C and A), blend together well, like the octave. When people "harmonize" by ear they almost automatically sing in thirds and sixths. Not all intervals blend this well. Seconds (for example, C and D) and sevenths (C and B) refuse to blend at all. Somewhere in the middle are fourths (C and F) and fifths (C and G). While they may sound a little odd or hollow, to most ears they are not unpleasant.

Bach was proud of the musical skills of his family. As they started the day with their "Morning Devotions," surely they sang in harmony. Incidentally, this painting bears no relationship to the actual Bach family: it was done in 1870 by a California artist living in Germany, Toby Rosenthal.

A **chord** (note that it is not spelled "cord") consists of three or more tones sounding together. The most fundamental chord is the **triad** [pronounced TRY-add]. A *tri*ad needs three tones, and these three tones must have letter names forming an every-other-letter pattern, such as C-E-G. (The notes can be moved around, however, so that a triad might be arranged as E-G-C or G-C-E.) When the pitches of any chord are spread out over time and occur one at a time, the result is a **broken chord,** sometimes called an **arpeggio** [pronounced ar-PEJ-ee-o].

Just as the two pitches forming an octave blend together, the three tones of a triad mingle and *create a new sonority.* The poet Robert Browning (1812–89) recognized this phenomenon when he praised a composer who could, out of three tones, create "not a fourth sound, but a star." Chords with more than three un-duplicated tones have an active quality compared with the more static sound of triads. Writers often describe such harmony as "rich," compared to the "lean" sound of triads. A few of the "richer" chords will be singled out in connection with the historical era in which they developed.

Wagner begins the *Prize Song* ⑤³ from *Die Meistersinger* with a simple triad played twice by the orchestra before the tenor enters.

Chords are given names in traditional studies: a Roman numeral that reflects the position in the scale of its lowest tone and a word that describes the function of that note in the scale. For example, the C-E-G chord in the key of C is called a "I" chord because C is number "one" in the scale. It is also called the **tonic chord** because C is the tonic note of the C scale. The tonic chord is stable: it provides a convincing ending. A more active chord is that on G (G-B-D), the fifth tone of the scale, called a V chord or the **dominant.** It demands to move on, generally to the tonic. Less active than the dominant, yet less stable than the tonic is the chord on F (F-A-C), the fourth tone of the scale, the IV chord or the **subdominant.** "Twinkle, Twinkle, Little Star" needs only these three chords for its harmonization, as follows:

Twinkle, twinkle, little star, How I wonder what you are.

I   I   IV I IV   I   V   I

Up above the world so high, Like a diamond in the sky,

I V   I   V   I   V   I   V

Twinkle, twinkle, little star, How I wonder what you are.

I   I   IV I IV   I   V   I

A "three-chord guitar player" knows only the three primary triads I, IV, and V, but they are enough to enable the player to harmonize thousands of songs. Three more chords, built on the second, third, and sixth tones of the scale, are almost as necessary. Frequently, composers embellish these basic chords with chromatic tones as well. Beethoven, for example, wrote a series of variations on the melody we know as "America." One of the variations (ex. 6.1) shows a surprising number of chromatic notes enriching the harmony.

Example 6.1

      PART ONE FUNDAMENTAL ELEMENTS

Traditional blues songs, such as Bessie Smith's *Lost Your Head Blues* (76), are based upon the I, IV, and V chords, in a highly structured order. Pachelbel's *Canon in D* (17) reveals an equally structured order, but with two more chords added to the I, IV, and V chords.

B

Consonance and Dissonance

The technical term for the restful, stable, blending quality we noticed in the octave and the triad is **consonance.** Conversely, **dissonance** refers to a lack of blending. Just as the intervals described above vary in the degrees to which they are consonant or dissonant, chords also vary. As we noted, the tones of the triad blend very well: it is consonant. Add a B to a C-E-G triad and a dissonant chord results.

In ordinary language, people often confuse "discord" with dissonance and equate both with something unpleasant. In music the dissonance may indeed have an aggressive, spiky quality, but dissonance need not be considered negatively. Rather, dissonance generates tension and activity, whereas consonance is the *relaxation of tension.* For instance, "Chop Sticks" (ex. 6.2) begins with a dissonance of a second, F and G, which is immediately smoothed out with a consonant third, E and G.

Example 6.2

In musical terms, dissonances **resolve,** that is, they progress or move to tones that form consonances—at least, we expect them to do so. Just as people need some tension in their lives, drama needs conflict, and food needs spices—so music needs dissonance.

Most of the music we study that was written before this century will seem generally consonant; there is some dissonance, but it is too fleeting to describe here. A marked rise in the dissonance level is obvious in some of our twentieth-century orchestral selections, for example, in *The Housatonic at Stockbridge* (74) by Ives, in *The Rite of Spring* (68) by Stravinsky, and, in its very beginning, in *Montagues and Capulets* (73) from Prokofiev's *Romeo and Juliet* ballet suite.

Major and Minor

The terms **major** and **minor** apply to harmony as well as to melody. For example, the C-E-G triad is a major triad; lowering the E to an E-flat makes it a minor triad. While a piece written in a minor key may include some major chords, the tonic chord (the one built on *do*) will be a minor chord, and that chord sets the tone of the entire piece. The small difference in physical terms creates a big difference in emotional climate. To recall the *Prelude to Carmen* yet again, the Toreador song, in major, and the Fate motive, in minor, point up this contrast. A statement such as "major's glad and minor's sad" is an exaggeration, yet enough truth remains in this old cliché to make it worth considering, if only to be alert for exceptions.

The titles of many larger compositions indicate that the work begins in a specific minor key, but they fail to tell the student that a particular movement of that work might be in major. This is true of several works we study: Mozart's *Symphony No. 40 in G Minor,* Beethoven's *Symphony No. 5 in C Minor,* Tchaikovsky's *Symphony No. 4 in F minor,* and Brahms's *Symphony No. 4 in E Minor.*

D

Harmonic Progressions and Tonality

"Progress" in its nonmusical sense means to advance, to improve. **Harmonic progressions,** a series of chords, do not improve anything, but they do seem to advance—to *go somewhere.* This concept of harmony has been operating, in Western music at least, for the past three or four centuries. Two chords are enough to establish a progression, as in John Lennon's recording of his song "Imagine." The piano accompaniment begins with the progression of I to IV, repeated several times. Only when the orchestra enters does the harmony become more varied and change at a more frequent rate.

Each chord in a well-chosen progression adds to the sense of moving along toward the ending. Characteristically, the ending employs the V chord (often enlarged by one note in a way we shall study later) followed by the I chord. To hear how strongly ingrained is the sense that a harmonization *must* end on a I chord, try substituting a IV chord at the end of "Twinkle." It will not hurt your ears, but it will seem strange. Sometimes the ending progression is IV to I. These chords provide the harmony for the concluding "Amen" in hymn singing.

In our discussion of melody we noted that playing a scale and stopping on *ti* would create an almost physical need to finish the scale because of the magnetic force of *do*. The central importance of one tone is known as **tonality,** a concept we first met in relation to melody, but it supports harmony as well. Listen to a scale with the simple harmonies of example 6.3. Lingering on the V chord that accompanies *ti* before moving to the I chord at the end will furnish an even more dramatic proof of our expectations regarding tonality and how important a role is played by harmony.

Example 6.3

In this scale harmonization, the letters above the scale refer to a system of chord notation found in popular music, in which chords have letter names, not the Roman numerals of traditional harmony. In this system, the I chord, C-E-G, is called simply a "C chord." Whatever the key in which the chord occurs, the letter name remains the same. Both systems, the Roman numerals and the letter names, are valid.

7 MUSICAL ELEMENTS: TEXTURE

PREVIEW   Just as fabric is woven out of vertical and horizontal threads, the notes of music can be regarded in two dimensions: the simultaneous (vertical) and the successive (horizontal). Three terms, each ending with "-phony," identify three possibilities for the treatment of melodies: monophony, polyphony, and homophony.

In music, a melody may occur by itself, with no accompaniment at all. Two or more melodies may sound at once. Or a melody may be accompanied in some fashion. Three basic terms identify these possibilities: (1) monophony, (2) polyphony, and (3) homophony. [All three words are pronounced with an accent on the second syllable. When they occur as adjectives, as in monophonic, polyphonic, or homophonic, the accent falls on the "-phon" syllable. "Phon" is the Greek word for sound.] These words are known collectively as **texture,** a term coming from the Latin *texere,* meaning to weave. Speaking more generally, texture sometimes refers to the idea of "thick" or "thin," just as we describe fabric as thick or thin.

A

Monophony

The first "-phony" word is **monophony.** The "mono" in this word indicates a single musical line. If you sing by yourself, you produce monophony. A hundred people could join you, everyone singing only that melody—it is still monophony. Although monophony is generally associated with vocal music, it also applies to a single melodic line played by instruments. The duplication of a monophonic line at different octaves, which happens when men and women sing together, or when instruments of both high and low pitch ranges play, does not affect it as monophony. In many cultures monophony remains the standard, and historians believe that it was the original kind of music. For Western ears, a melody without any accompaniment seems unusual because, as we shall see, Western music evolved in the Middle Ages to include added sounds.

Any Gregorian chant, as in our *Alleluia, Dies sanctificatus* (2),will demonstrate monophony. Both Debussy's *Prélude à l'après-midi d'un faune* (65) and Stravinsky's *Rite of Spring* (66) begin monophonically with a single instrument playing (you will hear the flute in Debussy and the bassoon in Stravinsky).

The second of our two "-phony" words, **polyphony,** can result from the combination of as few as *two musical lines,* making a literal reading of "poly-" as "many" misleading. The lines of polyphony are often referred to as **voices,** even in instrumental music. In **nonimitative** polyphony, the first main type, different melodies are combined. For example, the beginning sections of "Old Folks at Home" and "Humoresque," a melody by the Romantic composer Antonin Dvořák, happen by accident to combine well. ("Old Folks at Home" is shown in example 7.1 in the left hand; "Humoresque" is in the right hand.)

Polyphony

Example 7.1

Of course the nonimitative polyphony that we shall study is the intentional product of trained musicians.

The fourth movement of Bach's *Cantata No. 140* (29) is a complex web of nonimitative polyphony. At first, a flowing string melody is opposed by a steady bass line. With the entrance of tenors, three individual lines fit together. The second movement of Haydn's *String Quartet, op. 76, no. 3* (32) is a set of variations on a memorable melody. Variation I demonstrates nonimitative polyphony, as one violin plays this melody and the other violin decorates it with an elaborate, completely different, line.

Any familiar round, such as "Row, Row, Row Your Boat" (ex. 7.2), will demonstrate **imitative** polyphony, the second main type. A group of singers starts the melody. While this group continues, a second group enters at a fixed number of beats later, singing the same melody from its beginning. Rounds are planned to accommodate a certain number of voices, usually three or four. "Row, Row, Row Your Boat" can be sung in four parts. We call this type of polyphony "imitative" because each entrance imitates what was previously sung. A more academic term for round is **canon.** While rounds can be continued indefinitely by simple repetition, a canon usually reaches a definite stopping point.

Example 7.2

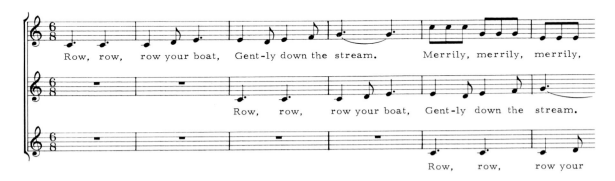

In a more complicated form of imitative polyphony, successive entries of the main melody alternate between *do* and *sol*. Listen, for example, to the round "Row, Row, Row Your Boat" in the arrangement given here (ex. 7.3). In it, successive entries begin alternately on C and G.

Example 7.3

In the *Kyrie* of Josquin's *Pange lingua Mass* , the four vocal lines imitate each other. For an instrumental example, we can turn to the most rigorous form of imitative polyphony, the fugue, as in Bach's *"Little" Fugue in G Minor* ㉖ , for organ.

When used for vocal music, both types of polyphony present an inherent problem: it is difficult to understand the text because different words are being sung at the same time by the different voice parts. If clarity of words is considered essential, polyphony might not seem the most appropriate vehicle for a religious text. Yet as we will see, polyphonic sacred music has existed for centuries, though not without controversy. A Roman bishop in 1549 complained that "while one voice says 'Sanctus,' another says 'Sabaoth,' still another 'Gloria tua,' with howling, bellowing, and stammering, so that they more nearly resemble cats in January than flowers in May."

C

Homophony

Quite different is the third "-phony" texture, **homophony.** It is generally defined as the texture in which a prominent melody is supported by an accompaniment of some sort. It also comes in two varieties. In choral music, as in a harmonization for soprano, alto, tenor, and bass, homophony results when all voices move in the same rhythm, singing the same syllable at the same time, though each voice maintains its own independent line. This first type of homophony, often referred to as **chordal style** or **homorhythmic,** can occur in instrumental music as well. When all voices move in the same rhythm, today's listener is apt to hear chords instead of separate lines and to interpret the highest voice as the melody, with the lower voices relegated to accompaniment status. For example, a choir sings "Silent Night" in a standard, four-part harmonization (ex. 7.4) and no doubt the altos, the tenors, and the basses all regard their own lines as nice melodies, well worth your attention. But the listener concentrates on the soprano tune.

Example 7.4

Haydn's *String Quartet in C, op. 76, no. 3* (31) begins with all four instruments playing together homorhythmically, giving us a demonstration of chordal style.

A second kind of homophony is the texture consisting of a melody with a *contrasting* type of accompaniment. Much piano music is homophonic, the pianist playing a melody in one hand, while the other hand supplies various chordal patterns. For a simple example, a piano beginner could play "Silent Night" in the style shown here (ex. 7.5), with the melody played by the right hand and the left hand supporting it with chords.

Example 7.5

Chopin's *Nocturne in F-sharp* (45) shows the second kind of homophony, melody-plus-chords, as does Schubert's *Die Forelle* (43), in which the vocal line is clearly set apart from its piano accompaniment.

Much music lies between the extremes of polyphony and homophony. Distinctions become blurred, as the musical lines of an accompaniment compete with the melody for the listener's attention. For variety, many pieces include all three types of texture.

The *Hallelujah* chorus (24) from Handel's *Messiah* begins with all voices singing homophonically in chordal style. This chorus also includes a brief moment of monophony and many passages of nonimitative polyphony, easily recognizable because two different sets of words are sung. Victoria's *Ave Maria* (12) begins with monophony and contains passages of imitative polyphony as well as chordal-style homophony.

8 MUSICAL ELEMENTS: FORM

PREVIEW In this brief chapter, we introduce the essential idea of musical form as we analyze the separate phrases of a familiar melody.

Most compositions have a shape, a pattern, some sort of organization. We call these shapes **musical forms.** They are created by repetition and by contrast. Listeners seem to have two deeply seated needs: a need for unity and a need for variety. Too much unity—too much repetition—produces boredom. Too much variety—too many contrasting ideas—creates confusion. Successful musical compositions display a delicate balance between these opposing forces.

Throughout history, musical forms have evolved and acquired names, such as sonata-form and rondo. Believing that such forms are best studied as they arise in our chronological survey, we have left them for later.

A

Phrases and Musical Form

Melodies ordinarily divide into **phrases,** a basic unit of music. Phrases are somewhat akin to short sentences in ordinary language. Analogous to the words of a sentence, the tones of a musical phrase seem to hang together. Though musicians often argue about how long a phrase is, an easy way to identify the ending of a vocal phrase is to note where the singer breathes, just as one does in ordinary speech at the end of a sentence. Phrases are less obvious in instrumental music, but it is usually possible to hear them. (Caution: people often discuss a given performer's "phrasing," making this word a general term for individual musical interpretation.)

At the ends of most phrases a **cadence** occurs. This is a kind of musical punctuation mark, functioning like a comma or a period in language—or an exclamation mark, in many cases. A cadence gives a *sense of ending,* which is communicated by any or all of these melodic or harmonic elements: a longer tone, a downward motion of the melody, a progression of the harmony such as a dominant chord resolving to a tonic chord. Often a slight pause identifies a cadence. In vocal music the poetic structure of the words customarily shapes the phrases, and since four-line stanzas are common in poetry, musical phrases are commonly grouped together into sets of four. Although the composer of instrumental music is free to choose otherwise, the number four seems to prevail.

To discover the form of a melody, we begin by identifying the individual phrases, with punctuation marks of the text offering possible clues. Letters of the alphabet show the results of analysis, with "a" indicating the first phrase or its exact repetition, "b" denoting a contrasting phrase, and "a'" standing for a varied repetition. Since the phrases of a well-made song share common elements, deciding whether a given phrase demonstrates a varied repetition (a, a') or a contrast (a, b) is sometimes difficult. For a sample demonstration, see the familiar song "Deck the Halls" (ex. 8.1).

Example 8.1

The first two phrases are identical musically. Word differences do not matter. The music of the last phrase parallels that of the first until the last "fa-la-la" refrain, which is clearly different. That accounts for an "a" label. And though the third phrase differs in pitch contour, and for that reason gets a "b" label, it relates to the other phrases because it essentially preserves their rhythm pattern. The resulting form, aaba (or aaba', to be exact), is a common, eminently successful one. Even more common is aba, as in "Twinkle, Twinkle, Little Star." The traditional name for aba or aaba forms is **ternary.**

Composers expand the basic form-building concept as seen in these songs to larger dimensions, which are measured in minutes instead of seconds. Capital letters, as in ABA, reflect this larger time frame.

Analyzing "Deck the Halls"

Chopin's *Nocturne in F-sharp* ㊺ is in ternary form, with its somewhat agitated B section flanked by a quiet beginning and ending. The *Minuet* of Mozart's *Symphony No. 40* ㊱ demonstrates a large ternary form, with the gentle B section (the "trio") representing a marked contrast to the more aggressive music surrounding it.

Analysis of works in ternary form can show that composers make many decisions in choosing the ways this form is handled. Is the B section a strong contrast or merely a slight change of character? Is the return of A a sudden event, or did the composer throw out hints that it was coming? If A is changed in its return, how drastic are the changes? Such analysis will guide listening in fruitful ways.

The same human need for unity and variety is shown in architecture as well as in music. The two wings of this sixteenth-century French chateau are an architectural parallel to the ABA form in music.

THE PERFORMANCE OF MUSIC 9

PREVIEW Studying about music is no substitute for listening to it. In this chapter we discuss some topics that relate to the listening experience: live music compared to recordings, the problems of musical titles, and performance variables—the reasons why performances of a work will differ.

Unique to the art of music is the need for an intermediary between composer and listener. We can read a book unaided or look at a painting all we like, but someone else must perform music for most of us. Much about the performance of music is taken for granted by those who make it themselves, but the novice needs an introduction to a few basic ideas.

A

For practical reasons, most of the listening you will do as part of your class study will undoubtedly be done with recordings. They have many advantages. They make repeated listening to musical works possible, which is a necessary condition if you hope to uncover the countless beauties within them. Comparing various interpretations of a work is easy with recordings. In fact, some great performers of the recent past have left a permanent legacy of their abilities. Some types of contemporary music exist only in recorded form.

Live Music Compared to Recordings

Despite all the advantages of recordings, a live performance offers values unattainable otherwise. Chief among them is spontaneity. Admittedly, live performances seldom match the technical perfection of recordings, where careful editing can snip out mistakes and create a perfect rendition from a number of imperfect ones. Still, in a live concert situation, every performance is a fresh, new experience. Being part of a group which has assembled specifically to share in the experience of listening helps many people concentrate on the music. Also, the sheer sound of many performing media, such as the pipe organ or a large orchestra in a reverberant hall, cannot be duplicated on recordings, no matter how expensive the audio equipment.

Conductor Zubin Mehta consults by telephone with the sound engineer in a recording session with the Los Angeles Philharmonic Orchestra. Plastic drapes the seats in order to increase reverberation time in the hall. (Photograph David Weiss, © 1990)

An often neglected consideration of a live performance is that it gives the listeners something to *look at.* The motions of the performers usually reflect the phrases, the rhythms, and the underlying mood of a piece. With nothing to watch, as when one listens to recordings, it becomes all too easy to lose focus and to lapse into daydreaming. For these and other reasons, you are strongly encouraged to seek out live performances. Indeed, you may be required to attend concerts as part of your class work. If you have never before attended a concert of "classical music," some preparation before the event is wise. Review the discussion of "movements"

Students make up this orchestra at UCLA, but they dress in the color universally adopted for professional performers—black.

in our Rhythm chapter (you certainly do not want to be the one who starts to applaud prematurely); read about the composers represented on the concert; arrive early enough to read the program notes, if there are any. In fact, these are good practices even for an experienced concert-goer.

You should also know that certain conventions are associated with most concerts. The performers all dress in a similar style, often wearing formal evening attire. No one introduces the music; the program tells everything you need to know (or so the theory goes). A level of silence is expected that may seem repressive—but people are listening. Coughing is most distracting and conversation is unforgivable.

As well as attending live concerts, you can also benefit from televised performances of music, which are increasingly available for purchase or rental as videocassettes. Not only do they supply the visual element that is missing in listening to recordings, but they can also show some aspects of performance that a concert audience never sees. For example, the televised view of the conductor as the orchestra sees him (it's almost always a him on television, although a few women conductors are working in mid-size orchestras these days) can provide fascinating revelations about that conductor's own reactions.

diminuendo

Copyright © Annetta Hoffnung.

B

What You Need to Know about Titles

A short poem by Alfred, Lord Tennyson (1809–92) can tell us something about all titles. Read the poem as it stands here:

He clasps the crag with crooked hands;
Close to the sun in lonely lands,
Ringed with the azure world, he stands.
The wrinkled sea beneath him crawls;
He watches from his mountain walls,
And like a thunderbolt he falls.

Non-Russians attending a concert in Russia can still follow the program, aided by Italian tempo terms that are standard the world around, and the K. numbers that identify works by Mozart.

ПРОГРАММА

I отделение

Соната до мажор для скрипки и фортепьяно (К-6)

Allegro

Andante

Менуэт I. Менуэт II

Allegro molto

Соната фа мажор для скрипки и фортепьяно
(К-377)

Allegro

Тема с вариациями. Andante

Tempo di minuetto

II отделение

Соната ре мажор для скрипки и фортепьяно
(К-306)

Allegro con spirito

Andantino cantabile

Allegretto. Allegro

Did you know what the poem was about? Does the title, "The Eagle," help you understand it? Similarly, in music a piece needs its title to attain its full effect. From that title, as well as from the composer's name, the experienced listener gains information that affects the expectations brought to that piece. Even the most inexperienced listener needs a full title in order to locate recordings or to track down references to a work. One particularly necessary word in titles is **opus,** Latin for "work," sometimes abbreviated as **op.,** plural "opp." This word indicates the chronological position of a given work in a list of that composer's output. Sometimes "opus" is restricted to published compositions. Such numbers help distinguish among pieces with similar titles—*which* symphony, *which* sonata.

For some composers, numbers preceded by letters, such as "K." (for Mozart), "D." (for Schubert), or "BWV" (for J. S. Bach), may appear in lieu of opus numbers. In addition, titles may include a number, Symphony No. 5, for example, and a reference to the key, such as "in C Minor." For some compositions titles appear in an English translation and in the original foreign language as well.

Even if you do not understand a title fully when first you meet it, it has value simply as a label. Rest assured that these matters will be explained, eventually.

C

Each performance of a given composition will differ from the next. For example, listening to several recordings of a work that we study, such as Mozart's *Symphony No. 40 in G Minor,* K. 550—a title that illustrates some of the possibilities just mentioned!—will quickly reveal that conductors have decidedly different ideas about it. (At last count, more than forty compact discs of this symphony are available.) Some of these performances seem louder, or faster, or smoother, or more accented than others, even though all the orchestras are playing the notes that Mozart wrote down. The elapsed time can vary. These and many other possible differences are summed up here as **performance variables.** Their existence is a fundamental, though often overlooked, part of music.

Performance Variables

Some people mistakenly assume that a composer does all the essential work and that a performer simply follows the composer's directions, much as carpenters build houses by faithfully following architects' blueprints. This analogy is invalid for any performing art. For example, every actor playing Hamlet recites "To be, or not to be," but interprets Shakespeare's words a bit differently. A powerful reason for music's performance variables is the widespread belief that music needs **expression,** that is, those elements of performance that vary in subtle ways with the performer.

Expressive performance in music can be compared to the different meanings a simple phrase acquires as it is repeated with a change of emphasis. "*I* am going" means that while I am going, you are not. "I *am* going" suggests certainty. "I am *going*" implies that staying is no longer possible. A speaker communicates the meaning of a phrase by emphasis on a word, by tiny hesitations, by speeding up or slowing down, and so on. Musicians do something similar. By emphasis on some notes, by subtle alteration of tone colors, by minute fluctuations in speed, they indicate what they think is important in these notes. They express what the music *means* in musical ways.

Musicians take some cues from **expression marks,** which are signs and marks in the musical score that give details of expression to the performer. Suggestions regarding dynamics, tempo, or how notes are to be connected or separated or given special stress are only a few of the many possibilities for expression marks. They have been employed by composers of the past four centuries to supplement the pitches and rhythms specified in music notation. A few of these expression marks

The director of a ballet company functions like the conductor of an orchestra. Here the dancers in a *Nutcracker* production of the San Francisco Ballet gather around their director for a last-minute pep talk before taping their performance. (Courtesy of San Francisco Performing Arts Library and Museum, Henri McDowell collection.)

are part of the vocabulary of technical terms we study. The closer the music is to the present day, the more likely it is that the composer's directions are extremely detailed. Even so, considerable room is still left to the performers. In pursuit of musical expression, musicians also follow many traditions and conventions beyond what is shown in the musical score.

Even if two musicians agree on a detail of expression, they may still perform it differently because they want an individual interpretation. In our culture, we are not satisfied simply with being part of a group; we expect credit and attention for our own work. Perhaps as a result, today highly individualistic performers reap the greatest rewards.

Another reason for performance variables has to do with history. In earlier times, the performer of a piece was very often its composer as well and therefore found it unnecessary to write down any interpretative directions in the music. For music of the Middle Ages, even the basic notes themselves may need deciphering. In playing music of the Baroque period, performers may add extra notes, improvising them on the spot.

Drawing by Lorenz;
© 1987 The New Yorker
Magazine, Inc.

"You have to admire the concept—early music performed on the original instruments."

When people talk about the "performance practice" of an era or want to know if "period instruments" are being played, they refer to **authenticity in performance,** which is the ideal of recreating performance styles that prevailed when the composition was new. In recent years some musicians have become increasingly aware of the possibilities in reconstructing earlier performing conventions. They revived earlier or "original" forms of instruments, because most of our instruments have undergone much change as they have evolved historically.

Regardless of how historically correct the actual instruments they play might be, some musicians seek diligently to perform in an authentic manner, guided by scholarly research. Others feel that the quest is hopeless because elements of musical life are so different today. For example, our concert halls are much bigger; our listening habits have changed. For many reasons, recordings of a very early work may differ so dramatically that they scarcely sound like the same piece. We shall refer frequently to this challenging, elusive, yet fascinating topic.

10 IDENTIFYING MUSICAL ELEMENTS

PREVIEW   No new content appears in this chapter. You can use it as a review of concepts outlined in Part One. Try to identify these musical elements as they appear in the specific examples listed.

This chapter provides a checklist of selected pieces, some of which were listed as suggested listening experiences in Chapters 3 through 8. They are described or analyzed in the listening guides that appear in historical context later in this book. Consequently, if your curiosity is aroused by any one of them, you have a source of information to help satisfy it. As in many self-questioning activities, the process itself is more valuable than are the actual answers. The purpose of this study is to provide some guided practice in concentrated listening.

Listen to a selection from the list of musical pieces that follows, and try to decide whether or not it clearly demonstrates any of the items described in the list of concepts that follows the list of pieces. If your authors believe that it does, the number for that selection appears after that concept. The absence of a selection's number does not necessarily constitute a "no" vote. There might be no clear "right" answer, or we may think it unreasonable to expect students to associate the concept with this particular work.

The titles listed appear in condensed fashion in order to save space; more information is supplied in the Index of Composers and Titles. Roman numerals identify separate movements or sections of a larger work.

To help identify tone colors, we append a brief, general description of the tone colors found in each selection. For some pieces, the sounds could quite possibly differ markedly from one recording to another, for reasons explained earlier as a part of the "authenticity" discussion.

1. Bizet: *Prelude to Carmen* (1) (orchestra)
2. Bach: *Toccata* (only) *in D Minor* (27) (organ)
3. Gabrieli: *Canzona* (14) (small instrumental ensemble)
4. Strauss: *Also sprach Zarathustra* (64), beginning (orchestra)
5. Tchaikovsky: *Symphony No. 4,* III (60) (strings begin; orchestra)
6. Verdi: *La donna è mobile* (56) (orchestra, tenor)
7. Victoria: *Ave Maria* (12) (four-part choral group)
8. Chopin: *Nocturne in F-sharp* (45) (modern piano)
9. *Estampie* (9) (early instruments, one flutelike, one cellolike)
10. Mozart: *Symphony No. 40,* III (36) (orchestra, no percussion)
11. Gregorian chant: *Alleluia: Dies sanctificatus* (2) (male choir)
12. Josquin: *Kyrie* (10) (four-part choir, possibly with instruments)
13. Schubert: *Die Forelle* (43) (modern piano, vocal soloist)
14. Handel: *Hallelujah* (24) (orchestra, four-part choir)
15. Joplin: *The Entertainer* (77) (piano)
16. Haydn: *String Quartet,* I (31) (two violins, viola, cello)
17. Prokofiev: *Montagues and Capulets* (73) (orchestra)
18. Bach: *Cantata No. 140,* IV (29) (strings, organ, tenors)

a. Begins in duple meter. 1, 3, 4, 5, 8, 13, 14, 15, 16, 18.
b. Begins in triple meter. 6, 9, 10, 12.
c. Is nonmetrical, or meter not obvious at first. 2, 7, 11, 17.
d. Contains a tuneful melody. 1, 6, 13, 15, 18.
e. Begins in minor. 2, 3, 7, 10, 12, 17.
f. Begins in major. 1, 4, 5, 6, 8, 13, 14, 15, 16, 18.
g. Contains some monophony. 2, 7, 11, 14.
h. Contains imitative polyphony. 3, 7, 12.
i. Contains homophony in homorhythmic style. 5, 7, 14, 16.
j. Contains homophony in melody-plus-accompaniment style. 1, 6, 8, 13, 15.

Music before the Renaissance

11 INTRODUCING STYLE PERIODS

PREVIEW   In this chapter, we outline the role that style periods will play in the remainder of this book. We give some dates for the major style periods, explain why there are limitations to this kind of study, and suggest the topics that we will cover for each style period, once the Renaissance is reached.

Any study of an art work raises basic questions, such as: Where did it come from? Who created it? When was it made? Why was it made? One way to begin answering such questions is to consider the work as the product of a particular **style period.** "Style" is one of those general terms we meet constantly. A person's life-style is the sum of that person's habits, preferences, and so on. Similarly, a composer has a style, a tendency to handle musical elements in an individual way. Just as people have styles, historical periods exhibit certain general characteristics that stamp the music, or the paintings, or the literature, as a product of that particular era. Since the style periods are related to history, we shall study them in a chronological order.

A

Dates for the Style Periods

Endless scholarly debate has produced little agreement upon exact dates for the style periods. To simplify matters, we have employed a module of 150 years beginning with the Renaissance. Dividing 150 into two seventy-five-year spans provides a suitable date to locate the division between the Classic and Romantic eras. All of these dates, it must be remembered, are approximate. Rarely did some specific landmark event occur in the targeted year, although the death of J. S. Bach in 1750 provides an exception.

450 to 1450: Middle Ages
1450 to 1600: Renaissance
1600 to 1750: Baroque

1750 to 1825: Classic
1825 to 1900: Romantic
1900 to date: Twentieth Century

B

The notion of style periods creates certain expectations in the minds of the listener. You should remember, however, that the names given to style periods and the traits connected with them were products of historians who looked at developments in hindsight after they had taken place. As is true of most generalizations, you cannot take the dates and ideas too literally. Music did not change by 180-degree turns in the landmark years. Every period includes forward-looking artists who introduce new ideas that gradually become fully accepted and eventually standardized. As these ideas degenerate into mechanical formulas with the passage of time, conservatives try to preserve them while a new set of radicals introduces their new ideas. Consequently a good deal of overlapping occurs in any given period.

Limitations of the Style Period Concept

Parallels exist between music and the other arts in a particular era. For example, in much Renaissance art it is easy to see the qualities of serenity and repose that you can hear in Renaissance sacred music. Such parallels cannot be carried to extremes because each art has its own individual character. Indeed, style period changes did not occur at the same time in all the arts. In fact, music tends to lag behind the others, as if history were some sort of competition!

C

The discussions of each style period cover three major areas: (1) the treatment of the characteristics of *sound* and the elements of *music* studied in Part One, especially in relation to authentic performance practices; (2) the musical *developments* for which the period is best known; and (3) the role of *composers* in the era, including biographical material about the most prominent figures together with representative examples of their music. Your knowledge of history may enable you to establish additional connections, beyond the few events that we mention, between historical events and the changes that took place in music.

Topics Covered in Each Period's Discussion

Following a brief look backwards at the ancient Greeks, we devote the remainder of Part Two to the Middle Ages. Because so much about this era is still being studied, the topics just mentioned will be covered more generally than the periods that lie closer to our time.

12 THE ANCIENT GREEKS AND MUSIC

PREVIEW In a long look backwards, we start with the ancient Greeks, although we will not study any examples of their music. The culture of the Greeks is a foundation of Western civilization. Their ideas about music in its relationship to numbers and its place in society still affect us.

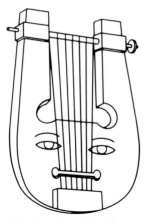

The Greek god Apollo played harplike instruments called lyre or kithara.

One might expect a chronological study of music to begin with the music of prehistoric peoples. After all, a history of art can begin with cave paintings or with monuments such as Stonehenge. Unfortunately, because musical instruments are so perishable and written records so scanty, the attempt to discover the "origins" of music has produced more speculation than fact. We can turn to the ancient Greeks instead, looking back to perhaps 500 B.C. Their myths and gods are part of our language; their architecture is still widely copied. Although they left a few fragments of music, written in a rudimentary kind of notation that scholars have deciphered and performed, the resulting sounds are far less important to us than are their ideas about music. Indeed, we will meet many terms of Greek origin, among them rhythm, melody, and harmony. For that matter, "music" itself comes from the Greek "Muses," the nine goddesses who presided over literature, the arts, and sciences.

Music was vital to the ancient Greeks. Apollo, the god of light and order, poetry and prophecy, was also the god of music. He favored a disciplined sort of music played on a small, harplike instrument (lyre or kithara). Even today we think of harps as associated with heaven. Apollo's opposite was Dionysus (Bacchus to the Romans), the god of wine and revelry, who played the aulos. This instrument with two pipes, one for each hand, sounded somewhat like an oboe and was considered suitable to accompany orgies! The Greeks developed several scales that we would recognize as close to our present-day scales. Some of the most famous Greek philosophers, notably Plato and Aristotle, wrote extensively about music. Their theories still influence us.

This famous drawing of Pythagoras engaged in testing the relationships of music and numbers dates from a 1492 book by Gafurrius: *Theorica Musices,* Milan, 1492. (Courtesy of The Music Division, The New York Public Library at Lincoln Center, Astor, Lenox and Tilden Foundations.)

A

Music and Numbers

One Greek idea about music involves the relationships between the lengths of sounding strings and the pitches they produce. Pythagoras (c.582–c.507 B.C.), whose name you might know in connection with the right-angle triangle, is credited with discovering at least some of these relationships. He found that strings with a 2:1 ratio in their lengths produce an octave. By extension, the ratio of 3:2 results in the interval of a fifth; 4:3 results in a fourth; 5:4 results in a third, and skipping ahead, 9:8 results in a second. Our scale is derived from these proportions, which provide the elaborate numerical and musical basis that underlies music theory.

Reasoning from this basis, the Greeks connected the tuning of strings, which could be tested by the sense of hearing, to numbers, which belong to the intellect. This persuaded them that the entire universe made sense because it was governed by numbers. A connection between music and mathematics persists today in the common, though unproved, notion that musical and mathematical talents go together.

The decorations on Greek vases supply much information about the kinds of instruments used by the ancient Greeks. The performer pictured on this vase of c. 475 B.C. is playing an instrument with two pipes, perhaps an aulos. (Courtesy of the J. Paul Getty Museum, Malibu, CA.)

Some Greeks claimed that music had ethical properties, that it was a moral force. This conception of music bears the philosophical label of **ethos.** Following this logic, the Greeks believed that the "wrong" kind of music would corrupt; "good" music elevated people. Consequently, Plato (c.427–347 B.C.), in planning his ideal society, put music foremost in the education of the young. He did not intend, however, that those young male aristocrats who were being groomed to run society should become virtuoso musicians. Indeed, Plato's pupil Aristotle (384–322 B.C.) advised that the young should study music because it was impossible "to produce good judges of musical performance from among those who have never themselves performed." In other words, the young should learn only enough to evaluate music; they should not try to attain a professional's skill. In Aristotle's view, being a musician is not "the proper occupation for a gentleman; it is rather that of a paid employee." Slaves, as mere entertainers, acquired virtuoso technique as an occupational requirement. Needless to say, the social standing of performing musicians was low—a prejudice that lingered until quite recent times.

For the Greeks, music possessed almost magical properties. It could "tune" the soul, inspire noble actions, cure the sick, charm wild animals. In Greek mythology the singing of the great musician Orpheus tamed wild animals and enabled him to descend into Hades to steal his beloved Euridice from death. Of course, the Greeks were not alone in attributing amazing powers to music. The Old Testament (in 1 Sam. 16:23) relates that David cured Saul's madness by playing the harp and that Joshua's trumpet caused the walls of Jericho to come tumbling down (in Josh. 6:20).

Lest you think that the Greeks exaggerated the powers of music, please note that today music therapists work in mental hospitals. Not too many years ago, the music education profession claimed that "a boy who blows a horn will never blow a safe." Currently, a few zealots in the United States, China, the USSR, and elsewhere, fear that rock music will undermine society. The Greek concept of ethos, that music has a moral character, may be worldwide in scope and timeless.

13 INTRODUCING THE MIDDLE AGES (450–1450)

PREVIEW   The Medieval period stretches roughly a thousand years, which is too long for us to do more than point up some highlights: Gregorian chant, the rise of polyphony, the Mass, and medieval secular music.

The **Middle Ages,** or the **Medieval** period, lasted from about 450 to 1450. If a more specific date for its beginning is wanted, the so-called "Fall of Rome" in 476 furnishes a possibility. No consensus exists about a suitable boundary between the Middle Ages and the Renaissance. Art historians tend to place the beginning of the Renaissance considerably before 1450, the year commonly accepted by musicians. Music and art historians alike divide this lengthy span of time into shorter units: Early Middle Ages, Romanesque, and Gothic. The Gothic period itself is divided into smaller units by music historians. Because the music coming from the Middle Ages is not yet part of the concert repertoire, we do not need this terminology.

Although the unifying force of the Roman empire had begun to wane long before the "Fall," chaos followed that momentous event. The familiar term for these years, the "Dark Ages," had a basis in fact as the accomplishments of the Greeks and Romans slipped from general view. Feudalism, though hardly a substitute for the once-mighty power of Rome, provided a basis for political power. The Roman Catholic church, now universally accepted, found itself not only the record-keeper of whatever civilization remained but also the chief educational establishment. Almost everyone else was illiterate. Though surely music making occurred outside the church's sphere of influence, the monks took little interest in any secular music. Consequently the early development of music unfolds chiefly in sacred music, preserved for us by the religious orders. Similarly, the history of medieval art is the history of Christian art with its concentration on religious themes.

Much about medieval music remains shrouded in mystery. We do not know how the music actually sounded. Scholars today vigorously debate how to decipher the notation system developed in the Middle Ages. Early music lacks bar lines. Rarely is the text placed directly under the notes to which the syllables should be

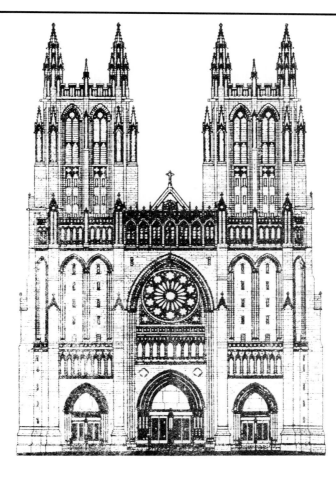

Gothic architecture, with its pointed arches, is represented by countless European cathedrals that have been preserved for centuries. This style is widely imitated in the United States, as in the Washington National Cathedral in Washington, D.C. © Washington National Cathedral, used with permission.

sung. Even if we were sure about these matters, uncertainties would linger about appropriate vocal techniques. Manuscripts are silent about instrumental participation—if there was any. Though literature of the times mentions instruments and medieval artists often included musicians in their paintings, such sources fall short of providing scientific evidence. For example, the instruments played by angels might have charmed the heavenly host, not mere mortals on earth. Of necessity, therefore, recordings of medieval music must be based on educated guesswork.

Just as we know little about the architects and sculptors whose work we still see in the great cathedrals, the list of medieval composers specified by name is relatively short. For centuries, artists labored collectively and anonymously for the greater glory of God: receiving individual credit for one's contribution was not a goal. Furthermore, because the medieval attitude valued authority so highly, people did not so much compose as arrange. Putting old things together into newer forms

The Old Testament figure King David adorns the monastery of Santiago de Compostela, Spain. As in many medieval sources, he is shown playing an instrument. (Photograph by Sam Adams.)

was the way things were done then. Only toward the end of the Middle Ages do the names of individual creative artists appear consistently.

Admittedly, we have outlined only a few of the many developments in this era. The simplest way of filling in the numerous gaps left here is to consult a historical anthology of music and its accompanying recordings. One representative anthology, *Masterpieces of Music Before 1750*, compiled by Carl Parrish and John F. Ohl, furnishes some examples for Part Two. They are identified with the abbreviation MOM and the appropriate number. Recordings for this anthology have been reissued on compact discs.

GREGORIAN CHANT 14

PREVIEW One prominent musical heritage of the Middle Ages is the monophonic chant sung in church services, usually called Gregorian chant. We study its origins and styles, the ways it is performed, and its specific musical qualities, learn how it affected all music, and examine one particular chant.

Quite early the church fathers had realized that singing a sacred text renders it more powerfully than speaking it. In fact, one prominent church leader, St. Basil the Great (c.330–c.379), claimed that the singing of psalms had a delightful effect: "By the pleasantness and softness of the sound heard we might receive without perceiving it the benefit of the words, just as wise physicians who, when giving the fastidious rather bitter drugs to drink, frequently smear the cup with honey." So developed the tradition of singing sacred texts in the church **liturgy,** a highly organized system of worship services and rituals.

Gregorian chant is still sung in religious communities in America, particularly on special occasions. This photograph was taken at the Prince of Peace Abbey in Oceanside, California.

Gregorian chant is the customary designation for the music sung in the medieval church. Approximately three thousand chants are known. That quite extraordinary number resulted because the liturgy included many different services and texts. Both parts of this label, "Gregorian" and "chant," need explanation. St. Gregory the Great, who reigned as pope from 590 to 604, is the subject of many legends which attribute the chant composition to him. One legend claims that a dove, representing the Holy Spirit, sang the chants into the pope's ear, and he in turn dictated them to his scribe, who wrote them down. Rather than composer or compiler, Gregory appears to have functioned as an administrator—not the last one in history to get credit for what his subordinates did.

Nor are the chants always "chanted." Although some are little more than the recitation of syllables upon one repeated tone with a downward inflection at the ends of the phrases, others are much more melodic. Indeed, another term for Gregorian chant is **plainsong.** Some Gregorian chants are "tuneful" enough to find a place in both Protestant and Catholic hymnbooks today. The Episcopal hymnal of 1982, for example, lists almost sixty hymns with a plainsong source. Gregorian chant continues to figure in church services today, though less prominently than before.

The chants differ greatly in the ways that pitches and syllables are related— a relationship determined by the role of a particular chant in a particular service. At one extreme stand those chants that match each syllable to a single note. Not surprisingly, this effect is called **syllabic.** (Most familiar songs today are syllabic.) At the opposite extreme stands the **melismatic** style, in which a single syllable is stretched out over as many as twenty different notes. This stretching-out process is called **melisma.** Some melismatic chants resemble Middle Eastern improvised song or perhaps cantorial singing in the synagogue. Somewhere between lies the **neumatic** style, with two or three pitches per syllable.

Scholars today cannot agree on how to interpret the early chant notation, some of it dating from the tenth century. Consequently, performances differ widely in respect to tempo, the duration and the degree of stress that is given the individual notes, pitch levels, how many singers perform, and other matters as well. Recorded performances of chants are sung either by members of religious orders whose varying traditions govern how it should be rendered or by groups of professional musicians who depend upon the research of the religious orders. The Benedictine monks at Solesmes [pronounced so-LEM], in the northern part of France, have pioneered in the scholarly study of chant.

Whether in live or recorded performance, chant will not set feet tapping. It was not designed primarily for the listeners' pleasure. It is *functional* music—a prayer or scripture reading set to a melody so that the sound can float easily down

Pope Gregory is pictured here with a dove singing into his ear. His scribe has poked a hole in the curtain that separates them so he can see better.

the cathedral. In order to experience the proper effect of this music you must transport yourself back to a dimly lit medieval cathedral whose vaulted ceilings make the music reverberate almost ceaselessly. This music evokes another world, one of mystery and great beauty, but it is only one aspect of the experience. All the senses are involved, as the worshipper sees a beautiful building and richly adorned vestments, smells the incense, tastes the elements of the Sacrament, touches the holy water and the materials—and hears music and the word. Even nonbelievers can enter this world through its music.

C

Specific Musical Qualities of the Chants

1. Chants are monophonic: they have only one musical line.

2. Chant texts are in Latin, the universal language of the Roman Catholic church and of Western civilization at the time. There is one striking exception: there are three Greek words in the Kyrie, an important chant discussed later as part of the Mass.

3. Based on prose texts, most chants are **nonmetrical.** That is, there is little sense of a regular beat. In some hymnlike chants, settings of poetic texts, a regular meter results from a pattern of stressed and unstressed syllables.

4. Chants have a limited pitch span, the range of an octave or less. Within that octave, scalewise motion prevails. Skips are few and usually small. These restrictions make the line easy for untrained voices to sing.

5. The melodic line is based not on the scales we know today as major and minor, but rather on earlier scale forms called **church modes** or simply **modes.** In order to hear the slightly unusual sound of modal scales, caused by the different ways the whole-steps and half-steps are arranged, play the white keys of the piano from one D to the next, then repeat this process starting with E, F, and G. Of the remaining pitches, A and C are omitted from this discussion because they are the keynotes of today's major and minor scales, which are survivors of two modes. One began on C, our major scale, and one on A, the original version of our minor scale (natural minor). For that reason, we frequently say that a piece is in the **minor mode.** Playing from one B to the next produces a theoretical scale that composers avoided in practice.

Each of the modal scales bears a Greek name, though the Greek scales and the church modes of the same name are not identical. While each mode has an individual quality, the ones on D, E, and G share a common feature: they end with a whole-step. Our major scale and the most commonly encountered form of the minor scale (harmonic minor) end with a half-step, *ti* going to *dô,* a feature that underlies tonality by creating a strong sense of completion. Most modal music lacks the same sense of completion because of the whole-step cadences.

Incidentally, modal scales are not confined to Gregorian chant. The Beatles, having discovered modes, based their song "Eleanor Rigby" on the **Dorian** mode, which is D,E,F,G,A,B,C,D. (That song begins with the pitches F,G,A,F,D; F,G,A,C,B,A,B . . . .) The perennial folk song "Greensleeves" is in the Dorian mode, although it is slightly modified at some phrase endings. *Fantasia on Green-sleeves,* a hauntingly beautiful arrangement of this tune (ex. 14.1), was composed by the twentieth-century English composer Ralph Vaughan Williams (1872–1958). (His name is indexed under V as if it were hyphenated.)

Example 14.1

Our Gregorian chant example is the following:

 CD1

Alleluia, Dies sanctificatus (2:04)
②

    This Alleluia is part of the Mass for Christmas Day. Like all alleluias, it is melismatic. It is also modal, using the Dorian tones of D to D but with a range of A to A. The low A is reached only once, on the first syllable of the word "venite." Most of the melodic motion is conjunct, with one leap of a fifth.

Example 14.2

(0:00)
1   Alleluia (as in ex. 14.2). Note how the last syllable is extended.

(0:21)
2   Dies sanctificatus illuxit nobis: venite, gentes, et adorate Dominum, quia hodie descendit lux magna super terram.

(1:37)
3   Alleluia, as in item 1.
        (Translation of item 2: A holy day has dawned upon us: come all ye peoples and adore the Lord. For today a truly great light has descended upon the earth.)

    It might be useful to compare this chant with *Alleluia: Vidimus stellam,* #2 in the Masterpieces of Music series. This latter chant is for January 6, or Epiphany, the "twelfth day of Christmas," celebrating the visit of the Wise men from the East bearing gifts for the baby Jesus. In both, the music for "alleluia" is the same; that for the middle portions differs slightly.

In this twelfth-century manuscript, Guido (on the left) demonstrates his methods of music teaching by use of a monochord.

D

How Gregorian Chant Affected Music

Until the late Renaissance, most musicians grew up in a church setting and received their training there. They absorbed the chant as their musical language; in fact, scholars speak of chant as providing the "soil" out of which music grew. Our system of musical notation evolved from early attempts to write down the chants and the subsequent musical developments based upon them.

For centuries musicians orally transmitted chant melodies to succeeding generations. Matters changed when the emperor Charlemagne ruled the Holy Roman Empire (786–814). Church leaders, wishing to ensure greater uniformity in church practices, began ever so slowly to develop a notation for chant. At first the notation resembled little strokes, curves, and dots, which produced a rough graph of melodic ups and downs. While these symbols did not specify exact pitches, they guided singers through a melody if they already had some idea of how it went. Sometime after the year 1000, Guido d'Arezzo (c.991–c.1033; the name is usually indexed under G) developed the musical staff. He placed symbols on lines and spaces to indicate specific pitches, a concept underlying our notational system. He is also credited with the familiar scale syllables: *do-re-mi-fa-sol-la,* although Guido sang "ut" for *do.* Guido's system lacked a *ti;* to sing more than six tones one shifted the whole pattern up or down. (Not until about 1600 was a seventh syllable added, and then it was called *si.* In English-speaking countries, the syllable *ti* is sung instead.)

The old symbols gradually turned into square- or diamond-shaped heads. Only in the Renaissance did the familiar rounded shapes for noteheads appear.

Music notation went through a long evolutionary process. The examples shown here come from the following centuries: (1) 10th; (2) and (3) 11th; (4) 12th–13th; (5) 12th and still today; (6) 14th–15th; (7) 15th–17th; (8) and (9) modern notation.

One crucial difference exists between the early notation system and our present one. For us, lines and spaces have an *absolute* value. For example, the A on the second space of the treble clef signifies a tone vibrating 440 times per second, the tune-up A. The medieval system was purely *relative*; it simply showed up and down pitch relationships as in *do, re, mi*.

To the present day, Gregorian chant appears in medieval notation. Church musicians and others treasure its simple, yet elegant portrayal of line. Examples of chant that are printed in textbooks often show them with the ancient symbols transcribed into quarter and eighth notes, although scholars are by no means as sure about the rhythm as they are about the pitches.

Not content with the enormous chant repertoire they already possessed, medieval musicians found an outlet for their creative energies by adding new words or new music, or both, to the services. Such unofficial additions varied from place to place: most of them have disappeared. One, however, proved immensely popular and is still sung today. That is the **Dies irae** [pronounced DE-es E-reh] from the Requiem Mass (the Mass for the dead). This chant (ex. 14.3), metrical because of its poetic structure, is syllabic, with one syllable per note.

Example 14.3

Di - es i - rae, di - es il - la, Sol-vet___ sae - clum in fa - vil-la

(The remainder of the first verse in Latin is: Teste David cum Sibylla./ Quantus tremor est futurus,/Quando judex est venturus,/Cuncta stricte discussurus. A translation that preserves the meter and rhyme scheme reads: Day of wrath and doom impending! David's word with Sibyl's blending, Heaven and earth in ashes ending.)

This chant even migrated to secular music as a symbol of Death and the Last Judgment. As we shall see, the Romantic composer Berlioz quoted this melody in the fifth movement, "Dream of a Witches' Sabbath," of his *Symphonie fantastique.*

Although the bulk of the chant repertoire was the product of anonymous churchmen and churchwomen, in a few cases we do know the names of individual composers. One of them, Hildegard of Bingen (1098–1179), has attracted considerable attention in recent years, and recordings of her music are available. That music is monophonic, with unusually wide pitch ranges, set to her own imaginative poetry. The abbess of a nunnery in Germany, she wrote six major books, composed a liturgical morality play, and corresponded with popes and kings, who sought her advice. Though sometimes referred to as "Saint Hildegard," she was never canonized.

THE DEVELOPMENT OF POLYPHONY 15

PREVIEW   The monophonic Gregorian chant served as a foundation for anonymous composers to add new musical lines, creating the earliest forms of polyphony. We show some stages in its evolution, examine three examples of early polyphony, and discuss its effect on music.

In the ninth century, anonymous monks began to embellish Gregorian chant with an added, improvised musical line. In so doing they created the earliest form of polyphony and at the same time set Western music on a path that led to the music we know today. We can never know precisely just why these singers were attracted to polyphony, but art reveals a possible parallel. With color and gold leaf, painters beautifully decorated, or "illuminated," manuscript copies of the Bible. Musicians enhanced the solemnity of the service by "decorating" it with these new polyphonic compositions. In response to the pervasive doctrine of church authority, it made sense to begin with what was already given, the chant, and add to it. A preexisting melody that serves as a basis for added polyphony is called a **cantus firmus** (from the Latin meaning "fixed song"), abbreviated **C.F.**

A

These first forms of polyphony are known collectively as **organum,** a Latin word with the literal meaning of "instrument" or "tool." While at one time this word designated the musical instrument we know as the organ—a connection that certainly looks logical—organum became associated with the polyphony of the ninth through the twelfth centuries. Anonymous authors of ninth-century treatises described rules for improvising polyphony. Their musical illustrations show an added layer of melody to a C.F., the preexisting Gregorian chant.

At first, judging from what we can see in the earliest examples, organum was very simple. The added part moved slavishly in **parallel motion** to the C.F. at a fixed interval of a fourth or a fifth above or below. To modern ears, accustomed to the rich diet of triads and full chords, this sound is hollow. But in the Middle Ages only fourths and fifths were expected; the third was allowed only under special

Some Examples of the Evolution of Polyphony

The cathedral at Chartres in France was completed by 1220. At least that is when the roof was done, although the spire of the tower on the left was not added until about 1507. Its stained glass windows make the cathedral a must-see for tourists.

circumstances. A more advanced kind of organum resulted from two voices beginning in unison, then moving to the fixed interval for a segment in parallel motion, and finally converging upon the unison, as in *Rex caeli, Domine* (ex. 15.1). The original chant is the upper voice.

Example 15.1

Rex cae-li Do-mi-ne ma-ris un-di-so-ni,

CD1

(0:00)
1   Rex cae-li Do-mi-ne ma-ris un-di-so-ni,

(0:07)
2   Ti-ta-nis ni-ti-di squa-li-di-que so-li,
        (The music of phrase 1 repeats for phrase 2.)

(0:14)
3   Te hu-mi-les fa-mu-li mo-du-lis ve-ne-ran-do pi-is.

(0:23)
4   Se ju-be-as fla-gi-tant va-ri-is li-be-ra-re ma-lis.
        (Phrase 3 employs similar music, beginning at a higher pitch. Phrase
        4 repeats it.)

        (A translation begins: King of the Heavens and the sea . . . .)

Rex caeli, Domine
(:34) MOM #6 ③

Eventually **contrary motion** appeared: one voice rises, the other falls. Often the two voices cross. Even more advanced was **melismatic organum,** in which the notes of the C.F. were stretched into a series of dronelike tones. Over each of these tones an elaborate melisma unfolded. This process resulted in much longer compositions, but it must have been difficult to recognize the original chant. Perhaps that did not matter, for the authority of the chant still remained. Only the pitches for the first word of *Benedicamus Domino* (ex. 15.2) appear in the recorded excerpt. Since most of those tones simply extend the opening note, D, the relaxing of tension when that tone changes (to C) at the excerpt's end is dramatic.

Benedicamus Domino
(:50) MOM #8 ④

 CD1

Example 15.2

11

(Translation: Let us bless the Lord.)

The last stages of organum date from around the year 1200. This development is associated with the cathedral of Notre Dame in Paris, a supreme landmark of early Gothic architecture. Its cornerstone was laid in 1163, but work on it continued until the fourteenth century. Not only can we associate a specific place with this music, but thanks to a keen observer, we have the names of two composers who worked at Notre Dame: Leonin and his pupil, or follower, Perotin. (Neither their first names nor their dates are known.) These compositions, written for as many as four voice parts, demonstrate new concepts of rhythm. At Notre Dame, measured, or metrical, rhythm appeared. Only triple meter was allowed—the sacred number three of the Trinity (Father, Son, and Holy Ghost) dominated medieval thinking. As in melismatic organum, the original chant tones were stretched out to great length and performed by the lower voices, perhaps with instruments.

 CD1

Perotin: *Alleluya (Nativitas)* (2:00) MOM #9 ⑤

One syllable, the "al-" that begins *Alleluya (Nativitas)*, is all our recorded excerpt gives (ex. 15.3). Above it the two upper voices, that is, the parts composed by Perotin, sing in measured rhythms and use only a few note values. Rests frequently interrupt the music, so the singers appear to be singing "ah, ah, ah," or whatever vowels are appropriate. The rhythmic patterns these upper parts create are physically involving, forming a decided contrast to the stability of the original chant.

Example 15.3

B

How Organum Affected Music History

Organum changed Western music in many ways. It needed better-trained singers than did Gregorian chant—singers who could read the notation that had evolved for this music, singers who could render their own parts against the competition of other musical lines. Organum, probably reserved for soloists, might have needed instrumental support, if only to help singers with the pitch. At least, art work of the period depicts instrumentalists and singers together. Offering an exciting contrast to monophony, the sonority of organum provided a stimulus to medieval composers. Thus encouraged, they developed even further the concept of simultaneous sounds, in short, the foundation of our harmony and of texture.

Plate 9 As in the Santiago cathedral sculpture, we see an artistic reference to King David's love of music. This is from an illumination dated c. 1240–50. (Courtesy of J. Paul Getty Museum, Malibu, CA.)

Plate 10 This fancifully decorated chant notation has a surprising touch—the donkey playing a harp in the lower left-hand corner. This manuscript is dated c. 1260–70. (Courtesy of J. Paul Getty Museum, Malibu, CA.)

Plate 11 The great cathedral of Notre Dame in Paris has been the site of music history since the laying of its cornerstone in 1163. It is situated by the Seine River, which cuts through Paris. (Photograph by Val Villa.)

Plate 12 The highly original Italian artist Giotto (c. 1267–c. 1336) painted this fresco, called *Deposition*, on the walls of a chapel. It shows human mourners frozen in their grief and weeping angels flying in the clouds.

Plate 13   This French tapestry is given a title, "Time." It dates from the early 1500s, but its stylized figures and unnatural scale give it a medieval look. Notice the instruments being played.

Plate 14 The Italian artist Botticelli (c. 1445–1510) is best known for his *Birth of Venus,* which pictures the nude goddess in a pose characteristic of Greek sculpture. Showing an unclothed body and alluding to ancient Greece are Renaissance characteristics.

Plate 15 The five-hundredth anniversary of the birth of Martin Luther, the towering Renaissance figure and an ardent supporter of music, was marked by the issuance of this postage stamp in 1983. (Copyright 1983 U.S. Postal Service)

Plate 16 Images of mother and child are everywhere at Christmas time. Stamps appear with Madonna portraits by Italian Renaissance painters, as in this 1986 issue with a placid Mother painted by Pietro Perugino (c. 1450–1523). (Copyright 1986 U.S. Postal Service)

THE
MASS 16

PREVIEW We discuss the two divisions of the Mass: Proper and Ordinary; then give the Latin (and Greek) texts for the five movements of the Ordinary, with their translations. Two Masses by composers of the late Middle Ages in France, Machaut and Dufay, furnish examples.

The vast chant repertoire functioned as one component within a grand liturgical framework. Organized to cover systematically (and often dramatically) the life and teachings of Christ, the church year began with the season of Advent, a solemn time of preparation for the Incarnation, Christ's birth at Christmas. Similarly, a wide range of church services, from short and simple to long and elaborate, allowed clearly focused daily worship. Irresistibly, the texts of these services invited musical setting.

For our purposes, the most important church service is the **Mass,** which is the ritual commemoration of Christ's Last Supper (the "communion" service). The word "missa" comes from the priest's formula of dismissal at the end of the service, "Ite, missa est," or "Go forth, it is ended." ("Missa," the Latin word for Mass, or its French equivalent "Messe" frequently identifies references to a particular Mass.) We include in this chapter a portion of Machaut's *Notre Dame Mass,* which in French is the *Messe de nostre dame.*

A

The Mass includes some twenty separate items. While every component can be spoken, about half may be sung in a "High" or "Solemn" Mass. Of those sung items, some of the texts remain the same for every occasion that a Mass is held, or, as the church says, "celebrated." These five parts—Kyrie, Gloria, Credo, Sanctus/Benedictus, and Agnus Dei—are known as the **Ordinary** of the Mass.

Other parts of the Mass change from one day to the next. For example, the Mass for Christmas day contains some texts specifically intended for December 25 only. These variable portions are called the **Proper** of the Mass because they

The Ordinary and the Proper of the Mass

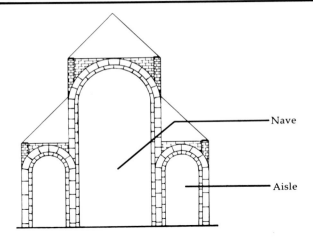

Romanesque churches are marked by rounded arches, as this cross section of a typical church shows.

Nave

Aisle

are appropriate, or proper, for a particular day. The Gregorian chant *Alleluia, Dies sanctificatus* studied in Chapter 14 belongs to the Proper of the Mass.

The Mass could be sung in unadorned Gregorian chant. When composers of the late Middle Ages began to set the Mass in the new polyphonic style, they concentrated on the texts of the Proper. Not until the 1300s, apparently, did they conclude that it made better sense to set those texts that would be sung constantly rather than those restricted to one or two occasions a year. They began, therefore, to concentrate on the Ordinary texts. In a musical context, references to the Mass normally imply the Ordinary.

By the time of the Renaissance, composition of polyphonic Masses was a standard practice. Throughout subsequent music history, composers have continued to write Masses that represent supreme monuments of their creativity. They have done so whether or not they had affiliation with the Roman Catholic or, indeed, any church. That composers have been drawn to the Mass stems in part from the universality of the Latin text, free as it is from any nationalistic ties and thus implying a message for all. Because Latin was the official language of the church, church music in Latin could be sung in any country, regardless of the native tongue. While the Catholic church in the 1960s (by actions of the reform-minded Vatican Council II) approved the celebration of the Mass in the **vernacular** (the language of the congregation), its broader musical traditions remain.

There are many modern translations of the Mass. Some reflect social changes and alter sexist or archaic language, with, for example, "people" replacing "men" and "you" replacing "thou." Since we are considering the Mass from an historical viewpoint, we supply a traditional translation.

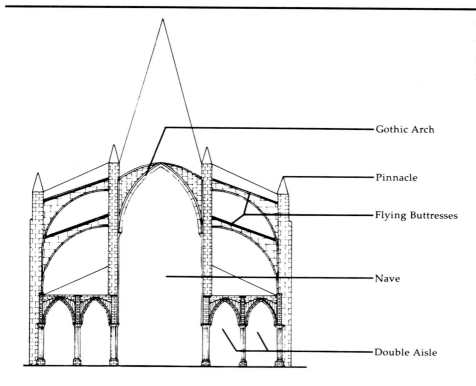

Gothic Arch

Pinnacle

Flying Buttresses

Nave

Double Aisle

Gothic churches can be identified by their pointed arches and the buttresses that helped support these structures.

1. Kyrie [pronounced KEAR-ee-ay]. This humble petition has the shortest text. (The words are Greek, the only non-Latin words in the Mass.) The three-fold repetitions reflect the central importance of the number three, signifying the Trinity. Even with these repetitions, composers often desire a more extensive movement. Consequently, they usually repeat these words further, as many times as they think necessary, aided by the resources of polyphony. Typically, the Christe section forms a subtle contrast to the two Kyrie sections, which are more apt to be alike musically. In fact, a kind of musical ABA form often results.

The Five Movements of the Ordinary

1	Kyrie eleison (three times)	Lord, have mercy
2	Christe eleison (three times)	Christ, have mercy
3	Kyrie eleison (three times)	Lord, have mercy

2. Gloria. A great hymn of praise, the Gloria begins with the intoning of the opening text phrase in Gregorian chant, either by the celebrant or by a soloist or a section of the choir. The choir then responds with "et in terra pax." Setting this lengthy text polyphonically throughout can produce too long a movement, at least too long for the service, which is the reverse of the Kyrie situation. Composers are apt, therefore, to resort to homophony, which has the advantage not only of getting through the text more quickly, but also of allowing important, solemn phrases to be heard clearly.

1	Gloria in Excelsis Deo	Glory be to God on high, and on
2	Et in terra pax hominibus bonae voluntatis.	earth peace good will to men.
3	Laudamus te, benedicimus te, adoramus te, glorificamus te.	We praise thee, we bless thee, we worship thee, we glorify thee,
4	Gratias agimus tibi propter magnam gloriam tuam.	We give thanks to thee for thy great glory.
5	Domine Deus, Rex coelestis	O, Lord God, heavenly King,
6	Deus pater omnipotens.	God the Father Almighty.
7	Domine Fili unigenite, Jesu Christe,	O Lord, the only begotten Son, Jesus Christ;
8	Domine Deus, Agnus Dei, Filius Patris.	O Lord God, Lamb of God, Son of the Father,
9	Qui tollis peccata mundi: miserere nobis;	Thou that takest away the sins of the world: have mercy upon us.
10	Qui tollis peccata mundi: suscipe deprecationem nostram;	Thou that takest away the sins of the world: receive our prayer.
11	Qui sedes ad dexteram Patris: miserere nobis.	Thou that sittest at the right hand of the Father: have mercy upon us.
12	Quoniam tu solus sanctus, tu solus Dominus, tu solus altissimus. Jesu Christe.	For thou only art holy, thou only art the Lord; thou only, O Christ, with the Holy Ghost,
13	Cum sancto spiritu, in gloria Dei Patris. Amen.	Art most high in the glory of God the Father. Amen.

3. Credo [pronounced CRAY-doh]. "I believe" is the meaning of this Latin word, although some modern translations read "we believe." Presented here is the central statement of Christian faith. Since the list of things to be believed is extensive, this component has the longest text of the Ordinary items. Like the Gloria, the Credo begins with a Gregorian phrase chanted by the celebrant; likewise, it frequently includes homophonic sections. Certain phrases of the Credo text are often highlighted musically. Slower note values or a marked change in pitch levels might emphasize a central doctrine, such as the profound mystery conveyed in "et incarnatus est" (item 7).

1 Credo in unum Deum	I believe in one God,
2 Patrem omnipotentem, factorem coeli et terrae, visibilium et invisibilium.	the Father Almighty, maker of heaven and earth, of all things visible and invisible.
3 Et in unum Dominum, Jesum Christum, Filium Dei unigenitum, et ex Patre natum ante omnia saecula.	And in one Lord, Jesus Christ, the only Son of God, eternally begotten of the Father.
4 Deum de Deo, lumen de lumine, Deum verum de Deo vero.	God of God, Light of Light, true God of true God,
5 Genitum, non factum, consubstantialem Patri: per quem omnia facta sunt.	begotten, not made, being of one substance with the Father, by whom all things were made;
6 Qui propter nos homines, et propter nostram salutem descendit de coelis:	Who for us men and for our salvation came down from heaven:
7 Et incarnatus est de Spiritu Sancto ex Maria virgine, et homo factus est.	And was incarnate by the Holy Ghost of the Virgin Mary, and was made man.
8 Crucifixus etiam pro nobis, sub Pontio Pilato passus, et sepultus est.	He was crucified also for us, suffered under Pontius Pilate, and was buried.
9 Et resurrexit tertia die secundum scripturas;	And the third day he rose again according to the Scriptures,
10 Et ascendit in coelum sedet ad dexteram Patris.	And ascended into heaven, and sitteth at the right hand of the Father.
11 Et iterum venturus est cum gloria judicare vivos et mortuos, cujus regni non erit finis.	And shall come again with glory to judge both the living and the dead, whose kingdom shall have no end.
12 Et in Spiritum Sanctum, Dominum et vivificantem, qui ex Patre Filioque procedit.	And in the Holy Ghost, the Lord and giver of life, who proceedeth from the Father and the Son.
13 Qui cum Patre et Filio simul adoratur et conglorificatur.	With the Father and the Son together is worshipped and glorified.

14 Qui locutus est per Prophetas. Et unam sanctam Catholicam et Apostolicam Ecclesiam.	Who spake by the prophets. And [I believe] in one holy Catholic and Apostolic Church.
15 Confiteor unum baptisma in remissionem peccatorum.	I acknowledge one Baptism for the remission of sins.
16 Et expecto resurrectionem mortuorum, et vitam venturi saeculi. Amen.	And I look for the resurrection of the dead, and the life of the world to come. Amen.

4. Sanctus/Benedictus. Many composers separated the Benedictus from the Sanctus, thus creating six movements instead of five for the Mass cycle. Given the shorter texts, polyphony is more likely. Both Sanctus and Benedictus end with the same textual phrase, "Hosanna in excelsis," usually set to the same music. The Sanctus directly links the Christian church and its Jewish heritage. The beginning words, "Holy, holy, holy," come from the Old Testament, Isaiah 6:3, and appear in the Jewish service as the *Kedushah,* "Kodosh, kodosh, kodosh."

1 Sanctus, sanctus, sanctus	Holy, holy, holy,
2 Dominus Deus Sabaoth,	Lord God of hosts;
3 Pleni sunt coeli et terra gloria tua.	Heaven and earth are full of thy glory.
4 Hosanna in excelsis.	Hosanna in the highest.
5 Benedictus qui venit in nomine Domini.	Blessed is he that cometh in the name of the Lord.
6 Hosanna in excelsis.	Hosanna in the highest.

5. Agnus Dei [pronounced AHN-yoose DAY-ee]. The short text of this simple, heartfelt petition allows scope for polyphonic repetition. Of the three phrases, the first two are identical. The third ends with a universal cry: "Dona nobis pacem" (grant us peace). Because of this text distribution, a corresponding musical division into three sections is traditional. Occasionally composers have separated the third phrase and cast it as an independent movement.

1 Agnus Dei, qui tollis peccata mundi: miserere nobis.	O Lamb of God, that taketh away the sins of the world; have mercy on us.
2 (repetition of 1)	O Lamb of God, that taketh away the sins of the world:
3 Agnus Dei, qui tollis peccata mundi: dona nobis pacem.	grant us peace.

Most Masses follow the plan just outlined, although composers sometimes expanded separate phrases into independent movements. Indeed, making a complete work based on only one of the five Ordinary sections is possible, as shown in the Glorias by the Baroque composer Antonio Vivaldi and the modern composer Francis Poulenc (1899–1963). The **Requiem Mass,** or Mass for the dead, so-called because it begins with the words "Requiem aeternam dona eis Domine" (Give them eternal rest, O Lord), is organized differently. While it includes some added sections, of which the "Dies irae," mentioned earlier in Chapter 14, is undoubtedly the most distinctive, it omits the Gloria and Credo.

C

Guillaume de Machaut [pronounced ma-SHOW] (c.1300–77) served both royalty and the church. His holy orders notwithstanding, he became France's leading poet and composer of secular music. He is best known for his *Notre Dame Mass*. (The title refers to "Our Lady," Mary, the mother of Jesus, not to the cathedral building in Paris.)

Machaut and his Polyphonic Mass

Legend has it that the *Notre Dame Mass* was sung at the coronation of Charles V in 1364. While music historians no longer believe this to be true, surely some grand occasion mandated its composition. It is memorable because it is both a masterpiece and also the *earliest polyphonic setting of the Ordinary of the Mass by one composer* who planned it as a musical whole. A four-part (male) chorus sings this Mass, each part confined within a limited range, all crowded together in the center of the pitch spectrum. Historians speculate that instruments (unspecified) might have replaced a voice part or two, or reinforced them all. Consequently, recordings of this work differ considerably, with some including various instruments and others relying only on voices.

The text of the Agnus Dei falls into three segments. So too does the Gregorian chant Agnus Dei tune that provides the foundation for Machaut's polyphonic setting. If only the first segment is sung, the correct designation is "Agnus Dei I." In Machaut's setting, "Agnus Dei II" contrasts musically with "Agnus Dei I," although the words are the same. "Agnus Dei III" is set to the same music as "Agnus Dei I," even though the last phrase of the text differs.

Machaut: *Agnus Dei,* from *Notre Dame Mass* (1:11 in MOM #13, Agnus Dei I only; 3:19 complete Agnus Dei) (6)

The composer Machaut (as we spell it) was born in the town of Reims in northeast France. Near the magnificent cathedral, a street bears his name.

In this Agnus Dei, rhythm functions as a powerful unifying device. The two lower parts move in relatively long note values, while the two upper voices exhibit an amazing variety of quicker, often syncopated note values. As one admiring authority observes, "Like the basic structure of a Gothic cathedral, the rhythmic unity of Machaut's Mass provides an unobtrusive but unshakable support for its wealth of decorative detail."

While the parts seem independent, for much of the time the voices declaim the same syllable at the same time. The cadences demonstrate the distinctive, empty sound of a fifth (*do-sol*). Triads were allowed in the Middle Ages, but not at endings. (The fifths are identified below, on the syllables in capital letters.)

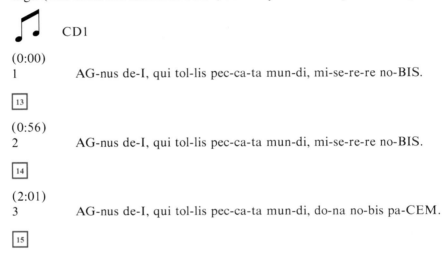

CD1

(0:00)
1   AG-nus de-I, qui tol-lis pec-ca-ta mun-di, mi-se-re-re no-BIS.

13

(0:56)
2   AG-nus de-I, qui tol-lis pec-ca-ta mun-di, mi-se-re-re no-BIS.

14

(2:01)
3   AG-nus de-I, qui tol-lis pec-ca-ta mun-di, do-na no-bis pa-CEM.

15

D

Dufay and the Cyclic Tenor Mass

Born in or near Cambrai, France, Guillaume Dufay [pronounced Doo- FAH-ee] (c.1400–74) was celebrated during his life as the greatest composer of his time and as the teacher of many famous musicians. A bachelor of law, a wine expert, and a cathedral canon, he held positions in many European musical centers, serving powerful patrons and singing in the papal choir, Europe's most famous musical establishment. Through his widely circulated compositions and through his pupils, he exerted enormous influence on his own century and beyond.

According to one recent view, Dufay's *Missa Se la face ay pale* may have been intended for the wedding of Charlotte of Savoy and Dauphin Louis (the future Louis XI) held in Chambéry in 1451. Whatever the occasion, this Mass magnificently illustrates the most impressive musical achievement of the fifteenth century: the **cyclic Mass,** a musically unified setting of the Mass Ordinary. In a cyclic Mass, all five components of the Ordinary are based upon a single cantus firmus (C.F.), a preexisting melody placed in the tenor, that is, in the next-to-lowest voice of a polyphonic piece. The C.F. is identified in the title of the individual Mass. Taking the general idea from English composers, Dufay transformed the cylic Mass by expanding it to a four-voice texture and grafting on additional unifying devices of his own. Howard M. Brown has stated that under Dufay's influence, "the tenor mass became the most common type of polyphonic setting of the Mass Ordinary for the next century."

Earlier composers invariably chose a liturgical melody for their C.F. Dufay apparently was the first to select a secular piece for this purpose. For the Mass we study, his choice of his own chanson may seem surprising, for its melody is a love song. We show its first three phrases (ex. 16.1). A translation begins: "If my face is pallid, know the cause is love. It alone doth cause it." Dufay placed the C.F. in the tenor, in notes of longer value than those of the newly composed parts.

Example 16.1

This music is typically sung by an all-male choir. Scholars once believed that instruments customarily supported the voices, or substituted for one or even all of them in portions of the music; more recent research has cast doubt on this assumption. Consequently, though recordings of this Mass are few, they are likely to differ greatly.

 CD1

Dufay: *Kyrie I,* from *Missa Se la face ay pale* (2:09) ⑦

The Kyrie begins simultaneously in all four voice parts, which sing independent lines shaped in graceful, gently curving, melismatic arches. These lines unfold in a freely flowing rhythm that is much simpler than Machaut's angular configurations. Placed below the C.F., a strong, supporting bass line allows greater harmonic freedom and a new sense of harmonic direction. Prominent in the cadences reached on the last syllable of "eleison" is the full sound of a triad. Dufay's fondness for triads produced a "sweeter" sound than that characteristic of fourteenth-century French composers. The many entrances on "Kyrie" overlap, continuing until a final cadence is reached. This one, however, is an empty fifth, the "correct" ending for Machaut as well.

The "Christe" section, which follows immediately, is in two and three voices, without the C.F. For "Kyrie II," Dufay returns to four voice parts and restores the C.F.

17 MEDIEVAL SECULAR MUSIC

PREVIEW Examples of both vocal and instrumental secular music appeared in the Middle Ages. We have chosen a monophonic song in a vernacular language paying tribute to the power of love. An instrumental piece most likely was planned for dancing.

During the Middle Ages, secular rulers gradually gained political power at the expense of the church. Princely courts supported musical establishments in the twelfth and thirteenth centuries. Consequently, some examples of secular music begin to appear in old manuscripts. Song texts were in the local or vernacular languages, such as French and Italian, that had been evolving from Latin.

A

Vocal Music

The earliest court music celebrated chivalry, that ideal code of honor which every knight claimed to uphold. Many poems with melodies have been preserved, with the earliest dated around 1100. While some songs dealt with the Crusades, the favorite topic—as always—was love. Although some paintings show a singer with an instrument, the songs are thought to be monophonic. The instrument simply duplicated the singer's line or contributed an introduction or a postlude. The French singers were known as **troubadours** (in southern France) and **trouvères** (in northern France). Though his role as a trouvère was slight, King Richard I of England (1157–99), usually called "the Lionhearted," wrote two poems that survive, one of them with music. The German equivalent of a troubadour, a **minnesinger,** provided the model for the Romantic composer Richard Wagner's hero in his opera *Tannhäuser.* ("Minne" is an old German word for "love.")

As is the case with church music, scholars are still not certain about the rhythms of these songs. Modern editors usually cast them in a definite meter, as in the following trouvère song, which dates from the twelfth to thirteenth centuries.

Or la truix is monophonic, like Gregorian chant. You can see that these two phrases (ex. 17.1) are very similar, both beginning with a motive, *mi-sol-fa-mi-re-mi*. They form a musical unit, which is repeated in items 3 and 4 below.

Or la truix (:55)
MOM #4 ⑧

Example 17.1

The text begins:

 CD1

(0:00)
1 Or la truix trop durete, voir, voir!
   A ceu k'elle est simplete.

⌗ 17

(0:14)
2 Trop por outre cuidiés me taius,
   Cant je cudoie estre certains,

(0:25)
3 De ceu ke n'a verai des mois. voir, voir!
   C'est ceu ke plus me blece.

(0:38)
4 (Text of 1 is repeated, as is the music.)

(A translation begins: I find it hard to woo her, because she is so simple.)

Toward the end of the Middle Ages composers wrote polyphonic vocal music based on decidedly secular texts dealing with love, hunting scenes, and the like. We have already met one such composer, the French poet-musician Machaut. Another, the Italian Francesco Landini (c.1325–97) was also a poet-musician. Blinded as a child, his disability did not prevent him from learning to play the organ. He composed no sacred music, specializing instead in appealingly melodic polyphonic songs called **ballate** (plural of ballata). Reflecting their dance origins, ballate have considerable rhythmic interest. Landini's name is also associated with a characteristic melodic cadence formula of the time: *ti-la-dô*.

The Italian composer of the late Middle Ages, Landini, is shown here playing an "organetto." The music that surrounds him is from one of his madrigals. (A museum in Florence houses this manuscript.)

B

Instrumental Music

Many of today's instruments had "ancestors" that flourished in medieval times. Far more than early stages of a perfection yet to come, they are interesting and valuable in their own right and in recent years have attracted new interest. Just as medieval people enjoyed strong colors and highly seasoned food, they liked colorful instruments with individual timbres. The louder ones they regarded as outdoor instruments; the quieter ones belonged indoors.

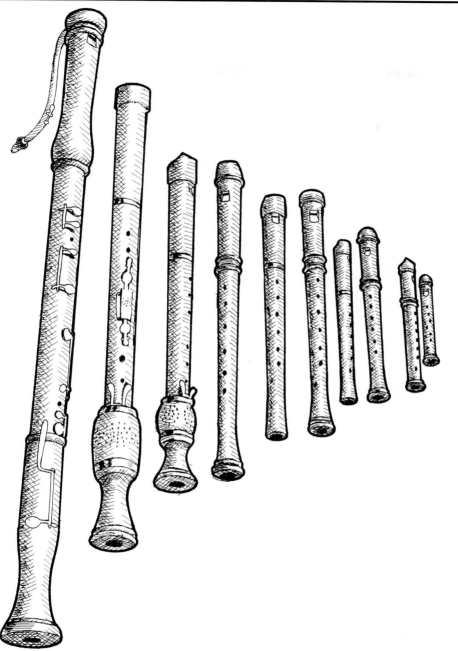

Recorders come in many sizes, from the tiny "sopranino" to the bass.

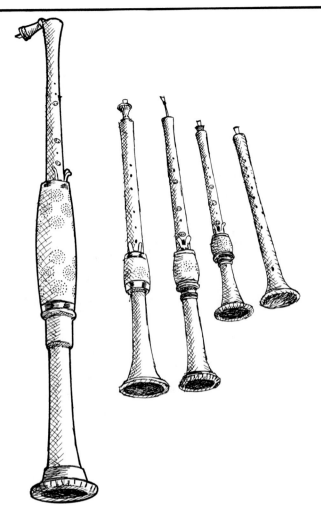

Shawms are played with a double-reed mouthpiece. The slight bulge in the middle and the flared shape at the end are distinctive.

Medieval instruments fall into the same families that we outlined in Part One. There was a bowed string instrument, the **fiddle** (not to be confused with the colloquial term for the modern violin). A medieval woodwind instrument, the **recorder,** has reappeared dramatically in this century. The player holds it in a vertical position and blows into its end, producing a soft, rather breathy tone. (Recently, students have begun elementary music training by playing inexpensive plastic versions of the recorder. Guaranteed not to disturb anyone within earshot, the recorder is an ideal instrument for educational purposes.) Other woodwind instruments, with mouthpieces consisting of two reeds bound together, can be compared to the modern oboe or the bassoon. An example is the **shawm,** with its strident, distinctive sound quality. The shawm is straight, with a flare at the bottom.

As for the brass instruments, except for the addition of valves, today's trumpet differs little in appearance from its medieval ancestor. The early trumpets could play only the notes the player's lips could control, which is the limitation of the bugle today. The present-day trombone looks much like its ancestor, the **sackbut.** All trombonelike instruments have a sliding mechanism that allows for a complete range of pitches. Percussion instruments have long existed. Indeed, a vase dating from the year 3000 B.C. pictures a large bass drum, and actual instruments from ancient Egypt have survived. So we can reasonably assume that various types of drums, cymbals, and bells thrived in the Middle Ages.

Medieval instruments came in varying sizes. For example, recorders covered the entire pitch range from soprano to bass. Several instruments of the same type might form an ensemble, although the more characteristic medieval sound resulted from a combination of different types of instruments.

Keyboard instruments date from this era. Many sources testify that large, impressive pipe organs existed in the Middle Ages. Remarkably, an organ in Sion, Switzerland, usually dated from 1380, is still playable. In contrast, art work shows small portable organs that ladies could hold in their laps. One hand played the keyboard; the other pumped the bellows that forced air into the pipes. While there may have been harpsichords and clavichords this early, we shall postpone discussion of these keyboard instruments until the Baroque period.

A very old instrument, the lute has undergone a revival of late in the hands of performers such as Paul O'Dette. The sharply-angled neck makes this instrument unique. (Photograph © Claire Rydell.)

Lutes were as common then as guitars are today. (Lutes, too, have made a comeback.) Both are plucked string instruments and sound much alike, although they look quite different. Guitars have flat backs, straight fingerboards, and six strings. Lutes have a round back, a bent fingerboard, more than six strings, and resemble in shape a half-pear.

 CD1

Estampie (1:24)
MOM #12 ⑨

Because the medieval composers did not specify their instrumentation, modern performers of early music must decide which instruments to choose. For that matter, often no distinction existed between vocal and instrumental music: a piece could be sung or played at will. Some music that might have been intended for dancing has survived, as in this thirteenth-century example, *Estampie* (ex. 17.2). Not surprisingly, some scholars relate its title to a Germanic word meaning "stamping" or "beating." With its lilting triple meter in a rhythm pattern that alternates half notes and quarter notes, this music invites dancing. In performing the two instrumental parts of this particular estampie, a recorder for the upper part contrasts nicely with an early string instrument on the lower part. As in sacred music, the favored intervals for the strong beats are the octave and the fifth, with their characteristic hollow sound.

Example 17.2

The Renaissance

18 INTRODUCING THE RENAISSANCE (1450–1600)

PREVIEW   We begin this chapter with a brief historical background of the Renaissance, list the composers we will study, and show how the characteristics of sound and the elements of music that were outlined in Part One function in Renaissance music.

"**Renaissance,**" with its literal meaning of "rebirth," may seem an exaggerated term to describe a style period. Yet to people who called the years after the Fall of Rome the "Dark Ages," the dramatic changes wrought by the Renaissance built a new world. Day conquered night. A revival of art, literature, and learning spread over Europe, much of it inspired by a renewed interest in the cultural heritage of ancient Greece and Rome. This factor is less important for music than for the visual arts, since artists and architects had ancient art to copy, while no models of Greek music were available for composers. Still, Greek ideas about music remained influential. Shakespeare echoed Plato in attributing ethical powers to music when he included these lines in *The Merchant of Venice,* act V, sc. 1:

> The man that hath no music in himself,
> Nor is not mov'd with concord of sweet sounds,
> Is fit for treasons, stratagems, and spoils;
> The motions of his spirit are dull as night,
> And his affections dark as Erebus.
> Let no such man be trusted.

No one event or year serves as a starting point for this era. Changes in the various artistic fields took place at different times, especially in different areas of Europe. Some art historians identify the beginning date as early as 1350; in music the year 1450 is more often chosen. Ending the Renaissance and starting the Baroque era at 1600 is generally accepted.

Many exciting discoveries involved the physical world. As we all learn in school, in 1492 Columbus (c.1451–1506) set out to sail around the earth, discovering the New World in the process. Copernicus (1473–1543) proved that planets revolve around the sun. One historian summed up the importance of the Renaissance as "the discovery of the world and of man." A questioning attitude toward authority and established wisdom made these discoveries possible and they, in turn, had momentous consequences.

Printing from movable type transformed intellectual life. Johann Gutenberg (c.1400–68) is credited with this invention (around 1450). The Venetian printer Ottaviano Petrucci (1466–1539) began to print music in 1501. Printing made it possible for compositions to be transmitted throughout the musical world. Music, in short, became an article of commerce. Because printed scores were expensive, manuscript scores remained an important means of distributing music for centuries.

The **Protestant Reformation** dealt the Roman Catholic church a devastating setback, breaking the church's domination of society and in the process affecting all the arts. In 1517, Martin Luther (1483–1546) set that Reformation in motion as he made public his arguments with the church he had been attempting to reform from within. Luther himself, a former monk who loved music passionately, played the flute and the lute, wrote hymn texts, and is credited with composing some hymn tunes still in common use. His most widely sung hymn, "A Mighty Fortress Is Our God" (Ein' feste Burg), was later nicknamed the battle hymn of the Reformation. The Lutheran denomination he founded valued music highly and allowed ample opportunity for congregational singing during the service. (In the Catholic service the congregation did not sing.) Some of the Lutheran hymns were adaptations of popular songs of the day, a practice Luther is supposed to have defended by asking, "Why should the Devil have all the good tunes?"

Other reformers, such as John Calvin (1509–64), established separate Protestant denominations, and King Henry VIII's differences with the Roman Catholic church resulted in the new Church of England (Anglican). Vast changes occurred in the kinds of music needed by the various new Christian denominations. Meanwhile, Catholics fought back with the Counter-Reformation, a movement that aimed at reform from within. Its musical consequences are illustrated in the life of Palestrina.

Secular music blossomed as society became increasingly interested in worldly matters. Creative artists in all fields employed secular as well as religious subject matter, desiring that their works would please people as much as earlier generations wanted to please God. While religious subjects dominate medieval art, Renaissance art is decidedly secular, with the human body shown as freely as in ancient Greece.

Michelangelo (1475–1564) is best known for his Sistine Chapel ceiling paintings, but his sculpture is equally impressive. His larger-than-life statue of David for the city of Florence shows the youthful hero, poised and yet tense, ready to throw the sling shot that brings down Goliath.

A book printed in 1528 (*The Book of the Courtier* by Baldassarre Castiglione) quoted courtly conversations praising music in extravagant terms like these: "I am not satisfied with our Courtier unless he be also a musician, and unless, besides understanding and being able to read music, he can play various instruments. For no medicine for ailing spirits can be found more decorous or praiseworthy in time of leisure than music, a most welcome food for the spirit."

B

Renaissance Composers

In the Renaissance, individual creativity flourished. In sharp contrast to the general anonymity of medieval workers, many Renaissance composers are known to history. Two important composers worked in the transition years between the Middle Ages and the Renaissance. We have met Dufay and his polyphonic Mass cycle based on his own secular song. Johannes Ockeghem [AHK-a-gem] (c.1420–96) was hailed for his mastery of complex canonic techniques.

Employed by church or nobility, composers wrote to order whatever their situation demanded. Besides the figures we study in individual chapters—Josquin

Orlando Laſſo. a 6.   XXXIIII.   Basso.

Anto e quel. Dal vivo fonte de la tua bontate, ch'ogni gente arrichiſce in ogni etate,

& ogni corpo & ogni mente paſ-   ce, quanto in terra tra noi more e rinaſ-

ce   orna et   ac- cende d'alta caritate,   co-   ſa non è   ch'ignud'o

The pitches shown by the diamond-shaped notes in this music are clear enough, but the lack of bar lines might cause difficulties for a modern musician. At the end of each line is a little squiggle that alerts the reader to the pitch that will come on the next line—a useful convention that has not survived.

Desprez, Palestrina, Victoria, Weelkes, and Gabrieli—we should also mention the following artists. A contemporary of Palestrina, the astonishingly versatile Orlando di Lasso (1532–94) was one of the most prolific composers of all time. A master of sacred polyphony, he also wrote madrigals and other secular music in several national styles. (Sometimes his name appears in its Latin form as Lassus.) Don Carlo Gesualdo, Prince of Venosa (1560–1613), gained renown for his Italian madrigals. Gesualdo's harmony is unusually dissonant for his time, but it is not his music alone that earns him a place in the history books. Scandal engulfed his name after he murdered his unfaithful wife and her lover. Two Englishmen, Thomas Morley (1557–1602) and John Dowland (1563–1626), cultivated secular music, particularly madrigals. The multitalented William Byrd (1543–1623) composed glorious church music (for both the Catholics *and* the Anglicans) as well as madrigals and keyboard compositions.

C

The Characteristics of Sound in the Renaissance

1. The overall *pitch* span expanded, reaching farther down into the bass range. There was still no absolute standard for pitch, although the musical scores gave more definite indications for it than had previous ages. Even so, present-day musicians often choose to perform a Renaissance piece at a different pitch level from that shown in the score.

2. *Dynamics* were seldom indicated in the musical score. When a late Renaissance composer whom we study, Giovanni Gabrieli, wrote the indications "*piano*" and "*forte*" into a piece for brasses (*Sonata pian e forte,* 1597), he earned a special place in history.

3. *Tone color* in this era displays a new feature: the sound of choral music without instrumental accompaniment. An Italian phrase designating this effect is

a cappella, which literally means "in the style of the chapel (or church)," because in Rome's Sistine Chapel the choir normally sang unaccompanied. It may be that only in that place was a cappella singing a standard practice. Elsewhere, instrumental support, especially from an organ, might have been added routinely, but nothing in the score calls for it. Renaissance choral music employed not only the four-part grouping of soprano, alto, tenor, and bass that we know today but also expanded groupings of five or six parts that could fill a reverberant cathedral with a rich sonority.

In this era the soprano and alto lines were entrusted to boys or to **counter-tenors**—men who have been trained to sing above the standard tenor range. An all-male choir can attain a unique purity and blend. In performing this music today a few choirs, particularly in England, perpetuate the all-male tradition. Because well-trained boy singers are so scarce (and because boys are reaching puberty at a younger age than in earlier times), most choirs today have females sing the upper parts.

Vocal music continued to be more important than instrumental music. As the composer William Byrd said, in the spelling of the time, "There is not any Musicke of Instruments whatsoever, comparable to that which is made of the voyces of Men, where the voyces are good and the same well sorted and ordered." Instruments supported voices or played vocal music. Composers did not seem much concerned with writing specifically for instruments until the late Renaissance. They did, however, continue a long tradition of writing for various keyboard instruments, showing that they recognized that such instruments posed unique challenges.

Many of the medieval instruments lived on, such as the recorder, shawm, trumpet, and sackbut. A new string instrument, the **viol,** came in at least three sizes: smaller viols were held on the player's lap; the largest viol, the **viola da gamba,** or **gamba** for short, was held between the player's legs. ("Gamba" means "leg.") Softer and somewhat more nasal in sound than today's string instruments, viols differ from them in several obvious details of construction. For example, a viol has six strings instead of the string family's four. New to the woodwind family was the **crumhorn** (also spelled krummhorn), a double-reed instrument shaped like the letter J. The lute became the leading domestic Renaissance instrument.

Unlike their medieval predecessors, who happily combined instruments of different families, Renaissance musicians preferred **consorts,** which were ensembles composed of instruments of varying sizes all of the same family.

D

The Elements of Music in the Renaissance

1. *Rhythm* was consistently metrical, although today's listener probably does not feel an obvious beat or pulse, at least in sacred vocal music. Metrical patterns are clearer in instrumental music, since much of it is dance-related. In this era duple meter rose in prominence as triple meter lost its preferred position.

2. *Melody* continued to perpetuate the characteristics of Gregorian chant in setting limits to ranges and controlling skips carefully. Scalewise motion prevailed.

Hans Burgkmair's woodcut (early 1500s) of the emperor Maximilian and his musicians shows what a wide variety of instruments might be used in the Renaissance. In the foreground from left to right are a small organ, harp and drums. A sackbut rests on top of the drums. Partially shown on the table is a viola da gamba, a flute, recorders, and a crumhorn. Singers are in the background.

3. *Harmony* experienced a dramatic change as the sound of the triad (*do-mi-sol,* for example), especially at final cadences, replaced the hollow sound of the fifth (*do, sol*) that was so characteristic of the Middle Ages. While there is little sense of an inevitable progression to the tonic, a concept associated with the Baroque period, still the overall harmony sounds quite "normal" to our ears. Though dissonance was allowed, it was approached carefully and immediately resolved, rarely disturbing the serene surface of the music.

The composers wrote in the medieval modes. Evidence suggests, however, that the performers might have made alterations which produced sounds that are surprisingly close to our major and minor scales. Scholars are far from agreement regarding these possible alterations, and consequently modern editions of Renaissance music may show accidentals placed above or below the staff instead of in the normal position, immediately to the left of the affected note. You may hear some fundamental differences in performances, especially in respect to the seventh

The J shape of the crumhorn is visually distinctive. Equally so is its intense sound.

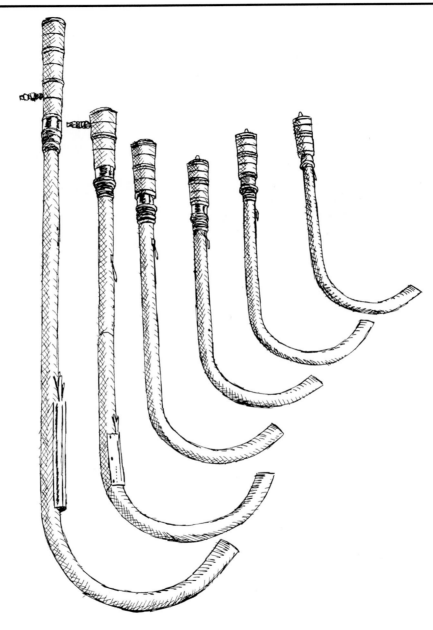

note of the scale at cadences. If this tone is raised, the end result is the "*ti* to *dô*" effect, the cornerstone of our feeling for tonality.

4.   Renaissance composers specialized in imitative polyphony, the prevailing *texture* of the time. In writing polyphonic music, a composer utilizes a technique known as **counterpoint,** a word which literally means "note against note," the style of the earliest polyphony. More generally, counterpoint stresses the linear aspect of music as melodies are fitted together. As a contrast to the prevailing polyphony, Renaissance composers relied on chordal-style homophony in which all voices move in the same rhythm, singing the same syllable at the same time.

5.   The *form* of Renaissance vocal music grew out of the text. Each separate phrase had its own musical motive. Each motive was imitated polyphonically, with the individual voice parts entering in turn. This process produced what is known as **points of imitation.** Usually, as one point of imitation was finishing another was beginning, resulting in much overlapping of imitative entrances.

19 JOSQUIN DESPREZ

PREVIEW Born in northern France, Josquin became an international figure whose music is still acclaimed. He demonstrated a mastery of polyphony as well as a concern for the relationship of text syllables and music. We study a movement from a Mass by Josquin that perpetuates the Medieval tradition of basing Masses upon preexisting melody.

IOSQVINVS PRATENSIS.

Josquin Desprez.

While the name of Josquin Desprez [prounounced GHOS-can day-PRAY] (c.1440–1521) can cause some confusion—he is called "Josquin" about as often as "Desprez"; his last name occurs in a variety of spellings—his stature is undisputed. Acclaimed in his lifetime and after his death as the finest composer of his generation, this truly international figure was born in an area of Northern France and later spent many fruitful years in Italy.

As signs of the enormous esteem in which Josquin was held at the time, his music circulated widely in print; composers wrote laments to mark his passing; sixteenth-century music theorists and literary figures alike praised him enthusiastically. Two remarks have become particularly celebrated. Martin Luther astutely observed that "He [Josquin] is the master of the notes, which must express what he desires; on the other hand, other choral composers must do what the notes dictate." Another story, something of a backhanded compliment, illustrates Josquin's temperament. A talent scout, hunting for a composer to grace an Italian duke's establishment, advised against hiring Josquin, recommending that the composer Heinrich Isaac (c.1450–1517) be employed instead. He admitted that Josquin was the better composer, but "he composes when he wants to, and not when one wants him to, and he is asking 200 ducats in salary while Isaac will come for 120." Nor has Josquin's fame diminished with the passage of time, as a 1971 International Josquin Festival and Congress held in New York City dramatically illustrated. His art remains as relevant today as it was 450 years ago.

Josquin cultivated secular French chansons, sacred motets, and Masses, his supreme achievement. Composing music of a new size, sensuous beauty, and expressive power, he demonstrated an awe-inspiring mastery of every polyphonic device, many of which reached back to the medieval period. At the same time, Josquin and his contemporaries evinced a new concern for the relationship of words and music. Earlier composers did not customarily show in their scores how the syllables should align with the notes, a task that present-day scholars have to complete so that the music can be performed. We take it for granted that word accents should match musical accents, a topic that authorities refer to as "declamation," but this concept emerged only in the sixteenth century. Josquin achieved additional musical variety and spaciousness by pitting high voices against low, additional richness by writing chains of ear-pleasing thirds and sixths, additional propulsion by an increased rhythmic vigor, and a clearer sense of shape by a strong drive to final cadences.

A thirteenth-century Latin hymn whose text begins: Pange lingua gloriosi corporis mysterium (Tell, o tongue, the mystery of the glorious body) provides the title of this Mass, composed late in Josquin's life. It also provides the principal musical motives for the Mass, making it a "paraphrase Mass," that is, one based on preexisting musical materials. Each individual phrase of the text receives its own musical motive, which is treated imitatively. Generally, the imitation comes in at an interval of an octave or a fifth, and at the composer's choice of time interval. While the score shows only four voice parts, some recordings employ various instruments as well. Our recording employs two instrumental quartets. They accompany voices in the two "Kyrie" sections and also are heard alone. These recordings also differ in respect to tempo and to degree of metrical accent.

Josquin: *Kyrie*, from *Missa Pange lingua* (Pange lingua Mass) (5:09) ⑩

 CD1

(0:00)
1a
[19]

Tenor begins with "Kyrie" (ex. 19.1) in triple meter, singing a melodic line taken from the first notes of the hymn, soon answered by bass. Before either line has completed the "eleison" word of the text, the soprano and alto have entered in a similar pairing. Then bass and tenor are paired once more in an entrance on "Kyrie." Such duets are a hallmark of Josquin's style. All four voices move in independent lines to a cadence on "-son," a medieval-sounding cadence on an empty fifth.

Example 19.1

Ky - ri - - e   e - - - lei - - - - - - - - - - son,

(0:47)

1b

In our recording, the viols give a preview of the "Christe" music (item 2), which they then accompany.

(2:03)

2a

20

"Christe" is begun by the bass, in duple meter, with a melodic line (ex. 19.2) taken from the third phrase of the hymn and answered by the alto. Both voices proceed on to a brief duet. Tenor, answered by soprano, sings the same "Christe" motive that began item 2a, and the two voices then execute a similar duet.

Example 19.2

Chri - ste_____, Chri - ste_____

"Eleison," the next text word, finally appears. An extended flourish for tenor embellishes the minor-chord cadence.

(3:24)

2b

Now the sackbuts provide a preview; here, of the second "Kyrie," (item 3), which they will accompany.

(4:14)

3

21

The concluding "Kyrie" returns to triple meter, but with a new melodic line (ex. 19.3), first begun in soprano and immediately answered by alto. After their duet, similar entrances occur in tenor and bass, which are soon joined by the remaining voices. Again the cadence on "-son" is embellished before the final conclusion on an empty fifth. This is the first time a true resting place identifies the mode, which is the mode based on E (E,F,G,A,B,C,D,E). Throughout, Josquin's text setting projects the words convincingly, with enough melismas to impart an impressive sweep to his melodic lines.

Example 19.3

Ky - ri - e   e - - - - -lei - - - - - - - - - - - - - - - - - son

(An English translation and discussion of the Mass text is in Chapter 16.)

GIOVANNI PIERLUIGI DA PALESTRINA 20

PREVIEW With a career centered in Roman church music, Palestrina made his reputation as a master of Renaissance imitative polyphony. His alleged role in "saving" polyphonic church music from the reform-minded Council of Trent is the subject of legends. As an example of his elegant contrapuntal style, we have selected a movement from one of his most famous Masses.

A town near Rome supplied the name for Giovanni Pierluigi da Palestrina (1525–94). His name simply means that he was "from Palestrina." He spent most of his adult musical career working as singer or music director in Roman churches, including the Sistine Chapel. Although Palestrina wrote secular madrigals in his youth, an "indiscretion" for which he later apologized, he is best known for his hundreds of motets and his 104 Masses. Many were published in his lifetime; after his death his sons published more of them. Publication was a contributing factor to his ongoing fame. Unlike his contemporaries, whose music slipped from view after their deaths, his music continued in favor.

Palestrina's reputation remains high to the present day, partly due to two factors associated with his name. He was such a supreme master of the flowing counterpoint associated with the Renaissance that eighteenth-century theorists formulated a teaching technique based on it, one still found in the curriculum. "Palestrina counterpoint" provides a method to control the intervals used and the balance of skips and conjunct motion.

The second factor to make his name immortal is his role as the "savior of church music." Like most legends, this one contains a grain of truth, even though his role in the rescue operation was probably overstated. The story begins with the Council of Trent (1545–63), which was convened by the Roman Catholic church as part of its Counter-Reformation. In its plans to reform the church from within, the Council directed some attention to sacred music. As the English historian Charles Burney (1726–1814) reported later, the church fathers, "having been offended and scandalized at the light and injudicious manner in which the mass had been long set and performed, determined to banish Music in parts entirely from

Palestrina presents his First Book of Masses, 1554, to the pope in this frontispiece.

J. Hodgson. Sculp.

the church." A decree issued in 1562 ordered that singing should be constituted so as "not to give empty pleasure to the ear, but in such a way that the words may be clearly understood by all, and thus the hearts of the listeners be drawn to the contemplation of the joys of the blessed."

Polyphony came under fire on the grounds that the multiple parts obscured the words. According to one account, Pope Pius IV was ready to ask the Council to ban polyphony. Palestrina, however, convinced him through several of his Masses that despite the multiplicity of vocal lines, words could be intelligible in polyphony. At any rate, the threatened ban never materialized. One particular Palestrina work, the *Pope Marcellus Mass* (Missa Papae Marcelli), is often credited with "saving church music" and therefore is dated from the years 1562–63. Indeed, it shows unusual clarity of text setting. Pope Marcellus's name might appear in the title because of actions he took in 1555 during his three-week tenure as Pope. He recommended to the papal choir that composers of sacred music allow the words to be heard more clearly. Since Palestrina sang in the choir, we know he heard this recommendation.

Unlike the *Pange lingua Mass* by Josquin, which took musical motives from a preexisting Gregorian chant, the *Pope Marcellus Mass* is freely composed. In other Masses, Palestrina employed the borrowing technique, as in his famous Mass *Aeterna Christi munera,* which takes its material from the hymn with that title.

Palestrina would have said that he wrote this Mass in the "Ionian" mode, the mode we know as C major. It calls for a six-voice choir: soprano, alto, two tenor parts, and two bass parts. Since voices are constantly entering and leaving, a shifting number of sounding parts at any one moment achieves considerable variety.

Palestrina:
Benedictus, from the
Pope Marcellus Mass
(3:25) ⑪

As did Josquin, Palestrina sets each phrase of the text to its own musical motive. When one phrase of the text is finished, a new one begins. Often the phrases overlap, with the new section beginning before the old one has reached a cadence.

 CD1

(0:00)
1

22

Only soprano and tenor begin (ex. 20.1) with independent lines on "Benedictus," creating an ethereal, floating sound. A second tenor, then an alto, soon enter, also with independent lines. (The accidentals under the music reflect possible pitch changes, depending upon a conductor's decision.)

Example 20.1

Be - ne - di

(0:51)

2

23

Tenor sings "qui venit" (ex. 20.2), beginning a series of imitative entrances, as the remaining voices of the quartet enter separately with these words.

Example 20.2

qui   ve

(1:30)

3

24

Alto sings "in nomine Domini," (ex. 20.3), beginning another section with many imitative entrances of the (new) motive. All voices finish together on "-ni," a cadence on the dominant. This will make the concluding phrase, "Hosanna," seem more final.

Example 20.3

in   no -   mi -   ne_____ Do - mi -   ni_____

(2:29)

4

25

"Hosanna in excelsis" is the last phrase of the Benedictus text and also of the Sanctus, which precedes the Benedictus, so it is traditional that the music for this phrase repeats the music from the Sanctus. Beginning with only four parts in homophonic style, the "Hosanna" section soon adds the two basses for a strong, weighty foundation. The initial homophony then gives way to complex polyphony with independent lines. All voices come together on "-sis" to end on a full-sounding, C major chord.

(An English translation and discussion of the Mass text is in Chapter 16.)

TOMÁS LUIS DE VICTORIA 21

PREVIEW   We study a motet by Victoria, a Spanish composer who wrote only church music. Similar in its unaccompanied sound to a Palestrina Mass, Victoria's motet shows more variety of texture.

Tomás Luis de Victoria (1548–1611), the greatest Spanish composer of the Renaissance, spent his life serving church music as an organist and chapel master. (His name sometimes appears in its Italian form as Tommaso Luigi da Vittoria.) Although his Italian contemporary Palestrina, who might have been his teacher, is better known today, Victoria still ranks high. Unlike Palestrina, who was married and consequently ineligible for the priesthood, Victoria was an ordained priest. All of Victoria's compositions are on Latin sacred texts, which he set with an unusual sensitivity to the specific meanings of the text.

Victoria: *Ave Maria*
(2:28) ⑫

Ave Maria is a **motet** for a four-part a cappella choir. The sixteenth-century motet is a polyphonic composition, based on a freely chosen sacred Latin text. The Mass and motet are very similar in musical styles. Victoria's motet begins by quoting a Gregorian chant melody for the "Ave Maria" text (ex. 21.1). The next three phrases of the original chant melody contribute additional musical motives as the motet continues. As its listening guide shows, this piece happens to demonstrate all three types of texture. Because the sound of *Ave Maria* is similar to that of the Palestrina Mass movement described in the preceding chapter, the two pieces invite comparison and contrast. In response to its intimate text, Victoria's motet offers more musical variety and generates greater intensity. Note throughout the numerous text repetitions that serve to heighten expressivity.

This is the title page of an edition of Victoria's Masses, published in Rome in 1583.

THOMAE LVDOVIC
A VICTORIA ABVLENSIS
MISSARVM LIBRI DVO
QVÆ PARTIM QVATERNIS, PARTIM
QVINIS, PARTIM SENIS,
CONCINVNTVR VOCIBVS.

Ad Philippum secundum Hispaniarum Regem Catholicum.

ROMÆ
Ex Typographia Dominici Basæ.
M D LXXXIII.
CVM LICENTIA SVPERIORVM.

Example 21.1

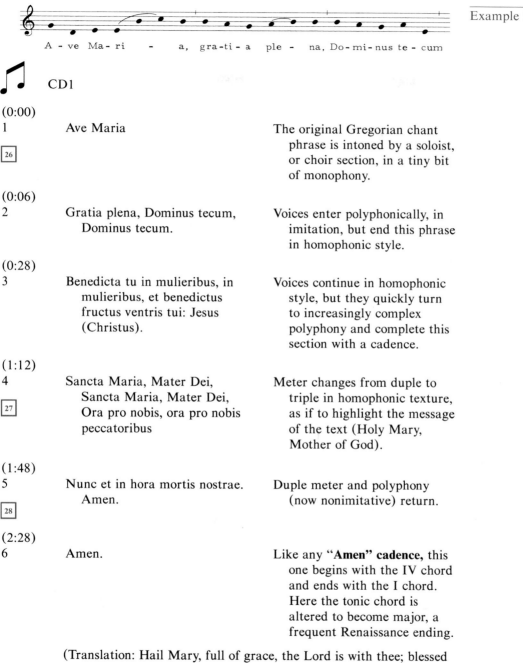

A - ve Ma- ri - a, gra-ti- a ple - na, Do-mi-nus te- cum

CD1

(0:00)
1

26

Ave Maria

The original Gregorian chant
phrase is intoned by a soloist,
or choir section, in a tiny bit
of monophony.

(0:06)
2

Gratia plena, Dominus tecum,
Dominus tecum.

Voices enter polyphonically, in
imitation, but end this phrase
in homophonic style.

(0:28)
3

Benedicta tu in mulieribus, in
mulieribus, et benedictus
fructus ventris tui: Jesus
(Christus).

Voices continue in homophonic
style, but they quickly turn
to increasingly complex
polyphony and complete this
section with a cadence.

(1:12)
4

27

Sancta Maria, Mater Dei,
Sancta Maria, Mater Dei,
Ora pro nobis, ora pro nobis
peccatoribus

Meter changes from duple to
triple in homophonic texture,
as if to highlight the message
of the text (Holy Mary,
Mother of God).

(1:48)
5

28

Nunc et in hora mortis nostrae.
Amen.

Duple meter and polyphony
(now nonimitative) return.

(2:28)
6

Amen.

Like any **"Amen" cadence,** this
one begins with the IV chord
and ends with the I chord.
Here the tonic chord is
altered to become major, a
frequent Renaissance ending.

(Translation: Hail Mary, full of grace, the Lord is with thee; blessed
art thou among women, and blessed is the offspring of thy womb,
Jesus. Holy Mary, Mother of God, pray for us sinners, now and in
the hour of our death. Amen.)

22 THE RENAISSANCE MADRIGAL

PREVIEW Still sung today are Renaissance madrigals, which are secular vocal pieces at first set to Italian poetry. We discuss their performance and special features, leaving a specific example for the next chapter.

The Renaissance **madrigal** is a type of secular vocal music that developed in Italy and later migrated to England. Madrigals remain favorites with singing groups even today because they flatter the voice. Though conceived for one singer to a part and for this reason placed in the category of "vocal chamber music," they are often performed by larger groups. Based on short texts with subject matter that is typically amorous (be the approach poignant or playful), they appeal to contemporary audiences as well. Madrigals originated in the early 1500s, set to the verse of great Italian poets such as Petrarch (1304–74) and his imitators. The second half of the century saw the flowering of the Italian madrigal, produced by some of the masters whom we mention on other pages, such as Monteverdi and Gesualdo. The prolific Luca Marenzio (1553–99), who served both nobility and church, published over four hundred madrigals.

A

Performing the Madrigals

The reactions of an audience were of little concern for the first singers of madrigals. Tradition says that aristocrats sang madrigals for their own entertainment as they sat around a table. In order to participate, these aristocrats learned to read music, just as they knew how to paint, to write poetry, and to manage the affairs of state. Even today we think of someone with multiple talents, like Leonardo da Vinci (1452–1519)—painter, sculptor, architect, engineer, scientist—as typical of the Renaissance.

In madrigals, as in church music, the unaccompanied or a cappella sound is assumed, although instrumental support might have been welcomed for practical reasons. (Perhaps these amateurs needed a little help to stay on pitch!) Designed for public performance and festive occasions, highly complex madrigals in which instrumental participation was likely appear late in the Renaissance.

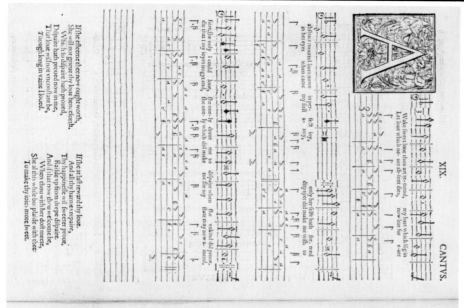

John Dowland's music was often printed in "table-book" form; that is, some parts were printed upside down, others vertically, so that singers seated around a table could all read from the same score.

The English composer Thomas Morley wrote *A Plaine and Easie Introduction to Practicall Musicke,* 1597, which is often cited as proof that all aristocrats in Morley's England possessed the musical literacy needed to sing madrigals. He described the embarrassment of a young nobleman who discovered a great lack in his education because others could sing and he could not:

> But supper being ended and music books being brought to the table, the mistress of the house presented me with a part earnestly requesting me to sing; but when, after many excuses, I protested unfeignedly that I could not, every one began to wonder; yea, some whispered to others demanding how I was brought up, so that upon shame of mine ignorance I go now to seek out mine old friend Master Gnorimus, to make myself his scholar.

B

Special Features of Madrigals

The late Renaissance ideal, that the music should enhance the words to which it was sung and express the emotions of those words, found its most obvious outlet in the madrigal. Many madrigals exhibit **word painting,** a term that refers to the way musical devices can reflect the meaning of specific words in the text. Most examples of word painting are quite obvious: a phrase such as "rising up" would move up the scale, a reference to "running" would move in faster rhythm values than would an allusion to "crawling." A reference to "eternity" would be set with long notes, while high pitches would suggest "heaven."

Non-Italian musicians composed their madrigals to the poetry of their own countries. During the reign of Queen Elizabeth I (1533–1603), who, like her father Henry VIII, was well-trained in music, the English madrigal flourished. Characteristic of many lighter English madrigals is the **fa-la-la** refrain, as in the Christmas carol, "Deck the Halls with Boughs of Holly," analyzed in Chapter 8 to show phrase relationships. The happy English madrigal tended to be homophonic, although its fa-la-la refrain might display some polyphony. Serious texts in English or Italian were more apt to be polyphonic, usually with the message "She doesn't love him."

THOMAS WEELKES 23

PREVIEW English composers eagerly embraced the madrigal. Among them was Thomas Weelkes, whose madrigal celebrating Queen Elizabeth I we study. Its text, naturally enough in English, is full of word-painting examples.

A major composer of English church music, Thomas Weelkes was born in 1576 and died in London in 1623. His main musical occupation was that of organist-choir master in provincial cathedrals. While he wrote much fine choral music for the English church, his chief fame stems from his madrigals, which he began to write as a very young man.

In 1601, twenty-three English composers compiled and published a collection of madrigals as a tribute to Queen Elizabeth I, no doubt as a sort of public relations gesture. "Fair Oriana" was their mythological name for her in these madrigals. Diana, the Roman goddess of virginity, and her nymphs and shepherds also appear in them, representing the Queen's subjects. *As Vesta Was From Latmos Hill Descending* was Weelkes's contribution to this volume. Unfortunately, the Queen lived only a couple of years longer. After her death madrigals fell from favor, their word painting now criticized as childish and ridiculous. Weelkes lived for two more decades, but his best days were past.

Vesta is written for a six-part group: two sopranos, alto, two tenors, and bass. Like the Palestrina and Victoria selections in preceding chapters, *Vesta* lacks written accompaniment, thus implying the a cappella sound. Unlike them, *Vesta* has a marked rhythmic drive and is, of course, in English. It includes several striking examples of word painting involving melodic direction, speed of note values, and changes in texture, most of them so obvious that they need no explanation. They are simply indicated here as occurring on the italicized words of the text.

Weelkes: *As Vesta Was From Latmos Hill Descending* (2:51) ⑬

This collection of madrigals to honor Queen Elizabeth was edited by Thomas Morley, one of the mos prominent of English madrigal composers.

CANTVS.

MADRIGALES

The Triumphes of Oriana,
to 5. and 6. voices: com-
posed by diuers seuerall
aucthors.

Newly published by Thomas Morley,
Batcheler of Musick, and one of
the gentlemen of hir
Maiesties honorable
Chappell.

1601.

IN LONDON
PRINTED BY THOMAS ESTE,
the assigne of Thomas Morley.

¶ Cum priuilegio Regiæ Maiestatis.

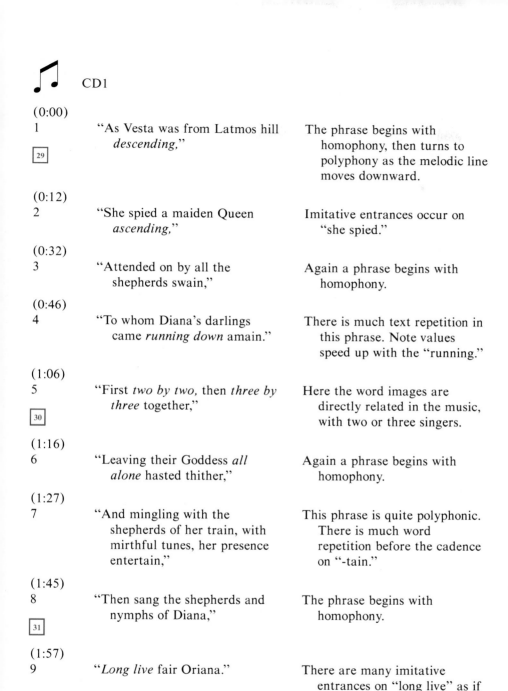

CD1

(0:00)
1

29

"As Vesta was from Latmos hill *descending,*"

The phrase begins with homophony, then turns to polyphony as the melodic line moves downward.

(0:12)
2

"She spied a maiden Queen *ascending,*"

Imitative entrances occur on "she spied."

(0:32)
3

"Attended on by all the shepherds swain,"

Again a phrase begins with homophony.

(0:46)
4

"To whom Diana's darlings came *running down* amain."

There is much text repetition in this phrase. Note values speed up with the "running."

(1:06)
5

30

"First *two by two,* then *three by three* together,"

Here the word images are directly related in the music, with two or three singers.

(1:16)
6

"Leaving their Goddess *all alone* hasted thither,"

Again a phrase begins with homophony.

(1:27)
7

"And mingling with the shepherds of her train, with mirthful tunes, her presence entertain,"

This phrase is quite polyphonic. There is much word repetition before the cadence on "-tain."

(1:45)
8

31

"Then sang the shepherds and nymphs of Diana,"

The phrase begins with homophony.

(1:57)
9

"*Long live* fair Oriana."

There are many imitative entrances on "long live" as if to assure the Queen that her loyal subjects hail her in all corners of her empire. The bass sings his line on very long tones indeed.

24 GIOVANNI GABRIELI

PREVIEW To an unusual degree, the specific locale where Gabrieli worked affected his music. We study an instrumental piece that was planned for the unique acoustics of St. Mark's church in Venice, Italy.

Giovanni Gabrieli (c.1553–1612) succeeded his uncle and music teacher Andrea Gabrieli (1510–86) as chief musician at St. Mark's church in Venice, Italy. Venice, famous for its canals, gondolas, and flamboyant architectural styles, was an important trade center, a wealthy and independent city-state, and a showplace for art and music. The church, together with the plaza in front of it, lies at the center of this fascinating city. St. Mark's was built to a unique architectural plan, with two galleries for musicians. It thus offered opportunities for divided choirs of instruments and of voices. In this setting, the physical placement of the musicians resulted in sounds coming from differing locations, one moment simultaneously, the next moment in alternation. "Stereophonic" sound is not just a twentieth-century interest.

Gabrieli: *Canzona on the Ninth Tone* (for eight parts) (Canzon per sonar noni toni) (3:26) ⑭

With the late Renaissance came a new emphasis on instrumental music. This purely instrumental piece alternates between imitative sections in duple meter and homophonic sections in a fast, triple meter. It begins with a rhythm pattern characteristic of canzonas: long-short-short. The "ninth tone" part of the title is the way a Renaissance composer would identify the key (Aeolian mode: A, B, C, D, E, F, G). Today we would say it was in A minor.

Because Gabrieli, like his fellow composers, rarely specified the instruments he wanted, his canzonas can be played by a variety of instrumental groups, including brasses, recorders, viols, and organ. In this canzona, the two groups, of four instruments each, sometimes play simultaneously; sometimes they alternate.

♪ ♪ CD1

(0:00)
1   m1   The first group of instruments begins with imitative entrances
[32]   exploiting the characteristic rhythm mentioned above: long-short-
         short. Toward the end of this section the second group enters.

(0:57)
2   m16 After a tiny pause the first of the triple meter sections (ex. 24.1)
[33]   begins in a fast tempo. The two groups alternate in playing.

Example 24.1

(1:26)
3   m38 The duple meter and the rhythm pattern of item 1 return. In
[34]   addition, new rhythm patterns appear.

(2:04)
4   m49 Similar to item 2, this section continues the rhythms and the
[35]   alternation of groups found there.

(2:32)
5   m70 A return of the duple meter of item 1 emphasizes the canzona
[36]   rhythm in quick alternations of the instrumental groups.

(3:06)
6   m79 As if to sum it all up, a brief return of triple meter is followed by a
         full-sounding, emphatic ending on a major chord, a frequent final
         chord in Renaissance music.

Today's visitor finds St. Mark's as fantastic a sight as ever, especially with the rain-covered plaza forming mirror images of the church. (Photograph © Claire Rydell.)

The Baroque

INTRODUCING THE
BAROQUE PERIOD (1600–1750) 25

PREVIEW In this introductory chapter, we give a brief sketch of historical events, list the major composers to be studied and mention several others, show how the characteristics of sound and the elements of music function, and outline four important special features of Baroque music.

The label "Baroque" came from art historians. Originally referring to large, irregularly shaped pearls, the term by extension meant something eccentric or imperfect. When applied to works of art produced between the years 1600 and 1750, the word has shed any negative connotations, although a faint implication of "excessive" or "extravagant" still clings to it. Baroque art projects tension and activity. Europe is dotted with churches built in the Baroque era, vast in scale, with many curved forms giving the effect of movement and complexity.

By historical coincidence, both 1600 and 1750 are years in which something specific happened. The oldest surviving opera—opera is the subject of the next chapter—dates from 1600, and the death of Johann Sebastian Bach marks the end of the period. The early years of the Baroque saw many exciting new things happening in music. These we outline briefly. Since the public is more familiar with music from the later years, the early 1700s or "high" Baroque, the majority of our examples represent that time, and our generalizations reflect the later practice.

A

The continuation of the bloody hostilities between Protestants and Catholics that had scarred the Renaissance continued during the Baroque period. *Absolute monarchs,* such as Louis XIV of France (1638–1715) and Frederick the Great of Prussia (1712–86), reigned with authoritarian efficiency, protected by the divine

Historical Background

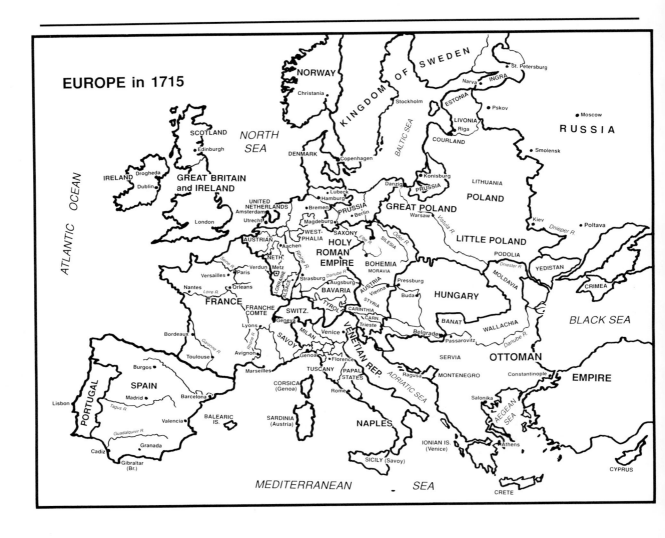

EUROPE in 1715

right of kings. Their power was so great that the "Age of Absolutism" is a historian's way of describing these years. Incidentally, both of these rulers participated actively in the arts: Louis danced in the royal ballets, and Frederick played the flute. Johann Joachim Quantz (1697–1773), resident composer of the Prussian court, left over five hundred pieces for—not surprisingly—the flute.

Advances in *scientific thinking,* begun in the Renaissance, continued in the work of geniuses such as Galileo Galilei (1564–1642). John Locke (1632–1704) believed that natural law operated in human affairs as in science. His essays attempted to prove that governments were formed because people yielded to society their own individual powers. The name of Sir Isaac Newton (1642–1727) always reminds us of the laws of gravitation, but he also explored the nature of light and developed the elements of calculus. As the poet Alexander Pope (1688–1744) expressed it, much more colorfully:

Nature and nature's laws lay hid in night:
God said, "Let Newton be," and all was light.

Landscape architects designed elaborate formal gardens, impressive evidence of their desire to control nature. Not to be outdone, composers attempted to be more "scientific" and "rational," compiling checklists of musical techniques and organizing music in more systematic ways.

B

Baroque Composers

Only a few opera composers worked directly for the public, writing music that a paying audience supported. Many composers served as music director for royal courts, a position identified in German as **Kapellmeister** (in Italian as maestro di capella and in French as maître de chapelle). Such courts were numerous, especially in the area known today as Germany, at that time a patchwork of small governmental units. They wrote music "on demand" and then directed it in performance to satisfy their employers' desires for a constant supply of new music.

As in the Renaissance, most of the composers were church musicians, affected as professionals by the continued divisions in the church. Catholics still needed polyphonic Masses and motets for their professional musicians to sing. The Lutheran service stressed the congregational singing of chorales and included the cantata, both of which we shall explore in the Bach chapter. Other Protestant denominations seemed less convinced about the value of music, especially instrumental music, in the service. The Calvinists, for example, reflecting the views of their founder John Calvin, contented themselves with unaccompanied singing of metrical versions of the Psalms. Today's church hymnals contain some of the Calvinist melodies, including one usually sung to the text beginning "Praise God from whom all blessings flow." Calvinists banned instruments, even the organ, despite the many references to music in the Old Testament, as in Psalm 150:

Praise him with the timbrel and dance: praise him with stringed instruments and organs. Praise him upon the loud cymbals . . .

We give individual chapters to Monteverdi, Pachelbel, Vivaldi, Handel, and J. S. Bach, all well known today. Many other composers deserve mention. In this era, distinctly national styles of composing emerged: Italian, German, French, and English. Consequently, composers are often discussed in groups according to their nationalities.

The Italians include Girolamo Frescobaldi (1583–1643), a celebrated organist whose compositions greatly influenced the development of Baroque keyboard music. Giacomo Carissimi (1605–74) is recognized in the main for his oratorios. The fame of Alessandro Scarlatti (1660–1725) rests chiefly on his many operas—and on being the father of Domenico. Born in the same year as Bach and

Handel, Domenico Scarlatti (1685–1757) is best known for his keyboard compositions. Living and working in Spain for most of his life, he wrote over five hundred sonatas, many of which exploit dazzling effects unique to keyboard instruments, such as hand-crossing. (Caution: Scarlatti's sonatas are one-movement works. The implications of "sonata-*form,*" a topic for the Classic period discussion, do not apply to the Baroque use of "sonata.") Arcangelo Corelli (1653–1713), a violin virtuoso and a perfectionist, is regarded as the founder of modern violin technique. His compositions for strings were seen as models; in fact, he was an early "specialist composer," concentrating on instrumental music only.

Germany produced a great number of composers. Linked together were three whose last names all begin with "S" and who were born just a year or two apart: Heinrich Schütz (1585–1673), widely considered the greatest German composer before Bach; Johann Hermann Schein (1586–1630); and Samuel Scheidt (1587–1654). The organist Dietrich Buxtehude (c.1637–1707) greatly influenced Bach. Also linked to Bach's career was the extraordinarily prolific Georg Telemann (1681–1767), who suffered the historical misfortune of being the Leipzig town council's first choice for the job eventually given to Bach.

The court of King Louis XIV dominated French music and, indeed, all French art. Holder of several important posts in Paris, Marc-Antoine Charpentier (c.1645–1704) composed for both church and the stage. His influential contemporary and arch rival Jean-Baptiste Lully (1632–87) developed a type of music, the French overture, which we shall discuss in connection with Handel. François Couperin (1668–1733), the organist for the Royal Chapel, demonstrates French tastes magnificently. His harpsichord suites are unusual in providing programmatic (storytelling) titles. A nearly forgotten French composer, Jean Joseph Mouret (1682–1738), composed a *Rondeau* which has become familiar as the theme music for Public Television's "Masterpiece Theater." Jean-Philippe Rameau (1683–1764), whose operas ruled the French stage for thirty years, created the modern science of harmony.

The Englishman Henry Purcell (1659–95) wrote a short opera, *Dido and Aeneas,* which contains a profoundly moving lament sung by the opera's heroine, the doomed Dido, Queen of Carthage. People at one time thought Purcell wrote *Trumpet Voluntary,* a piece often played as processional music in American weddings. It is actually the work of Jeremiah Clarke (c.1673–1707). A work that Purcell really did compose furnished a melody for the twentieth-century English composer, Benjamin Britten (1913–76), who based his *Young Person's Guide to the Orchestra* on a theme from Purcell's *Abdelazer.*

C

The Characteristics of Sound in the Baroque Era

1. *Pitch* began to be standardized in the Baroque era, at about one half-step *lower* than today's A 440, or about A 415. Many performers today play authentic instruments (or modern reproductions) built to accommodate this pitch standard. Compared to the Renaissance, the overall pitch spectrum expanded. Accordingly, instruments were built to play in wider ranges.

PART FOUR THE BAROQUE

Plate 17   In his colorful *Procession in Piazza San Marco,* the Venetian painter Gentile Bellini (c. 1427–c. 1507) memorably portrayed the ceremonial role of the church of St. Mark's in his city. Begun in 1063, the building, an architectural blend of Byzantine and Italian influences, confirms that Venice served as a meeting ground for East and West.

Plate 18 Gianlorenzo Bernini (1598–1680) created the *Ecstasy of St. Theresa* in life-size marble. It pictures the saint as she is being pierced by an angel's flaming arrow. Golden light streams from heaven. The turbulence of the entire scene is typically Baroque.

Plate 19 The monastery church at Ottobeuren, in the Bavarian area of Germany, attracts countless tourists because of its spectacular, colorful interior. Completed in 1725, it is one of the most magnificent examples of Baroque architecture. (Photograph by G. Russell Wing.)

Plate 20 Two elderly wandering musicians fight over a place to play in the painting *Beggars' Brawl,* by the French artist Georges de La Tour (1593–1652). One wonders if their instruments will survive being used as weapons in their brawling, an unusual subject for a seventeenth-century painter. (Courtesy of the J. Paul Getty Museum, Malibu, CA.)

Plate 21 Jerome Prager, a Los Angeles harpsichord maker, built this elaborately carved and decorated harpsichord, modeling it on one made in France in 1749 and now housed at the Paris Conservatoire. (Courtesy of Jerome Prager, Harpsichord Maker, Los Angeles.)

Plate 22 This organ, located in a university studio, is built with its keyboards directly attached to the mechanism that allows the pipes to sound. Such organs are said to have "mechanical action."

Plate 23 Sometimes the organ pipes that are trumpetlike in sound are horizontally mounted. Their sound then goes out directly. Most unusual are the carved faces that appear to be blowing these pipes in this organ from Valdedios, Asturias, Spain. (Photograph by Sam Adams.)

Plate 24   The American musical comedy has become a universal favorite. Those of Jerome Kern occupy a special place, as this 1985 stamp attests. (Copyright 1984 U.S. Postal Service)

Plate 25 The impact of the Metropolitan Opera spreads far beyond its New York location. Its facade appears on this 1983 stamp, issued to mark the founding of the Metropolitan 100 years ago. (Copyright 1983 U.S. Postal Service)

Baroque tuning systems differed from today's system, which is called **equal temperament.** "Temperament" refers to any system of tuning in which intervals are "tempered." That is, they deviate from the pure, or acoustically correct, intervals derived from the principles of Pythagoras. Equal temperament divides the octave into twelve mathematically *equal* half-steps. The advantage of equal temperament is that all keys sound alike as far as the *do-re-mi* relationships are concerned. The disadvantage is that all intervals except the octave are slightly out of tune, a circumstance of which most listeners are unaware. In the Baroque era those scales using mostly the white keys of keyboard instruments produced intervals that were acoustically *pure* or at least bearable, but those scales needing more than two black keys produced some intervals that were badly out of tune. Composers avoided those scales and, consequently, those tonal centers.

During the Baroque period, musicians made many experiments leading to equal temperament. Some writers mean by the term **unequal temperament** these experimental Baroque tuning systems in general. They made all keys more-or-less in tune. Bach tuned his own harpsichords with various temperaments, which accounts for the title he gave to his *Well Tempered Clavier.*

2. *Dynamic* changes were seldom indicated in musical scores. When they appear, these changes do not occur gradually, as if going uphill or downhill, but in *definite stages,* as if going up or down stairs. Because of this staircase analogy, such changes in volume are called **terraced dynamics.** On keyboard instruments with two or more manuals that can be set up to produce contrasting dynamic levels, that is, almost all organs and many harpsichords, terraced dynamics can result from simply changing manuals. With instrumental ensembles, these changes result from adding or removing instruments in groups. Of course, in all these situations the tone color is altered as well as the dynamic level, and it is possible that Baroque composers were as interested in the contrast of tone colors as in the contrast of dynamics.

To what extent singers and non-keyboard instrumentalists made dynamic changes by singing or playing louder or softer is not known. However, maintaining a rigidly constant volume is unnatural. Consequently, performers of Baroque music feel free to alter dynamics, at least in a subtle way, regardless of the lack of any instructions to do so in the score. Whatever the indications given by the composer, the actual volume produced was less than we are accustomed to today. For one thing, the instruments themselves could not be played as loudly as today's. The listener who has heard Baroque music only through recordings, where the dynamic level can vary with a simple twist of a dial, has no real idea of the composer's original conception of volume.

3. *Tone color* shows several important new aspects. During the late Renaissance, the instruments of the string family, the **violin, viola, cello,** and **bass,** evolved into their present forms, eventually displacing the Renaissance viols. (Occasionally you see "'cello," an abbreviated form of the full name of the instrument: "violoncello." Note the spelling—it is *not* vio*lin*cello.) The bass is often called a "string bass" or a "double bass." Baroque string instruments differed from today's

A German composer and theorist, Michael Praetorius (1571–1621) wrote extensively on instruments and performance practice. This title page is from one of his books.

versions in several ways. For example, the strings were made of gut instead of metal and the bows were shorter. Not only were the string instruments softer overall, but the tone was not as smooth and rich as we expect today. In the early Baroque period, Italian violin makers such as Antonio Stradivari (1644–1737) built the wondrous string instruments that remain unsurpassed, treasured by those performers fortunate enough to play them. What makes them so special—varnish? proportions? wood? Scientific research to answer these questions is still inconclusive.

The woodwind instruments, although superficially resembling their present-day counterparts, were of a simpler construction. They had fewer keys and their pitch ranges were smaller. The older recorder coexisted with the newer **flute,** which was unique in being held parallel to the floor. For that reason, it was called a transverse flute, a term still found occasionally. Unlike today's metal flute, the Baroque instrument was made of wood. Its tone was breathier, less penetrating. **Oboes** came in several varieties, and **bassoons** were important in ensembles. Both oboe and bassoon are **double-reed** instruments: two thin pieces of cane bound together are compressed between the lips of the player. The sound of both oboe and bassoon is intense and nasal, rich in harmonics.

Brass instruments, the Baroque **trumpet** and the **French horn,** were "natural" instruments, lacking valves or pistons. The player's lips alone create different pitches. Trumpet players enjoyed high status, because the trumpet had been associated with the nobility and with ceremonial functions since the fourteenth century. The extraordinary difficulties of trumpet music resulted from its placement in the very high ranges. Trombones, softer than today's models, reinforced vocal lines.

The only percussion instrument that appeared consistently was the **timpani,** the plural of "timpanum," or "kettledrum." These drums always occur in pairs, and sometimes in multiple pairs. In Baroque music, the timpani usually play when the trumpets do, helping to reinforce the aura of royal ceremony.

Music was written for specific instruments and various instruments were often combined, though the standardized orchestra does not appear until the Classic era. Still, composers apparently did not restrict a given work to a single kind of sound. As we shall see, Baroque composers often recast music—their own or other people's—for a different performing medium. Such a piece is known as a **transcription.**

Like the strings, the keyboard instruments reached an unsurpassed level of excellence. Several of today's instrument makers copy them, using the surviving originals as models. Much Baroque music simply calls for a **clavier** (the German term for keyboard or keyboard instrument, sometimes spelled as "klavier"), without specifying which instrument. The piano, a novelty in the Baroque, was not commonly found until the Classic era. (The oldest surviving piano is dated 1720.) Strictly speaking, therefore, playing Baroque music on the piano is historically incorrect, although pianists do not hesitate to do so.

The mechanism of the **harpsichord** *plucks* strings, unlike the hammers of a piano, which *hit* strings. The sound, a distinctive, rather brittle "twang" as the strings are plucked, dies away quickly. The plucking force does not change with finger pressure; consequently, the fingers do not control the volume level on the harpsichord as they do on the piano. Some instruments have two keyboards, each controlling one or two sets of strings. The sets contrast slightly in tone color and in some models produce tones in different octaves. The two keyboards make possible the "terraced dynamics" mentioned earlier. A player can "couple" or link the manuals together, so that both keyboards play at once, though the fingers press only the lower keyboard. This creates a fascinating visual effect—it's magic! Despite its soft volume, a harpsichord can penetrate louder sounds when it is played in ensembles, one of its most important functions. Incidentally, harpsichords have become very popular recently: you can purchase a kit and make one yourself at a relatively modest cost.

A number of pipes made of wood or metal attached to a source of air under pressure make up an **organ,** the most complex of all instruments. (There are, of course, modern electronic substitutes for the pipe organ, which are related to it in approximately the same way that plastic is related to wood, or polyester to silk.) Today, electric blowers provide the air pressure: in earlier times boys or men pumped bellows. The air in the pipes vibrates when activated as the player depresses keys. Magnetic switches control this activation in most modern instruments, but before the use of electricity was introduced, a direct mechanical connection linked keys and pipes. Organs employing such mechanical action are known as **tracker organs.** Similar to the harpsichord's revival, the tracker organ has undergone a rebirth in this century. Players believe that this mechanism allows for a more sensitive control of the instrument.

A set of pipes, or a **rank,** in an organ consists of one pipe for each key on the keyboard. The pipes in each rank vary in size according to pitch and share a distinctive tone color, which in some ranks is reminiscent of various wind instruments. They also share a specific shape: square, conical, or cylindrical. The mechanism that controls a rank of pipes has a lever or a knob called a **stop,** which the organist adjusts ("draws" in organ parlance) to have the rank available. When someone is said to be "pulling out all the stops," that person is throwing all available resources into a task. (Actually, this saying is somewhat faulty: organists almost never play all the stops of an organ simultaneously.)

Organs differ greatly in size: five or six ranks may suffice for a practice organ; some Baroque organs contained as many as sixty ranks of pipes. The Crystal Cathedral, located in southern California, claims to house the world's largest organ, with 280 ranks. The ranks of an organ are arranged in groups controlled by two, three, and even four keyboards (not quite as large as piano keyboards, with fifty-six to sixty-one keys) called **manuals.** There is also a **pedal** keyboard for the feet, with a range of thirty to thirty-two keys. The pedal's chief responsibility is the low bass range, going down nearly to the bottom of the pitch spectrum, but it can also control higher pitches and in much Baroque music plays an independent line. As is the case with the harpsichord, finger pressure on the keys does *not* affect volume; that is determined by the number of ranks sounding at any given moment. Always the *organist decides* which of the ranks will play at a particular time, guided somewhat by tradition, and by the composers' wishes, when known. Consequently, the same piece on the same organ can sound remarkably different, depending upon who plays it.

The **clavichord** is a small keyboard instrument in which delicate little metal tangents hit strings. The dynamic level is very soft indeed, making it better for home practice than concert giving. Still, Baroque musicians valued its ability to respond even slightly to finger pressure. The experiments that led to the modern piano capitalized upon this feature.

D

The Elements of Music in the Baroque Era

1. Baroque *rhythm* is distinctive, marked by a steady, motoristic beat and the reiteration of the same basic rhythmic patterns throughout a piece. For the first time in history, bar lines appeared in the musical scores, showing that meter was taken for granted. Composers were no more specific about indicating how tones should be connected than they were about indicating dynamics. Research into Baroque sources, however, has convinced performers who strive for authenticity that a somewhat detached manner of playing was the norm. Today's standard, a completely smooth connection, **legato,** was employed only in special circumstances or when specifically called for by the composer.

2. Baroque *melodies* are often quite long and complicated. Frequent skips and big ranges make them better suited to instruments than to voices, although the composers expected singers to demonstrate the same agility they required of instrumentalists. Sequences abound. Melodies contain **ornaments,** which are little embellishments to the line. Some ornaments are written into the music, either by means of small notes that do not count rhythmically or by special signs that performers learn to interpret. Others the performers were expected to improvise. Of the many different types of ornaments, we will mention just one, the **trill.** It results when a given note alternates rapidly with the note immediately above it. Trills often occur near the ends of musical sections, and consequently they can function as a signal to the listener. Baroque vocal melodies frequently display exuberant melismas, a text-setting effect we first noted in Gregorian chant. In it, one syllable is stretched out over many notes.

3. Baroque *harmony* perpetuated the triads of the Renaissance. Supplementing a triad with a fourth tone creates the richer sound of a **seventh chord.** For example, the notes G-B-D create a triad; adding an F forms a seventh chord, which is a chord demanding a resolution.

The most important harmonic concept of the Baroque period involved tonality. As described earlier, tonality, in the general sense that one central pitch dominates the others, is a very old feature of music, found worldwide. A more specific meaning of the term limits it to the developments that took place in the 1600s, when a growing interest in harmony and chords supplanted earlier habits of thinking melodically. In this more specific sense, tonality is confined to two scales, major and minor, contrasted to **modality,** which is music based on the old church modes. To avoid confusion, we shall refer to **major/minor tonality.**

With major/minor tonality operating, each chord and each tone have a specific function in relation to the all-important tonic chord and tonic note, *do.* For example, the dominant chord, especially when enlarged with a seventh as just described, has essentially only one function, to precede the tonic. (This function may be evaded temporarily, but must eventually be fulfilled.) As a result of major/minor tonality, music now seems to "go" somewhere and, even more important, it seems to arrive.

This development is so important for music that the entire period from about 1600 to about 1900 is often said to be based on the **tonal system,** rather than the modal system. The tonal system allows composers to change tonal centers, or keys, in the course of a piece, a process called **modulation.** Modulation enabled a composer to repeat musical ideas, each time in a different key. This capability led to longer compositions, as it offered a new way of producing variety while ensuring unity. In fact, almost every piece we study from now on contains modulations. (A little eavesdropping as vocal students practice their warm-up exercises will allow you to hear constant modulation: they repeatedly sing a short pattern, a half-step higher each time.)

For an example of modulation in miniature, we can recall the familiar song, "Deck the Halls," analyzed in Chapter 8. Look closely at the third phrase of this song. We saw that it differs melodically from the other three, but it also modulates to the key of the dominant, the fifth tone of the scale. This process begins with the first "fa-la-la" (where there is a b-natural). Modulation is completed with the concluding "fa-la-la," which now sounds like a *mi-re-do,* using as the new *do* the tone that originally was *sol.* No sooner is the modulation accomplished than the harmony flip-flops back to the original key, and the fourth phrase, like the first two, clearly begins on that original *sol* which an instant earlier sounded like a new *do.*

4. *Texture* in the Baroque era showed more variety than in the Renaissance. While polyphony continued to attract composers, and is indeed dominant in the late Baroque, homophony, a single melody clearly set against its accompaniment, was favored in the early years. A composer like Handel enjoyed the variety allowed by mixing textures within the confines of one piece.

5. New *forms* developed. The ternary principle (ABA) is shown in many a vocal composition, while binary form (AABB) provided the structure for much instrumental music. Composers wrote fugues, a word that designates a method of operation rather than a fixed form. We will also meet continuous variations.

1. Fundamental to Baroque performance is the idea of **improvisation**—creating music as it is being performed. At a minimum, soloists, both vocal and instrumental, were expected to embellish their own melodic lines, especially when a section of music was repeated. Keyboard players were able to improvise entire compositions, so the task of improvising accompaniments (see item 2) must have seemed relatively easy. Though the art of improvisation died out in the nineteenth century as composers demanded greater control over their products, currently it is being revived, along with other Baroque performing practices.

2. Most Baroque music requires a special kind of accompaniment called **basso continuo** ("continuous bass"). This term refers to a shorthand method of indicating an accompaniment by means of a bass line supplemented with some numbers and symbols that specify what chords are wanted. While based upon the composer's harmony, the actual pitches produced by a keyboard player are supposed to be improvised on the spot. One performer might exhibit great creativity, while another's rendition or realization of the part might be simple and unimaginative.

Reinforcement of the bass line comes from one or more low-range instruments, such as the cello, bass, or bassoon. Basso continuo confirms that Baroque music is solidly anchored to its bass line. Not too many years ago, performing groups routinely omitted the basso continuo on grounds that keyboard players no longer knew how to interpret the symbols. Today, groups again consider it essential, although variables in performing situations will determine how audible it actually is to a listener.

3. A third fundamental idea of the Baroque is given a rather odd-sounding label: the **doctrine of the affections,** a translation of the German *Affektenlehre.* By this word, German theorists meant that music was expected to express particular *affects,* or emotions. Certain musical figures and devices were associated with certain moods, feelings, or emotions. A celebrated theorist, Johann Mattheson (1681–1764), left a systematic treatment of this doctrine that has been widely quoted:

> Since joy is an *expansion* of our vital spirits, it follows sensibly and naturally that this affect is best expressed by large and expanded intervals. Sadness, on the other hand, is a *contraction* of those same subtle parts of our bodies. It is, therefore, easy to see that the narrowest intervals are the most suitable.

The most obvious application of the doctrine of the affections occurs in Baroque vocal music. In a general way, it applies to most Baroque music. This theory reminds us of Renaissance word painting, but there is an important difference. Word painting applied to *single* words, or to brief sections of a piece. In Baroque music, an *entire* piece or movement embodied a single affect, maintained throughout. This theory helps account for the single-minded quality of Baroque pieces, the sense that the material has been thoroughly exploited by the time the work concludes.

4. Our fourth fundamental idea is the **concertato** principle. Both "concertato" and the closely linked term "concerto" refer to contrasts and combinations of various colors and groupings, both instrumental and vocal, within a Baroque composition. One voice or instrument may contrast with another, one group with another, or a group with a solo. This principle explains a readily audible difference from the Renaissance. In texture and sound, a Victoria motet is relatively homogeneous; a Vivaldi concerto movement is not.

The word "concertato" has long proved troublesome. Writers once stressed opposition, contention, even combat between the assorted forces. More recent scholars prefer to derive the adjective "concertato" from the Italian verb "concertare," meaning to reach agreement. As one advocate puts it, "In a musical concerto diverse and sometimes contrasting forces are brought into a harmonious ensemble." In another place, he concludes that "the desired agreement is always a triumph over some natural opposition." Equally applicable to all of the Baroque composers we study, the concertato idea invites the listener not only to take sensuous delight in the rich, diverse instrumental and vocal sounds of each given moment, but also to rejoice in their ultimate reconciliation.

OPERA 26

PREVIEW Because we will encounter opera in all suceeding periods, in this chapter we discuss some general features of opera: its history in brief, beginning with its origins in the Baroque; its essential components; and some of its specific elements: recitative, aria, ensemble, and chorus.

A *drama presented in music* is an **opera.** This Italian term, actually the plural of the word *opus,* simply means "work." The earliest operas were called *opera drammatica in musica,* or "dramatic works set to music." Music adds an important dimension to the drama, as it sometimes emphasizes the verbal and visual messages—and sometimes contradicts them. Opera lovers continually debate the relative importance of its elements: drama, music, and spectacle. They are equally important—a case of the whole being greater than the sum of its parts.

Though we expect characters to sing their roles, in many operas characters speak some dialogue, which is a traditional feature of the later, related forms of operetta and musical comedy. No precise distinction separates these terms, but "operetta," a term meaning "little opera," implies a more European outlook. Jacques Offenbach (1819–80) is considered the father of the modern operetta. The Englishmen Gilbert and Sullivan created a characteristically English form of operetta, with Sir Arthur Sullivan (1842–1900) writing music that often wittily parodies opera's more pretentious forms. By the 1920s, the term "musical comedy" came to be associated with the delightful works of twentieth-century Americans such as Jerome Kern (1885–1945), whose *Show Boat,* 1927, has remained a perennial favorite. Some other terms that describe opera, such as "opera seria," "opera buffa," and "grand opera," refer to distinctions we lack space to cover here.

A

Opera History in Brief

A long history of music as an adjunct to spoken drama led to opera as we know it. The Greek plays incorporated sung choruses. In medieval churches, liturgical dramas employed music to enhance the appeal of the religious stories. The

These are pages from the original printed score for *Euridice,* the oldest surviving opera.

LE MVSICHE
DI IACOPO PERI
NOBIL FIORENTINO
Sopra L'Euridice

DEL SIG· OTTAVIO RINVCCINI
Rappresentate Nello Sponsalizio
della Cristianissima

MARIA MEDICI
REGINA DI FRANCIA
E DI NAVARRA

IN FIORENZA
APPRESSO GIORGIO MARESCOTTI·
M D C·

(a)

(b)

Florentine Camerata, a group of Italian noblemen who met during the late Renaissance years, studied Greek tragedy and decided that all of its text was sung. In an attempt to imitate those Greek dramas, they invented opera. The earliest preserved opera, *Euridice,* dates from 1600. Early operas consist mainly of **recitatives** [pronounced reh-se-ta-TEEVS], which are solo vocal lines in a free, speech-like rhythm. Accompanied by basso continuo, recitatives are not tuneful. Instead, the composers strove to heighten the expressivity of the words, especially the individual emotions for each character. These early operas enjoyed success. Opera developed rapidly, with a public opera house appearing as early as 1637 in Venice.

Soon opera was enriched with **arias,** which are more songlike than recitatives and are accompanied more elaborately. The addition of choruses widened the sound spectrum. Fantastic, amazingly elaborate staging treated the audiences to a dazzling spectacle as well. By the end of the century, opera was a leading musical institution in Italy. Patterns of opera developed that had far-reaching influences in other countries, particularly France. As we shall see, Handel spent many years producing Italian-style operas in England. For four centuries, opera has remained a vital force. Baroque opera is enjoying a healthy revival today. The operas of Mozart, Verdi, and Wagner rank among the most impressive achievements of Western culture. Adaptable to changes of style and taste, opera continues to be written in this century.

Australia takes great pride in the eye-catching architecture of the Sydney Opera House.

Opera has always been *costly.* Ticket sales alone cannot underwrite the production expenses, so support for opera must come from other sources. Civic or national pride may result in direct taxpayer support for opera. In most areas of the United States, to the contrary, opera depends upon individual and corporate contributions, with some help from foundations. Consequently, the unfortunate notion has arisen that an opera audience consists of unmusical rich people, for whom attendance is a status symbol. (In countries such as Italy, where state support makes low ticket prices possible, people go to the opera much as Americans go to sporting events.) There is no need for prejudice to keep a newcomer away from opera. Opera productions are increasingly available for everyone, with local and regional opera companies dotting the country. Opera America, a Washington, D.C. organization, lists more than one hundred opera companies. Public television stations frequently broadcast opera, and videocassettes of many operas can be bought or rented at modest cost.

Opera has many *conventions,* just as any art form does. Stage time is not "real time." Of course, it is not natural for people to sing as they lie dying, or, for that matter, to sing instead of speak, but if opera's conventions are accepted, they fade into the background while the irresistible beauties of opera engage the listener.

B

1.   Opera is built on *dramatic subject matter,* which is often a tragedy with an unhappy ending. Greek mythology provided the subjects for the earliest operas. The drama may have considerable merit on its own, because many operas are adaptations of already-famous plays, such as those by Shakespeare, Beaumarchais,

The Essential
Components of Opera

THE GIRLS

By Franklin Folger

"I can't say I'm too much for opera but I simply love getting dressed for it."

and Victor Hugo. Admittedly, not all operas rest on so strong a foundation—it is no coincidence that daytime television dramas are known as "soap operas." Usually, a composer collaborates with a writer who prepares the **libretto** (Italian for "little book," the text for the opera). A successful libretto accommodates the various vocal components, to be mentioned later, and maintains the dramatic values of the story. Prior to the twentieth century, librettos were cast in verse form. Rarely do composers also write their libretti (Italian plural of libretto), but some have done so, most notably two composers who otherwise have little in common: Richard Wagner, whose work we study in Part Six, and the American Gian Carlo Menotti (born 1911), best known for his Christmas-season television opera *Amahl and the Night Visitors*.

Language, one of the joys of opera, can cause problems for the neophyte. The libretto is usually written in the language spoken by the writer and composer. Their language, in turn, does not necessarily relate to the locality pictured on stage. This fact can confuse the newcomer who wonders why Carmen, so obviously Spanish, is singing French. And why she is singing French when the audience speaks English is a related issue.

In many European countries, the libretto is customarily translated into the local language, but most major United States opera companies refuse to do this. It is true that translations often do violence to the original text—a possibility summed up in an Italian pun: "Il traduttore è un traditore," which means "The translator is a traitor." There are practical reasons for not singing translations. Many opera singers already know their roles in the original language and are understandably reluctant to relearn them in another. English is a difficult language in which to sing anything at all. Good, singable (that is, with an appropriate number of syllables and with accents similar to the original), idiomatic translations of opera libretti are enormously difficult to produce, but enough have been written to prove that it is possible.

Translations that appear in printed libretti (and in this book) to be read while listening to a recording are another matter entirely. These are usually literal, concentrating on the meanings of words. This is done because in most situations the composer had a particular reason for putting each word or syllable in a specific place. To show this, it is necessary to follow the original word order as much as possible, even when English would place the words differently. Such translations do not pretend to be singable, let alone poetic or literary.

The problem of text comprehension is addressed in many opera houses by means of "supertitles." These are translations projected on a screen above the stage while the performance is in progress. Even this device meets with objections—usually from those experienced opera-goers who need no such help—because the translations can be distracting. Sometimes, seeing a bit of Italian dialogue turned into prosaic English like "Thank you" seems oddly humorous to the audience. Filmed and televised operas almost always project a translation on the screen, one of the many reasons for recommending them to the student. Some operas are written in English, which for English speakers should result in better understanding of the drama.

2. Though operas are occasionally presented in concert form, generally they are *staged* and the staging director often gets as much press attention as the conductor. Directors may see fit to update the action, devise new motivations for the singers, and in effect create a new work. One version of *Carmen,* for example, has been transplanted to 1936, with the Spanish Civil War providing occupations for the characters. Another opera we study, *Rigoletto,* has been shifted, in one production, to New York with a Mafia chief as the Duke. All the complications of any dramatic production are involved—scenery, costumes, lighting—all demanding special (and expensive) workers and equipment. Some stages make startling visual effects possible: characters descend from the ceiling, or disappear through a trap door in the stage floor. Of course, filmed versions of opera give designers free rein for their ideas, unhampered by the restrictions of a stage.

3. An opera should be accompanied by an *orchestra,* which is usually out of sight in an orchestra pit. Opera workshops might have to make do with the accompaniment of one or two pianos. The entire production is under the musical direction of the orchestra's *conductor,* although rehearsal pianists, vocal coaches, and chorus masters have all participated in the musical preparation. The orchestra accompanies the singers, of course: it also has moments when it plays alone. Traditionally, an **overture** is played before the curtain rises. Certain traditions accompany the choice of formal structure for an overture. Ending it with a brilliant flourish is one of those traditions, although in many cases the overture does not come to a full stop and Act I begins without pause. In such cases, the label of "Prelude" is often given. Forecasting the mood of the particular opera is another of the traditions. One or more prominent themes from the opera may appear in the overture. Indeed, some overtures are best regarded as a preview of tunes, heard in a kind of medley. Detached from their context, many opera overtures or preludes are played in orchestral concerts.

Other moments for orchestra alone may occur, especially between acts or when interludes are needed to cover set changes. Suitably arranged and assembled into **suites,** these orchestral selections can make attractive concert music, as is the case with the *Carmen Suites.* Since the arrangements might be done by someone other than the composer, it is possible for the music to be changed from its original form.

4. *Singers* represent a variety of ranges and vocal types. Six main types are basic: soprano, mezzo-soprano, alto, tenor, baritone, and bass. The qualifying term "lyric" is given to a "light" voice, while "dramatic" denotes a "heavy" voice. Specialized categories exist also, such as the **coloratura soprano** (a soprano who can sing very high virtuoso passages). The demands made on all the voices are extraordinary, especially the need to project over an orchestra in a large auditorium.

Since the nineteenth century, some traditions have become associated with the casting of opera roles. For example, the heroine is apt to be a soprano; her mother, or friend—or enemy— will be an alto or mezzo-soprano. Both vocally and dramatically, Carmen, a mezzo, is an exception as a heroine. Tenors are usually heroes who get the girl; baritones or basses are fathers, kings, wise men—or villains.

In spite of the importance of the drama in opera, the singers in most companies are chosen first for their vocal ability and second for their acting skills or physical resemblance to the character they portray. A beautiful voice can create powerful illusions—the mature tenor *is* the ardent young lover. Besides, by the time an opera singer has matured vocally, he or she is not so young anymore.

Another seemingly odd tradition is the **trousers** or **breeches role,** which is a male role portrayed by a female singer. Most of these women-in-pants are taking the part of a teenager. Improbable as it may seem, the boy in the drama may be young enough that his voice has not changed—but he is old enough to be interested in girls! Some of these roles result from changes in social mores. Baroque opera had many parts for **castrati**—male singers who had been castrated as children in order to preserve the high range of a boy's voice. When they matured, their voices combined adult male strength and female range with an unusual quality that the audiences of the time seemed to relish.

This barbaric custom eventually died out, leaving today's director to solve the problem: who sings this beautiful music? One solution is to employ females in trousers or perhaps a countertenor. If the director deems it acceptable, moving the melody down an octave allows a tenor or baritone to sing it in his normal range.

5. Some operas also contain a *ballet* or at least some dancing. This element varies considerably by nationality. For example, the French long thought that ballet was essential to an opera and saw to it that an opera lacking one would fail.

C

Solo recitatives and arias make up the bulk of opera. These two components appear in Baroque cantatas and oratorios as well. Although no one goes home whistling them, recitatives carry the chief dramatic action in opera. In recitatives, a rapid, speechlike quality is maintained, the musical inflections resemble those of language, and words are not repeated any more than they are in normal conversation. Basso continuo provided a sparse accompaniment for recitatives in Baroque opera. Such a recitative is said to be **secco** or "dry." Though written with rhythmic values, a recitative is usually performed with metrical freedom.

The term "accompanied recitative" refers to one with more elaborate orchestral accompaniment, in a sense blurring the distinction between recitative and aria. That distinction, generally clear enough in the Baroque and Classic eras, becomes less clear in the Romantic period when maintaining continuity assumed greater importance.

The "songs" in operas occur in the arias, which are metrical and fully accompanied. In the late Baroque, **da capo arias** (ABA) were the norm. After a contrasting B section, the composers simply called for a return to the beginning, the meaning of "da capo." Singers were expected to improvise embellishments to the music of the A section when they repeated it. Also typical was the orchestral introduction to the aria, the so-called "motto" beginning, which forecast the theme to be sung. These two traditions did not die completely with the Baroque, but lingered on even as new traditions arose.

Arias customarily contain much word repetition. Viewed dramatically, characters tend to *reflect* upon what has just happened in the preceding recitative.

Recitative, Aria, Ensemble, Chorus

Some arias can be compared to soliloquies in drama, in which a character expresses his or her innermost thoughts. Although the audience can hear these thoughts, they are inaudible to the other characters on stage. Other arias are like extended monologues.

The characters in opera often sing together, in duets, trios, quartets—and there is at least one famous sextet (from Donizetti's *Lucia di Lammermoor*). Such numbers are known as **ensembles.** If two or more characters in a play spoke their lines simultaneously the audience would be confused; in opera it is possible to understand the general messages of each singer in an ensemble, even though the individual words get lost. Conflicting emotions make up the stuff of the larger ensembles, while duets allow a pair of singers to unite their voices into one thought. An important operatic tradition since Mozart's time is that the acts end with soloists and chorus, if there is one, singing together in an **ensemble finale,** a tour de force of the composer's art.

A **chorus** appears in many, but by no means all, operas. It is made up of unidentified people: a group of soldiers, courtiers, fellow workers—whatever the drama calls for. The actual number of singers in the chorus may be dictated by the size of the stage and the size of the budget. The chorus may participate in the action or make some comments on it. Their costumes provide local color, and they, as a group, form a contrast to the solitary lead characters. In some operas, the chorus is as important as any principal singer. For example, in *Boris Godunov* the chorus represents the very soul of the Russian people.

Plate 26   Opera is far more understandable when a translation of its libretto is projected on a screen for the audience, as in this supertitle from a production of Wagner's *Tristan und Isolde*. (Courtesy of Los Angeles Music Center Opera.)

Plate 27 Pieter Bruegel the Elder (c. 1525–69), Dutch painter, depicted the seasons in a series of paintings. One of them, *The Return of the Hunters,* pictures winter in the same realistic way that Vivaldi's music (*Four Seasons*) does.

Plate 28 This monument to Bach stands in the square of Eisenach, the small German town where he was born. (Photograph by G. Russell Wing.)

Plate 29 A gold-plated record with "Sounds of the Earth" was placed on the Voyager spacecraft prior to its exploration of outer space in 1977. One of the "sounds" was, of course, music by J. S. Bach. (Courtesy of NASA.)

Plate 30 This 1973 poster by David Lance Goines offers stylized forms symbolic of the four New Testament Apostles. Bach's name is added as an allusion to his status as the "fifth Apostle" because of his magnificent religious music.

Plate 31   The French painter Jacques Louis David (1748–1825) recalled the days of
ancient Rome in the *Oath of the Horatii*, 1784. The brothers of the Horatius family
swear to win in the coming battle, or die, oblivious to their weeping sisters. Typical of the
Classic ideals is the balance shown by the arches and placement of figures.

Plate 32 In *The Fountain of Love,* 1748, the prolific and successful François Boucher (1703–70) painted a pastoral scene of the French aristocracy. The superficial fantasies he turned out were typical of Rococo tastes. Musical instruments find their way into the picture as well. (Courtesy of the J. Paul Getty Museum, Malibu, CA.)

Plate 33   This monument to Mozart stands in a park in Vienna. (Photograph by G. Russell Wing.)

Plate 34   In this 1830 painting, *Liberty Leading the People,* the French artist Eugène Delacroix (1798–1863) gives us an allegory of Revolution, full of Romantic excitement. Liberty carries the tricolor banner of the French republic, advancing over dead bodies as she leads the people in this turbulent scene.

CLAUDIO MONTEVERDI 27

PREVIEW Centered in Italy, Monteverdi's career spanned two eras. Although he wrote many beautiful madrigals in a late Renaissance style, we prefer to consider him in our Baroque coverage because his name is associated with the earliest operas still sung today. We will study one of them—the last opera he composed.

FIORI POETICI
Raccolti nel Funerale
DEL MOLTO ILLVSTRE;
E Molto Reuerendo
SIGNOR CLAVDIO
Monte verde
Maeftro di Cappella della Du-
cale di S. Marco .
Confecrati
DA D. GIO: BATTISTA
Marinoni, detto Gioue :
Maeftro di Cappella del Do-
mo di Padoua
ALL' ILLVSTRSSIMI
& Eccellentiffimi
SIG. PROCVRATORI
Di Chiefa di S. Marco .

In VENETIA, Preffo Francefco Miloco.
Con Lic. de Sup. MDCXLIV.

Monteverdi is surrounded by instruments on the title page of a volume of his music published just after his death.

Claudio Monteverdi's life (1567–1643) spanned the close of the Renaissance and the early years of the Baroque. Born in the Italian city of Cremona, famous for its violin makers, he was trained there in the polyphonic techniques of the sixteenth century. As a child he wrote motets, and he soon became a leading madrigal composer. After service as a court musician for the Duke of Mantua, in 1613 he became the music director at St. Mark's in Venice, where the Renaissance composer Giovanni Gabrieli had worked.

In serving the nobility, Monteverdi came in contact with a new kind of music, opera. He then created the first Baroque operas that have more than historical interest for listeners today. Opera demanded a different composing manner, or as he called it, a "second practice." He contrasted the differences between the old and the new styles in a famous explanation. The first, or old, practice was polyphonic, in which the music "was the mistress of the words." But in the second, new, practice, composers were "chiefly concerned with the perfection of the setting, in which the words are mistress of the harmony." His first operas unfold primarily in an extended recitative style, with simple basso continuo accompaniment, thus allowing the words to dominate over the music. Probably his best-known work is *Orfeo* (1607), based on the Greek legend of Orpheus, the singer whose magical powers charmed the wild beasts. In this story, Orfeo descends to the Underworld, hoping to retrieve from death his beloved Euridice. When he first learns of her death, he sings a powerfully expressive recitative, *Tu se' morta, mia vita* (You are dead, my darling), that is a standard component of anthologies.

Monteverdi: *The Coronation of Poppea*

Monteverdi's last work, written in 1642 when he was seventy-five, is *The Coronation of Poppea* (L'incoronazione di Poppea), now considered the finest opera of its century. Unfortunately, the surviving manuscripts for this work are incomplete, consisting of bass lines, vocal lines, and some sketchy notations for the instrumental interludes. It is almost certain that portions of this opera were contributed by other composers. Performances today, therefore, are essentially reconstructions and consequently can differ greatly. The discussion here is based upon Raymond Leppard's televised production of the opera at Glyndebourne, England, and upon his edition of the score (1977), which differs in some respects from scores edited by G. F. Malipiero (1913) and Alan Curtis (1989).

Because the basso continuo bears so much of the burden in this opera, Monteverdi took for granted a variety of chord-playing instruments to avoid monotony. Thus you might hear a harpsichord, harp, lute, guitar, or a small organ in various portions of the opera, each adding harmony to the bass line. Strings make up the accompanying orchestra throughout, although trumpets may sound a festive note in the Coronation scene.

The librettist for this opera, G. Francesco Busenello, provided Monteverdi with a story drawn from Roman history. Two thoroughly amoral characters defeat

The triumphant conclusion of *The Coronation of Poppea* is portrayed in this photograph of a production by the Santa Fe Opera company. (Photograph by Hans Fahrmeyer.)

their adversaries in the opera, with the help of the gods. Not only do these gods hover above the mortal characters throughout much of the action, but the god of Love actually descends to save Poppea from a would-be murderer. ("*Deus ex machina*" is the Latin phrase that describes this sort of godly intervention in human affairs, a frequent feature in ancient Greek and Roman plays.) Yet Monteverdi's music, while it cannot redeem these characters, makes them understandable in human terms.

In the Prologue to the opera, the gods Fortune, Virtue, and Love argue, trying to show which of them is most powerful in managing human affairs. Love, claiming that he is the strongest, tells the story of Poppea and Nero as proof. Nero, the notorious Roman emperor in A.D. 54–68 (he did far worse things than his legendary fiddling while Rome burned), has fallen in love with the beautiful courtesan Poppea, who is shamelessly eager to become empress. Obstacles to their union are Poppea's husband (Nero's good friend), Nero's wife (a noble lady), and Nero's trusted advisor and former tutor, Seneca, who strongly argues that the match is against the best interests of the state. After Nero exiles their respective mates and orders Seneca to commit suicide, Poppea gets her wish. The opera ends with her coronation.

Poppea is sung by a soprano, the voice expected for the heroine. In Monteverdi's time the part of Nero would have gone to a castrato. Today's choices are to employ a tenor or to have a soprano sing the role dressed as a male. Either way, the Baroque idea of the high voice as heroic is preserved.

CD1

Coronation Scene
(2:45) ⑮

(0:00)

1 *r201 The scene begins with a minute-long, martial-sounding instrumental Sinfonia that features many repetitions of a four-note motive, all on the same pitch. During this Sinfonia, a male chorus assembles, representing the Consuls and Tribunes of the Roman government. **Sinfonia** (note the resemblance to "symphony") was the name for an instrumental piece that served as an introduction to what comes next.

[37]

(0:50)

2 r202 Tenors and basses solemnly sing these words, at first in unison. After "Augusta," they sing in two independent parts that echo each other polyphonically:

[38]

A te, a te sovrana augusta,	To you, august sovereign,
con il consenso universal di Roma	with the universal consent of Rome,
indiadediam la chioma;	we crown you.
a te l'Asia, a te l'Africa s'attera,	Asia and Africa bow before you,
a te l'Europa, e'l mar che cinge e serra quest'Imperio felice	Europe and the ocean that surrounds this happy empire
hora consacra, e dona questa del mondo imperial corona	and the Gods grant you this imperial crown.

On the word "imperial," the men's voices demonstrate a "trillo," a kind of Baroque ornament which consists of many repetitions of the same pitch.

(The following Sinfonia is omitted in our recorded performance.)

3 r206 Another instrumental Sinfonia, in a fast duple meter over a quickly moving bass line, accompanies the exit of the chorus.

r indicates that rehearsal numbers are used here because measures are not numbered in the Leppard score.

CD1

(0:00)
1   r208   A brief orchestral introduction to the duet of Nero and Poppea
                unfolds in a flowing triple meter. The duet is a variation form, one in
    [39]   which new features are added to a constantly repeated bass line or
                repeated chord progression. Since the variations proceed without
                interruption, this form is known as **continuous variations.** Pieces
                based on this principle bear various titles, often employed
                inconsistently, one being **ground bass.** The foundation for the ground
                bass is a simple line that descends right down the scale: *dô-ti-la-sol,*
                a pattern that repeats several times. Soaring above the strict bass
                line are the sensuously intertwining voices of the lovers as they
                sometimes echo each other and sometimes blend in polyphonic lines
                that employ the "love" intervals—thirds and sixths.

Duet of Poppea and Nero
(3:08) ⑯

Pur ti miro, pur ti godo,	I look at you, I love you,
pur ti stringo, più non peno,	I embrace you, I suffer no longer,
mia vita, o mio tesoro.	O my life, O my treasure.

(1:09)
2   Abandoning the ground bass, Monteverdi moves to a free musical
    [40]   structure. The performance tempo might accelerate here, with this
                text:

Io son tua, speme mia,	I am yours, all my hope,
dillo, dì, tu sei pur, speme mia,	all I wish, my delight, all my hope,
l'idol mio, dillo dì, sì, mio ben,	my wish, my delight, yes, my love,
mia vita, sì, sì, sì, sì.	my life, yes, yes, yes, yes.

(1:57)
3   r211   A slower tempo might mark the return of the words and music of
    [41]   item 1, shorter this time, with fewer repetitions of the ground bass,
                before the voices blend in a melting unison conclusion.

28 JOHANN PACHELBEL

PREVIEW Recent attention to one of his instrumental works has introduced the name of the German-born organist Pachelbel to the general public. We study that piece as a demonstration of two Baroque compositional principles.

The organist Johann Pachelbel [pronounced PAHK-ul-BEL] was born in Nuremberg, Germany, in 1653 and died there in 1706. A leading composer of Protestant church music, he was known especially for his organ compositions. Highly respected in his day, he was never completely forgotten. In the past few years the general public has taken a renewed interest in his work, due to the popularity of his *Canon in D*. (Its German spelling, "Kanon," often appears.)

Instrumental music gained new stature in the Baroque era, challenging and ultimately rivaling vocal music for attention. Lacking the framework supplied by a text, composers had to create formal patterns to shape instrumental music. *Canon in D* demonstrates two favorite compositional principles of the Baroque period: canonic writing and variation form.

Pachelbel: *Canon in D* (4:45) ⑰

The "canon" in the title of this piece (date of composition unknown) refers to the way the three violin parts enter in canonic style, one following another just as singers do in a simple round like "Row, Row, Row Your Boat." In addition, the entire piece is a set of continuous variations over a ground bass, a form we met in the closing duet sung by Nero and Poppea in Monteverdi's opera. Pachelbel's bass line contains eight notes: *Dô-sol-la-mi-fa-do-fa-sol*. Quickly establishing the key of D major, as shown in the first two measures of example 28.1, this line remains unchanged during the progress of the twenty-eight continuous sections that make up the work. The three violin parts enter in down-the-scale lines at first, as shown in example 28.1, then increase and decrease in complexity of rhythmic patterns. By the time the third violin part has arrived at any new pattern, the first violin has begun still another type of variation technique.

Example 28.1

 CD1

(0:00)

1   m1 Depending upon the performers' decisions, a keyboard
          accompaniment of organ or harpsichord (the basso continuo) may be
          heard as the cellos and basses begin. Then the first violin part enters
          in notes that match the speed of the bass line (quarter notes) and the
          other two parts follow in turn. At the fourth appearance of the
          ground bass, the first violin notes come twice as fast (eighth notes).

42

(0:54)
2   m11 With the sixth appearance of the ground bass, the notes are four
times as fast (sixteenth notes).

43

(1:33)
3   m19 Here, with the tenth appearance of the ground bass, begins the
quickest motion of the violin parts (thirty-second notes).

44

(2:12)
4   m27 At the fourteenth appearance of the ground bass, the violin parts
return to the slower motion of sixteenth notes.

45

(3:48)
5   m47 Syncopation is introduced for the first time at the twenty-fourth
appearance of the ground bass. From here to the end, the parts show
a variety of rhythms, with simple eighth notes prevailing at the final
cadence.

46

Many recorded versions of this piece should more properly be called transcriptions, because they have been so freely arranged. Recording artists demonstrate an amazing variety of performance styles in regard to tempo, articulation,
and dynamics. Performers sometimes relate their dynamic levels to the speed of
the violins' notes, for example, becoming louder with the sixteenth notes and softer
with the eighths.

An engraving from the early 1700s shows a "student serenade," with instrumentalists joining singers in their outdoor performance.

29 ANTONIO VIVALDI

PREVIEW Trained as a priest, the Italian violin virtuoso Vivaldi wrote hundreds of instrumental works. Most of them feature the concertato principle, the contrast of differing musical forces. We study a concerto grosso by Vivaldi.

Born a few years earlier than Bach and Handel, Antonio Vivaldi [pronounced vee-VAHL-dee] (1678–1741) until recently was overshadowed by them. Bach, however, thought enough of Vivaldi's string compositions to arrange some of them for keyboard, and Vivaldi's music has won increasing attention in this century. Born in Venice to a musical family, Vivaldi became a violin virtuoso himself, writing challenging music for his instrument. Much of his output was composed for his pupils, the girls at a Venetian orphanage where he taught the violin. Although trained for the priesthood, he spent more time in music than in church, blaming his poor health for his failure to say Mass.

Amazingly prolific, Vivaldi wrote operas, sacred music, and more than four hundred concertos for a wide variety of instruments, including violin, flute, cello, trumpet, guitar, and even the mandolin. Most of these compositions belong to a type of music known as **concerto grosso.** Developed in the middle Baroque, a concerto grosso is a multimovement work for a small group of soloists, such as two violinists, accompanied by a somewhat larger orchestra, usually of strings plus basso continuo. The virtuoso soloists are pitted against the orchestra, composed of players with more modest skills. Baroque solo concertos employ the same basic plan with only one soloist.

The standard concerto grosso plan calls for a three-movement pattern of fast-slow-fast, with the fast movements in **ritornello form.** "Ritornello" literally means "little return" and refers both to a returning theme and to the form those returns create. In ritornello form, the movement begins with a musical theme played by the entire group in the tonic key. The ritornello then alternates with contrasting ideas played by the soloist or the solo group. The ritornello's returns are usually fragmentary and in different keys, until a complete, final return in the tonic.

Vivaldi's best-known work, written c.1725, is the *Four Seasons,* a set of four concertos, each portraying a season of the year. To make his musical descriptions clearer, Vivaldi supplemented the score with sonnets which he probably wrote himself. At the appropriate place in that score, a letter identifies which line of the sonnet applies. In the listening guide, the lines of the sonnet (as translated into English) appear in quotation marks directly above the musical item that is identified in the score. As in the Renaissance madrigal with its word painting, here nonmusical ideas are given musical representation. The resulting images can be almost literal, as in the chattering teeth caused by winter's cold (item 9), or they can merely evoke a quiet scene, as in the slow movement.

Vivaldi: *Four Seasons,* IV: *Winter.*

CHAPTER 29 ANTONIO VIVALDI **165**

CD1

First Movement:
Allegro non molto
(3:45) ⑱

"Trembling, chilled in the frigid snows"

(0:00)
1   m1   The ritornello begins in the tonic key of F minor, as low strings play
[47]   a throbbing figure, each note repeated many times. Violas, then
             second violins enter, each on a higher pitch, each playing the same
             repeated-note idea. With the first violin's trills added to the repeated
             notes, the "trembling" is more audible. (Performances vary in
             respect to the clarity of these trills.)

"Under the harsh breath of the terrible wind."

(0:45)
2   m12   The solo violin plays completely alone in rapid, descending notes.
             Soon the orchestra interrupts the soloist twice with bits of the
             ritornello.

(1:09)
3   m18   As the soloist concludes, the orchestra begins the ritornello again
[48]   with its repeated notes.

"Running with the feet stamping rapidly."

(1:23)
4   m22   Rather abruptly, the orchestra changes ideas with very fast figures
             that really do seem to "stamp."

(1:35)
5   m26   As the orchestra finishes, another solo begins, this time accompanied
             only by the basso continuo.

(2:00)
6   m33   Again the orchestra interrupts with brief, repeated-note comments.

[49]

(2:16)
7   m38   Similar to the beginning of the movement, this ritornello appearance
             is in a major key (E-flat).

(2:37)
8   m44   Here the soloist is accompanied only by basso continuo.

"Teeth chattering from the overwhelming cold."

(2:45)

9   m47   The chattering idea is communicated by means of high, quick, repeated notes. During this passage there is no bass line.

50

(3:16)

10   m56   The orchestra returns to the "stamping-feet" figures of item 4 to close the movement vigorously.

 CD1

"Spending quiet, contented days by the fire, while outside the rain soaks all."

Second Movement:
Largo
(2:36) ⑲

(0:00)

1   m1   Supported by a pizzicato accompaniment (raindrops?) over repeated bass notes, the solo violin's tranquil, legato melody (ex. 29.1) memorably illustrates the technique of sequence. The viola contributes long, sustained tones. Depending upon the performers, the keyboard basso continuo may be quite prominent. Appropriately, this movement is in a happy, major key.

51

Example 29.1

(1:08)

2   m9   After a tiny rest for the soloist, the second half of the movement follows. It is much like the first, except that it begins in a different key (the dominant). The soloist might play an unusually long trill at the cadence.

52

The third movement, like the first, is fast and in minor, with several different musical ideas that illustrate the sonnet's literal images of winter: "Walking on the ice at a slow pace,/Going about cautiously, for fear of falling./ Running about, slipping, falling to the ground,/Again making way on the ice and running hard/ Until the ice breaks and separates./Feeling the rush through the iron portals;/Of the Sirocco, Borea and all the warring winds."

The sonnet concludes on a positive note: "This is winter, but such that brings joy."

A. Vivaldi

30 GEORGE FRIDERIC HANDEL

PREVIEW The German-born Handel became a naturalized Englishman. His successful career as composer and producer of Italian-style operas floundered after the public lost its taste for them. He then turned to oratorios. We concentrate on one of them, *Messiah,* the work which the average person associates with the composer. We discuss the misconceptions that surround this work and select five portions of it for study.

George Frideric Handel.

The lives of the two leading composers of the Baroque era yield fruitful comparisons. Less than one hundred miles separate the German towns where George Frideric Handel (1685–1759) and Johann Sebastian Bach were born—in the same year. (Handel's name often appears in its original German form as Georg Friederich Händel. However, he anglicized it when he became a British subject.) His birthplace was the town of Halle. Unlike Bach, he did not spring from a musical family. His father, a barber-surgeon who expected his son to be a lawyer, discouraged the child's first musical explorations. (There is a famous story that he had to practice in the attic at night, secretly, by moonlight.) Impressed with Handel's musical gifts, a local nobleman persuaded the father to allow him to study music. He made rapid progress in performance on keyboard instruments and in composition.

In accordance with his father's expectations, Handel obediently began law studies, but he soon abandoned them; his heart was in opera. He visited Italy, where opera and new forms of instrumental music flourished. There he quickly established a good reputation as a composer, while meeting and learning from the prominent Italian composers of the time.

In 1712 Handel moved to England, where he stayed the rest of his life. He rapidly became a favorite of English musical circles and of the Royal court, teaching the princesses their music lessons. Most of his compositional energy went into operas, which he produced himself. Consequently, he prospered as long as operas sold well at the box office. In 1728, an opera produced by a rival company appeared. *The Beggar's Opera,* assembled by John Gay from popular tunes and ballads, was in English and dealt with the lower strata of society. Packing the audience appeal of today's musical comedy, it was a runaway hit. A parody on the Italian-style operas that Handel was composing, its success should have warned Handel that the public had grown tired of his operas' artificialities. Indeed, Handel's opera company went bankrupt, though he stubbornly continued to compose operas until 1741.

During this period, Handel began to experiment with **oratorios.** Oratorios resemble operas in that they require similar performing forces: soloists, chorus, orchestra, and the same two basic vocal components of recitative and aria. Also, though they are not staged, oratorios are often written to a narrative libretto. The Old Testament proved to be a favorite source. In *Samson,* for example, the hero laments his blindness and argues with Delilah, while the chorus represents both of the opposing sides in the drama—the Philistines and the Israelites. Oddly enough, Handel's most famous oratorio, *Messiah,* which we study later, is not typical, because it lacks the specifically narrative quality of most oratorios. He planned his oratorios for concert performances, for an evening's entertainment. Audiences responded favorably to English texts and the familiar Biblical stories. Handel, as a businessman, no doubt was happy that oratorios were cheaper to produce—no scenery, no costumes. Indeed, his oratorios restored his financial health. Because he did not change his style, he could recycle the music of some of his operas into his oratorios.

Actually, Baroque composers expected to revamp music for new situations, and apparently thought nothing of using someone else's music. It was considered a form of borrowing, to be repaid with "interest" by further developing the music that had been borrowed. No copyright laws existed and few were concerned about plagiarism or originality. Besides, composers worked in haste. Handel wrote *Messiah* in twenty-four days and then wrote *Samson* in the next six weeks. Not surprisingly, portions of *Messiah* have been traced to earlier music. For example, the chorus *For Unto Us* was originally an Italian chamber duet.

In his last years, even though blind and in failing health, Handel continued to conduct and supervise productions of his works. Upon his death in 1759, he was honored by burial in Westminster Abbey, the resting place of so many great English citizens. Three thousand mourners attended his funeral.

A

No other composer is so linked in the general public's mind to a single work as is Handel. Many people associate him only with *Messiah,* probably the most frequently performed choral work in English-speaking countries. This is doubly unfortunate: not only did he create a wealth of other beautiful music, but what the public *thinks* it knows about this work is incorrect. We shall concentrate on clearing up some misconceptions, starting with the title itself. It is simply *Messiah*—no "The."

Handel, Typecast as the Composer of Messiah

MESSIAH.

AN

ORATORIO

Compos'd by Mr. HANDEL.

MAJORA CANAMUS.

*And without Controverſy, great is the Myſtery of Godlineſs :
God was manifeſted in the Fleſh, juſtified by the Spirit,
ſeen of Angels, preached among the Gentiles, believed on in
the World, received up in Glory.
In whom are hid all the Treaſures of Wiſdom and Knowledge.*

DUBLIN Printed by GEORGE FAULKNER, 1742.

Messiah was *not* conceived as a Christmas piece, although many productions today occur during the Christmas season, which is logical, since the first third of this work does deal with the birth of Jesus. Actually, it was first given as a charity event in Ireland (in 1742) in the penitential season before Easter, when opera was forbidden. It received rave reviews, as this sample from the *Dublin Journal* demonstrates: "On Tuesday last Mr. Handel's Sacred Grand Oratorio, the MESSIAH, was performed at the New Musick-Hall; the best Judges allowed it to be the most finished piece of Musick. Words are wanting to express the exquisite Delight it afforded to the admiring crowded Audience." Its acceptance in England was slower. Once it became associated with charitable purposes there also, it gained enormous popularity, eventually becoming a British national institution.

Messiah is *not* church music, although the text is drawn from the Bible. Because people are confused about the religious aspect of *Messiah*, they wrap a badly fitting mantle of piety around the composer and think of him, incorrectly, as chiefly a composer of sacred music.

Nor was *Messiah* designed for massed choruses of several hundred singers, with orchestras to match. A 1784 festival performance in Westminster Abbey can be blamed for—or credited with—starting this tradition. (Cities such as Los Angeles, San Francisco, and Chicago have a tradition of "sing-along" *Messiah* productions, where as many as three thousand singers gather and run through—or should we say run over?—the choruses.) Though millions have heard it sung only by amateurs, it is *not* an ideal work for them to sing because of its stiff vocal challenges, chiefly the extended melismas.

The recent interest in authentic performance practice has resulted in a wealth of *Messiah* performances, both recorded and live, rendered in a style that Handel might recognize. Playing from the original orchestral parts instead of an orchestration later made by Mozart makes for a more authentic instrumental sound. Small, professional choruses, closer to the twenty or so singers in Handel's chorus, plus lively tempos, freely added ornamentation, and imaginative basso continuo realizations have brought renewed life and respect to this venerable work—and in the bargain, additional respect to its composer as well.

B

Handel's Music

Two of Handel's multimovement orchestral suites, originally planned for outdoor performance, the *Water Music* (1717) and the *Royal Fireworks Music* (1749), are well known, not least because of the delightful stories told about their first performances. For example, the *Water Music* was played from a barge to entertain the king and his court as they enjoyed an excursion on the Thames river. At the first performance of the *Royal Fireworks Music* the fireworks display got out of control, the crowd stampeded, and the chief technician went mad. At least the music survived. Handel had scored it for a large group of brass and woodwind instruments, adding strings for a possible later performance. Until recently, these works were usually played in arrangements for full symphony orchestra made by Sir Hamilton Harty (1879–1941) and others.

Surprisingly, Handel wrote little solo organ music, despite his own virtuosity on that instrument. He did leave some organ concertos, works which he himself played between acts of his oratorios. He improvised much of the organ part, so that, unfortunately, the scores as he left them fail to provide a complete picture of what he played. His harpsichord suites are also incompletely written, leaving the performer much freedom.

Messiah is but one of his many oratorios. Others are becoming better known of late, with *Judas Maccabeus* and *Israel in Egypt* frequently performed. His thirty-nine operas, and indeed almost all Italian-style Baroque opera, were considered impossible to perform for generations, because many of the principal male roles were written for castrati. The increasing number of performances of Handel's operas in this century shows that that problem can be solved. As witness, his *Agrippina* and *Julius Caesar* are available in videocassette form. One of his operas, *Xerxes* (or *Serse*), contains a lovely melody, *Ombra mai fu,* which has been arranged countless times for both vocal (with new words) and instrumental performance. It is familiarly known— inaccurately—as "Handel's Largo" (ex. 30.1).

Example 30.1

Another well-known Handel melody, an eternal favorite with voice students, is *Where'er You Walk,* a da capo aria from the oratorio *Semele* (ex. 30.2).

Example 30.2

Wher- e'er you walk,   cool gales shall fan the glade.

Handel: *Messiah*
selections

A complete performance of this work takes over two hours, although the increasingly rapid tempos adopted recently have trimmed its running time considerably. For our purposes, five of its approximately fifty separate movements will demonstrate Handel's style. (The numbers following the titles given below identify the selection in the complete work. Various editions differ slightly.) Handel scored it for four soloists, a four-part (male) chorus, and a small accompanying orchestra of strings, oboes, bassoons, and, at climactic places, trumpets and timpani. Of course, a basso continuo must be employed. There is no one definitive score for *Messiah,* because Handel constantly revised his works to fit the needs of a particular performance. He might give a bass solo to an alto, for example, or change the length of an orchestral interlude. Consequently, performances of this work can differ in such respects. The text was compiled by Charles Jennens (1700–73), a wealthy English gentleman, who selected passages from both the Old and New Testaments.

 CD1

The Sinfonia adopts some style characteristics of the **French overture,** the first standard type of overture, developed by the French composer Jean-Baptiste Lully. Such pieces begin in a solemn, majestic, slow tempo and feature dotted rhythms, which in Baroque music are customarily associated with the pomp and ceremony of splendid royal occasions. French overtures then continue with a section in imitative polyphony, at a fast tempo, and often close with a brief restatement of the opening mood.

I. Sinfonia (#1) (or "Overture") (3:00) (20)

(0:00)
1

53

The piece begins with dotted rhythms, in slow tempo, in the minor mode. All instruments play together in homophonic style.

(0:32)
2

54

The opening music is repeated. Some performers choose to play the repeated music softly, although Handel left no such instructions.

(1:04)
3

55

A polyphonic section begins, allegro, with the theme in a high range. Other entrances occur, each one lower in pitch; then Handel develops the subject at some length.

(2:46)
4

56

A slowing down of the tempo recalls the majestic style of the overture's beginning. It ends, as it began, in minor.

 CD1

A tenor solo, this movement is called a recitative in some scores, in others an **arioso,** a term referring to a small aria. This particular solo shares characteristics of both aria and recitative. It resembles an aria because it contains some word repetition, is usually metrical, and has a full accompaniment—characteristics that define an aria. It lacks only the aria's customary formal structure: an ABA pattern, including a theme played by the orchestra to begin and end the aria. *Comfort Ye,* however, changes style completely near the end, turning into a brief recitative with no word repetition, free rhythm, and a

II. Comfort ye (#2) (2:56) (21)

bare minimum amount of accompaniment. Perhaps to make this solo sound more "comforting," Handel writes in the major mode.

(0:00)
1

57

The orchestra begins with a short motive of *mi-mi-mi-mi-sol,* which will return between the phrases sung by the tenor.

(0:14)
2

58

"Comfort ye, my people, saith your God. Speak ye comfortably to Jerusalem,"
The orchestra both supports and echoes the tenor's lines.

(1:40)
3

59

"and cry unto her, that her warfare is accomplished, that her iniquity is pardon'd."
The accompaniment is interrupted dramatically on "cry," then resumes.

(2:33)
4

60

"The voice of him that crieth in the wilderness, Prepare ye the way of the Lord, make straight in the desert a highway for our God."
The style shifts abruptly to recitative. The placement of the accompanying chords occurs with, or in between, words. The final cadence of recitatives is almost always a simple one, dominant to tonic.

  CD1

***III. Ev'ry valley** (#3)*
(3:24) ㉒

Another tenor solo, this aria begins immediately after *Comfort ye* and remains in the same E major key. It shows aria characteristics in that it is quite melodic, contains much word repetition, is strongly rhythmical, and is fully accompanied.

(0:00)
1

61

An orchestral introduction announces the melody (ex. 30.3) that the tenor will soon sing.

Example 30.3

(0:20)
2

"Ev'ry valley shall be exalted, and ev'ry mountain and hill made low,"

62

The exuberant and extended melismas Handel wrote for the word "exalted" are challenges to the virtuoso singer.

(0:59)
3

"the crooked straight, and the rough places plain."
Word painting is evident. "Crooked" moves quickly from low to

63

high, and "plain" is emphasized in long, drawn-out notes. Both words contrast with the fancy treatment given to "exalted."

(1:37)
4

"Ev'ry valley shall be exalted, and ev'ry mountain and hill made low; the crooked straight, and the rough places plain."

64

These previously heard words return, treated in similar style.

(2:18)
5

"the crooked straight and the rough places plain."
At this cadential point, the accompaniment slows down and the

65

singer frequently adds embellishments.

(3:01)
6

The singer's opening melody is played once again, as it was in the introduction.

 CD1

This stirring chorus, appropriately in the major, employs the standard four parts: soprano, alto, tenor, and bass. This chorus resembles an aria in some musical respects, such as the role of the orchestra and the abundant word repetition and melisma. It alternates between two textures, as the listening guide reveals.

IV. For unto us (#11)
(3:54) ㉓

(0:00)
1

In a lively tempo, the orchestral introduction begins with the melody that the sopranos will soon sing (ex. 30.4).

66

Example 30.4

(0:14)
2

67

"For unto us a Child is born, unto us a Son is given,"
Imitative entrances unfold in this order: soprano, tenor, alto, bass, with melismatic flights on "born."

(0:59)
3

68

"and the government shall be upon His shoulder, and His name shall be called:"
A new motive using dotted rhythms is also treated polyphonically. (Surely it is no accident that dotted rhythms, associated with royalty, occur on the word "government.")

(1:16)
4

69

"Wonderful, Counselor, the Mighty God, the Everlasting Father, the Prince of Peace."
All parts sing the same syllables together in homophonic texture, over an accompaniment of very quick notes.

(1:26)
5

70

"unto us a Child is born . . ."
Words that have already been heard in items 2, 3, and 4 return, and the alternation of textures continues in different keys.

(2:52)
6

71

"For unto us a child is born. . . ."
All four parts sing these words together. As voices continue, now in pairs, the sound thickens.

(3:35)
7

72

The orchestral conclusion is in the style of the introduction.

♫ CD1

V. Hallelujah (#39)
(3:42) ㉔

This is undoubtedly the most famous of all Handel choruses. At one of the first London performances of *Messiah,* the king of England got to his feet when it began. (Perhaps he thought the work was over, but this chorus is only the end of Part Two, with Part Three yet to come.) Of course, when the king stands, everyone stands, and so a tradition was born. To this day, the audience rises when this movement begins. This chorus resembles *For unto us* in its variety of textures, something Handel did frequently, in its major mode, and in its amount of word repetition, but there are no melismas in *Hallelujah.* Trumpets and timpani add excitement to this chorus and reinforce its triumphant message.

(0:00)

1

73

A short orchestral introduction has time only to introduce the opening rhythm.

(0:07)

2

74

"Hallelujah!"
The many repetitions of this word peal out in homophonic texture. Orchestral fanfares echo the rhythm of "Hallelujah."

(0:35)

3

75

"For the Lord God Omnipotent reigneth."
Now all voices and instruments produce the same melody (ex. 30.5) as they sing and play together, creating a bit of monophony, which is quickly followed by a return to the "Hallelujah" style.

Example 30.5

(0:47)

4

76

Combining the melody of item 3 with "Hallelujah" produces a passage of nonimitative polyphony.

(1:12)

5

77

"The kingdom of this world is become the Kingdom of our Lord and of His Christ."
With another shift in texture, voices and instruments move generally together in homophonic style, in a section traditionally sung softer, with a dramatic crescendo when these words are repeated.

(1:31)

6

78

"And He shall reign for ever and ever."
Imitative entrances start with the bass and move upward, supported by instruments playing the same lines.

(1:53)

7

79

"King of Kings, and Lord of Lords, for ever and ever."
Polyphony continues with long, drawn-out notes in the upper voices, rising ever higher. At the same time, the remaining voices and the instruments continue together with "for ever and ever" and "Hallelujah."

(2:32)

8   "And He shall reign for ever and ever."

80

The polyphony of item 6 begins the final section of this movement as the preceding phrases of the text return. The final choral acclamation is the familiar "Amen" cadence.

For someone familiar only with amateur performances of an incomplete *Messiah,* a modern recording will prove a revelation. If time allows for only a few selections, it is interesting to compare those just studied with others. The dotted rhythms of the *Sinfonia* also can be heard in choruses, particularly in *Behold the Lamb of God* (#22), the opening of Part Two. All of the soloists have recitatives and arias. Sopranos relish a florid display piece, *Rejoice greatly* (#18). The darker alto voice fits the melancholy of *He was despised* (#23). The tenor has more to sing than the two solos just described; later comes his *Behold and see* (#30). And many a bass has wondered how it is possible to sing such an aria as *The trumpet shall sound* (#48), which demands bass voice power and soprano agility.

Handel

JOHANN SEBASTIAN BACH 31

PREVIEW Born in the same year as Handel, Bach stayed close to his German roots, spending the last half of his career as a church music director in Leipzig. Almost forgotten after his death, his music experienced a dramatic revival in the Romantic period. We study examples of his ensemble (orchestral) works, organ compositions, and church cantatas.

Heredity and environment collaborated to make Bach a musician. Because there were several composers named Bach, one must include his initials or cite his full name to distinguish Johann Sebastian Bach [pronounced BAHKH] (1685–1750) from his sons or other relatives. His was a musical family, unique in the number of musicians it fostered, supplying central Germany with at least eighty town musicians and church organists over a period of three centuries. A genealogy traces the family origins to a Viet Bach, who died before 1578.

Born in the small town of Eisenach, Bach began his musical education at home. His father taught him to play the violin; his brother taught him the keyboard instruments. This way of learning a craft, from the family, was standard for most skilled trades of his time—and music *was* a skilled trade. Much of his education was self-directed as he copied out scores and heard some of the great organists of his day.

Before he was twenty Bach was a virtuoso organist, a church musician. He had embarked upon a series of small-town positions, none of which offered him the kind of organ he wanted or the musical challenges he craved. Late in 1705 he took a leave from his Arnstadt post (greatly overstaying his leave in the process) and traveled in the dead of winter to Lübeck to hear the organist Dietrich Buxtehude, whose Sunday afternoon concerts attracted musicians from all over Germany. (Buxtehude was looking for a possible successor. Both Bach and Handel might have been interested in the job, but one condition restrained them both— the necessity of marrying Buxtehude's daughter, considered elderly at age thirty!)

Johann Sebastian Bach.

From 1708 to 1717, while serving the Duke of Weimar as court organist and chamber musician, Bach wrote most of his organ music. When he asked for release

Bach never traveled far from his birthplace. This map of Germany shows the cities that were important to his career.

Potsdam • • Berlin

• Cöthen
• Halle
• Mühlhausen • Leipzig
Eisenach • • Weimar Dresden •
Ohrdruf • • Arnstadt

GERMANY

from his position to move to a new job, his employer thought his request too insolent. The court history relates that "he was placed under arrest in the County Judge's place of detention for too stubbornly requesting his dismissal." After almost a month in jail, he was released "with notice of his unfavorable discharge."

Fortunately, Bach's next employer, the young, music-loving Prince Leopold of Cöthen, treated him as an equal. At Cöthen, serving as court music director (Kapellmeister), he composed most of his orchestral and chamber music. Church music was not part of his duties since the prince, a Calvinist, observed simple court services. Despite this, Bach was so content in his situation that he would have remained there the rest of his days had the prince not married an unmusical princess. The prince's interest in music waned and with it Bach's enthusiasm for his post.

In 1723 Bach settled in Leipzig (after World War II a part of East Germany), a "free" or self-governing city of some 30,000 people. He reluctantly accepted the grudging offer made by the town council to be **cantor** (church music director) for St. Thomas's church and director of music for the city. (Bach's era knew nothing of a separation between church and state!) Historians have assumed that his religious convictions played a part in his decision to return to church music, for a cantor ranked below a Kapellmeister in status. This position included the musical responsibility for the four principal churches of the city plus teaching at the St. Thomas choir school.

Astonishing as it may seem today, Bach was the council's third choice, or as one member of the council put it: "Since the best man could not be obtained, lesser ones would have to be accepted." The town council's actions make more sense to us once we understand that a cantor's primary task was to compose cantatas for the church service and Bach had not written very many when interviewed. A prolific, amiable composer like Telemann, the man the council really wanted but couldn't get, would have pleased them more. Bach's fame as an organist counted for little, since the cantor was not expected to play for the church services.

Although the position at Leipzig carried considerable prestige, the town fathers withheld the support Bach felt church music deserved. He faced numerous difficulties. The organs were second-rate; the choirboys admitted to the school that was part of the establishment too frequently lacked talent; the instrumentalists were on a par with the singers. Bach described his grievances in a letter to a friend, noting that his expenses were greater than he had expected and his income was less— especially when there was good weather and few funerals. He portrayed his "masters" as "strange folk with very little care for music in them," and complained that he was "subjected to constant annoyance, jealousy, and persecution." Despite his professional disappointments, Bach stayed in Leipzig the rest of his life. No better situation ever came his way.

Bach's convictions about church music stemmed from his religious faith. Bach's own copy of the Bible, with his underlinings and marginal comments, was rediscovered in the late 1960s. It shows that Old Testament accounts of the splendor of temple music under King David influenced him greatly. It also shows that although he was frustrated with the earthly representatives of the church, his faith remained secure. Further evidence for his religious views comes from his music. At the ends of the scores for his cantatas and Passions he wrote the initials "S.D.G.," standing for a Latin motto: "to God alone be glory." For him, no real difference existed between sacred and secular music, and he often turned secular music into sacred by changing the texts.

Unlike Handel, Bach was a family man who never traveled very far from home. Married twice (both wives were musical), he fathered twenty children, but when he died in 1750 only nine of them were living. Given child mortality and life expectancy figures in those days, that was a normal situation. Four of his sons became distinguished composers, all trained by their father. But the Bach family's strong traditions did not last much longer. It is shocking to read that his surviving sons allowed Bach's widow to die in poverty. By 1843, at a ceremony unveiling a belated statue to J. S. Bach, only one grandson was left to represent this distinguished family.

Bach: His Fall and Rise

Even before he died in 1750 Bach was out of touch with the trends of his times, in both religion and music. An emerging rationalism weakened his Lutheran church. And musical tastes changed: people now regarded Bach's intricate polyphony as old-fashioned. In fact, in 1737 a prominent German music critic described Bach's music as "bombastic and confused." Bach devoted his last years in Leipzig to writing monumental works that far exceeded the demands and the resources of his position—or of anyone else's, for that matter. Indeed, a famous late work, the *Art of Fugue,* bears no indication to show what performing medium it was planned for.

Following Bach's death the memory of his compositions soon faded except within the small circle of his pupils and admirers. His posthumous reputation was that of a virtuoso organist. For example, his obituary, written by one of his sons, claimed: "With his two feet, he could play things on the pedals which many not unskillful clavier players would find it bitter enough to have to play with five fingers."

Imagine the reactions of Bach and the members of the Leipzig town council if by some miracle they had been resurrected in 1985. In that year the Western world celebrated the tricentennial of Bach's birth, together with those of Handel and Domenico Scarlatti, and the quadricentennial of Heinrich Schütz. They would learn that when polled in 1964 American musicologists ranked Bach as the number one composer of all time. They would have seen scholars examining every single note Bach wrote and debating the chronology of many of his works. The scholars' research tools of handwriting analysis and paper dating would amaze them. How astonished Bach and the council members would be to learn that a spacecraft launched in 1977 carried a recording of Bach's music!

Surely the evidence of Bach's stature in 1985 would have flabbergasted the council members, who saw in him only a competent and cantankerous church musician. But would he be so surprised? Though writing for the future was not the way composers worked in the Baroque period, in everything Bach was exceptional. And we know he was supremely self-confident.

Composer Felix Mendelssohn, whom we study in Part Six, had much to do with the "rise" of Bach. In 1829 he conducted a performance of the master's *St. Matthew Passion,* a work almost forgotten since Bach's death. The renewed interest in Bach's music that this performance inspired set in motion the **Bach Revival.**

One of the first tasks of the Bach Revival was to publish all of Bach's music in scholarly editions, an effort that took several decades and, in a new Bach edition, still goes on. Although Bach himself published a few compositions, much of his music circulated only in copies made by pupils and family. A great deal of editorial work has been needed, therefore, to decide questions of authenticity and accuracy. Even though nearly fifty large volumes resulted initially, we know that much of what he wrote has been lost.

Another scholarly task was the compilation of a numbering system for Bach's music, a system that supplies **BWV** numbers for titles. "BWV" stands for "Bach-Werke-Verzeichnis," a catalog compiled by Wolfgang Schmieder in this century. Sometimes that number appears with an **S** instead, as a way of acknowledging Herr Schmieder. The renewed interest in Bach that Mendelssohn helped generate has never faded. To the contrary, each passing decade sees an ever greater acclaim for him.

Bach's supremacy is often explained as the result of his unique ability to synthesize the national styles—Italian, French, and German—and the various musical ideas of his day into one unified whole. He summed up what had already been done, treating each kind of music in a definitive way, as if he wanted to write an encyclopedia of musical possibilities. Still, such rational explanations of Bach's supremacy neglect the emotional power of his music. The aura of absolute rightness and utter conviction in every measure is profoundly moving. Listeners sense that Bach's intellectual control extended far beyond what they can hear in the music and see in the score.

The existence of hidden layers in Bach's music transcends the purely musical. Various kinds of symbolism fascinated him. For example, the number three, the Trinity, is central to Christian theology. Consequently, some scholars believe that Bach wrote in the key of three flats, or divided a work into three sections, in order to make a religious statement. His *Prelude and Fugue* for organ, BWV 552, in the key of E-flat—three flats—includes a prelude having three themes and a fugue in three sections.

Another kind of symbolism involved his own name, possible because in the German musical alphabet, the letter B means B-flat and H means a B-natural. So **B-A-C-H** forms a musical motive: B-flat, A, C, B-natural, which he incorporated in his last composition, the *Art of Fugue*. (As a tribute to him, many later composers, among them the Romantics Liszt and Schumann and the modernists Schoenberg and Webern, have quoted this motive in works with titles such as "Fugue on B-A-C-H.") Additionally, the game involved arithmetic based on the alphabet, as follows: A = 1, B = 2, C = 3, H = 8. The sum of these is fourteen and there are scholars who consider it no accident when Bach put fourteen notes into a musical theme or when fourteen of anything can be counted in his music.

B

Prelude No. 1 from the *Well Tempered Clavier* may seem familiar for at least two reasons. Millions of piano students have worked on it—it is reasonably easy to perform—and it was appropriated by the French composer Charles Gounod (1818–93) as an accompaniment for a melody he wrote. Later his melody was adapted to the "Ave Maria" text. References to that often-performed song list the composer as "Bach-Gounod." The *Prelude's* basic procedure is typically Baroque: the style of broken chords (one chord note played at a time) found in the beginning measures (ex. 31.1) continues throughout.

Bach's Music

Example 31.1

The entire *Well Tempered Clavier* consists of two volumes, each containing twenty-four preludes and fugues. The first prelude, just mentioned, and its fugue are in C major, the second set in C minor. Next comes a C-sharp major pair, followed by a C-sharp minor pair, and so on until Bach had covered all tones of the chromatic scale with twelve major and twelve minor keys. Some of these keys were rarely encountered in Bach's era; his experiments in temperament or tuning systems made these key choices possible and that is why "Well Tempered" begins the title. Notice that the title does *not* refer to "clavi*chord*." As we said earlier, "clavier" means any keyboard instrument.

Although the orchestra as we know it, a standardized group, is a product of the Classic era, Bach wrote four multimovement orchestral suites. The term **suite** designates a group of dance types, composed for both keyboard instruments and ensembles.

The four standard dances of a Baroque suite produced a truly international form: allemande (German), courante (French), sarabande (Spanish), and gigue (English). Optional dances might be included as well. The dances were "stylized;" that is, nobody really danced to them, but the original meter, tempo, and general character remained.

Bach's third orchestral suite, in D, includes a movement called "Air." In the nineteenth century, when a violinist arranged the music for solo performance upon the lowest string of the violin and called it "Air for the G string," it became famous as a separate piece.

The fourth suite, in B minor, concludes with a *Badinerie,* a light-hearted dance in **binary** form, which is also the form of the *Air* just mentioned. Binary form, as the "bi-" implies, consists of two parts, each of the parts repeated exactly, AABB. The labeling of "A" and "B," while traditional, is misleading. The motives or themes are basically the same in both parts; the degree of contrast encountered in a ternary form, ABA, is alien to binary form. Key relationships account for the chief differences between the A and the B sections: the A section moves to a cadence and a full stop in a new key; the B section works its way back to the key of the beginning. In the *Badinerie,* the flute soloist outlines a triad-based motive (ex. 31.2) which begins each section, making it easy to follow the form.

Example 31.2

PART FOUR THE BAROQUE

Few examples of Bach's own musical handwriting have survived. This one is a bourrée, one of the optional dances in a Baroque suite.

Beginning piano students play delightful little pieces that are often attributed to Bach, with titles such as *Minuet in G* or *Musette*. They are found in the *Notebook for Anna Magdalena Bach* (Bach's second wife, a fine musician herself), a collection compiled for the family to play. More advanced players study his *Inventions,* which train fingers—and minds—to perform polyphonic lines. Though people constantly play his keyboard music on the piano, he wrote little or nothing for that instrument. The earliest surviving pianos date from the 1720s, but many years passed before composers wrote specifically for them. As might be expected, Bach wrote much great organ music. To this day, organists build their technique upon his mighty preludes and fugues.

An important part of Bach's work was based on centuries-old German hymn tunes called **chorales** [pronounced with an accent on the last syllable], some of them attributed to Martin Luther himself. Placing the traditional melody in the soprano, Bach supplied harmonic lines for alto, tenor, and bass. These chorale harmonizations are so perfectly realized that music students still use them as models when learning to write harmony, just as Palestrina's Masses and motets furnish models for counterpoint. Bach's **chorale preludes,** settings for organ of German hymn tunes, reflect with remarkable sensitivity the text messages of the original hymns. The chorales also function as a key ingredient of the cantata, as we shall see.

Making up a large proportion of his collected works are the compositions for choir, soloists, and various combinations of instruments. Bach's *B Minor Mass* requires virtuoso performers to master its difficulties. No one is sure why he wrote it, although scholars have speculated that the beautiful score he sent to the Elector of Saxony was meant as a job application. We do not know if he ever heard it performed as a whole. With each phrase of the text forming a separate movement, it is much too long for a Catholic service. Only the first two items of the Mass, the Kyrie and the Gloria, could have been sung in a Lutheran service.

Bach lavished unusual care on his manuscript of the score, in some movements recycling music he had written over a two-decade period. Some scholars think he composed the Mass as a kind of encyclopedia of musical forms, for in this work he covered a thousand years of music history. For example, the Credo begins by quoting an ancient Gregorian chant; the Sanctus pits two choral groups against each other and supports this elaborate Baroque structure with trumpets and timpani. Ever conscious of the text meanings, Bach made a particularly dramatic contrast between two movements in the Credo: the closing, hushed moments of the *Crucifixus* (He was crucified) and the exuberant beginning of the movement that follows immediately, *Et resurrexit* (He rose again).

Also difficult to perform, although his Leipzig congregations did hear it, is Bach's awe-inspiring *St. Matthew Passion.* **Passions** are musical settings of the Bible accounts (the writings of Matthew, Mark, Luke, and John) of Jesus's last days. Bach's Passions are much like oratorios, and they include a prominent part for a tenor soloist who sings the Biblical narration in a recitative style. Solo arias reflect upon the dramatic events. The chorus plays two roles: the crowd in the drama and the congregation, which sings settings of chorale tunes, as if commenting on the action like a Greek chorus. Some chorales appear more than once. For example, Bach included *O Haupt voll Blut und Wunden* (O sacred head, now wounded), the so-called "Passion chorale," five times in the *St. Matthew Passion,* each time with a different harmonization, as if to highlight the message of the particular stanza.

About two hundred of Bach's cantatas have survived. We will study one of them, No. 140. Another cantata, No. 147, includes a movement known in English as *Jesu, Joy of Man's Desiring.* This music (ex. 31.3) has been arranged many times for instrumental performance.

Example 31.3

The melodic line given here shows triplets, a detail of rhythm notation. Three notes take the same amount of time as would two notes of the same value, if the number "3" were not there.

Bach: *Brandenburg Concerto,* No. 5, in D. First movement, allegro. (9:56) ㉕

Written in 1721, this piece is a concerto grosso. It resembles the *Four Seasons* by Vivaldi in its adherence to the concertato principle, notably in the contrast between two forces, a small group of soloists, called the **concertino,** and the larger accompanying group or "orchestra." In Bach's six *Brandenburg Concertos*—their dedicatee was the Margrave of Brandenburg—the concertino differs for each work. For the fifth, it consists of flute, violin, and harpsichord. In this piece, as in most Baroque ensemble music, a keyboard player "realizes" the basso continuo; that is, fills in the chords above the bass line. Consequently, the harpsichordist functions both as a soloist and as a part of the accompanying orchestra.

The opening words in the conversation belong to the orchestra, as it announces the ritornello (ex. 31.4) (we met "ritornello" in studying Vivaldi). As the example demonstrates, many of the notes of this theme are played twice, creating an active, typically Baroque sound. The ritornello appears in complete form only twice, at the beginning and the end of the movement. Portions of it return eight times, some fragmentary, some beginning at the point where the previous entrance had left off.

Example 31.4

Between the ritornello appearances, the concertino is occupied with its own set of themes, one of them taking a six-note motive from the third measure of the ritornello. It features the notes *re-mi-re-fa-mi-la,* the notes circled in example 31.4. Another interchange of themes occurs in this piece. The orchestra quietly plays the first eight notes of the ritornello at several points, at moments where you might expect it to be concerned with its accompaniment role. (For the curious reader, these moments can be found in the following measures: 10, 11, 13, 35, 36, 37, 44, 49, 109, 110, 112, 114, 145, and 146.)

CD2

(0:00)
1a   m1   The orchestra (and the solo violin) play the complete ritornello, a duple meter melody. It begins in disjunct motion, moving upward along the D major chord, then descends in conjunct motion.

(0:21)
1b   m9   The concertino enters with the first of its themes, which begins with a downward scale line, *dò-ti-la-sol.* Relatively soon, another theme moves upward in quick triplets.

(0:47)
2a   m19   The orchestra returns briefly with only two measures of the ritornello, now played in a new key (the dominant).

(0:51)

2b   m21   Cutting off the orchestra, the concertino begins with the *re-mi-re-fa-mi-la* motive mentioned above.

(1:12)

3a   m29   The orchestra returns with more of the ritornello, resuming at the point of interruption in 2a.

3

(1:19)

3b   m31   The concertino is prominent with still another theme, this one featuring longer notes played echo style.

(1:40)

4a   m39   Here the orchestra's version of the ritornello is changed to minor.

4

(1:47)

4b   m43   The harpsichord leads, as the *dô-ti-la-sol* theme is developed. Soon the harpsichord is prominent with a virtuoso display of scale playing.

(2:29)

5a   m58   The orchestra enters as the ritornello is returned to the tonic key.

5

(2:36)

5b   m61   Now it is the *re-mi-re-fa-mi-la* theme which is developed as it is exchanged between flute and violin.

(3:02)

6a   m71   Bach begins a completely new section here, in minor, as if to prevent matters from becoming too predictable. Almost every motive is immediately echoed.

6

(3:28)

6b   m81   A subtle change in motives marks the beginning of this item. Flute and violin echo each other with overlapping motives, as the bass line gently descends.

(4:05)

6c   m95   Long trills played by flute and violin hint that a cadence is near.

(4:20)

7a   m101   Rather abruptly, the orchestra recalls the ritornello's first two measures, in the dominant key, and then flute and solo violin engage in a dialogue.

7

(4:45)
7b m110 The concertino returns to the opening theme, *dô-ti-la-sol* as in 1b. Soon the upward-moving triplets return.

(5:12)
8a m121 The orchestra returns with the ritornello, now almost complete.

8

(5:23)
8b m126 The concertino develops the *re-mi-re-fa-mi-la* theme.

(5:53)
9a m136 The orchestra returns with the middle segment of the ritornello.

9

(6:00)
9b m139 As in item 4b, the harpsichord is conspicuous with a display of technique.

(6:39)
10a m154 A unique feature of this piece, a long, dazzling harpsichord solo,
10 begins with a relentless treatment of the *dô-ti-la-sol* theme. When Bach reworked this piece in order to send it to the Margrave, he vastly extended this solo, forecasting what became the solo cadenza in the Classic era.

(8:12)
10b m189 A new pattern in the left hand changes the sound of the harpsichord
11 solo, as a low tone (A) is struck thirteen times. Although a cadence is long overdue, it is evaded. Once again there is an emphasis on the same low tone and again a cadence is evaded.

(9:32)
11 m219 Finally, as if to say, "Enough, J. S.!," the orchestra enters with a
12 complete version of the ritornello, played as it was in the beginning to bring the movement to a neat, logical close.

With the unusual title of "Affettuoso" (meaning "tender"), the second movement of this work is in a slow tempo. Only the three soloists play. Their parts present two contrasting motives, both of which appear in inversion as well as right-side-up. The movement is built on a thorough canonic treatment of these motives.

The third movement recalls the first in tempo (Allegro) and in its flashing passages for the harpsichordist. Unlike the first movement, the third allows no battle of themes, for both soloists and accompanying orchestra play together with dancelike themes. The movement begins with the soloists playing, quite literally, solo. The violin starts with a lilting motive that is treated fugally, with entries from the flute, then from each hand of the harpsichordist in turn. Almost thirty measures go by before the accompanying orchestra joins in the merriment.

Bach: *"Little" Fugue in G Minor* for Organ, BWV 578 (4:11) ㉖

A **fugue** is like a canon or round. Its roots lie in Renaissance vocal polyphony. There is no such thing as "fugue-form," only a general procedure, and fugues differ greatly. The one predictable feature is that a fugue begins with its "tune," properly called a fugue **subject,** first presented monophonically. Subjects can be as short as four notes or as long as several measures. Appearances of the subject are called **entries.** These entries occur in a standardized arrangement at the beginning of a fugue, starting with pitches centering on the tonic and alternating with the same melodic line, now centering on the dominant. The entries are described as if they were being performed by singers. If, for example, the subject begins in the lowest register, it is said to be in the "bass voice." It could just as well begin in the "soprano." Fugues usually have three or four voices, or that many separate lines, though fugues in five or six voices are possible.

Each fugal voice continues to spin its melodic line in counterpoint while another voice enters with the subject. In some fugues the line produced by the continuation of the voice is distinctive enough that it becomes almost as important as the subject itself. When this happens the continuation is called a **countersubject** and it accompanies each entry of the subject.

After all voices have entered, the composer begins a series of modulations to other keys before returning to the tonic for the final entry, which for many listeners gives a sense of ultimate triumph over difficulties. Between entrances of the subject, **episodes** may appear. These are passages without a complete subject, although motives from it may occur.

Other possible ingredients of a fugue include certain devices of counterpoint, among them **augmentation** (notes made uniformly longer) and **diminution** (notes made uniformly shorter). Some subjects work equally well upside down, that is, in **inversion.** Where the original line went up, the inverted would go down, and so forth. For example, "America" begins: *dô, dô, rê, ti, dô, rê.* An inverted "America" would begin: *dô, dô, ti, rê, dô, ti.* If one voice enters early, before another voice has completed the subject, this tightening effect is called **stretto.**

Fugues are usually paired with a prelude, toccata, or fantasia. This one, to the contrary, is an independent fugue. Nicknamed "Little" to distinguish it from the "Great" one in the same key, it has been arranged more than once for orchestra. Orchestral transcriptions might help a student who experiences difficulty following a fugue in an organ performance. The variations in tone color in any orchestral transcription highlight the sections for the novice listener.

Highlighting the entries of a fugue is precisely what the organ cannot do, although when an entry occurs in the bass range, played by the pedal, an organist can elect to make its tone color more aggressive. But changing tone colors to point up an episode was probably not the way to play fugues in the Baroque—the organist kept the same tone colors throughout, and that is the currently approved way to play fugues. Consequently, a fugue demands concentration on the music, not on the sound.

 CD2

(0:00)

1a   m1   The first entry of the subject (ex. 31.5) is in the highest range, the "soprano."

Example 31.5

(0:18)

1b   m6   The second entry follows, four notes lower, in the "alto." The soprano continues with a new contrapuntal line in steady sixteenth notes, the countersubject.

(0:41)

1c   m12   Entry three begins in the "tenor," in the tonic key, while the alto continues with the countersubject.

(0:59)

1d   m17   Entry four is in the "bass," an octave lower than entry two. This line is given to the pedal division of the organ. A long trill in the soprano line competes with the bass line for the listener's attention.

(1:16)

2   m22   Now that all four voices have entered, the subject drops out and an episode begins. Episodes usually change keys frequently. This one employs several sequences.

(1:26)

3a   m25   Entry five begins—or does it? Starting in the tenor, the subject then moves up to the soprano, a most unorthodox thing to do. During the last half of this entry, a long, sustained tone called a **pedal point** is played by pedal. (This association is not as obvious as it might seem. Pedal points can occur in any pitch range.)

(1:54)
3b m33 Entry six begins in the alto, for the first time in a major key.

(2:22)
3c m41 Entry seven begins in the bass (pedal), also in major.

(2:38)
4 m45 A second episode occurs, with sequential movement again a feature.

16

(2:56)
5 m50 Entry eight occurs in the soprano, in minor.

17

(3:12)
6 m55 A third episode begins. Longer than the other two, it moves steadily upward in pitch, as if to build tension as the end approaches.

18

(3:42)
7 m63 The last entry begins in the bass (pedal). As in the earlier pedal entries, it is cut short, eliminating the sixteenth notes, which might be cumbersome on the pedal. The final cadence demonstrates a standard practice for Bach: ending a minor mode piece with a major chord.

19

Bach: *Toccata in D Minor,* for organ, BWV 565 (Toccata, 2:48) (27)

Toccata derives from an Italian word meaning "to touch." Consequently a toccata is a "touch" piece, calling for some dexterity. A Baroque toccata was a keyboard piece in several sections, in a free, idiomatic style with full chords and running passages, and quite possibly including some passages in an imitative style verging on short fugues. Reflecting this pattern, this work begins in the free style: the fugal portion concludes with a section recalling the display character of the Toccata's beginning. Actually, the "and Fugue" portion of the title as it usually appears for this work is inaccurate: "Toccata" is sufficient.

This work was composed as early as 1705 when Bach was a very young organist, eager to show off both his and the organ's capabilities. We do not know what role, if any, such pieces might have played in the church service of Bach's time. Despite the work's universal popularity with organists and the public, perhaps influenced by its appearance in such classic movies as the "Phantom of the Opera" and "Twenty Thousand Leagues Under the Sea," some scholars have doubted that it was written by Bach. From start to finish, many musical details seem uncharacteristic of him. For example, the opening flourish in octaves is unusual, and the final cadence of the fugue (the "Amen" cadence that we have met many times before) is unique because the last chord remains minor. No copy in

Bach's own handwriting survives to prove that he was indeed its composer, but that is true of many of his works. It may seem surprising that after two hundred years, historians still are not sure about the authenticity of some works. Research continues. In music, as in any field of inquiry, the last word is yet to be said.

 CD2

(0:00)

1   m1   The Toccata begins (ex. 31.6) with an ornament, a type of figure

[20]   called a **mordent,** consisting of: note, down a step, back up to the original note. It is followed by a down-the-scale figure. The opening passage ends on a dramatic chord constructed one note at a time, then resolved.

Example 31.6

(0:39)

2   m4   Fast triplet figures occupy the player until another dramatic chord

[21]   interrupts and the passage concludes.

(1:13)

3   m12   A contrasting section begins, which might be played to highlight

[22]   possible echo effects. It ends with that same dramatic chord.

(2:03)

4   m22   Quick broken chords race down the pitch spectrum and back up,

[23]   leading to an ending in which the pedal division of the organ is featured in a brief solo.

The fugue continues immediately with a lengthy subject in uniformly quick notes. Some elements of the fugue are untypical of Bach, such as the eventual entry of the subject as a pedal solo. An unusual amount of free material separates some entries, including flourishes for the hands that cry out for echo treatment. For the conclusion, the fugue style vanishes altogether, replaced by the show-off, almost willful nature of the opening toccata.

In the Baroque period, the **cantata** was a relatively short (roughly a half-hour), composite work in several movements, for voices with instrumental support. While secular cantatas existed, our focus is on those composed for the church.

Bach: *Wachet auf, ruft uns die Stimme* (Cantata No. 140)

Bach's church cantatas, each a sermon in music, relate to particular days in the Lutheran church calendar, in the same way that the items in the Proper of the Catholic Mass are "appropriate" to specific days. Composed in 1731, this cantata is frequently sung today in church and in concert performance. Three of its movements are based on a hymn text and tune dating from 1597. In each of these movements, Bach treats the chorale tune differently. The remaining movements include recitatives and duets, which are elements borrowed from opera.

A four-part choir of soprano, alto, tenor, and bass is supported by strings and oboes. A French horn duplicates the soprano line in the first movement, and the bassoon reinforces the bass line. In a church setting, an organ for basso continuo is appropriate, of course.

The text of this cantata deals with the parable of the wise and the foolish virgins. Representing Christian believers, the wise virgins were prepared to meet the bridegroom (Christ) with oil in their lamps. (Through lack of forethought, the lamps of the foolish virgins had gone out.) Reflecting the generally cheerful character of the text, the three movements that are based on the chorale are in major. The form of the chorale melody itself (ex. 31.7) is a venerable one, the "bar" form, AAB. Each of the movements based on the chorale follows this same form.

Example 31.7

The eyebrow-shaped symbols above the music of example 31.7 are **fermatas**. They indicate a possible prolonged duration. They are placed in chorales at ends of phrases. At the end of the second staff of this chorale is a **repeat sign** (a thick and a thin line paired with two dots). It instructs the performers to go back to the beginning and perform the music again.

PART FOUR THE BAROQUE

(0:00)
1

24

Recalling the style of a concerto grosso, this cantata begins with an extended movement in ritornello form. In a dignified triple meter, the orchestral ritornello contains at least three ideas. First comes a dotted-rhythm pattern, alternating between strings and oboes, then a syncopated figure, also alternating, and finally fast scale passages. As the voices enter, they are accompanied by ritornello material. Sopranos sing the chorale in long notes. Under them, the remaining voices sing animated polyphonic lines, freely derived from fragments of the chorale tune.

Movement I: Wachet auf, ruft uns die Stimme (6:51) (28)

(0:33)
2

25

Wachet auf, ruft uns die Stimme	Awake, call to us the voices
Der Wächter sehr hoch auf der Zinne,	of watchmen from the high tower.
Wach auf, du Stadt Jerusalem!	Awake, you town of Jerusalem!

(1:44)
3

26

The ritornello returns, as in item 1. The next stanza is set to the music of item 2.

(2:15)
4

27

Mitternacht heisst diese Stunde;	Midnight is the hour.
Sie rufen uns mit hellem Munde;	They call to us with clear voices:
Wo seid ihr klugen Jungfrauen?	Where are you, wise virgins?

(3:27)
5

28

Again the ritornello separates the stanzas and returns in fragments thereafter.

(3:50)
6

29

Wohl auf, der Bräutgam kömmt,	Be happy, the Bridegroom comes.
Steht auf, die Lampen nehmt! Alleluja!	Get up, your lamps take. Hallelujah!
Macht euch bereit Zu der Hochzeit,	Make yourselves ready for the wedding.
Ihr müsset ihm entgegengehn!	You must go to meet him.

(6:15)

7   As in a concerto grosso, a complete statement of the ritornello
     rounds off the movement.

30   CD2

Movement IV: *Zion*   (0:00)
hört die Wächter   1a   Strings in unison play a flowing melody almost continually, which
singen   functions as a ritornello. The strong supporting bass line moves for
(3:59) 29   31   the most part in even note values, creating two-part polyphony.
                           When the unison voices of the tenor section enter (1b), singing the
                           chorale tune with some tiny embellishments, the result is a trio, a
                           favorite polyphonic Baroque texture.

(0:41)

1b   Zion hört die Wächter singen,   Zion hears the watchmen
                                                  singing.

      Das Herz tut ihr vor Freuden   Her heart is, for joy, springing.
         springen,
      Sie wachet und steht eilend auf.   She wakes and rises quickly.

(1:08)

2a   As the tenors complete their stanza, the string melody begins a
      restatement of the music of 1a.

32

(1:48)

2b   Ihr Freund kommt von Himmel   Her Friend comes from heaven,
         prächtig,
      Von Gnaden stark, von   With grace, strong in truth.
         Wahrheit mächtig,
      Ihr Licht wird hell, ihr Stern   Her light is bright; her star
         geht auf.   shines.

(2:14)

3a   Again the tenors complete their stanza and leave the string melody
      exposed.

33

(2:39)

3b   As the tenors begin the third stanza of the chorale, Bach changes his
      pattern slightly. The chorale phrases here are shorter; the
      instrumental lines separating these phrases are longer.

      Nun komm, du werte Kron,   Now come, Thou worthy crown.
      Herr Jesu, Gottes Sohn,   Lord Jesus, God's son.
      Hosianna!   Hosanna!
      Wir folgen all   We follow
      Zum Freudensaal   To the joyful hall
      Und halten mit das Abendmahl.   And observe the Lord's Supper.

When Bach wanted to publish some of his music toward the end of his life, he arranged this movement as a chorale prelude for organ called *Wachet Auf* (often translated as "Sleepers Awake!"). It is the first of the six so-called Schübler chorales. His method could hardly have been more logical: he set the string melody for the right hand, the chorale tune for the left hand, and the bass line for the pedal. Omitted, of course, is the harmony implied by the basso continuo.

This homophonic setting of the chorale as a four-part congregational hymn is the simplest one and the most sublime. Sopranos sing the notes of the original chorale accompanied by alto, tenor, and bass lines written by Bach. All voices are duplicated by the supporting instruments. Bach's richly harmonized result is a standard in most modern hymnals.

Movement VII: *Gloria sei dir gesungen (1:42)* ㉚

 CD2

(0:00)
1

34

Gloria sei dir gesungen	Gloria be sung to you
Mit Menschen- und englischen Zungen,	With men's and angel's tongues,
Mit Harfen und mit Zimbeln schon.	With harps and beautiful cymbals.

(0:31)
2

35

Von zwölf Perlen sind die Pforten	Twelve pearls are the gates
An deiner Stadt; wir sind Konsorten	At your city; we are consorts
Der Engel hoch um deinen Thron.	Of the angels high above your throne.

(1:00)
3

36

Kein Aug hat je gespürt,	No eye has ever seen,
Kein Ohr hat je gehört	No ear has ever heard,
Solche Freude, des sind wir froh,	Such wondrous joy that we delight in,
Io, io, ewig in dulci jubilo.	Io, io, evermore in dulci jubilo.

The Classic Period

32 INTRODUCING THE CLASSIC PERIOD (1750–1825)

PREVIEW   The Classic period covers a relatively short span of years, with the American and French Revolutions dominating the historical background. Three prominent composers occupy us in this period— composers whose life spans and working conditions allow for interesting comparisons. Again we relate the characteristics of sound and the elements of music to this period.

The words "classic" and "classical" have several meanings. "Classical music" in ordinary language is a general label for the opposite of "popular music." "Classic" may also refer to a lasting model of excellence, as in a "classic" automobile— something timeless, something always in fashion. Then there is a usage of "classic" as opposed to "romantic," to describe two opposing tendencies which occur throughout art history: the one characterized by stability, clarity, balance, objectivity, and moderation, and the other associated with unrest, exaggeration, experimentation, and subjectivity. When we refer here to a **Classic period** with a capital C, we mean the years 1750 to 1825, although these other meanings of "classic" may have some application as well.

A dictionary definition of "classic" relates it to the art of ancient Greece and Rome. The mid-eighteenth century saw a renewed interest in antiquity. Archeologists excavated the ruins of Pompeii; sculptors used classical statues as a basis for their figures; painters portrayed Greek or Roman subject matter. Since little music survived from antiquity, some other justification for applying the term to music was needed. In looking back at the late eighteenth century, nineteenth-century musicians detected a similarity between the balance, the clear proportions, and the disciplined look of Greek art and the elegant proportions in the music of Haydn and Mozart. So they called that music "Classic." Whether or not this is an appropriate term for Beethoven's music as well is still open to debate. He remained committed to the general Classic principles, but some historians want nonetheless to place him with the nineteenth-century Romantics.

The major composers of the Classic period lived in or near the city of Vienna, the present capital of Austria, then and now a thriving center of commerce and art. The center of the mighty Hapsburg Empire, a crossroads city, Vienna was constantly affected by every European conflict. It was also the place to hear the various national styles of music. Because of the city's importance, this era is often called the "Viennese Classic period."

Since J. S. Bach died in 1750, that is a logical year to *end* the Baroque. Well before 1750, however, new trends had made it possible for critics to claim that Bach's music was old-fashioned. All the arts should be entertaining, or so a younger generation maintained. Symptomatic of this new emphasis is a definition of music by the historian Charles Burney: "the art of pleasing by the succession and combination of agreeable sounds."

Some historians find a need to place a **preclassic** or transition period between the Baroque and a full-blown Classic era. One label for this intermediary time span is taken from a development in French art of this time, **Rococo.** The term refers to shells and shell-form that furnished the principal motifs of Rococo art. A lighter, "prettier," more decorative form of expression was cultivated in music as well as art.

Just as Baroque and early Classic overlap, so do Classic and Romantic at the other end of the time span. Romantic tendencies were already stirring in the early 1800s. Indeed, some historians, contending that Classic and Romantic periods form one continuous era, refuse to set any boundary year between them. Many, however, focusing on Beethoven's death in 1827, find a certain logic in rounding off that boundary at 1825.

A

By the Classic period, the intense religious conflicts of the Baroque era had subsided. Agnosticism flourished, as trumpeted by such writers as the French philosopher François Voltaire (1694–1778) and the Swiss-born political writer Jean Jacques Rousseau [pronounced roo-SO] (1712–78). The English poet and artist William Blake (1757–1827) spoke for those outraged by agnosticism when he wrote:

Historical
Background

> Mock on, mock on, Voltaire, Rousseau:
> Mock on, mock on, 'tis all in vain!
> You throw the sand against the wind,
> And the wind blows it back again.

A faith in human *reason* as the best guide to human behavior was the basis for the *Enlightenment* (c. 1687–1789), an important eighteenth-century intellectual movement. Rationalism, skepticism, and a confidence that social injustice could be corrected were characteristic of Enlightenment thought. The Hapsburg Emperor Joseph II, who reigned from 1780 to 1790, personified the enlightened, liberal monarch. Enlightenment philosophy fueled the American Revolution, with its ideals of "life, liberty, and the pursuit of happiness." Indeed, the author of the Declaration of Independence, Thomas Jefferson (1743–1826), third American president, provides a splendid example of Classic ideals. Scholar, architect, statesman, writer, he was musically trained as well. His self-designed home in Virginia (Monticello) is a monument of Classic architecture, a revival of the Italian Renaissance style.

The beginnings of the *Industrial Revolution* appear in the Classic era. The steam engine, the cotton gin, Franklin's experiments with electricity—these and many other developments eventually transformed our material lives.

Taking inspiration from the American Revolution, the *French Revolution,* which erupted in 1789, had a tremendous impact on Europe. Society was traumatized as Louis XVI, Marie Antoinette, and many aristocrats in French society went to the guillotine. A rising middle class gained power. The reaction to the chaos of revolution thrust Napoleon (1769–1821) to center stage. Soon he had embroiled most of Europe in bloody wars.

B

Classic Composers

Haydn and Mozart perfected the mature Classic style and Beethoven vastly extended it. Their lives invite comparison, for they demonstrate the changing position of musicians in society during this period. At its outset, composers functioned within the **patronage system.** Either they were hired servants of a noble family, for whom they wrote and performed new music to be heard by an invited audience of aristocrats, or they were church musicians. By the end of this period, the composer had become a free-lance artist who composed because he or she felt an inner need. The music was heard and appreciated by a large public. For the first time in history, the idea arose that music did not have to serve a functional purpose; it could exist for its own sake.

Besides the three giants just mentioned, a number of "others" deserve to be better known by the general public. Two were sons of J. S. Bach. Carl (or Karl) Philipp Emanuel Bach (1714–88) was associated with the court of Frederick the Great of Prussia. Johann Christian Bach (1735–82) worked in London, where he encountered and influenced the child Mozart. (London was one of the many stops on the Mozart family tours.) Christoph Gluck (1714–87), though German born, drew on Italian and French influences as he developed a new type of opera that profoundly affected later composers, especially Mozart, Berlioz, and Wagner.

The turmoil of revolution and war naturally affected music. Fewer kings and aristocrats could support musical establishments. On the other hand, a rising middle class created a growing audience which paid for admission to concert halls. Indeed, one of the Enlightenment ideals proclaimed that culture belonged to everyone, not just to the nobility. Ultimately, the concert hall became the center of musical life. Public balls needed dance music, and outdoor entertainment called for light-hearted music with titles such as Serenade, Divertimento, and Cassation. The middle class wanted music lessons for its children and relatively simple music suitable for amateurs. Playing piano duets or singing songs provided home entertainment in Classic society, somewhat analogous to television viewing today. Even the major composers we study did not scorn to supply these demands.

While Catholic and Protestant churches alike conservatively perpetuated the musical practices of the Baroque period, the dying of religious fervor was accompanied by a decline in the amount of attention that composers gave to religious music. Even though Haydn and Mozart were both practicing Catholics who wrote monumental examples of sacred music, their secular music took much more of their time. And Beethoven, something of a free-thinker, wrote little church music, although his *Missa Solemnis* towers over most other Mass settings.

C

1. The *pitch* spectrum continued to expand in both directions, a development that can be seen most easily in the keyboard instruments we describe. Tuning in equal temperament and standardization of pitch, both begun in the Baroque era, were gradually accepted. Although in Baroque music the "outside" lines of bass and soprano receive the emphasis, Classic music shows a more even distribution over the entire pitch spectrum.

The Characteristics of Sound in the Classic Era

2. More *dynamic* indications appeared in Classic music. Instead of the terraced dynamics of the Baroque, composers began to supply directions for *gradual* changes in volume, using the words "crescendo" and "decrescendo" and the special signs for them. Also new was the concept of a sudden, strong accent: **sforzando** (abbreviated sfz). The interest in gradual changes of dynamics affected even the conservative world of church music. Builders began supplying organs with shutters, like giant Venetian blinds, which enclosed some, though never all, of the pipes. As the organist opens or closes the shutters, gradual changes in volume result because more, or less, sound can emerge.

3. Composers showed an increasing interest in *tone color,* as new instruments came into being, older ones changed, and instrumental groups became standardized. During the Classic era the piano became the all-purpose keyboard instrument, ultimately displacing the harpsichord. The earliest piano builders, around 1710, had attempted to overcome the dynamic inflexibility of the harpsichord and the limited volume of the clavichord. Early pianos were wooden-framed, with thin strings and hard, leather-covered hammers that *struck* the strings instead of plucking them as do the plectra of a harpsichord. (Because hammers strike strings, the piano is essentially a percussion instrument.) The tone of the early piano has a bright, almost clattery sound, one that dies away or "decays" quickly. The pianist varied dynamics by changing finger pressure, a capability that gave the instrument its full name: "pianoforte." In other words, it could easily go from soft to loud. The pitch range of early pianos was about five octaves, like the harpsichord. It gradually expanded to six and one-half octaves by the end of Beethoven's life.

The piano continued to evolve in the Romantic period. Today's piano, therefore, is not at all the instrument for which the Classic composers wrote so sensitively. Recently, some pianists, as a result of their studies of performance practice, have come to prefer a *Classic piano* for Classic music. Such pianists use the term **fortepiano** for their authentic instruments or reproductions.

The early forms of the piano are smaller than today's grand piano. "Fortepiano" is the label pianists currently apply to surviving instruments or replicas of them. (Courtesy of the Metropolitan Museum of Art, New York, Crosby Brown Collection of Musical Instruments.)

Another major difference in sound occurred as composers gradually did away with the basso continuo, although its use continued in opera recitatives well into the nineteenth century. Instead of expecting a keyboard player to improvise a chordal background, composers wrote all the notes they wanted played. Standardized instrumental ensembles developed, allowing a composer to write string quartets or symphonies and know that in all music centers an appropriate group could play the music.

During the Classic era, the term **chamber music,** originally intended to distinguish music played in private households from church music, acquired the meaning we give it today: small instrumental ensembles, with only one player for each part. It is an intimate, often intricate art, distinct from the broader symphonic style. Since each player is alone on his or her part, unlike the situation in orchestral music where several performers are required for each string part, no conductor is needed. In a form of musical democracy, all the players help make musical decisions. (Traditionally, orchestral conductors wield absolute power.) Under eighteenth-century patronage, chamber music was the delight of a relatively small audience listening in "chambers," their private drawing rooms. Today chamber music is generally heard in larger-than-ideal halls simply because a large audience is necessary to pay the bills.

The most important of the chamber music groups is the **string quartet** (or just "quartet"), which consists of two violins, a viola, and a cello. While it might seem reasonable to expect a bass and only one violin, the bass is not flexible enough to converse on equal terms with the violin. The components of a **string trio** are just what you would expect: one each of violin, viola, and cello. But a **piano trio** does

A string quartet plus a piano is called a "piano quintet." This chamber music group, shown here rehearsing, sounds its best in a home environment rather than a large concert hall. (Courtesy of IMA Concerts, Los Angeles.)

not employ three pianos; it is composed of a violin, a cello, and one piano. **A piano quartet** uses a string trio plus a piano. Other possible combinations involve an instrument added to a string trio or quartet. In such cases, that instrument is named in the title, as for example a **flute quartet.**

A standardized pattern for the **orchestra** emerged in the Classic era, with the four sections described in Chapter 3. The *string* section was (and still is) routinely grouped into first and second violins, violas, cellos, and basses. (Incidentally, though playing "second fiddle" in life means taking a secondary role, second violin parts are just as necessary as first.) Exactly how many musicians were expected for each part is not always known, but the orchestra in the German town of Mannheim in 1756 included twenty violins and four each of violas, cellos, and basses. This, however, was an exceptional orchestra in both size and reputation. The *woodwinds* employed pairs of flutes, oboes, clarinets, and bassoons; the *brass* section included pairs of trumpets and French horns. The one *percussion* instrument was the timpani. Since orchestral string sections are considerably larger today, conductors reduce the number of string players when playing Classic music if they wish to approximate the balance between strings and winds that the composers intended. An orchestra with a reduced number of string players is sometimes called a **chamber orchestra.**

Regardless of the actual number of performers, in Classic music the strings tend to dominate the sound and play almost constantly. The woodwind resources add variety, especially when themes are repeated. The brass section is usually reserved for cadences and climaxes, with possible reinforcement by timpani.

The one member of the string section in today's orchestra who draws some individual attention is the **concertmaster,** the principal first violinist, who is the last to walk onstage before the conductor's entrance. He or she may receive a certain amount of applause before signaling the oboe player to sound the "440 A" for the final round of tuning. (The concertmaster has many responsibilities behind the scenes as well, sometimes functioning as an assistant conductor.)

During the Classic era, a number of changes were made in the construction of instruments and in their employment in the orchestra. *Woodwind* instruments became easier to play as more keys were added to control finger holes. The flute vanquished the recorder in the same way that the piano defeated the harpsichord. One of Mozart's favorite instruments, the **clarinet,** won a permanent place in the orchestra. The clarinet's range is unusually wide, with a marked variation in tone quality from low to high. Impudent, almost squeaky in its highest tones, its bottom range is smooth and rich. Beethoven added the **piccolo** and the **contrabassoon** to the orchestra. The name "piccolo" is derived from the Italian "flauto *piccolo*" (little flute). Half the size of the flute, the piccolo plays an octave higher. Small but mighty, it can penetrate the sound of the entire orchestra. In contrast, the contrabassoon, which plays an octave lower than the bassoon, is not easy to hear in the orchestra. It is so long that its tube is folded back upon itself.

The role of the *brass* instruments changed in the Classic era. No longer did the trumpet explore the virtuoso heights; parts became simpler. Late in the period the trombone was added to the orchestra. Though the timpani continued to be the orchestra's only *percussion* instrument in regular use, cymbals, bass drum, and triangle appear in a few Classic scores, often to produce a pseudo-Turkish sound. (The Viennese never forgot that a Turkish army had actually surrounded Vienna in 1683. They seemed to enjoy parodies of their enemies' music.)

The concern for authentic performance has recently expanded from a focus on Baroque and earlier music to Classic music. Performing it with reduced-sized orchestras is by now a standard practice. Just as a few pianists are accepting the fortepiano, some directors have created ensembles in which players perform on antique Classic instruments or reproductions of them. A new clarity and sparkle result.

D

The Elements of Music in the Classic Era

    1. *Rhythm* patterns are seldom as consistent within movements as they were in the Baroque period; instead, *contrasting* rhythm patterns help realize the Classic ideal of variety. Tempo and meter usually remain constant; what a listener might interpret as a change in tempo is more likely a change in rhythm pattern.

2. Classic *melodies* are often singable *tunes*. Some sound as if they could be folk songs, although they usually are not. Unlike the complex, richly ornamented lines of Baroque melodies, they tend to fall into clearly marked, symmetrical phrases. Melody moves into the forefront of musical elements. Haydn is reported to have said, "If you want to know whether a melody is really beautiful, sing it without accompaniment."

3. Classic *harmony* perpetuates the same basic chords that the Baroque knew. In many respects Classic harmony is simpler than was Bach's. Chromatic chords (chords based on tones of the chromatic scale) do appear from time to time in Classic music, attracting attention with their appealing richness.

The chords of Classic harmony tend to change less rapidly than they did in the Baroque period, contributing to a greater sense of stability. The biggest difference in harmony between the two eras, however, comes from the fact that Classic composers employed the *major mode* so consistently that works in the minor mode bear a special emotional quality. Mozart, for example, wrote only two of his twenty-three piano concertos and two of his forty-one symphonies in minor. Besides the *Symphony No. 40* in G minor that we study, there is also an early one in this same key, number 25. It provided the music with which the Mozart-based film "Amadeus" begins.

4. *Texture* changes dramatically in this era: now *homophony is standard and polyphony is the exception*. Although Haydn, Mozart, and Beethoven were masters of counterpoint, their contrapuntal passages make contrasting statements in an otherwise homophonic work. The homophony that we found in Renaissance music arose from similar rhythmic motion in all parts. A second type of homophony, in which a melody is clearly set off from its subordinate and contrasting accompaniment, figures prominently in the Classic era. We still find this texture the norm in music. For example, a beginning pianist takes it for granted that the right hand will play the melody and the left hand will accompany it with chords in some fashion. One particular Classic accompaniment style spread so widely that it acquired a name, **Alberti bass,** from the name of a minor Italian composer, Domenico Alberti (c.1710–40), who used it constantly. Essentially a form of broken chord, the tones are played in this order: lowest, highest, middle, highest.

5. Some of the *forms* of Classic music will seem familiar because they were Baroque staples. We shall make return visits to theme-and-variation and binary form, but rondo will be new. Ternary form, or ABA, is present in every era. Most important is sonata-form, complicated enough to require its own chapter.

In general, Classic composers help a listener follow their forms by clearly separating their subdivisions. Often they are contrasting, with tiny pauses articulating the sections. Repeated-chord cadences add emphasis to the endings, whether of a section or of a whole movement.

Though this painting by the English caricaturist Thomas Rowlandson (1756–1827) is entitled *Concerto Spirituale,* the ferocity with which the performers attack their instruments makes a joke of the title. (Courtesy of Huntington Library, San Marino, CA.)

CHAPTER

THE SONATA CONCEPT 33

PREVIEW   "Sonata" merits an individual chapter because the term can mean several things. It *may* refer to **sonata-form,** a form that evolved in the Classic period. Its three main sections: exposition, development, and recapitulation, are outlined below. Two other sections are not always present: introduction and coda. "Sonata" may simply be part of a work's title, with no structural implications. Multimovement works such as symphonies, which include at least one movement in sonata-form, make up an overall design that demands attention.

EXPOSITION
1. Theme I, in tonic key
2. Transition
3. Theme II, in new key
4. Closing theme, in the new key

DEVELOPMENT
Many keys
A variable number of subsections

RECAPITULATION
1. Theme I, in tonic key
2. Transition
3. Theme II, in tonic key
4. Closing theme, in the tonic key

A

The Three Sections of Sonata-Form

Sonata-form, which emerged in the mid-1700s as an outgrowth of the binary and ternary forms cultivated in the Baroque period, caught on with composers of all nationalities. A crowning achievement of the Classic period, it allows for both unity and variety in a dramatic way. Extraordinarily flexible, its outlines have helped shape countless works. With modifications, it remains in favor to the present day. The outline given above might create the mistaken impression that writing sonatas is as simple as following a cooking recipe. Just as chefs may rely on a basic recipe yet add their own creative touches, composers adapt sonata-form to their own individual styles. No two movements in sonata-form are exactly alike.

   1.   Exposition. The main themes are "exposed" here.

   a.   Theme I (it might be better to say "first theme *group,*" because several musical ideas may be announced). This theme unfolds in the *tonic* or "home" key, the key referred to in the title of the complete work, as in Mozart's symphony in

"G minor," or Haydn's quartet in "C." Seldom is the theme "tuneful," but it is often based on a distinctive motive.

b. **Transition.** Composers frequently conceal the beginning of this section. Just as often they make it obvious with a change to a more vigorous or brilliant style. Its most important function is to *modulate,* or change key. Some writers refer to the "tensions" of this area, caused by a sense of changing keys as a new key is prepared for Theme II.

c. **Theme II.** The second theme is *always* in a different key. In works in major keys, Theme II occurs in the **dominant**—that key whose tonic is the fifth tone of the scale of the original key. In works in minor keys, Theme II occurs in the **relative major**—that key whose tonic is the third tone of the original scale. Since that is a major key, the major mode of Theme II will then provide a contrast with the minor mode of Theme I.

Conventional wisdom long maintained that the two themes must differ markedly in character, and that there should be changes of instruments, rhythm patterns, pitch and dynamic levels, and the like. It is true that Theme I often tends to be more forthright and direct than Theme II, perhaps simply to catch the listener's attention at the beginning. But these contrasts are not fundamental to sonata-form; indeed, Themes I and II can share motives. It is the contrast of keys that is essential.

d. **Closing theme.** This theme continues in the key of Theme II and confirms it. As in the transition, the beginning of this area is often not obvious. Composers frequently recall here some of the musical ideas or motives first heard in Theme I.

In works by Classic period composers, the end of the exposition is usually easy to sense, punctuated as it is with repeated chords and a tiny pause. By placing a repeat sign here, composers specified that the entire exposition should be repeated. Even though a return to the original key results, there is seldom any modulation to prepare this change. As a listener, you may find that performers, to save time, have decided *not* to repeat the exposition. The music then proceeds directly on to the development. You cannot know in advance whether or not this will happen. Performers who strive for authenticity can be expected to observe the repeat sign.

2. **Development.** Although each one is unique, a development section typically falls into perhaps three or four subsections. In each subsection, the composer works out the materials in some particular way. Because there are few predictable features (other than frequent changes of key), you cannot expect an outline of the development section as for the exposition and recapitulation. Any of the materials presented in the exposition may return, often in new ways as themes are broken down into motives and motives are altered and recombined. Other common features of Classic period development sections are polyphony and the exploration of the minor mode. On occasion, completely new material may appear. Modulation is frequent, and much activity seems to be going on. The sense of "tension" associated earlier with the transition is especially marked here. As the development nears its end, the composer customarily prepares for the recapitulation and a return of the original key by emphasizing the fifth tone of that key (the dominant) in a passage called **dominant preparation.**

3. Recapitulation. In ordinary language, people refer to a "recap" as a condensation of something already said. But in sonata-form the recapitulation is *not* at all a summary. It is a *restatement* of the exposition, with alterations (indicated below) that are necessary because the keys change.

a. Theme I. As in the exposition, this section is in the tonic key and sounds much the same as before, although there may be some subtle changes in tone colors. Now that the tonic key has been restored, the rest of the movement stays in that key. Writers often compare this portion of sonata-form with the effect of returning home after a journey.

b. Transition. In pitch levels at least, this section *must* be changed from its counterpart in the exposition, because no modulation is necessary. A master composer can generate remarkable tension in a transition section despite the fact that it ends up in the same key in which it began.

c. Theme II. This section occurs here in the tonic key, which produces at a minimum a different pitch level. Differences are more pronounced at this point for sonata-form movements in the minor mode because the composer has a choice: Theme II may now appear in the minor mode, or remain in the major mode as in its first appearance in the exposition.

d. Closing theme. This section is similar to its counterpart in the exposition, except for the necessary key adjustments. In some Classic works the composers indicated that the development and recapitulation sections *together* should be repeated. It is less common today for performers to observe the development-plus-recapitulation repeat.

B

1. Introduction. While most sonata-form movements start right out with the exposition and its Theme I, some are prefaced with an introduction in a slow tempo. The tempo terms that identify movements always show this, as for example: "Largo—allegro," with largo the tempo of the introduction. The exposition begins with the allegro. Slow introductions serve at least two principal purposes: dramatic, to attract the audience's attention; musical, to allow the composer to begin the allegro in ways otherwise not possible. While you will probably find no obvious thematic resemblance between the introduction and the rest of the movement, many subtle relationships often exist.

2. Coda. As with introductions, so too with codas. After the recapitulation is complete, composers frequently add a coda or a concluding section. Codas can serve to reinforce the sense of closure. They vary widely in size, from a few punctuating chords to a massive section comparable to another development. A coda might contain something new; more often it restates what has already been heard.

Additional Features of Sonata-Form

C

Sonata: The Title and the Form

1. As early as the mid 1500s, the word "sonata," deriving from *sonare* (to sound), meant "sound-piece." It identified instrumental music as opposed to vocal music. A sonata, then, is an instrumental work for one or two players, in more than one movement. There are sonatas for piano alone and sonatas for a melody-playing instrument, such as violin or flute, with a keyboard accompaniment. Usually both instruments have equally demanding parts and the two performers should share equal billing. The title of "sonata" is no guarantee of "sonata-form." For example, no movement of a Baroque "trio sonata" could be in sonata-form, since that form did not yet exist.

2. Some writers like the term "sonata-*allegro* form." This can be misleading because sonata-form movements in slow tempo abound.

3. Works that are not titled "sonata" at all are shaped by sonata-form, as in numerous Classic period Mass movements and opera numbers. Countless movements in sonata-form can be found in music written for chamber music groups such as trios, string quartets and quintets; orchestral works such as symphonies (hence the term "symphony orchestra") and concertos for soloists and orchestra; and in many independent, single-movement works, such as overtures.

D

The Complete Multimovement Work

No generally accepted label serves to identify the pattern formed by an *entire* three- or four-movement work that includes at least one movement in sonata-form. Especially in the Classic era, compositions with differing titles, such as "sonata," "symphony," "concerto," and "quartet," share a general pattern of tempos, forms, and qualities, as shown in the following outline and discussion.

Movement:	FIRST	SECOND	THIRD	FOURTH
Tempos:	fast	slow	"minuet tempo"	fast
Forms:	sonata-form	ABA, theme-and-variations, rondo, sonata-form	minuet-trio-minuet	sonata-form, rondo, theme-and-variations, ABA
Qualities:	serious, dramatic	songlike	dance-related, in triple meter	serious, or "lighter"
Keys:	tonic	related or tonic	related or tonic	tonic

1. **First movement.** Allegro, in sonata-form. Often said to be serious, forceful, dramatic, grand, or brilliant. The most demanding of the four movements.

2. **Second movement.** Slower, perhaps adagio or at least andante. Possible forms include ternary and sonata-form, which we have met, and rondo and theme-and-variations, which we study in this period. Often songlike or lyrical, to contrast with the first movement, it relies less on developmental techniques.

3. **Third movement.** A dance-related movement in triple meter, most commonly a **minuet,** a favorite dance of the French aristocracy. (The spelling of "minuet" as "minuetto" or "menuet" varies with different nationalities.) In the Baroque period, dances had been grouped in suites. Perhaps retaining one stylized dance movement in the complete four-movement pattern was a bow to tradition. The tempo ranges from gracefully dignified to quite fast. Today, conductors differ remarkably in their choice of the "right" tempo for many minuets.

    Minuets usually consist of clear-cut phrases that fit the patterns dancers make as they go so-many-steps to the right, and then so-many-steps to the left. Customarily, the first third of the movement is clearly marked off as a minuet, cast in a binary form with each half repeated. A contrasting **trio** follows. Also in binary form and of similar length, it might as well be called a second minuet. The trio gets its name from the standard Baroque practice of scoring a second minuet for three players only. The lighter sound thus produced created a contrast to the first minuet. Although in most Classic trios the number of performers remains constant, other types of contrast arise. After the trio comes a return of the original minuet, typically performed without its internal repeats. At least, that has been the traditional practice. Citing authenticity, several recent performers are restoring such repeats.

    Some composers speeded up the minuet, turning it into a **scherzo.** The word literally means "joke," and scherzos characteristically exhibit a sense of humor, or at least a lighthearted quality.

4. **Fourth movement, or finale.** Allegro, in any of the forms listed for the second movement, with sonata-form and rondo the favorites. To achieve a "happy ending," the last movement is "lighter" than the first. Toward the end of the Classic period, a change in this expectation gradually occurred, with the last movement often the "heaviest"—a climax demanding a suitably emphatic conclusion.

    Possible variations in the multimovement pattern just outlined include a reversal of the order of movements two and three. Dispensing with the minuet, most concertos and sonatas consist of only three movements.

    In concerts, the performers usually pause briefly between the movements—long enough to turn pages or check their instruments. (This is *not* the time to applaud!) In some works, a transition connects a pair of movements, thus eliminating a pause, something we will see in Beethoven's *Symphony No. 5,* between the third and fourth movements.

Many scholars have sought to discover what makes the movements of a complete work hang together in spite of their obvious differences. While clear-cut thematic resemblances are seldom present in the Classic period, analysts can find subtle motivic relationships. Dealing with the obvious, the movements are clearly related by key. The first and last share the same tonic, even if the first is minor and the last major. At least one of the middle movements is in a **closely related key.** Keys are closely related if their scales have all but one of their pitches in common. Thus the key of C is closely related to the major keys of F and G, and the minor keys of D, E, and A.

We will meet several examples of complete multimovement works not only in the Classic period but in the Romantic era as well. The pattern is followed, with modifications, by several twentieth-century composers also.

JOSEPH HAYDN 34

PREVIEW   Born in Austria, Haydn, in an unusually long career, demonstrated the best qualities of the patronage system. He profited from his association with a wealthy, music-loving aristocratic family. His sense of humor found outlets in many "surprising" elements in his music. We focus on his instrumental music in theme-and-variation form.

(Franz) Joseph Haydn [pronounced HIGH-dn] (1732–1809) was born in an Austrian village to a working-class family who loved music and encouraged folk singing. His fine voice gave him the opportunity of becoming a choirboy in Vienna, where he acquired most of his musical education. While he could play the violin and keyboard instruments, he candidly admitted that he was a virtuoso on none of them.

Haydn spent almost thirty years as music director for the wealthy and noble Esterházy family in Hungary. Their lavish palace had rooms for concert and opera performances. Family members were enthusiastic performers, as well as listeners. Their estate was isolated geographically, but a constant stream of visitors kept Haydn informed of the latest trends. In fact, the isolation proved to be an advantage for Haydn, for as he said, "there was no one around to mislead and harass me, and so I was forced to become original." The situation allowed him to experiment and learn from his own efforts.

Haydn's position was that of a well-paid, highly honored servant. His contract, signed in 1761, stated that he should appear in a uniform, including "white stockings, white linen, powdered, and with either a pigtail or a tiewig." He promised in dealing with the musicians who reported to him to "abstain from undue familiarity and from vulgarity in eating, drinking, and conversation," to report daily to find out "whether his Highness is pleased to order a performance of the orchestra." And so on . . . Haydn might have chafed privately at the restrictions of his employment, but on the whole the patronage system worked very well for him. His music was given an immediate, competent performance for an appreciative audience—something of great value to any composer.

Haydn is shown here rehearsing with his musicians for a chamber music concert.

As a result of the conditions under which Haydn worked, he wrote much music that is seldom heard today. For example, his Highness was an amateur musician who played a string instrument called the baryton, now obsolete. Similar to the cello in range, it is unique in having extra strings, like guitar strings, which are plucked. Haydn found it advisable to write large quantities of music for the baryton, tailoring it to fit his patron's technique. Many operas are in Haydn's list of works, because opera was an important part of the palace entertainment. After long neglect, they are currently experiencing a revival.

Upon his death in 1790, Prince Nikolaus Esterházy was succeeded by his son, who, not sharing the family interest in music, dismissed the orchestra. Though Haydn kept his title and salary, he was essentially retired. At last he was free to leave the palace, to travel, and to compose for new patrons and publishers all over Europe. Two trips to London were enormously successful, resulting in tributes on a scale new to him. Soon he established his own home in Vienna. He was a friend to Mozart, and as we shall see, something of a teacher for Beethoven. His fame spread; he was honored and universally acclaimed. When he died at age 77 in 1809, a memorial service for him attracted "the whole art-loving world of Vienna."

A big city by the standards of the time, the Vienna that Haydn knew was a center for the arts. This illustration shows it as it looked in 1779.

Even invading armies paused to honor him, for Napoleon ordered his troops to guard Haydn's home.

A

The "Surprises" in Haydn

While every creative artist's personality is reflected to some degree in his work, with Haydn this factor seems unusually important. Cheerful and friendly, he had a decided sense of humor. Evidence for this quality is found in many compositions, with the so-called *"Surprise" Symphony,* more soberly known as No. 94, in G, the best-known example. We will discuss its second movement. A striking example comes from the finale of his *"Joke" Quartet,* op. 33, no. 2. Only after six attempts does the movement finally quit, much to the relief of an audience waiting for the proper moment to applaud! A subtler humor can be found in the minuet of his *Symphony No. 65,* in A. It is moving along sedately in the ONE-two-three pattern that is expected for a minuet, when without warning the accents change: ONE-two-THREE-four. They soon revert to ONE-two-three. Because of the repetition patterns in a minuet, the listener has several chances to sort it all out. Of course, the casual hearer who is only aware of the overall sound of a piece will probably notice nothing out of the ordinary.

Even when Haydn's music cannot be considered particularly humorous, and this is true of the majority of the measures he penned, there is always the possibility of the musically unexpected. Perhaps the phrases will not come out even; tonalities may change dramatically. Paradoxically, you can expect to be surprised.

Haydn's Music

Haydn played a key role in the evolution of the **symphony,** a multimovement work for orchestra that is one of the most important developments of the Classic period. Many of his symphonies bear nicknames, such as "Clock," "Military," and "Drumroll," attached to them by publishers. Among his most celebrated early symphonies is the *"Farewell"* Symphony, No. 45, in the highly unusual (for its time) key of F-sharp minor. The ending is unique. Detailed instructions in the score tell the performers when to stop playing and leave the stage, mostly one by one. By the finale's end, only the conductor and two violinists remain on stage. (There was method in this apparent madness—Haydn was letting the Prince know that his musicians needed some time off to spend with their families. The ploy worked.)

His best-known symphonies are his last twelve, numbers 93 to 104, written for performances in London, the largest city in the world at the time and a thriving musical center. The impresario Johann Peter Salomon had encouraged Haydn to compose these works. For these reasons they are frequently referred to as the "London" or the "Salomon" symphonies. A concerto for trumpet and one for cello are full of his engaging tunes.

Haydn has been called the "father of the string quartet." He wrote at least sixty-eight quartets during his long creative life, greatly influencing Mozart, who in turn dedicated six quartets to Haydn. (Actually, in an exchange unique in music history, the two composers learned from each other.) The established string quartet groups of today look upon Haydn's quartets as the foundation for their repertoire. Haydn composed many works for other chamber music groups as well.

Haydn's six late, large-scale Masses, for soloists, chorus, and orchestra, are frequently performed in concerts today. Most of their movements have structures strikingly similar to the symphonies. Also popular are his two oratorios, *The Creation* and *The Seasons,* inspired by the example of Handel, whose works he had heard in London.

Haydn: *String Quartet in C,* op. 76, no. 3 ("Emperor")

Hungarian musicologist László Somfai is convinced that this quartet conveys a patriotic message, especially in the second movement, which is based on a theme that gives the quartet its "Emperor" nickname. The history of the tune (ex. 34.3) begins in 1797, when Haydn composed a song, "Gott erhalte Franz den Kaiser" (God preserve Franz, the Emperor), to be sung at a birthday celebration for the Emperor. This song, which quickly achieved "hit tune" status in Vienna, eventually became the Austrian national anthem.

The patriotic message is more subtly expressed in the first movement, which begins with the notes: G,E,F,D,C in the theme (ex. 34.1)—an anagram of the first five words of the Emperor's birthday song if one spells "Kaiser" as "Caesar." And the gypsylike episode in that movement (at item 3b in the guide) has its own nationalistic flavor.

Example 34.1

Turning to more prosaic matters, both the first and the fourth movements of this work are in sonata-form. As is often the case with Haydn's forms, they are not particularly easy to follow. While his expositions always include two different tonalities, a contrasting theme might not coincide with the second tonality. Instead, Haydn frequently restates motives from Theme I in a new guise when the new tonality is reached. What we might choose to call Theme II occurs later with contrasting motives. This practice proves that it might be better to refer to "theme groups" rather than "themes." Nor can you count on Haydn's pauses to identify a new section.

 CD2

(0:00, repeat 1:51)

1a   m1   All four instruments begin the Exposition playing Theme I (ex. 34.1) in rhythmic unison. Several contrasting ideas, including scale figures in dotted rhythms, follow immediately.

37

FIRST MOVEMENT: Allegro (6:38) ③⑴

(0:28, repeat 2:19)

1b   m13   A tiny pause is *not* the signal for Theme II; instead more development of Theme I motives occurs.

(1:01, repeat 2:43)

2a   m26   Theme II (ex. 34.2) arrives (without any signal), solidly in the dominant key and consistently *forte*.

38

Example 34.2

(1:16, repeat 3:07)

2b   m33   A soft interruption recalls Theme I motives.

(1:30, repeat 3:22)

2c   m38   With a sudden *forte*, Theme II returns as in item 2a. An extended cadence follows. If the Exposition is to be repeated, a soft, short transition occurs here.

(3:37)
3a m45 The Development begins softly, with viola and cello playing a version
of Theme I motives.
[39]

(4:26)
3b m65 Viola and cello accompany with a rustic, dronelike sound. Such
repeated tones are characteristic of the bagpipe or the hurdy-gurdy,
instruments of the common folk. The accents on weak beats here
recall the rhythms of gypsy bands. Haydn seldom quotes actual folk
tunes, but he does seem sympathetic to the "people."

(5:00)
4a m79 Theme I returns, as above, 1a, beginning the Recapitulation with a
sudden *forte*.
[40]

(5:37)
4b m94 A decided pause is the signal that Theme II is almost, but not quite,
ready to return.

(5:47)
5a m98 Theme II does return, again *forte,* now in the tonic, as expected.
Some unexpected pauses and changes of tempo then occur.
[41]

(5:25)
5b m115 A brief recall of Theme II concludes the movement.

The second movement is in a favorite Classic form: **theme-and-variations,** a
form based on varied restatements of a theme. Instead of the *continuous* variations
on a repeated bass line or a repeated chord pattern that Baroque composers cultivated, Classic composers were more apt to write *separate* variations on an easily
followed tune. That tune might be original, it might be a folk song, or it might be
another composer's work. Sometimes the source is identified in the title of the piece.
A good example is Mozart's set of variations on *Ah, vous dirai-je maman,* a melody
sounding very much like "Twinkle, Twinkle, Little Star." Of course, the specific
techniques of variation are limitless, since any of the musical elements can be
changed, but some techniques are standard:

1. *Rhythmic*: change of meter; change of tempo; alteration of rhythmic figures.
2. *Melodic*: adding, or removing, tones; changing register (moving melody to a higher
    or lower octave); extracting a motive from the melody.
3. *Harmonic*: change of mode; elaboration of basic harmony; change in accompanying
    figures; reduction of a passage to its chordal structure alone.
4. *Tone color*: changing instrumentation.
5. *Texture*: polyphonic imitation of a motive; adding countermelodies.

♫ CD2

This movement is in the closely related key of G major. Although the possibilities for varying the tune are endless, in this movement Haydn concentrated on the addition of countermelodies. The theme remains intact—perhaps out of respect for the Emperor? A scale line connecting the two playings of the last phrase is the only melodic change.

SECOND MOVEMENT: Poco adagio; cantabile (6:39) ㉜

(0:00)

1   m1 The first violin presents the "Emperor" melody, with simple supporting harmonies produced by the other instruments. This theme (ex. 34.3) consists of five phrases, each ending with a longer note value. Repetitions create a pattern of AABCC.

⌷42⌷

Example 34.3

(1:19)

2   m21 In Variation I, the second violin plays the theme while the first violin spins an elaborate countermelody around it. (Viola and cello rest.)

⌷43⌷

(2:27)

3   m41 The theme moves to the cello for Variation II; countermelodies are played above it.

⌷44⌷

(3:45)

4   m61 In Variation III the viola gets the theme. Now the countermelodies are more complex, with subtle syncopations. Perhaps it is evidence of the democratic nature in a Haydn string quartet that all four instruments have had a turn playing the melody.

CHAPTER 34 JOSEPH HAYDN   219

(4:58)
5   m81   The melody returns to the first violin in Variation IV. Some minor chords enrich the harmony. In the second phrase, all four parts play an octave higher than in the first. During the third phrase, the cello plays a pedal point.

(6:15)
6   m100   A soft, brief coda completes the movement.

The history of the "Emperor" tune continued after Haydn's lifetime. In 1922, the Germans adopted this tune to words beginning "Deutschland, Deutschland über alles." It is still sung today with yet another set of words. This melody also appears in hymnals (tune name of "Austrian hymn"), often sung to words beginning "Glorious Things of Thee are Spoken."

The quartet's third movement returns to the C major tonality. It is a standard minuet-trio-minuet, with both minuet and trio in binary form, as is traditional. The fourth movement, in presto tempo, begins in C minor, a "surprising" feature for a work that began in C major.

HAYDN: *Symphony No. 94 in G* ("Surprise")

This symphony, first performed in London in 1792 with great success, is in the standard four movements and employs what was a large orchestra for the time, including trumpets and timpani. The first movement, Adagio cantabile—Vivace assai, is in sonata-form, preceded by a slow introduction. The third movement is a minuet, with a tempo marking of Allegro molto and the last movement another sonata-form, marked Allegro di molto. These three movements are in the key of G; only the second movement changes key, to C.

   CD2

SECOND MOVEMENT: Andante
(6:22) �33

The theme of Haydn's Andante movement is original with him, though it sounds much like a folk tune. (Its first half strikingly resembles "Twinkle, Twinkle" in rhythm and in melodic curve.) The basic theme is in binary form, AABB, and the listener might expect that in each variation the sections would repeat more or less exactly, following the shape of the theme. But only in the first variation does this happen. The other three variations show different ways to handle the repeats. So, although there are (strictly speaking) only four variations, in fact many more techniques of variation occur. Haydn forecasts these changes in the theme itself, where the famous "surprise" chord provides a conspicuous example of a modified repeat of an A section. In the quartet movement just discussed, Haydn seemed content with a limited number of variation techniques; in this symphony movement he exploited a wide variety of possibilities.

(0:00)

1a   m1   Violins begin with section A of the theme (ex. 34.4). It is even in
rhythm and disjunct, moving at first up, then down.

48

Example 34.4

(0:17)

1b   m9   Section A is repeated, this time softer, with pizzicato
accompaniment. The "surprise" chord occurs at the end of this
section.

(0:33)

1c   m17   Section B contains a more elaborate melody (ex. 34.5) and ends with
a phrase that resembles the start of the theme.

Example 34.5

(0:50)

1d   m25   The repeat of section B is varied with the addition of flute and oboe
playing a duetlike countermelody.

(1:07)

2a   m33   Second violins begin the theme; soon a high countermelody in
quicker notes is played by first violins.

49

VARIATION I

(1:24)

   . . Item 2a is repeated exactly.

(1:41)

2b   m41   The B section of the theme receives the treatment just described in
item 2a.

(1:57)

   . . Item 2b is repeated exactly.

VARIATION II	(2:14)		
	3a	m49	A loud, unison treatment of the theme begins, in the minor mode. Soon the theme is further altered, as Haydn modulates to a major key (E-flat).

50

(2:30)

. . Item 3a is repeated exactly.

(2:46)

3b   m57   Instead of proceeding to the B section of the theme, Haydn develops motives from the beginning. Rushing passages in the strings add excitement. This section ends with a downward line for violins alone that returns to the calm of the beginning.

VARIATION III

(3:22)

4a   m75   As the major mode returns, oboe plays a variation of the theme in which four quick notes substitute for the original two. Strings accompany in the same rhythm.

51

(3:39)

4b   m83   The ideas in item 4b are abandoned in favor of a new variation technique for section A. Here, violins play the original theme as oboe and flute play another duetlike countermelody.

(3:55)

4c   m91   The melody of the B section receives the treatment just used in item 4b.

(4:13)

4d   m99   Item 4c is repeated, with the brief addition of French horns the only new element in the repetition.

VARIATION IV

(4:29)

5a   m107   Much louder, this military-sounding variation features the addition of notes in quick values to the theme, with a heavy, off-beat accompaniment that creates a syncopated effect.

52

(4:46)

5b   m115   As in Variation III, the initial ideas are soon abandoned. Now the violins play a legato, soft elaboration of the theme in a dotted rhythm. The accompaniment on offbeats continues, but lightly.

(5:03)

5c m123 The violins continue the style of item 5b, using the B section melody.

(5:20)

5d m131 For the repeat of the B section, Haydn returns to the bold style of item 5a as the theme almost disappears.

(5:37)   *CODA*

6a m139 A brass fanfare competes with fragments of the theme; a sustained, unresolved chord ends this phrase.

[53]

(5:49)

6b m143 Motives of the theme appear softly in the strings over new, more elaborate harmonies. Repeated soft notes end this movement.

35 WOLFGANG AMADEUS MOZART

PREVIEW   Born in Salzburg, Mozart spent his last decade in Vienna. He was a good friend to the older Haydn, whose much longer life span overlapped his. Musical abilities that seemed miraculous to his contemporaries when he was a child prodigy stayed with him. He left a magnificent legacy of symphonies, operas, and concertos for us to explore.

Probably the most remarkable child prodigy in music history was Wolfgang Amadeus Mozart [pronounced MOH-tzart] (1756–91). He was born in Salzburg, today a part of Austria, then a small, independent state ruled by a prince-archbishop. Mozart's father Leopold, an excellent violinist and composer in his own right, was a musician at that court. He took charge of his son's entire education, including his musical training. Wolfgang studied the violin and keyboard instruments, although he progressed so quickly that it appeared he had been born knowing how to play. His older sister, nicknamed Nannerl, was almost equally gifted. Their father dedicated his life to the development and promotion of their talent. He took the children on long, exhausting European tours, during which they performed for the nobility and for royalty, such as George III of England, to great acclaim. (Nannerl's compositions met with her brother's approval but none of them survive. After she was widowed, she lived in Salzburg with her children, teaching piano to pupils eager to study with Mozart's sister.)

Mozart's travels and his childhood fame had both good and bad results: he learned a great deal in his travels and absorbed many musical influences, but after performing for Marie Antoinette it was difficult to settle down in provincial Salzburg. To please his father, who had sacrificed advancement in his own career in order to concentrate on his son's, he made the effort to work as a court musician and to accept his servant-class status. Mozart left many letters, so we know in detail both the situations of his life and his reactions to them. In one letter, he reported that at dinner he was placed "below the valets but above the cooks." The security of such a position did not compensate for the social and musical indignities that the young Mozart had to suffer. Furthermore, the Archbishop was a very

Wolfgang Amadeus Mozart.

This illustration of the Mozart family shows the talented children with their father.

difficult employer. After a celebrated row with his chief steward, ending, as Mozart reported, "with a kick on my arse . . . by order of our worthy Prince Archbishop," Mozart left Salzburg.

Mozart spent his last decade in Vienna. Here he hoped to find a more congenial patron; possibly, too, he needed to get away from his domineering father. Although a few minor court appointments came his way, economic security did not. At first he enjoyed remarkable success as a composer, performer, and teacher, but one thing father Leopold had not taught him was the fine art of managing money. Nor was his wife Constanze (Weber) any more practical. They were married in 1782 against his father's wishes, though their marriage was a happy one. Mozart's last few years saw his popularity with the fickle Viennese public decline, as people complained that his music was becoming overly complicated.

However, Mozart had never been one to cater to the public. Even Emperor Joseph II discovered that, when he complained to Mozart that a certain opera he had written contained "too many notes." "Exactly the necessary number, your Majesty," the composer replied audaciously. Still, the Emperor really did have a reason for what he said. In the opera in question, *Die Entführung aus dem Serail* (The Abduction from the Seraglio), Mozart had lavished so much attention on the orchestra that it competed with the singers for the audience's attention. This was not what an audience expected of a **Singspiel,** the category of German comic opera with spoken dialogue to which this work belongs.

Mozart's tragically early death in 1791 at the age of thirty-five was followed by burial in a mass grave. Today no one knows exactly where his body lies. Current historians claim that this was Viennese custom at the time. After his death, gossip circulated, including a rumor that he had been poisoned—speculation which continues today. According to recent medical research, his death is attributed to acute nephritis, although some blame the decline of his health on the exhausting tours of his childhood.

historians claim that this was Viennese custom at the time. After his death, gossip circulated, including a rumor that he had been poisoned—speculation which continues today. According to recent medical research, his death is attributed to acute nephritis, although some blame the decline of his health on the exhausting tours of his childhood.

In the 1985 movie "Amadeus," Antonio Salieri (1750–1825), branding himself as a second-rate composer, confessed to killing Mozart, but no evidence suggests that he did so. Incidentally, though this movie achieved great success and introduced Mozart to a new audience, it never claimed to be historically accurate. It did present substantial portions of his music in good, reasonably authentic performances, something that *cannot* be said of most Hollywood movies based on composers' lives.

One matter regarding Mozart's funeral has been settled: he was *not* buried to the accompaniment of a blinding rainstorm, a romantic tale that crept into early biographies. Research into Viennese records by Nicolas Slonimsky, the indefatigable editor of *Baker's Biographical Dictionary of Musicians,* reveals that the weather was mild that day. Ironically, Salzburg, the town Mozart was so eager to leave, is now the scene of an annual summer Mozart festival that attracts an international audience.

A

The Miraculous Mozart

A special quality sets Mozart apart—a quality that his father called "miraculous." Many anecdotes testify to his amazing childhood abilities. His father began teaching him when he was four; in about half an hour he could learn simple minuets. At age five, he was composing them. As a six-year-old he could point out minute differences in pitch. On his tours he demonstrated performance and improvisational skills that few adults could match. While in London, the prodigy was "scientifically" observed by a member of the Royal Society. In an official report, the observer expressed amazement at Mozart's ability to sight read an orchestral score and to improvise songs on command. In Rome's Sistine chapel, after one hearing of a carefully guarded work for double choir that was never supposed to be sung by any other group, he wrote it down in full.

Even if one rejects the explanation of Mozart's talent as a "miracle," it must be admitted that all his life he showed a fantastic inventiveness and productivity. In a letter to his sister accompanying a manuscript of a prelude and fugue, Mozart explained that he wrote the notes of the fugue while he was composing the prelude—in his head. Some sketches survive which prove that on occasion he worked out preliminary details before finishing a piece. He referred to the string quartets that he dedicated to Haydn as "the fruits of long and laborious endeavor," and the manuscripts confirm that he did have to work hard on them. Yet his music has a crystallike clarity and perfection; it seems beyond human limitations.

Mozart's music lives because it can be perceived on two levels. As he himself said, "there are passages here and there from which connoisseurs alone can derive satisfaction but these passages are written in a way that the less learned cannot fail to be pleased, though without knowing why." Haydn praised him as "the greatest composer known to me either in person or by name. He has taste and what is more, the most profound knowledge of composition."

B

Mozart's Music

Mozart excelled in every medium of his age, writing more than six hundred compositions. Since he did not assign them opus numbers, a scholar named Ludwig von Koechel (1800–77) [in German, Köchel, pronounced KER-shel] placed them in approximate chronological order and published a catalogue of the works in 1862. The "K." (or "KV.") number that appears with titles of Mozart works refers to numbers in this listing. (This catalogue has been revised several times, with additional research altering some of the K. numbers.)

Several of Mozart's compositions are familiar. The *Piano Concerto* in C, No. 21, K. 467, includes a hauntingly beautiful slow movement, with a theme (ex. 35.1) that begins in the strings, then is taken over by the soloist. In describing this concerto, program notes and record jackets frequently label it the "Elvira Madigan" concerto. This came about because Mozart's memorable theme was appropriated for the background music of the 1967 award-winning Swedish film of that title which tells the story of a doomed love affair.

Example 35.1

Equally familiar is a short *Piano Sonata* in C, K. 545, often attempted by students who think all of it is as easy as the first two measures—they soon learn better! The first movement's opening theme (ex. 35.2), *dô-mî-sôl-ti-dô-rê-dô,* is very distinctive. This makes the movement an easy introduction to sonata-form, since listening for that theme's returns will identify the repeat of the exposition and the start of the recapitulation. The sonata also provides a model example of Alberti bass (*do-sol-mi-sol*) in the left-hand accompaniment.

Example 35.2

Eine Kleine Nachtmusik (A Little Night Music), K. 525, illustrates a type of piece called **divertimento,** or serenade. Essentially an entertainment piece, it is as skillfully worked out as any symphony, and it follows the symphony's four-movement plan. A string quartet plus a bass, or an entire string orchestra, are the usual performance alternatives for this work.

Although Mozart wrote over forty symphonies, fewer than ten are performed with any frequency. His *Symphony No. 40* in G minor, K. 550 (discussed below) was the favorite of nineteenth-century composers, who thought it an early manifestation of the Romantic spirit. It and two other symphonies (No. 39 in E-flat, and No. 41 in C, nicknamed "Jupiter") are often linked together in a so-called "trilogy," although there is no evidence that Mozart planned them as a group. Indeed, we lack proof that they were ever performed in his lifetime. He composed all three in a six-week period in 1788—more testimony to Mozart's amazing creativity.

Besides his piano concertos, Mozart created several concertos for instruments not usually given solo opportunities, such as bassoon, clarinet, flute, and harp. His string quartets are basic to the chamber music repertoire. A group of six quartets was dedicated touchingly to Haydn, and Haydn's influence is clear. (The influence worked both ways—the older man learned much from his younger friend.)

PART FIVE THE CLASSIC PERIOD

Birdcatcher Papageno and Prince Tamino (with flute) are shown here as they appeared in a San Francisco Opera production of *Magic Flute*. (Courtesy of San Francisco Opera Collection, San Francisco Performing Arts Library and Museum.)

Even though left unfinished, the *Requiem Mass* is probably the best-known of Mozart's sacred works. It had—and continues to have—a troubled history. It was commissioned, through an intermediary, by a wealthy amateur who planned to pass it off as his own. Some claim that Mozart, already in declining health, began to fear that he was composing his own funeral music. He died before completing it, and his student Franz Xaver Süssmayr (1766–1803), whose handwriting almost duplicated Mozart's, later finished it from Mozart's sketches. Mozart's widow claimed that Süssmayr's role in completing the work was modest, while he, quite understandably, claimed it was extensive. To this day, scholars argue about how much of the work is genuine Mozart, although they agree that it is a masterpiece.

Opera is the field in which Mozart scored his greatest success. Today, many authorities consider him the leading opera composer of all time. Five of the seven operas upon which his present reputation rests are comedies, with serious—at times cosmic—undercurrents. While outwardly obeying the social conventions of his time, they often imply some carefully crafted rebellion against them. For example, the

Marriage of Figaro (an **opera buffa,** the term for a comic opera in Italian) tells the story of a servant who, with the help of his clever fiancée, outwits their master. An audience in 1786, composed largely of "masters" quite aware of the growing social unrest that would soon lead to the French Revolution, might well have found this subject touchy, if not downright dangerous.

Don Giovanni, ostensibly a comic opera, pictures another representative of the ruling class, the legendary womanizer Don Juan. Unrepentant to the end, even after a terrifying visit from the statue of the man he had killed in a sword fight, he is dragged down to the fires of hell. *The Magic Flute,* which we shall discuss later, is also a comedy. *Idomeneo* is a "serious opera" in the Italian style, a type known as **opera seria,** set in ancient Crete. Whatever the story Mozart used for an opera, he excelled in bringing the characters to life through his music.

Mozart: *Symphony in G Minor,* K. 550 (No. 40)

The G Minor symphony was considered by some in the nineteenth century to be the very image of a serene Mozart, full of "Grecian lightness and grace." Yet in this century, many commentators have rediscovered in it "passion and grief," disturbing qualities to an audience of Mozart's time that might have contributed to the loss of popularity he suffered toward the end of his life.

For example, all movements except the second are in minor and the composer refused even to end the minor-key movements with a consoling major chord. Minor keys are rarely found in Mozart's period; when they are, they are associated with a special emotional significance. He exploited motives relentlessly, both in melodic and in rhythmic forms. Most of the themes start on, or center on, the fifth tone (*sol*) of the scale, a tone with an active, unstable feeling. Also contributing to the overall sense of tension are sudden changes of volume and some strong—by Classic standards—dissonances.

This symphony is scored for an orchestra of one flute, pairs of oboes, clarinets, bassoons, and French horns, and strings. (Some conductors prefer to follow Mozart's first version of the symphony, which is without clarinets.) These modest forces are used economically, with full orchestra reserved for transitional passages and for cadences. Strings introduce most of the principal themes; woodwinds often vary a theme when it is repeated. Unlike most of Mozart's mature symphonies, this one lacks parts for trumpets or timpani, instruments normally absent from a minor-key work.

All of the movements except the minuet are in sonata-form, which is more evidence of serious content. The Minuet has the traditional ternary structure of minuet-trio-minuet. Most of the subdivisions of the movements are easily recognized because Mozart separates them with brief pauses.

CD2

(0:00, repeat 1:44)

1a   m1   Theme I (ex. 35.3), played by violins, is built on a basic motive of two eighths and a quarter, the first three notes of the theme, a breathless, almost "sighing" motive. Violas create an active accompaniment.

54

FIRST
MOVEMENT:
Molto Allegro
(6:54) ㉞
EXPOSITION

Example 35.3

p

(0:14, repeat 1:58)

1b   m14   Woodwinds enter softly, then reinforce a loud cadence in which the rhythm of the basic motive dominates.

(0:21, repeat 2:04)

1c   m21   Theme I is restated; soon the harmony takes a new turn as a modulation to a new key (B-flat major) begins.

(0:28, repeat 2:11)

1d   m28   The full orchestra interrupts the theme with a new staccato, *forte* figure that serves as a transition to Theme II.

(0:44, repeat 2:28)

2a   m44   After a pause, Theme II (ex. 35.4) begins, securely in the new key of B-flat major. It is shared by strings and woodwinds in dialogue, with a prominent part for clarinet.

55

Example 35.4

p

(0:53, repeat 2:36)

2b   m52   Theme II is restated, this time starting with winds. A crescendo follows. A melody rises, then falls to complete this section quietly.

CHAPTER 35 WOLFGANG AMADEUS MOZART   **231**

(1:15, repeat 2:57)

3a m73 The closing theme section begins softly, with a recall of the basic sighing motive played by winds.

[56]

(1:30, repeat 3:14)

3b m88 Vigorous descending scales emerge from item 3a. Soon the basic motive returns to add emphasis to the cadence. Two slashing chords complete the Exposition, which is marked in the score to be repeated.

DEVELOPMENT

(3:27)

4a m101 Two more chords create a striking change of key (to F-sharp minor). Theme I, slightly modified, returns softly in the strings.

[57]

(3:41)

4b m115 Lower strings interrupt and take over Theme I, while violins play a vigorous countermelody. The reverse soon occurs, as violins resume playing Theme I and the lower strings play the countermelody. This musical conflict lasts until the violins are left in control, playing only the basic motive.

(4:06)

4c m139 Violins softly play the basic motive and are echoed by winds.

(4:20)

4d m153 One last agitated moment occurs with a loud dialogue of motives opposed by strong wind lines. French horns stress the dominant of G minor (D) as the development nears its end. Soon a soft woodwind passage based on the basic motive leads into the recapitulation.

RECAPITULATION

(4:33)

5a m164 No break marks this entrance; in fact, violins enter with Theme I as the woodwinds are completing the passage started in 4d.

[58]

(4:45)

5b m177 Woodwinds enter softly, as in item 1b of the Exposition.

(4:52)

5c m184 Theme I is restated, as in 1c. Here immediate changes are made in it.

(5:00)

5d m191 Suddenly loud, a transition begins, at first very similar to 1d, but twice as long, even though no modulation is necessary. This section has the force of a second development section.

(5:36)

6a m227 After a pause, Theme II returns with the string-wind dialogue of 2a. The change to G minor gives the theme a darker hue.

(5:45)

6b m235 Theme II is restated, as in 2b. Also returning from 2b are the crescendo and the rising-falling line.

(6:12)

7a m261 The closing theme section begins softly with a recall of the basic motive in the winds, as in 3a.

60

(6:28)

7b m276 Loud, descending scales mark this section, as in 3b. Unlike 3b, the cadence here is incomplete.

(6:39)

8a m285 A coda begins softly, with Theme I treated imitatively.

61

CODA

(6:46)

8b m293 Insistent repetitions of the basic motive as in 3b add emphasis to the cadence. The movement ends typically, with three repeated chords.

CD2

SECOND MOVEMENT: Andante (in E-flat major) (8:40) ㉟ *EXPOSITION*

(0:00)

1a m1 Theme I grows out of groups of six repeated notes, contributed in turn by violas, second violins, then first violins (ex. 35.5).

62

Example 35.5

(0:17)

1b   m5   An answering phrase (ex. 35.6) moves generally downward. A quickly moving two-note figure (marked by an x in the example) flickers twice before the section is completed. This figure grows in importance as the movement progresses.

Example 35.6

(0:34)

1c   m9   Low strings begin the theme-building process, as in 1a. Above them, violins play a soaring countermelody.

(1:21)

2a   m20   A transition section begins with suddenly loud, then soft, notes.

63

(1:55)

2b   m29   Theme I returns, quite unconventionally, in a remote key.

(2:29)

3a   m37   Theme II (ex. 35.7) makes a soft, delayed entrance in a high range, with minimal accompaniment. It insistently repeats the *dô-sol* with which it begins.

64

Example 35.7

(3:00)

3b   m44   A loud, chromatic passage interrupts Theme II. After appearances of the two-note figure, a gentle cadence ends the exposition. The direction to repeat the exposition is seldom followed, except for "authentic" performances, because of the slow tempo and the resulting length.

(3:40)

4a m53 The development begins quietly, with a return of the repeated-note
motive of Theme I. Winds soon counter with *forte* repeated notes,
and the strings then answer. This conflict of motives continues as the
bass line rises.

[65]

(4:43)

4b m69 A bassoon entrance on Theme I softly suggests—falsely—that the
recapitulation has begun. However, the key is not "right," and a
dialogue of strings and winds prepares for the "real" recapitulation.

(5:04)

5a m74 Again, the start of a recapitulation is concealed, as it emerges out of
the development, with violas beginning Theme I, as in 1a.

[66]

(5:21)

5b m82 The music of 1b returns here.

(5:55)

6a m86 Suddenly loud, then soft, notes begin a transition section, similar to
2a, but now in a different key (F minor).

[67]

(6:27)

6b m94 The middle portion (1b) of Theme I returns at this point, followed
soon by the beginning portion (1a).

(7:26)

7a m108 Theme II returns, even more fragile than before in its transposition a
fourth higher to the tonic key.

[68]

(7:57)

7b m115 Suddenly loud, a chromatic passage interrupts, as in 3b. The section
ends as did the exposition; there is no coda. The score calls for a
repeat of both development *and* recapitulation together. Conductors
who observe the exposition repeat usually observe this one also.

CD2

THIRD MOVEMENT:
Menuetto (Allegretto)
(3:53) ㉞ MINUET

(0:00, repeat 0:13)

1   m1   A triad-based melody begins the A section of the minuet. Three-bar phrases (the first is shown in ex. 35.8) make the theme unique. Normally, a dance form has two- or four-measure phrases to fit the back-and-forth patterns the dancers make. A syncopation created by the tied note in the melody (marked by an x in the example) further complicates the rhythm.

69

Example 35.8

(0:13)

After a one-beat rest, the A section is repeated.

(0:25, repeat 0:50)

2a   m15   The melody of the B section (ex. 35.9) is quite similar to that of the A section. An opposing line to the melody creates an occasional pungent dissonance, as in the second full measure.

70

Example 35.9

(0:44, repeat 1:10)

2b   m36   Woodwinds smooth over the tensions of the B section as they begin this codalike passage. Strings join in to complete it. After a one-beat rest, the B section is repeated.

TRIO

(Trios, by tradition, contrast with their minuets. Some of the contrasts in this work are: major mode, a more legato style, two-measure phrases.)

(1:16, repeat 1:33)

3   m1   As in the minuet, the main melody of the trio's A section (ex. 35.10) is based on a triad. Strings begin this folklike melody; woodwinds develop it and then return the theme to the strings.

71

Example 35.10

After a one-beat rest, the A section is repeated.

(1:49, repeat 2:12)
4a   m19   A conversation of strings and woodwinds is featured in the B section, as the rising line of low strings is answered by the falling line of woodwinds.

72

(1:57, repeat 2:20)
4b   m27   French horns reinforce a return of the trio's beginning melody; then woodwinds and strings exchange roles, as in item 3.

After a one-beat rest, the B section is repeated.

(2:36)   *MINUET*
5   ml   At this point, tradition calls for the minuet to be played once more, ignoring the repeats for its A and B sections. Recently, some conductors have elected to observe the repeats.

73

🎵   CD2

(0:00)   *FOURTH*
1a   ml   Theme I (ex. 35.11) contains several contrasting ideas. It begins   *MOVEMENT:*
          with a soft, upward-moving figure based on a triad, a figure so   *Allegro assai*
74   commonly used in the Classic period that it had a name, the   *(4:46)* ㊲
          "Mannheim rocket." The rocket motive is followed by a *forte* answer
          in quicker notes.

Example 35.11

(0:29)
1b   m32   A busy transition passage continues the activity of 1a with a falling line. It ends with a decisive, three-chord cadence followed by a brief pause.

(1:04)

2   m71   Theme II (ex. 35.12) is played by soft strings, moving generally

75   downward as a contrast to the rocket motion of Theme I. Clarinet
and bassoon have brief solos.

Example 35.12

(1:33)

3   m101   A sudden *forte* begins the closing theme section, as busy as the
transition. Again a three-chord cadence marks the end. The score

76   calls for a repeat of the exposition.

DEVELOPMENT   (1:55)

4a m125   This symphony is famous for the startling way this development
begins, with a loud, unison statement of Theme I (ex. 35.13).

77   Tonality is almost destroyed as pitches of the theme are altered;
rhythmic security is lost because of unexpected rests.

Example 35.13

(2:05)

4b m135   As if to compensate for the jolting start, the development proceeds
more conventionally—for a time. Strings and woodwinds alternate
quietly in six playings of the rocket motive; then rocket motives
occur at *forte* level, each one beginning before the preceding one is
complete.

(2:52)

4c m187   Despite a short pause, the development is not over. A renewed
conflict of rocket motives occurs, ending abruptly on an unresolved
chord. A short pause follows.

(3:10)
5a m207 Theme I returns, played as in 1a but only half as long.

☐78

(3:24)
5b m222 A busy transition passage continues the activity of Theme I, as in 1b. Again there is a decisive cadence and a pause.

(3:47)
6 m247 Theme II returns, played softly by strings as in item 2. Now transposed to the tonic key of G minor, it is lower in pitch and somewhat subdued in mood. Again woodwinds are prominent.

☐79

(4:16)
7 m277 A sudden *forte* begins the closing theme section, as in item 3. There is a sense of rushing to an inevitable fate, the music remaining in minor to the very end. The movement ends abruptly, without a coda. The score calls for a repeat of both development and recapitulation, as was the case with the second movement.

☐80

Mozart wrote his last opera, *The Magic Flute,* to a German text that includes spoken dialogue. The libretto, by his friend Emanuel Schikaneder, is a fantastic mix of farcical comedy, solemn ritual, fairy-tale elements, Masonic ideals of brotherhood, and Masonic symbolism, particularly the number three. Whatever his motivations, Mozart created a masterpiece: sparkling entertainment on a surface level, and at a deeper level a profound statement of Enlightenment ideals.

In this drama, the dark forces of evil (represented by the Queen of the Night and her assistants) battle with the good (represented by Sarastro and his priests in their Temple of Wisdom). Good wins out. Two high-born lovers (Pamina and Tamino) attempt to attain wisdom, undergoing trials of fire and water. They are assisted and at times thwarted in their search by a host of characters, some comic, some threatening, who often appear in groups of three, the Masonic number.

Mozart: *The Magic Flute* (Die Zauberflöte)

♫ CD3

(0:00)
1 The overture is in sonata-form, preceded by a slow introduction. Three imposing chords establish a solemn mood (and reflect Masonic symbolism, as does the key signature of E-flat—three flats).

☐1

Overture (7:27) ㊳

(1:15)
2 The high-spirited exposition section begins with a repeated-note theme treated fugally. Classic opera overtures were often cast in sonata-form but the expositions were not repeated, perhaps reflecting an attitude of "let's get the show on the road."

☐2

(3:57)

3

3

To preface the development section, Mozart recalls the slow introduction music with its three imposing chords and thus reminds us of the opera's serious side. Then the lively mood of the first theme returns, though now in minor, and the development proceeds normally.

(5:23)

4

4

The recapitulation begins with the music of item 2. It concludes with a characteristic repeated-chord cadence.

As the curtain rises, an exhausted hero, Prince Tamino (tenor), is being chased by a most fearsome dragon. Before he faints, his cries of help are heard by The Three Ladies, attendants to the Queen of the Night. They come on the scene and, after they slay the dragon, leave before he regains consciousness. Soon Prince Tamino meets a friendly chatterbox of a bird-catcher named Papageno (baritone). The bird-catcher carries with him a set of pipes, which he plays frequently in a five-note up-the-scale run that serves as his musical identification tag. His aria, *Der Vogelfänger bin ich ja* (I am a bird catcher), describes both himself and his occupation. A visit from the Queen of the Night herself persuades the pair to go in search of her daughter, Princess Pamina (soprano), who, she claims, is held captive by Sarastro. Her aria, beginning with a recitative, *O zittre nicht, mein lieber Sohn* (Fear not, noble youth), explores the stratospheric range of the loratura soprano. (We eventually learn how evil she really is, but her character is not clear to Prince Tamino at first. Hint: She usually wears black.)

Armed with a magic flute and magic bells, prince and bird-catcher team up to seek the court of Sarastro, the high priest of the temple of Wisdom. Contrary to the Queen's point of view, he is keeping Pamina away from her evil mother. Sarastro's role is for a very low bass—one writer has said Sarastro sings music fit for God. This range allows him to project as great a contrast to the Queen as possible. (And he wears white.)

In Act Two, Papageno's dearest wish, to find a soul-mate, is granted. When she eventually appears, her name turns out to be Papagena (soprano). Pamina and Tamino, predictably, fall in love and suffer separations and misunderstandings. They must undergo trials, which are something like initiation rites.

 CD3

Scenes 28 and 29
(numbering systems for recordings and scores vary) *(13:38)*
39

(0:00)

1

5

As Scene 28 begins, Papageno is alone playing his little piping tune and calling out to his lost Papagena. Constitutionally unable to keep quiet as he had been ordered to do, he has been punished by losing her, or at least he thinks so because he hears no answer.

(1:17)
2

6

After a break in tempo, Papageno says he is weary of life and decides to hang himself if no one comes before he finishes counting one, two, three.

(3:24)
3

7

After dragging out his "eins, zwei, drei" as long as possible, Papageno bids farewell to the world in a slow, minor-key passage. He places the noose around his neck . . .

(3:59)
4

8

Just in time, Three Spirits (usually sung by boys) intervene. They remind him of his magic bells, which he then plays. After a delightful passage of bell sounds and folklike tunes, Papagena returns.

(5:37)
5

9

In the duet that follows, Papageno and Papagena breathlessly stammer each other's name, then plan their happy life together. That life will include many children, all of them the very image of their parents.

(8:27)
6

10

In scene 29, the Queen, her ladies, and her henchman, the evil Monostatos, who has been one of Sarastro's guards as a kind of undercover agent, sneak onto the stage. This soft, minor mode passage pictures the evil characters of the opera as they stealthily advance upon the Temple, telling each other to be wary. Monostatos reminds the Queen of her promise that he may marry her daughter.

(10:06)
7

11

Thunder and lightning defeat the forces of evil and they sink below the stage. Light floods the stage and the major mode returns for the finale.

(10:45)
8

12

Sarastro announces that the sun has now destroyed the power of evil. His priests (the chorus) proclaim that wisdom and beauty will forever abound, as Prince and Princess are reunited. Judging from the triumphant sounds of the final chords, all the parties should indeed live happily ever after.

Included among Mozart's twenty-three solo piano concertos are many of his greatest works. Indeed, because he often intended them for his own use, Mozart produced the largest group of masterworks in the solo concerto literature. Inherited from the Baroque is the exciting concerto principle, the contrast and cooperation between a soloist and the orchestra. Surviving also is the ritornello form of the concerto grosso and the solo concerto, now joined with Viennese Classic sonata-form in a new synthesis.

Under the guiding hand of Mozart's genius, four powerful influences united to raise his piano concertos to a supreme height. The Viennese symphonic style allowed him to achieve a perfect collaboration between soloist and orchestra. His operatic orientation equipped him to create musical drama with or without words. The perfection of the Viennese fortepiano enabled the keyboard to imitate larger ensembles, orchestral or operatic, to match the orchestra more successfully, and to incorporate a wide range of touches and expression. In the orchestra of the Classic era, winds gained a new prominence, providing the potential of winds, strings, and keyboard as a three-part ensemble to be combined and contrasted in countless ways. In the words of an admiring observer (1799), "The best *specimens* of good modern Concertos for the Piano-Forte, are those by *Mozart,* in which every part of the accompaniments is interesting, without obscuring the principal part."

To develop an appreciation for Mozart's exploitation of his resources, try following throughout a movement the shifting relationships between orchestra (Tutti, or T for short) and piano (Solo, or S). At the extremes, T may play alone or S may play alone. Between these extremes, T may accompany S or S may accompany T. Most magically, T and S may engage in dialogue as equals.

Mozart concertos invariably contain three movements. The first is a complex blend of ritornello form, familiar from the concertos of Vivaldi and Bach, with sonata-form. Typically, much of the movement's principal material is announced by the orchestra in a magnificent opening ritornello (T). The entrance of the soloist initiates an expanded restatement of this material (and new material as well) that unfolds in the manner of a sonata-form exposition (S). Near the end of a concerto first movement, the orchestra drives to a suspenseful chord, followed by the **cadenza,** a modestly proportioned improvisation in which the soloist combines material from the movement and virtuosic figuration appropriate for the piano.

Slow movements of concertos are much like slow movements of symphonies: songful, relaxed, in a related key, in any one of several possible forms. For third movements, Mozart recognized only two options: theme-and-variations or rondo, his choice for all but two of the piano concertos. Rondo form is one of the oldest and most serviceable designs in music. A **rondo** consists of a number of sections, the first of which recurs between subsidiary sections before returning finally to conclude, or round off, the composition. A typical analysis is ABACA. A Viennese audience expected rondos to be of a bright, cheerful character. With their lively tempos, dance rhythms, and songlike themes, Mozart's rondos positively sparkle.

Mozart: *Piano Concerto in B-flat, No. 27, K. 595*

Composed early in 1791, the final year of his tragically short life, K. 595 is Mozart's last piano concerto. Its sunny nature belies the disappointments and frustrations of that fateful year.

In the listening guide, we have added two terms to the A,B,C analysis. The **refrain** is the initial, or A, section of the rondo. Anchored firmly in the tonic key, it is clearly separated from what follows it by a strong cadence in that key. This section recurs throughout the piece. The term **couplet** (labeled B, C, D, as needed) refers to material placed between refrain statements. Usually in a different key (or mode), this material may either be derived from the refrain or contrast with it. Finales of the time, as a whole, often exhibit a fusion of the rondo principle of return (as in the listening guide sections labeled Refrain) with elements of sonata-form (key relationships, developmental processes, and recapitulation).

 CD3

(0:00)

1a   m1   The solo piano announces the songlike refrain theme (ex. 35.14), a lilting tune that begins by bouncing up and down the tonic chord. Supporting the connection of rondo and song is Mozart's own song from 1791, *Sehnsucht nach dem Frühling* (Longing for Spring, K. 596), set to a strikingly similar tune.

THIRD MOVEMENT: Allegro (8:31) ㊵ *REFRAIN #1 (A)*

Example 35.14

(0:09)

1b   m9   The refrain theme passes to the orchestra.

(0:17)

1c   m17   The solo piano presents the remainder of the refrain theme.

(0:33)

1d   m32   Continuing its solo, the piano returns to the music of item 1a.

(0:42)

1e   m40   An extended orchestral passage, developmental in character, featuring several moments for winds alone, leads to a typical three-chord cadence.

(1:09)

2a   m65   Solo piano leads again, now with a "solo entry theme," (ex. 35.15) similar in its rhythmic lilt to the main theme. In a few seconds, the strings join in with this theme as the piano moves to rapid scale flourishes while the tonality begins to shift.

COUPLET #1 (B)

Example 35.15

(1:24)
2b m79 Solo piano very briefly begins a variant of the refrain theme, then engages in dialogue with the orchestra.

(1:41)
2c m94 Solo piano again introduces another variant of the refrain theme, flirting with the minor mode as the dialogue continues.

(1:57)
2d m108 Again the piano is prominent, now introducing the closing theme (ex. 35.16), clearly in the dominant key. The orchestra restates the closing theme, and then all forces drive to a cadence on a sustained chord.

Example 35.16

(2:23)
2e m130 With the free rhythm and virtuoso flourishes of a cadenza, the piano's connecting passage, called a "lead-in," links the couplet with the following refrain statement.

REFRAIN #2 (A)

(2:51)
3 m131 Piano is allowed one phrase of the refrain theme. The orchestra restates only a part of that phrase. Mozart took no chances of boring his audience by giving the complete refrain.

15

COUPLET #2 (C)

(3:09)
4a m147 Abruptly interrupting the orchestra, the piano begins a lengthy solo passage, developmental in character and set in the minor mode.

16

(3:26)

4b   m163   The orchestra joins in the developmental process, using the refrain theme in a minor-mode version. All forces join in on another sustained chord. (After it, some performers improvise another "lead-in" before going on.)

(3:53)   *REFRAIN #3 (A')*

5a   m182   Solo piano begins the expected return of the refrain. Highly unexpected, however, is its key (E-flat, the subdominant).

17

(4:00)

5b   m188   To complete this sophisticated combination of refrain and couplet, woodwinds interrupt with the same musical motive that began the preceding couplet (4a). The developmental dialogue continues, with the piano having the last word.

(4:18)   *COUPLET #3 (B')*

6a   m204   Again the piano is alone with the solo entry theme of item 2a and again the orchestra joins in, restating the content of Couplet #1 but remaining in the tonic key.

18

(5:06)

6b   m247   The closing theme is given out by the piano, soon echoed by orchestra. All forces drive toward a cadence on a sustained chord.

(5:37)

7   Mozart has furnished a cadenza for this movement, a combination of   *CADENZA*
             thematic material and virtuoso figuration that provides an
19   inspirational model for today's pianists who would improvise
             appropriate cadenzas where Mozart did not supply them. As is
             standard in cadenzas, a trill signals the approaching end.

REFRAIN #4 (A)

(6:57)
8a m273 The piano begins alone with the theme, as in the first refrain, and is soon joined by the orchestra in a new combination of refrain elements.

[20]

(7:32)
8b m304 An orchestral passage, as in item 1e, leads to a *forte* cadence.

CODA

(7:53)
9   m323 One last outburst of pianism initiates a splendid example of how the piano can interact now with winds, now with strings. All forces combine for an exhilarating close.

[21]

LUDWIG VAN BEETHOVEN 36

PREVIEW   Blessed with an indomitable will, the German-born Beethoven succeeded as a free-lance musician-composer in Vienna, the same city where Mozart had failed to find adequate aristocratic support. Not gifted with Mozart's fluency, Beethoven had to struggle to compose; he struggled to come to terms with his deafness also. Perhaps as a result, his life has become a symbol for idealistic hopes. The symphonies and piano sonatas that we study blazed new ground.

Like Leopold Mozart, the father of Ludwig van Beethoven [pronounced BAY-toh-ven] (1770–1827) was a musician who recognized his child's talent early. By no means, however, was father Beethoven the equal of Leopold as musician, promoter, or parental model. Beethoven was born in Bonn, after World War II the capital of West Germany. From his father, a professional musician at the court, Beethoven learned to play the violin and the piano; he also studied with local teachers. He compensated for an inadequate elementary school education by reading widely all his life. While he showed musical talent as a child, he was not a "second Mozart," though his father attempted to pass him off as one. Beethoven's childhood was darkened by his father's alcoholism, which eventually forced young Ludwig to be the head of the household.

Beethoven's ability attracted attention from some noble families in Bonn. With their financial assistance he went to Vienna in 1792 to study with Haydn. One benefactor, Count Ferdinand Waldstein, sent him off with these words: "You are going to Vienna in fulfillment of your long-frustrated wishes. The Genius of Mozart is still mourning and weeping over the death of her pupil. With the help of assiduous labour you shall receive *Mozart's spirit from Haydn's hands.*" The linking of Haydn, Mozart, and Beethoven that began with the Count still continues today.

Beethoven was dissatisfied with Haydn as a teacher, so he received instruction from other teachers behind Haydn's back. Later, Beethoven took lessons in setting the Italian language from Salieri, whom we met while studying the life of Mozart.

This imaginative picture shows Beethoven composing furiously at his piano, oblivious to the chaos around him.

By 1800 Beethoven had attained considerable success in Vienna as a composer and as a virtuoso pianist. He had made valuable contacts with aristocratic circles; publishers were competing for his newest works. Just when the future looked brightest, Beethoven realized that he was growing deaf. The threat of deafness, to a musician who prided himself on his ability to hear, profoundly altered his life. It is true that composing can be an internal process involving the "inner ear," and consequently deafness did not end his creativity. But his performing career was eventually halted and he was obliged to become a "pure composer." His personality changed: he became morose and suspicious; his social life was hampered. When his hearing was completely gone, visitors communicated with him by writing in his "conversation books," nearly four hundred of which have been preserved.

As Beethoven began to realize that his deafness was incurable and would eventually become total, he sank into a depression. Evidence of his despair survives in a letter that he wrote to his brothers in 1802 but never sent. It was found among his papers after his death. Called the "Heiligenstadt Testament," after the suburban village in which Beethoven lived at the time, the letter explained that growing deafness had been responsible for his strange behavior. He described his despair and admitted that he had considered suicide—but his creative drive held him back: "Ah, it seemed impossible to me that I should leave this world before I had produced all that I felt I might, and so I spared this wretched life."

In front of the Beethoven Hall in Bonn, Beethoven's birthplace, stands this unusual modern sculpture. It looks abstract in a closeup view. When viewed from a greater distance, the familiar craggy features of Beethoven appear.

Beethoven fulfilled his promise to himself. A wealth of music in many styles testifies to his energy and artistry. He eventually solved the problem that Mozart apparently could not solve: how to win financial security without surrendering artistic and personal freedom. He persuaded some Viennese noblemen to guarantee him a yearly salary as long as he remained in Vienna. Though he refused to be properly obsequious—he once remarked that "it is good to mingle with aristocrats, but one must know how to impress them"—he managed to remain in their good graces. He also derived income from selling his music to publishers, after making sure he had driven the best possible bargain. A crowd of 10,000 attended his funeral in 1827, a testament to his position as the greatest composer of his time.

The same group of musicologists who in 1964 ranked Bach as the number one composer placed Beethoven second in line. The bicentennial of Beethoven's birth in 1970 was celebrated by scholarly conferences and the issuing of recordings of his complete works. His success created major aesthetic problems for composers who came after him. Few escaped his influence. Certainly the general public knows his name. Not many other composers appear in comic strips and on T-shirts!

PEANUTS Characters: © 1951, 1952 United Feature Syndicate, Inc.

A

*Beethoven: A Symbol
of Universality*

It is surely no accident that when large-scale public events are planned involving people of many nationalities, the music programmed will include something by Beethoven. For example, in December 1989, the entire world could witness a telecast of his *Symphony No. 9* from Berlin to celebrate the breaching of the Berlin wall. This symphony's finale is a mighty affirmation of the unity of all peoples. In it, Beethoven brings in vocal soloists and a chorus, giving them a setting of a text by the German poet Johann Christoph Friedrich von Schiller (1759–1805) called "Ode to Joy." (Our discussion of melody in Chapter 5 quoted that movement's musical theme.) In a way no other composer does, Beethoven transcends the boundaries that divide people. He has become a symbol of universalism, a heroic, mythical figure.

Both his life and his music explain why Beethoven has become a symbol for idealistic hopes. We admire his struggle to overcome the handicap of deafness. His musical manuscripts bear visual witness to another kind of struggle. He jotted down his musical thoughts in sketchbooks (more than 5,000 pages survive) which he carefully preserved, though he was notably careless in many other respects. Themes evolve in these pages, revised and reworked, often over a period of many years. His sketchbooks reveal that unlike Mozart, who composed for the most part with extraordinary fluency, Beethoven had to wrestle with his muse. (The sketchbooks also show that Beethoven's musical handwriting was unbelievably sloppy, causing enormous problems for his unlucky copyists.) His life offers an inspiring message for everyone: never accept defeat; struggle with whatever burdens life has given you.

Many compositions by Beethoven have a clearly idealistic slant. The *Egmont* incidental music accompanies a play by Johann Wolfgang von Goethe (1749–1832), which tells of a Dutch patriot. Though killed for his revolutionary activities, he nonetheless can be seen as a victor, as others carry on his fight to free their native land from foreign domination. The struggle for political freedom also plays a part in Beethoven's only opera, *Fidelio,* as does the theme of wifely devotion. (Beethoven's idealistic image of marriage was not tested in real life: he never married, although he talked of it.) In his third symphony, the *Eroica,* an even broader message can be read in the events which led to its title. At first, the symphony was named "Bonaparte" as a tribute to Napoleon, but when that ruler crowned himself Emperor and threw off any pretense to democracy, Beethoven angrily renamed the symphony as an "Heroic Symphony to the memory of a great man." (Beethoven was not completely consistent, however. Despite his democratic ideals, he clung to the "van" in his name because it, misleadingly, suggested that his was an aristocratic family.)

Beethoven's Music

As early as 1828, biographers divided Beethoven's musical output into three periods, and this division, with some refinements into subperiods, is still useful. With Beethoven, a very close relationship existed between his emotional life and his creativity, so biographers have found that the breaks between the periods coincided with important turning points in his life. In the first period, ending around 1802, his music is relatively conservative, as Beethoven paid homage to the prevailing Viennese style and yet displayed his own individuality. His best-known works, such as the *Symphony No. 3, Eroica,* come from the second, mature period, ending about 1812. The most complex works, such as his last five string quartets and the *Symphony No. 9,* date from his last or "transcendent" period, when he was completely deaf. More serene and introspective, they show great individuality of style.

A virtuoso pianist, Beethoven wrote much piano music, at first for his own use. Most of his thirty-two sonatas are a foundation of the pianist's repertoire. Probably the most famous is his *Sonata quasi una fantasia,* op. 27, no. 2, in C-sharp minor. Most people know it as the "Moonlight" sonata, although Beethoven had nothing to do with this nickname. The name came from a review in which the first movement was compared to visiting Lake Lucerne by moonlight. The sonata defies the usual expectations for a multimovement work by beginning with a soft, slow movement, not one in the standard sonata-form (ex. 36.1).

Example 36.1

Almost equally well-known are two challenging sonatas, also with nicknames: number 21, in C, op. 53, the "*Waldstein,*" and number 23, in F minor, op. 57, the "*Appassionata.*" But by no means does all of his piano music require virtuosity. Piano students can play some early sonatas and enjoy his *Minuet in G* and the rondo-shaped *Für Elise* (ex. 36.2).

Example 36.2

For his chamber music, Beethoven followed the superlative models of Haydn and Mozart. His works in this genre include sonatas for violin and piano and for cello and piano, trios, and sixteen string quartets.

All of Beethoven's nine symphonies are constantly performed, in contrast to the limited number of symphonies by Haydn and Mozart found in the standard repertoire today. The fact that there are only nine by Beethoven, compared to the number of symphonies traditionally given for Haydn (one hundred four) and Mozart (forty-one), and that Beethoven's are much longer, shows that he approached composition in a different way. Each symphony cost him much effort; each is strikingly individual in character. Generally speaking, the large, powerful, odd-numbered ones are better known than the even-numbered, although the sixth, the *"Pastoral,"* won a certain kind of fame when Walt Disney appropriated it for an episode in his movie "Fantasia." The ninth, mentioned earlier, is unique for its finale in which a chorus and four vocal soloists appear. All of his five concertos for piano and orchestra and the one for violin and orchestra receive frequent performances.

Though Beethoven left a number of songs and several works for chorus and orchestra, he seems to have felt more at home with instrumental music than with vocal music. Singers sometimes complain that his vocal writing is not "grateful" for them. For example, sopranos can become exhausted by the long passages in which he required them to stay in their highest range.

Beethoven scorned the physical limitations of everyone, just as he ignored his own. Three versions of his one opera, *Fidelio,* mentioned earlier for the idealistic themes of its dramatic component, testify to his enormous efforts in writing and rewriting. Like Bach's *B Minor Mass,* Beethoven's *Missa Solemnis* far exceeds the time frame of any church service; it memorably illustrates the expanded dimensions characteristic of several of his last period works. He "stormed the heavens" in those attempts, inspiring generations to follow.

Beethoven: *Symphony No. 5 in C Minor,* op. 67.

Beethoven's most famous work—some say it is the most famous musical work of all time—is his fifth symphony, finished in 1808. During World War II, it became known as the "V for Victory Symphony" because of a coincidental relationship between the letter "V" in Morse code, which is three dots and a dash, and the main motive of the symphony's first movement, three short notes and a longer one. When this symphony was played in wartime, it symbolized the hoped-for eventual victory of the Allied forces. This motive occurs in almost every measure of the first movement, and it makes return visits in later movements, a highly unusual technique at the time. Decades after the war, many listeners still hear in the concentration and strength of this work evidence that it is appropriate for such a symbolic use without the Morse code coincidence. Attempts to find a "message" in this symphony are hardly new; asked to interpret the work, Beethoven is reported to have said, "So Fate knocks at the door."

 CD3

(0:00, repeat 1:23)

1a m1 Two statements of the basic motive, three short notes and a longer note, played by strings and clarinet in unison make a memorable start. Then Theme I (ex. 36.3) grows out of the motive, as it is played at different pitch levels, with modifications, by the individual string sections. The short-short-short-long idea of the motive seems to remain intact, even when the fourth note is not really long, simply accented.

FIRST MOVEMENT: *Allegro con brio* *(6:58)* (41) *EXPOSITION*

Example 36.3

(0:23, repeat 1:40)

1b m22 After a tiny pause, there is a single statement of the motive and a continuation of Theme I. A dramatic crescendo follows, which supports the transition and modulation to the new key (E-flat major) to prepare for Theme II.

(0:43, repeat 2:04)

2 m59 The transition ends with a brief but dramatic signal from the French horns (ex. 36.4) that begins with the basic motive, then adds two more notes. Immediately, Theme II is begun by violins; soon woodwinds enter. The theme moves evenly in quarter notes, as a contrast to Theme I. But the basic motive is not forgotten; it rumbles along as played by the low strings, at first softly. The entire orchestra then builds a crescendo.

Example 36.4

(1:05, repeat 2:26)

3   m95 The closing theme begins with quicker notes. Soon the basic motive returns and brings the exposition to a definite close. Two silent measures make the sense of ending even clearer. [The exposition is marked in the score to be repeated.]

24

DEVELOPMENT

(2:44)

4a m125 An explosive statement of the motive begins the development. This is followed by a section which at first sounds like Theme I. Changes in tonality and a crescendo increase the tension.

25

(3:18)

4b m179 Violins recall the signal, which was played at 1c by the French horns.

(3:29)

4c m198 Strings answer winds in two-note groupings, an idea derived from the end of the signal that immediately precedes Theme II. As the music gets softer, the two-note groups are reduced to one note but the answering process continues.

(3:48)

4d m228 A sudden return of the signal interrupts the echoing chords; then a flurry of repeated motives leads without pause into the recapitulation.

RECAPITULATION

(4:01)

5a m248 Two dramatic statements of the motive begin the recapitulation. Now the entire orchestra plays. Theme I then returns, as before in 1a.

26

(4:19)

5b m268 Emerging out of a sustained chord, a brief oboe solo is a unique feature of this symphony, offering a respite from the driving motive. Such a solo is unusual for any Classic period work, although Haydn included some.

(4:34)

5c m269 Now the recapitulation proceeds more conventionally, almost as if to compensate for the precedent-breaking oboe solo. The musical content of 1b returns, but here pitch levels are changed, since no modulation is needed.

6 m303 Again comes the signal, now played by bassoons. (Some conductors give these notes to the French horns, assuming that Beethoven called for bassoons simply because the horn of his day could not play these notes.) Theme II is given to violins, as in 2, now in the key of C but in the major mode instead of the more conventional minor. As before, the basic motive mutters away, here in low strings and timpani. A crescendo follows.

`27`

(5:21)

7 m347 The closing theme section is very similar to that in the exposition. Again as in 3, a repeated use of motives leads to a definite-sounding cadence.

`28`

(5:37)   ***CODA***

8a m374 However, instead of stopping, Beethoven plunges on with a renewed battle of echoing motives in a characteristically long coda. (It is as long as the development section.)

`29`

(5:53)

8b m400 A new, more flowing theme is added in the violins on top of a continuation of the motive; soon the motion becomes more vigorous.

(6:17)

8c m440 Winds begin an echoing passage similar to one in the development (4c). Strings answer. Soon Beethoven repeats the beginning of the movement, with its short-short-short-long motives.

(6:46)

8d m483 Very quietly, strings recall Theme I, almost as if Beethoven dared to start this movement all over again. But the orchestra unites to brush aside the theme with forceful motives and the movement ends.

An unusual feature of this symphony is that Beethoven quotes the short-short-short-long motive in the last two movements and some people find a relationship in the second movement also. That second movement, Andante con moto, in the closely related key of A-flat, is a set of variations, actually on two themes. It contains a loud, triumphant figure (first heard beginning in measure 31, about one minute into the movement), the last four notes of which relate to the basic motive's rhythm of short-short-short-long. Here it is at a much slower tempo and with new pitch relationships, *do-do-re-mi*.

The third movement, in C minor, is given only a tempo label, Allegro. In some of his multimovement works, Beethoven substituted a **scherzo** for the traditional minuet. Except in name, this movement is a scherzo. Here the triple meter that is characteristic of a minuet is accelerated until only one beat per measure is felt, but the minuet structure (minuet, contrasting trio, return of minuet) is preserved. Beethoven recalls the basic motive of the first movement as French horns boldly play, quite early in the movement, the short-short-short-long rhythm pattern, here all on the same pitch, *sol*. The entire orchestra soon joins in to make it even more emphatic. After a contrasting trio in C major, highlighted by an almost-comical scrambling for notes by cellos and basses, the return of the opening music is mysteriously hushed. Now the strings play pizzicato, and the return of the basic motive, which earlier was played assertively by the horns, goes instead to soft woodwinds.

When the third movement appears to be almost ended, a magnificent surprise occurs. Beethoven writes a long, mysterious-sounding transition linking it to the fourth movement, Allegro. A sonata-form in C major, it literally explodes, triumphant and marchlike, with an expanded brass section that includes trombones. Later, near the middle of the movement (at measure 160, about three and a half minutes into the movement), the third movement's version of the basic motive returns, now starting in strings, as if recalling earlier struggles. After a recapitulation of the opening music, an extended, accelerated coda leads to one of the most emphatic conclusions in all music. After building up such momentum, Beethoven could not slam on the brakes!

Beethoven: *Piano Sonata in C Minor,* op. 13, "Pathétique"

Almost as familiar as the "Moonlight" sonata is Beethoven's "*Pathétique*" *Sonata*, op. 13, in C minor, a sonata with a nickname that he *did* authorize. ("Pathetic" in this context implies great emotion and feeling.) With its almost violent contrasts of loud and soft, this sonata shows how far from the gentle world of the harpsichord Beethoven had moved and how much he depended upon the emerging fortepiano. (Or was he predicting today's concert grand?) Beethoven wrote this rather somber work in the late 1790s, when he was apparently in a "C minor mood," using that key also for works included in his opp. 9, 10, 18, and 30. It was published in 1799. The first movement is in sonata-form with a slow introduction. While sonata-form is to be expected for a first movement, Beethoven's treatment of it is exceptional, as we shall see in its guide.

♪ CD3

FIRST MOVEMENT: Grave—Allegro di molto e con brio (7:43) ㊷ INTRODUCTION

(0:00)
1a   m1   Full chords in the lower half of the piano range command attention with their dotted rhythms. They also make dramatic dynamic
[30]   changes from loud to soft, a Beethoven characteristic.

(0:31)
1b   m5   A quiet melody, derived from the top notes of the beginning chords, alternates with returns of those chords.

(1:13)
1c   m10   A rapidly descending chromatic scale ends the introduction.

(1:17, repeat 2:52)   EXPOSITION
2   m11   Theme I (ex. 36.5) starts softly as the right hand moves upward in
            pitch. The "sf" sign indicates a sudden *forte,* which coincides with a
      31   syncopation here.
            The left hand accompanies with the low, rumbling sound of broken
            octaves. Contrasting ideas lead to a transition as the rumbling sound
            returns. A brief moment when the right hand plays alone signals the
            end of this section.

                                                                Example 36.5

(1:47, repeat 3:21)
3a   m51   Theme II starts with a four-note motive in even notes, first low, then
            high. (This theme calls for quick hand-crossing.) It is in the minor
      32   mode, although major at this point is conventional.

(2:17, repeat 3:51)
3b   m89   A change to major marks the start of this new melody, supported by
            a broken-chord accompaniment.

(2:34, repeat 4:08)
4a   m113 The closing theme features a running scale line over an "oom-pah-
            pah-pah" accompaniment.
      33

(2:41, repeat 4:15)
4b   m121 The closing theme completes the exposition by quoting Theme I.
            Two loud chords signal the end. [The exposition is marked in the
            score to be repeated. Besides the normal amount of variability
            concerning repeats of an exposition, there is a corrupt version of the
            score in print that calls for a return all the way back to the start of
            the introduction.]

| DEVELOPMENT | (4:26) |
| | 5a m133 Quite untypical of development sections is this restatement of the introduction music, in a higher key, the dominant. The restatement ends with another surprise, a modulation to an unrelated key (E minor). |

34

(4:53)
5b m137 Now, with a return to the Allegro tempo, the development proceeds conventionally. Both the transition theme and Theme I appear, and the rumbling sounds of item 1 are much clearer, now played in a higher pitch range.

(5:32)
5c m187 A single melodic line releases the built-up tensions of the development and descends to lead smoothly into the next section.

RECAPITULATION

(5:39)
6 m195 Theme I returns, as in item 2. Soon, pitch adjustments prepare for another harmonic surprise. Again, a brief moment when the right hand plays alone clearly signals the end of this section.

35

(5:59)
7a m221 Theme II returns, as in 3a, with the four-note motive and the hand-crossing. Here Beethoven explores the key of F minor, the subdominant, another unusual feature. Soon the passage is extended as he prepares for the "normal" key for a recapitulation, the tonic key of C minor.

36

(6:25)
7b m253 The broken-chord passage of 3b returns.

(6:42)
8a m277 As in 4a, a running scale line is supported by an "oom-pah-pah-pah" accompaniment to begin the closing theme.

37

(6:49)
8b m285 As in 4b, the closing theme continues with a quote from Theme I. Dramatic, powerful chords end the recapitulation.

(7:00)
9   m295   Again untypically, the introduction music returns briefly.

38

(7:26)
10   m299   Theme I makes a reappearance, quickly halted by five slashing
             chords.

39

The second movement, Adagio cantabile, in A-flat major, contains one of Beethoven's most singable melodies, sustained over a broken chord accompaniment. Both it and the third movement, Allegro, back to C minor, are in rondo form. Typical rondo patterns are: ABACA, the form of this sonata's second movement; ABACADA; and ABACABA, the form of its third movement. In the latter, the B sections are apt to function tonally like Theme II in sonata-form, and the C section is developmental. Here the main theme is easily followed because its first two returns are preceded by a pause.

The Romantic Period

37 INTRODUCING THE ROMANTIC PERIOD (1825–1900)

PREVIEW As in the other chapters that introduce a period, we begin with a review of the historical events. Because there are so many Romantic composers who are known to the general public, this division of the text is longer than other parts. Again we show how the characteristics of sound and the elements of music apply. We close with a discussion of some special aspects of Romanticism.

The **Romantic period** is often described as a revolt against the artistic and philosophical principles of the previous century. One derivation of the term "Romantic" relates it to "romance," the translation of a French term, *roman,* a long narrative. Free of the rules imposed on most literary types, the romance came to signify freedom of expression in general. We often link "romantic" to "love," but romantic love was only one of this era's hallmarks. Others are: freedom of form and spirit; an emphasis upon individuality, originality, and personal expression; the depiction of emotion; an idealization of faraway places and the past, particularly the late Middle Ages; a fascination with the supernatural and the sinister; an interest in—even a worship of—nature. When William Wordsworth (1770–1850) wrote:

> Come forth into the light of things,
> Let Nature be your teacher.

he expressed a common Romantic thought—that Nature is more to be trusted than society. Equally in love with nature, artists such as Joseph Mallord William Turner (1775–1851) carried landscape painting to new heights.

The Romantics believed that music, more than the other arts, could express inner feelings the most freely because music is not bound to words or things; it has the closest connections to the subconscious. The nineteenth-century critic Walter

Pater (1839–94) is famous for his phrase: "All art constantly aspires toward the condition of music."

However, caution is needed in applying these general ideas to specific composers or to specific works. Because the Romantic period placed such a high value upon individuality, great differences existed among artists in all fields. Making generalizations, always problematic at best, is especially risky in this complex period, full as it is of conflicting tendencies.

Unlike the dates for the Baroque period, those for the Romantic period have no specific events to justify them. As we explained earlier in the Classic period discussion, the Classic to Romantic shift is gradual, to say the least. Indeed, some historians refuse to acknowledge a dividing point. Early in the 1800s, hints of Romanticism appeared in Beethoven's music, so much so that he might be considered its herald, despite his commitment to Classic forms. And composers who died prematurely, like Schubert in 1828, barely lived into the Romantic period. Ending it with the year 1900 is convenient but may seem arbitrary, for many scholars believe that not until World War I is there a clear break. For that matter, many composers maintained a Romantic style well into the twentieth century. The Russian pianist/composer Sergei Rachmaninoff [pronounced rahkh-MAHN-in-ahff] (1873–1943), famous for his *Prelude in C-sharp Minor,* provides a good example.

A

Historical Background

After Napoleon met his Waterloo in 1815, society spent years recovering from the tremendous disruptions caused by the Napoleonic wars. Political unrest continued for decades, as unification proceeded slowly in both Italy and Germany, areas that had been previously divided into many small governmental units. A new interest in nationalism arose, with musical results that will be discussed later. The inventive geniuses who had set in motion the Industrial Revolution made it possible to develop industry as we know it. Partly as a result of that revolution, populations expanded tremendously as people flocked to the cities. New technology produced musical instruments abundantly and facilitated modifications and improvements in them.

B

Romantic Composers

The publication of music became more profitable for composers, and increased financial support came also at the box office as public concerts became the norm. Though many were amateur singers or pianists at home, the new audience was composed of middle-class people, less knowledgeable about music than the aristocratic patrons of Classic composers. **Virtuosity,** a performer's ability to excel in technically difficult music, especially impressed the new audience, and as a result composers wrote increasingly challenging music. Indeed, virtuoso performers were treated like present-day rock stars, complete with publicity, groupies, and scandals.

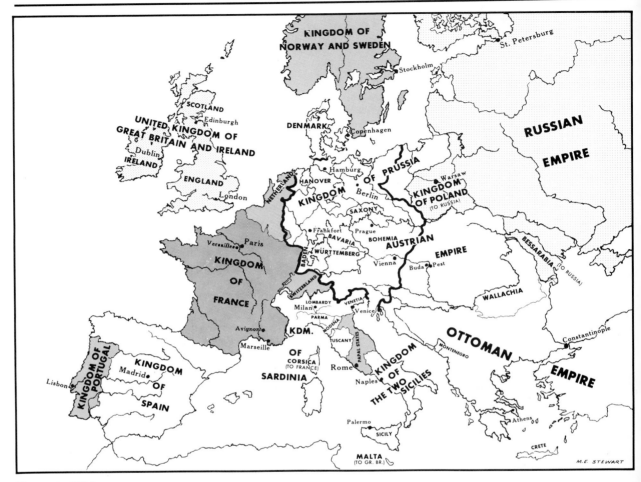

Europe in 1815.

Music was no longer a family trade, passed on from one generation to the next: instead, conservatories trained musicians. Nor were composers hired servants or skilled workers: now they thought of themselves as free spirits. Society might not understand them—a society from which they often felt alienated. The artist as a heroic "genius" who works only when "inspired" to create a "masterpiece" for "posterity" is a Romantic concept.

Earlier composers might be called "general practitioners." Bach, for example, composed numerous types of music, played all keyboard instruments, presided over the performances of his music, and taught. We shall study several Romantic period composers who might be called "specialists." To illustrate, Chopin

This picture shows Liszt at the piano, gazing soulfully at the larger-than-life bust of Beethoven. Listening to him with rapt attention are celebrities of the time, including Chopin to the left, with George Sand next to him. At Liszt's feet is his current mistress, modestly sitting with her back to the viewer.

concentrated on a single type of music, piano compositions, and performed only on the piano. Mendelssohn and Wagner were excellent conductors, but most composers preferred to leave this role to professional conductors. A few Romantic composers, among them Schumann and Berlioz, were also skillful writers whose essays on music are still read today. They took up their pens in a crusading mood, for they hoped to elevate the public's taste and reform the musical life of Europe.

In the midst of enormous changes, some composers held fast to earlier traditions and produced Masses and cantatas for church use as well as concertos, symphonies, quartets, and sonatas. The French composer Gabriel-Urbain Fauré [pronounced foe-RAY] (1845–1924) wrote a gentle *Requiem* (minus the threatening "Dies irae" of the official Mass text) that is a favorite with choral groups. Indeed, choral music flourished in this period, aided by the rise of large amateur singing societies. Even the oratorio was not dead, as those by the English composer Sir Edward Elgar (1857–1934) proved. However, he is best-known for his *Pomp and Circumstance* marches, the first of which is always linked with graduation ceremonies in this country.

Choosing the composers whose works will be studied here is a far more difficult task than selecting representative Baroque and Classic composers. Few would deny that Bach and Handel, and Mozart, Haydn, and Beethoven must be included and that they should receive the lion's share of attention. For the Romantic period, no such consensus exists. At least thirty-five composers cry out to be included.

Since this is clearly impossible, the fourteen who are allotted individual chapters were chosen to represent a broad range of Romantic styles. Many others are mentioned in association with a particular topic—as has already been the case in this section.

C

The Characteristics of Sound in the Romantic Era

1. The *pitch* spectrum continued to expand. For example, the piano keyboard was enlarged to seven and one-quarter octaves, or eighty-eight keys, its present compass. Another aspect of pitch, equal temperament, though it had begun much earlier, was finally universally accepted in the mid 1800s. An international conference met in 1885 to decide a standardized pitch. They chose a frequency for A of 435 instead of today's 440 A.

2. Composers specified *dynamic* changes with great precision, noting extremes such as pppp, ppp, fff, and ffff, even though most listeners would find it hard to distinguish between pppp and ppp. Crescendo and decrescendo signs constantly appear in the music and frequent fluctuations in volume levels are a part of a Romantic performance.

3. *Tone color* attained a new prominence in the Romantic period. Though Baroque and Classic composers wrote well for instruments, they thought of instrumental "color" as something applied later, after the "black-and-white" drawing of the notes had been done. With Chopin or Berlioz, the sound itself is as essential as the notes. Not surprisingly, this interest in tone color went along with the invention of new instruments and the physical modifications of old ones.

By mid-century, the **piano** became the instrument we know today. Manufacturers built upright pianos to meet the desire of almost every middle-class family to own a piano, which the daughters were obliged to learn to play. The Classic period's fortepiano underwent considerable evolution in the 1800s, an evolution made possible by advances in manufacturing. Heavier strings under greater tension necessitated a cast-iron frame and allowed for a greater range of volume, from whisperingly soft to thunderously loud. Felt-covered hammers produced a tone with a prominent fundamental that took a long time to die away, creating the illusion of a connected legato. Improvement in key action made lightning-fast repetition of tones possible—at least if the pianist had the technique to do it.

Foot-controlled **pedals** became a standard piano feature. All pianos have at least two pedals. The one on the right, the "sustaining" pedal, sometimes incorrectly called the "loud" pedal, raises dampers which ordinarily stop the strings from vibrating. This action allows the sound to continue even after the player's fingers have left the keys, making a thicker texture possible. The pedal on the left shifts the keyboard mechanism slightly, resulting in a softer, more muffled sound. (Some pianos have a third pedal in the middle, which sustains only those tones whose dampers are already raised by key action.) The large grand piano exhibited in 1855 by Steinway and Sons of New York represented the culmination of much technical change and put America on the map as an instrument-producing nation.

The Romantic infatuation with tone color eventually affected even the conservative world of the organ. Organs built in this era contained new varieties of pipes, designed to imitate orchestral instruments. Particularly in France, composers cultivated a "symphonic" style for the organ, calling for the constant changes in tone color and in volume that are characteristic of Romantic orchestral works. For example, César Franck [pronounced say-zar FRAHNK] (1822–90), in Paris, wrote such works as *Grande Pièce Symphonique*. Its title clearly indicates a performance on the new style of organ.

String instruments were not much changed in the Romantic period, although some technical modifications (to fingerboards, bows, and string materials) increased the possible volume level and caused a more brilliant tone color. With increasing frequency, string players began to use an older effect called vibrato. An oscillating motion of the *left* hand which creates a slight fluctuation of pitch, vibrato adds to the emotional quality of sustained tones. It is easy to see players using vibrato; it might seem harder to hear it.

Strings were employed in the orchestra in new ways. Cello and bass parts became independent from each other (earlier scores had them playing the same music with the bass sounding an octave lower). Orchestras required many more string players, with a total of sixty not unusual. The large number of string players resulted from two reasons: composers began to divide each string group to create new effects, and more players generated the volume needed to fill the large new concert halls.

Technical changes in wind instruments made them not only louder but also easier to control, especially in playing legato and in producing chromatic notes. No longer content with pairs, composers called for three or four each of wind instruments.

Expanding the top and bottom ranges of pitch, the *woodwind* section gained permanently the piccolo and the contrabassoon (sometimes called the double bassoon), which had previously been limited to cameo appearances in Beethoven's music. While the flute was hardly new, it acquired more keys and gradually shifted from wood to metal construction. The veiled, melancholy sound of the **English horn** enriched the woodwind section. Despite its name, the English horn is *neither English nor a horn*. Sharing many features of the oboe and playing a fifth lower, "alto oboe" would be a better name. Invented in the 1840s, the **saxophone** found a limited use in the orchestra, especially by French composers. It is a hybrid instrument, made of metal as is the brass family but played with a single reed, like a clarinet. Bizet's *L'Arlésienne Suites* contain striking examples.

As for the *brasses,* formerly restricted to the tones that the player's lips could control, the addition of *valves* or *pistons* to the trumpet and the French horn made a complete chromatic span of pitches readily available on these instruments. Composers enthusiastically responded, giving them more demanding parts and songlike melodies. The **tuba** now supplied the bass for the brass section.

The "alto oboe," or English horn, becomes prominent in the Romantic period. The English horn is slightly larger than an oboe, with a pear-shaped bell at the bottom and a slightly curved mouthpiece.

The *percussion* family also grew. Instead of a pair of timpani, a third and soon a fourth timpani allowed for quick pitch changes. (The tension on the drumhead can be changed to alter the pitch, but the timpani player needs time to do it.) Earlier novelties—triangle, bass drum, and snare drum—became routine members of the orchestra. Other additions included the cymbals, chimes, glockenspiel, celesta, castanets, and tambourine.

Though not a new instrument, the **harp** entered the orchestra. Both the player's hands pluck the strings, which are tuned to a diatonic scale, like the white keys of the piano. Foot-controlled pedals change the pitches of the strings to make a full chromatic scale possible.

With all these additions, the orchestra grew dramatically. By the late Romantic period, about one hundred players were needed. In response, professional **conductors** became increasingly necessary. In the Baroque period, whoever played the basso continuo directed from the harpsichord, or the first violinist assumed musical leadership with an occasional nod or a wave of a bow. But in the early 1800s an orchestra was led by someone standing in front of the group, using a **baton,** a short stick, to make the time-beating clear.

The German composer Carl Maria von Weber (1786–1826) is shown conducting. Rather than a baton, he uses a rolled-up sheet of paper.

A growing interest in individual interpretations of music further mandated the presence of the conductor, for the essential job is not merely to get the group started and stopped, but to establish a unique rendition. Since most of the conductor's work is accomplished in rehearsal, the public is seldom aware of the complexity of the task. A great conductor is able to inspire the musicians as a group to perform even better than they can as individuals. By the end of the century, the virtuoso conductor had become the dominant musical figure, a situation that continues to this day.

Romantic composers lavished great care on the details of their orchestral writing. The art of **orchestration** developed, a word that must not be confused with the familiar use of "orchestrate" to imply a carefully managed or staged event. Orchestration takes into account the individual properties of instruments, so they can contribute toward the particular sound the composer has in mind. Usually, the composer orchestrates a work; if someone else does it, that person receives credit.

D

1. Contrasting *rhythm* patterns are characteristic of Romantic style, as are considerable fluctuations of tempo, indicated in the score by signs for an accelerando or a ritardando. In addition, performers of Romantic music tend to make many subtle variations in tempo that are not written down exactly in the score, a

The Elements of Music in the Romantic Era

practice called **tempo rubato.** This word literally means borrowed or stolen time, on the theory that time taken from the beat will be repaid later. Deciding just how much rubato is appropriate poses a challenge: excessive rubato can stretch music out of shape but a too-rigid control of the beat can destroy the Romantic feeling of spontaneity.

2. The Romantic era was a time of *melody.* For voice and instruments alike, composers wrote singable, memorable melodies. When twentieth-century writers of popular songs and musical comedies needed fresh inspiration, they turned to Romantic period tunes. They grew rich stealing the music of many composers whom we study, and some of whom we can only mention, such as the Norwegian Edvard Grieg [pronounced GREEG] (1843–1907), whose music was appropriated for the 1940s musical *Song of Norway.* The original themes were not sufficiently symmetrical in phrase structure to meet the rigid requirements for commercial music, so they were mercilessly chopped down to fit into thirty-two-measure lengths and supplied with lyrics in the "June, moon, croon" style. But the songs sold, introducing the tunes of "great" music to millions. (A wry comment once circulated among musicians: "Everybody's making money but Tchaikovsky!")

3. *Harmony* became ever more complex. Found to a limited extent in the Classic period, chromatic chords, that is, chords based on any of the twelve tones of the chromatic scale, became common coin. Since all its invervals are half-steps and sound alike, a chromatic scale lacks a sense of beginning or ending. The highly chromatic harmony of some composers produced a similar effect. After a number of chromatic chords, a listener can easily lose track of tonality.

The simple triads of the Classic period were enriched with one or two additional pitches (which continue the every-other-letter pattern), resulting in seventh or ninth chords. Though not new, strictly speaking, these chords saw extra duty in the Romantic period. Other developments in harmony included frequent fluctuation between the major and the minor modes while retaining the same *do.* Another feature involved freer modulation to **remote keys.** Earlier composers usually restricted their modulations to *closely related* keys, that is, keys whose scales have all but one tone in common. All other keys are more or less remote or unrelated. Moving to a remote key carries a certain shock value; at the very least it offers a sense of surprise.

4. The Classic emphasis on homophonic *texture* continued in the Romantic era. However, accompanying patterns are often quite complex and varied, with countermelodies creating the effect of polyphony.

5. Similarly, the Classic *forms* continued in favor, but with important changes. In sonata-form, for example, composers generally eliminated the repeat of the exposition. Great contrasts between Theme I and Theme II became the rule, and the Classic restrictions on key relationships between themes and movements were relaxed. Though composers continued to employ the older forms, they articulated them less clearly. Instead of inserting pauses to mark off sections within movements neatly, as Mozart often did, they concealed the joints with continuous music. Not only was continuity within the movements a goal, but *links* between the movements appeared. Beethoven had led the way, connecting the third and fourth movements of his *Symphony No. 5.*

Again heralded by Beethoven in this same symphony, a new principle emerged, that of **cyclic form,** in which themes from earlier movements return in later ones. Another technique employed to unify large works is **thematic transformation.** A basic motive or theme, occurring in transformations of rhythm, pitch, harmony, and tone color, returns throughout a piece. Meredith Willson's Broadway musical *The Music Man* contains a simple example of thematic transformation. "Seventy-six Trombones" is basically the same tune as "Good Night, My Someone." Rhythmic changes make the difference between a marching tune and a waltz— and alter its basic character completely.

E

1. Romantic composers tended to exploit *extremes*. Their music called for both higher and lower pitches than ever before. Loud became even louder; soft became almost inaudible. Whirlwind tempos challenged the virtuosity of performers, and deliberate tempos tested the patience of the listeners. Pieces reached epic proportions: an hour or more for a symphony is not unusual, and some of Wagner's operas run five hours or more. At the opposite pole, composers wrote miniatures, as fleeting as leaves in the wind.

Special Aspects of Romanticism

2. Romantic art emphasized *the emotional force of music* in the service of individual expression. One need only consider the large number of terms in the music which furnish clues to the desired mood or the feeling, such as *con fuoco* (with fire), *mesto* (sad), and *gioioso* (joyful). The directive to play "expressively" dots Romantic scores.

3. **Nationalism** was an important political movement in the 1800s, particularly in the last half of the century. Its impact was strongest in nations that were struggling for unity and independence from foreign domination. Such causes attracted liberal minds, and many musicians were at least liberals, if not downright revolutionaries. Nationalism involved the writing of music that pictured favorably the composer's native country. Specific musical sources included folk melodies and characteristic dance rhythms. Scenes from a country's history could be the subject of an opera or a symphonic poem, a topic we touch on in outlining program music. Musical nationalism found its greatest acceptance in Russia, Bohemia (now a part of Czechoslovakia), and the Scandinavian countries, areas which had not produced composers on a world-class level earlier or where native art music had not been extensively developed. Jean Sibelius [pronounced sih-BAY-lee-us] (1865–1957), for example, made the world aware of Finland, especially with his *Finlandia* (1899).

Some composers, not content with mining the riches of their own heritage, responded to the sounds of other national groups, a concept that is sometimes called musical **exoticism.** As we saw earlier, the Frenchman Bizet put Spanish elements into his opera *Carmen.* The Italian Giacomo Puccini [pronounced poo-CHEE-nee] (1858–1924) pictured Japan in *Madama Butterfly* and China in *Turandot.*

4. **Program music** (the word is *not* "programmed!") was a powerful force in this era. The term is applied to *instrumental* music inspired by a nonmusical idea that is *authorized* by the composer, usually in giving the work its title. To make the story-telling qualities clearer, explanatory remarks are customarily attached to the score. As the "program" for the work, these explanatory remarks get printed in concert program notes, on record album jackets, and in books like this one.

We referred in Chapter 2 to the general idea that music can have representational qualities. It was certainly not new to the Romantics. In the Renaissance, word painting colored the madrigals. In the Baroque period, the "affect" of a particular piece, its ruling emotion, dictated the musical qualities of the entire composition. Vivaldi aimed at more specific descriptions in his *Four Seasons.* What was new in the Romantic period was the complexity of the stories told in program music and the emphasis placed on it, to the extent that some people feared, and others hoped, that it would supplant its apparent opposite—or rival—absolute music. This latter term refers to music (sonatas, symphonies, and the like) that is free of any overt connections with nonmusical ideas and that is usually described in terms of its form. Heated debates between the proponents of both types of music notwithstanding, the two are really intertwined. Extramusical ideas often exist in absolute music, and program music can be analyzed for its form alone, apart from its story.

Several types of program music can be distinguished. (a) The **symphonic poem,** also called **tone poem,** is a *one*-movement piece. It may be in one of the standard forms, with or without the use of thematic transformation. (Caution: despite the label, no "poem" accompanies the purely instrumental music.) (b) The **program symphony** has several movements, as is true of any symphony. It may employ the standard forms for those movements. (c) The **concert overture** is a one-movement, independent, programmatic orchestral piece. The concert overture evolved out of the operatic overture, which, detached from its opera, makes good concert material. Writing an "overture" as an independent piece to be played on a concert is just a small step. The title indicates some sort of programmatic content for it. Sonata-form was traditional for opera overtures in the Classic era, so it was natural that this form shaped many, though certainly not all, concert overtures. (d) Many plays have inspired **incidental music,** which is music for possible inclusion in the performance of a drama. As the word "incidental" implies, such music is not essential to the drama in the way that music is essential to an opera. We saw that, as evidence of his idealism, Beethoven had supplied incidental music for Goethe's drama *Egmont.* But of course, performances of that drama could take place without Beethoven's music. Still, the addition of an overture, music between acts, and perhaps a march or some dance music to accompany the action on the stage can enhance the audience's experience. Even when incidental music is played in concerts without the drama, its programmatic associations remain.

Akin to incidental music, even if not called that, is film music or background scores. Forgettable in most movies, a few film scores have entered the concert repertoire. Certainly, the "pop concert" audience will experience John Williams's score for "Star Wars." The history of such music dates back to the days of silent movies in the 1920s, when "background music" added atmosphere. Theaters installed a special kind of pipe organ, played by some skillful musicians who were (actually, a very few old-timers still *are*) near-geniuses in the art of improvising music to fit the movie.

Music for the ballet forms yet another type of program music, assuming that some sort of representation is conveyed by the dancers. Many ballets, of course, are purely abstract, and others adapt preexisting music.

In creating program music, composers have three basic tools. (a) The easiest way to work is to *imitate natural sounds.* Thus a timpani's thunderstorm is amazingly realistic, and a flute chirps and warbles as prettily as any bird. Some natural sounds translate into music so neatly that they turn into favorite devices. For example, the cuckoo—or even better, the cuckoo clock—is supposed to sound a descending third, *sol-mi.* So in Handel's organ concerto, titled *The Cuckoo and the Nightingale,* this motive was enough to account for the cuckoo part of the title. (b) Next come the *general associations* of mood and music that seem natural in our culture. In the Western world, a melody with a descending line, slow tempo, and in minor is regarded as "sad," while one with an ascending line, fast tempo, and in major, would be "happy." (c) *Specific associations* must be established in the mind of the listener for the program to make sense. For example, melodies from France and Russia fight it out, musically speaking, in Tchaikovsky's *1812 Overture,* but there is nothing particularly French or Russian about these tunes. Only the listener who knows the tunes in advance and who knows which country prevailed in 1812 will understand the "program" of this piece.

38 FRANZ SCHUBERT

PREVIEW   Blessed with the miraculous fluency of a Mozart, the Viennese native Schubert was granted an even shorter life. His life story is almost a stereotype of the struggling Romantic artist whose fame comes only when he is dead. Adhering to Classic forms in his instrumental music, he yet can be placed as a very early Romantic on the strength of his lieder (art songs).

Vienna is famous as the home of many great composers. While most of them were born somewhere else, Franz Peter Schubert [pronounced SHOO-bert] (1797–1828) was a native Viennese. His father, an amateur musician, played cello in the family string quartet. He was the proprietor and headmaster of a small school, an occupation without much social standing or monetary reward. A local organist who gave the young Schubert music lessons later reported: "If I wished to instruct him in anything fresh, he already knew it. Consequently I gave him no actual tuition but merely conversed with him and watched him with silent astonishment." Schubert's good voice earned him a place in the imperial court chapel as well as a place in a training school for singers. Here he received a thorough musical education, eventually becoming a pupil of Salieri. Though he played the violin and the piano, he did not often perform in public.

To assist his family financially, Schubert taught in his father's school while still a teenager himself. He was a poor teacher, probably because his attention was already fixed on composing. Indeed, some of his best-known songs date from these early years. Leaving his teaching post in 1818, he failed in his many attempts to find a satisfactory, permanent position. While his songs and piano music were selling well by 1828, he was decidedly underpaid—if not actually cheated—by his publishers.

Franz Peter Schubert.

Schubert's obvious genius and sunny disposition won him a circle of devoted friends. Some of them helped support him as best they could, but his financial condition was usually precarious. These friends often gathered for evenings of music making, with many of these performances providing Schubert's only opportunity

With friends gathered around, Schubert heard his songs performed, often by a retired opera singer who was one of the few friends Schubert had with musical influence. These gatherings were known as "Schubert evenings."

to hear his music. Not until the last year of his life was he able to organize a full-scale public concert of his works. When Beethoven died in 1827, Schubert was one of the thirty-six torch bearers in the funeral procession. That was about as close to being part of the musical establishment as he ever came. Today, his grave is next to Beethoven's in the Vienna central cemetery. After his tragically premature death in 1828, more widespread recognition developed for his music, especially his songs and piano music. However, his greatest instrumental works were hardly known until the 1860s, and it was not until the 1930s that his symphonies made their way into the standard repertoire.

Many people hold a stereotype of the Romantic composer: a person who lives only for music; is wildly impractical in worldly matters; will starve in a garret and be recognized as a genius only after premature death. Schubert comes close to fitting this stereotype, but even his fate was not quite this bad! Shy, self-effacing, he spanned two eras, the Classic period with its aristocratic patrons like Haydn's Prince Esterházy and the Romantic period, when composers worked as free-lance artists. Unfortunately, he could adapt to neither set of conditions. Never winning a satisfactory musical position, he lacked the self-confidence and the aristocratic contacts that enabled Beethoven to force society to listen.

A

Although Schubert wrote much glorious instrumental music, he long has been associated in the popular imagination with **art song,** in German, **lied** [pronounced leet], plural **lieder.** Lieder, which had existed for centuries, attained new stature in the Romantic period. Two contributing factors were the development of the

Schubert and the Romantic Lied

piano and the abundance of native German poetry. Composers were inspired by this poetry, much of it by supreme masters such as Goethe. Stimulated by the possibilities of the piano, an orchestra in miniature, they elevated the accompaniment to an equal partner with the voice. The best examples of the art song set fine poetry to distinctive melodies, contain accompaniments that enhance that poetry, and project a universal drama in microcosm. Some composers organized groups of songs into **song cycles,** which might be unified by the poetry of a single poet, or by poems that tell a more or less continuous story.

One way to build an art song is to repeat the same music for each of the poem's stanzas. Most familiar and popular songs are of this design, called **strophic.** A contrasting way provides ever-changing music for the succeeding stanzas. The term for this plan is **through-composed,** a translation of the German term *durchkomponiert.* In other words, the composing process continues all the way *through* a song. Through-composed songs are apt to be more dramatic than strophic songs, because the changing music can reflect the changing moods of the text.

Although a few songs are gender-specific, most of them can be sung by either a male or a female voice. Further, singers do not hesitate to have their accompanists change the notes of the piano part to a higher or a lower key to fit their particular range. Moving music to another key is known as **transposition.** Consequently, no one vocal timbre can be expected for any particular art song.

Schubert employed both the strophic and the through-composed plans in his more than six hundred songs, half of them written before he was twenty. Such quantity alone is amazing—he wrote eight songs on one day in 1815—but the quality is also unparalleled. With unusual sensitivity and imagination, he matched the words of the poetry to his melodies and accompaniments. The examples mentioned below will illustrate this.

B

Schubert's Music

Because Schubert's opus numbers are unreliable, the scholar Otto Erich Deutsch (1883–1967) prepared a catalogue of Schubert's works. The "D." numbers assigned for Schubert's music go up to almost one thousand and function similarly to the "K." numbers applied to Mozart's music.

Probably Schubert's best-known lied is *Ständchen* (Serenade) (D. 957, No. 4). In it, the serenader sings (ex. 38.1) to his beloved, hoping to induce her to come join him outside. Especially towards the end, the harmony fluctuates between the minor and the major modes (a Schubert trait), almost as if asking the question, "Will she or won't she?"

Example 38.1

Lei - se fle - hen mei - ne Lie- der   durch die Nacht zu dir,

Also famous is his *Ave Maria* (Ellens Gesang III, D. 839), sometimes thought, incorrectly, to be sacred music because of its opening words. Many editions show it set to the traditional Ave Maria text in Latin. The original German text, however, is a translation of poetry by Sir Walter Scott (1771–1832).

The piano part of a Schubert song magically creates an appropriate world for the particular text. For example, in the "Serenade" just mentioned, the piano imitates the strumming of a guitar. In *Gretchen am Spinnrade* (Margaret at the Spinning Wheel, D. 118), the piano's monotonously repeated figuration conveys the image of a whirring spinning wheel.

Schubert wrote two great song cycles (later we discuss a song cycle by Schumann). In picturing the fruitless travels of two alienated men, they mirror all too closely Schubert's own life. In *Die schöne Müllerin* (The Lovely Maid of the Mill, D. 795), the young man's journey follows the course of a stream, which provides the rationale for the rippling accompaniment in several songs—and which proves, in the last song, to be his final resting place. The other cycle, *Die Winterreise* (The Winter Journey, D. 911), portrays another wanderer, disappointed in love, dejectedly slogging through a bleak landscape in the dead of winter. Although a few happy moments come his way, his eventual resigned request to a begging organ-grinder is unbearably poignant. He asks: "Shall I go with you? Will you grind away on your hurdy-gurdy to my songs?"

Besides his songs, Schubert wrote much piano music, including sonatas that rank with those of Beethoven. His chamber music—trios, quartets, and quintets—shows a mastery comparable to that of Haydn and Mozart. The *Piano Quintet in A* (D. 667) is nicknamed "The Trout," because it contains a slow movement in theme-and-variation form based on the melody of his lied *Die Forelle* (described below).

Of Schubert's symphonies, the eighth, in B minor (D. 759), is the most familiar. It is nicknamed the "Unfinished," because only two movements were completed, although a third was started. No one knows why Schubert abandoned it, but since it is dated 1822, its incomplete state cannot be due to his early death. A lilting theme (ex. 38.2) in the first movement (Theme II of the sonata-form) has contributed to its popularity.

Example 38.2

pp

After Schubert's death, his symphonies gathered dust, unpublished. Two Romantic composers we shall study helped revive them: in 1837 Schumann discovered the score of Schubert's "Great" symphony in C (the ninth) and in 1839 Mendelssohn conducted its first performance.

Especially in respect to his instrumental music, Schubert could be placed with the Viennese Classic masters. Like them, he cultivated specific forms and adhered to absolute music. But he fits into the Romantic era as well. Illustrating his adventurous sense of harmony are many poignant shifts between major and minor modes. Almost shocking are his sudden key changes, often to unexpected keys. Another Romantic trait is his fondness for long, songlike themes in instrumental music. It is as if Schubert wrote songs all the time—whether they were to be sung or played made no difference.

Schubert: *Die Forelle* (D. 550) (2:04) ㊸

This song is strophic in form (the music of the first stanza is repeated for the remaining stanzas of the song). Although Schubert slightly modified the music for the third stanza, this change does not invalidate the strophic label. A bugle-call-like motive of *sol-dô-dô-mî-mî-dô-sol* dominates the happy-sounding vocal melody (ex. 38.3), in a major key.

Example 38.3

In   ein-em Bäch-lein hel - le, da   schoss in fro - her   Eil'

The accompaniment of *Die Forelle* (The Trout) plays a storytelling role, rippling and flowing as if depicting the fleeting movements of the fish in the stream. A short introduction (not included in modern scholarly editions) introduces this rippling theme. As interlude, it occurs between the stanzas. In the third stanza, the accompaniment loses its rippling theme and chords change more frequently, because of the text reference to muddied water. A return to the original style shows that the onlooker is resigned to the fate of the unfortunate fish.

In the German texts of songs printed in this book, brackets enclose repetitions of words that represent changes from the original poetry. Composers seem to have no qualms about this practice, a freedom that the poets involved do not always appreciate.

♫ CD3

In einem Bächlein helle
Da schoss in froher Eil'

Die launische Forelle
Vorüber wie ein Pfeil.
Ich stand an dem Gestade,
Und sah in süsser Ruh'
Des muntern Fischleins Bade
Im klaren Bächlein zu,
[Des muntern Fischleins Bade
Im klaren Bächlein zu.]

In a bright little brook
there darted about in happy
    haste
a playful trout,
past me like an arrow.
I stood on the bank
and watched, contentedly,
the merry fish bathe
in the clear little brook.

Ein Fischer mit der Rute
Wohl an dem Ufer stand,
Und sah's mit kaltem Blute,
Wie sich das Fischlein wand.

So lang' dem Wasser helle,
So dacht' ich, nicht gebricht,
So fängt er die Forelle
Mit seiner Angel nicht,
[So fängt er die Forelle
Mit seiner Angel nicht.]

A fisherman with his rod
stood right on the bank,
observing in cold blood
how the little fish wriggled to
    and fro.
As long as the clear water,
I thought, remains undisturbed,
he will not catch the fish
with his fishing gear.

Doch endlich ward dem Diebe

Die Zeit zu lang. Er macht
Das Bächlein tükkisch trübe

Und eh' ich es gedacht,
So zuckte seine Rute,
Das Fischlein, das Fischlein
    Zappelt dran,
Und ich mit regem Blute
Sah die Betrogne an,

[Und ich mit regem Blute
Sah die Betrogne an.]

But finally the thief [the
    fisherman] felt
the time was too long. He made
the little brook muddy,
    maliciously.
And before I knew it,
his rod was quivering
with the struggling little fish.

And I with my heart pounding
stared at the one who'd been
    betrayed.
(German text by Christian D.
    Schubart.)

The drama of the Erlkönig story appealed to artists as well as to the poet Goethe and the composer Schubert.

Schubert: *Erlkönig* (D. 328) (4:03) (44)

A hauntingly powerful setting of Goethe's ballad *Erlkönig* (translated variously as Erlking or Elfking) is one of Schubert's best-known songs. It is in fact a miniature drama, with one singer enacting all four roles (they are identified in the listening guide). A narrator describes a desperate situation: a father rides furiously through the night, clutching his dying, delirious son. The son, convinced he sees and hears the Erlking, the spector of Death, cries out to his father. The father's attempts to comfort the child are in vain. As the narrator's final words, rendered in a recitative style, must tell us, the child dies.

Each of the four characters has an individual sound, conveyed by Schubert's music and the skills of the singer, and reinforced by the virtuosic piano part. The Narrator is matter-of-fact, at least in the opening stanza. The Father's pitch range is low, as he tries to calm his child. Reflecting his growing fear, the Son's voice becomes ever higher throughout the song, with notes that are dissonant against the piano harmony. The Erlking, whose music is in major with a seductive, waltz-like lilt, betrays his true nature with his final snarling words.

Like *Die Forelle, Erlkönig* has a piano accompaniment that adds immeasurably to the drama, here creating impressions of night, terror, and nature as an ominous force. To mirror the changing moods encountered in the eight stanzas of Goethe's ballad text, Schubert rejects the strophic design of *Die Forelle* in favor of a through-composed arrangement that is tightly unified by vocal motives, accompanimental patterns, and the sound of the diminished-seventh chord harmony.

CD3

(0:00)

1a

43

The piano introduction sets the stage. Repeated octaves in the right hand simulate the sounds of the galloping horse; the ominous rising motive in the left hand (ex. 38.4) pictures the terror that grips both father and child, and establishes the minor mode. Both elements of this accompaniment color much of the song.

Example 38.4

(0:23)

1b

(Narrator)

Wer reitet so spät durch Nacht und Wind?

Es ist der Vater mit seinem Kind;

Er hat den Knaben wohl in dem Arm,

Er fasst ihn sicher, er hält ihn warm.

Who rides so late through night and wind?

It is a father with his child.

He has the boy in his arms,

he holds him close, he keeps him warm.

(0:57)

2

44

(Father)

"Mein Sohn, was birgst du so bang dein Gesicht?"

(Son)

"Siehst, Vater, du den Erlkönig nicht?

Den Erlenkönig mit Kron' und Schweif?"

(Father)

"Mein Sohn, es ist ein Nebelstreif."

My son, why do you so fearfully hide your face?

Don't you see, Father, the Erlking?

The Erlking, with crown and train?

My son, it's a misty streak.

(1:29)

3

(Erlking)

"Du liebes Kind, komm, geh
mit mir!
Gar schöne Spiele spiel' ich mit
dir;
Manch bunte Blumen sind an
dem Strand;
Meine Mutter hat manch'
gülden Gewand."

You lovely child, come, go with
me!
Beautiful games I'll play with
you.
Many colored flowers are on the
shore.
My mother has many golden
robes.

(1:52)

4

(Son)

"Mein Vater, mein Vater, und
hörest du nicht
Was Erlenkönig mir leise
verspricht?"
(Father)
"Sei ruhig, bleibe ruhig, mein
Kind;
in dürren Blättern säuselt der
Wind."

My father, my father, don't you
hear
what the Erlking softly
promises?

Be quiet, remain quiet, my
child.
In withered leaves rustles the
wind.

(2:14)

5

(Erlking)

"Willst, feiner Knabe, du mit
mir gehn?
Meine Töchter sollen dich
warten schön;
Meine Töchter führen den
nächtlichen Reihn
Und wiegen und tanzen und
singen dich ein,
[Sie wiegen und tanzen und
singen dich ein."]

Don't you want to come with
me, you fine boy?
My daughters will serve you
well.
My daughters lead the nightly
dancing.
And they rock you and dance
and sing to you.

(2:32)

6

48

(Son)

"Mein Vater, mein Vater, und
    siehst du nicht dort
Erlkönigs Töchter am düstern
    Ort?"

My father, my father, and don't
    you see over there
the Erlking's daughters in that
    place?

(Father)

"Mein Sohn, mein Sohn, ich
    seh' es genau,
Es scheinen die alten Weiden so
    grau."

My son, my son, I see it clearly.

It's the shining of old grey
    willows.

(3:00)

7

49

(Erlking)

"Ich liebe dich, mich reizt deine
    schöne Gestalt,
Und bist du nicht willig, so
    brauch' ich Gewalt."

I love you, you have a beautiful
    form.
And if you are not willing, I
    will have to use force.

(Son)

"Mein Vater, mein Vater, jetzt
    fasst er mich an!
Erlkönig hat mir ein Leids
    gethan!"

My father, my father, now he
    has taken hold of me.
The Erlking has done me harm!

(3:24)

8

50

(Narrator)

Dem Vater grauset's, er reitet
    geschwind,
Er halt in Armen das ächzende
    Kind,
Erreicht den Hof mit Müh' und
    Not:
In seinen Armen das Kind war
    tot.

The father shudders, he rides
    very fast.
He holds in his arms the
    sobbing child.
He reaches the courtyard in
    anguish.
In his arms, the child was dead.

CHAPTER 38 FRANZ SCHUBERT

281

39 FRÉDÉRIC CHOPIN

PREVIEW Another short-lived Romantic composer was Chopin, unique in his heritage: he was born to a Polish mother and a French father. He is the first of our Romantic composers to be tagged a "specialist." The center of his world was the piano. In his music Chopin imaginatively exploited its possibilities as it evolved from the Classic era's fortepiano into the concert grand as we know it today.

The next three Romantic composers we study, Chopin, Schumann, and Mendelssohn, are linked together because their life spans were so similar. Born within a few months of each other, they all died prematurely, like Schubert. The brief life of Frédéric Chopin [pronounced SHOW-pan] (1810–49) began near Warsaw, Poland. (Two different spellings of his first name are commonly seen: the Polish spelling as Fryderyk, and the French form shown here.) His father was a Frenchman who taught French in the local high school; his mother was Polish. Throughout his life the Polish heritage seemed dominant. He was educated in his father's school and at the Warsaw Conservatory. By the age of seven he was performing in public on the piano and composing. While still in his teens, he had developed the essential "Chopin" style of both playing and composing. His Opus 2, a set of variations on a theme by Mozart, received a rave review from the influential composer and writer Robert Schumann in 1830. (We meet Schumann in the next chapter.) At the age of twenty-one, Chopin played his first concert in Paris and was so well received that he settled there permanently.

Although zealous for Polish independence from Russia, Chopin never returned to Poland, even for a visit—understandable considering his frail health and the difficulties of travel in those days. Though he was a virtuoso pianist who could rival anyone in Europe, he disliked the hurly-burly of concert life. In his whole career, he gave barely thirty public performances. He saved his strength for a select audience in aristocratic salons.

After a concert Chopin played in London, a newspaper review praised not only his compositions but his performance: "It is the exquisite delicacy, with the liquid mellowness of his tone, and the pearly roundness of his passages of rapid

This statue stands in Poland as a monument to one of its most distinguished sons. (Photograph David Weiss, © 1990.)

articulation which are the peculiar features of his execution, while his music is characterized by freedom of thought, varied expression and a kind of romantic melancholy which seems the natural mood of the artist's mind." Chopin's success with aristocratic audiences allowed him to meet on equal terms with the leading figures in art, literature, and society. He taught piano, very profitably, to the members of that aristocracy and was also well paid for his compositions. (This Romantic composer had no intention of starving in a garret!)

Chopin's decade-long love affair with Madame Aurore Dudevant (1804–76), a writer with the pen name of George Sand, has been chronicled in novels (she herself wrote one of them) and in twentieth-century movies. She had adopted a man's name because it seemed unlikely that books by a woman would sell. A radical—she wore trousers now and then and even smoked cigars!—and a feminist, she was a domineering person who on the whole probably helped Chopin's career. At least, her care helped him live as long as he did (he suffered from tuberculosis, a major killer in those days). During the time they lived together he was musically productive. After they quarreled and parted, he lived only two more years. Three thousand mourners attended Chopin's funeral rites in 1849 and heard the *Requiem* by Mozart, written when that composer's even briefer life was slipping away.

Although musical *nationalism* is a movement generally associated with the political events of the last half of the century, a touch of nationalism colors those Chopin pieces that have Polish roots. Examples include the **mazurka,** a folk dance in triple meter, and the **polonaise,** a festive processional dance associated with nobility, in moderate tempo and also in triple meter. Indeed, Chopin made the polonaise a musical symbol of Poland. Unlike many Romantics, he did not link his music to literary subjects nor did he write program music. Some people claim, however, that his ballades are programmatic.

A

Chopin: The "Poet of the Piano"

Unlike most of the composers who preceded him, Chopin was a "specialist." Not only did he confine his own playing to the piano, but every composition he wrote includes the piano. Most of his works are for solo piano, although there are concertos for piano and orchestra, songs, and some chamber music. He liked the smaller forms, even the miniature: he would feel at home with today's slogans of "less is more" and "small is beautiful."

Chopin exploited the possibilities of the piano, possibilities that had grown as the instrument itself had changed. As the piano's action was improved, fast trills and repeated notes became more feasible. For shading, connecting, and sustaining tones, the pedal is essential in his music. Now a "singing" touch became a reality. Melodies could rival the human voice in legato connections because individual piano tones lasted so much longer. Characteristic of his style are songlike melodies in the right hand, often embellished when phrases are repeated, as in the style of Italian opera.

To support his lyrical melodies, Chopin developed new styles of accompanying. His music, often extremely difficult, is magnificently calculated *for* the instrument—some composers are said to have written *against* it! All pianists study his music, not only because it is graceful and beautiful, and appreciated by the audience, but also because they acquire an advanced piano technique in the process of learning it.

Still, the piano Chopin played was smaller than our big-sounding, nine-foot concert grand. Although most pianists play his music on today's instrument, the trend toward authenticity in performance may well encourage the playing of Chopin's music on his kind of piano.

A familiar piece by Chopin is the so-called *"Minute" Waltz,* more formally known as op. 64, no. 1. While the left hand plays the traditional "oom-pah-pah" waltz accompaniment, the right-hand melody (ex. 39.1) begins with a decided feeling of duple meter, caused by the repetitions of groups of four notes.

Example 39.1

Also famous, the *Polonaise in A-flat,* op. 53, reflects the stately quality of a Polish courtly procession. After a brief introduction, the main theme enters (ex. 39.2).

Example 39.2

The middle section of *Fantaisie-Impromptu,* op. 66, contains a lovely melody, one of those Romantic creations that suffered the fate of being transformed into an American popular song. Also part of everyone's background is the ominous dotted rhythm of the "Funeral March" from the *Sonata in B-flat Minor,* op. 35. Every pianist who wants to acquire the Chopin technique studies the twenty-four *Etudes,* opp. 10 and 25. Those who master their difficulties go on to play them in recitals, for they make ideal program material. The sixty-one *Mazurkas* span his entire career and show great varieties of mood.

With respect to form, Chopin was conservative. Although he did not apply sonata-form strictly in his larger works, he tended to rely on the general ternary principle: the opening theme returns after a contrasting section. He often employed the Baroque idea of working out one particular motive or pattern consistently throughout a piece. This technique can be seen in his *Twenty-four Preludes,* op. 28. While many in this collection are as difficult as the etudes, the ones in A major and E minor, both quite short, are well within the grasp of second-year piano students. Chopin wrote these preludes in all twelve major and twelve minor keys, following the example Bach set in his *Well Tempered Clavier.* The points of comparison in the two collections do not stop with choice of keys. For example, the first prelude in each set is made up of chord progressions which articulate the chord tones from the bottom up. (We met Bach's *Prelude No. 1* in Chapter 31.)

Although he did not authorize them, some of Chopin's pieces bear nick-names, coming from stories told by his friends or publishers. For example, the stormy *"Revolutionary" Etude in C Minor*, op. 10, no. 12, is said to have been inspired by Chopin's indignation at the Russian invasion of Warsaw in 1831.

What places Chopin firmly in the Romantic camp is his harmony. Often chromatic, it contains modulations to remote keys that earlier composers would not have dared. Now and then his harmony becomes so complex that all feeling of tonality is lost. Its revolutionary implications were not fully realized until the next century.

Chopin: *Nocturne in F-sharp,* op. 15, no. 2 (3:36) ㊺

Chopin's nocturnes are usually in ternary form (ABA'), often with a some-what turbulent middle part in between the quiet, rather slow beginning and ending sections. Because the word "nocturne" is associated with nighttime, someone has joked that the nocturnes represent a "dream-nightmare-dream" form. The sus-taining capabilities of the piano make it possible for the smoothly connected melody to "sing" over the wide-ranging, broken-chord accompaniment Chopin invented.

  CD3

(0:00)
1a   m1   The melody (ex. 39.3) begins with a generally conjunct motive of
      [51]   *mi-fa-mi-re-ti-sol-sol*, which becomes more disjunct. Soon it is
              increasingly decorated with quickly moving notes. The left-hand
              broken chords establish the major mode with simple harmonies.

Example 39.3

(0:35)
1b   m8   After an incomplete cadence, the melody begins to repeat. Soon it is
              embellished with many extra notes in an improvisatory style.

(1:07)
1c   m16   A complete cadence occurs; then a slightly contrasting phrase
              begins.

(1:42)
2   m24   Several repeated notes mark the end of the A section. The B section
      [52]   then begins, with a more elaborate pattern in the right hand. As the
              melody moves upward in pitch, the volume increases and the tempo
              becomes faster. Soon these processes are reversed, and the B section
              eventually dies away.

(2:23)

3   m48   A pause identifies the end of the B section and signals the return of
          the opening melody. Since the melody is even more decorated this
          time, and the section is shorter, the appropriate analysis label is A′.

(3:07)

4   m58   Another complete cadence occurs; then a short coda begins with a
          very high melodic line. As it descends in pitch, the music grows ever
          softer.

Although not authorized by Chopin, a nickname, "Butterfly," is often associated with this etude. Seemingly appropriate at the beginning of the piece, as
the melody softly flits up and down, it becomes less so when that melody grows
louder.

This brief, fast, major-key etude helps develop right-hand facility in playing
octaves and broken chords. The accompaniment also presents a challenge, as the
left hand swings back and forth between bass notes and chords, a familiar style
used in many types of music. In fact, ragtime depends upon it.

Chopin: *Etude in G-
flat*, op. 25, no. 9
(1:02) ㊻

   CD3

(0:00)

1   m1   The etude begins with a theme that repeatedly moves upward (ex.
         39.4).

Example 39.4

(0:29)

2   m25   The beginning theme returns. Chopin calls for it to be louder than
          before.

(0:43)

3   m37   A coda begins softly, with a repeated-chord pattern in the left hand.

40 ROBERT SCHUMANN

PREVIEW   Born in Germany, Schumann displayed literary skills and a vivid imagination at an early age. These qualities are seen in his essays, which he signed with the names of his imaginary companions, essays which helped further the careers of Chopin and Brahms. At first a specialist composer writing chiefly piano music, he turned to song writing in the year of his marriage to the virtuoso pianist Clara Wieck. We study one of his song cycles.

Born in the German town of Zwickau, Robert Schumann [pronounced SHOO-muhn] (1810–56) was the son of a bookseller and publisher. A highly imaginative child, Robert read widely in his father's collections and from an early age showed literary as well as musical talent. He contributed to his father's publications and composed pieces for his fellow classmates to perform. In his late teens, he was sent—unwillingly—to Leipzig to study law, but he skipped lectures in favor of improvising at the piano. Finally persuading his family to allow him to consider a musical life, he began piano study with a celebrated teacher, Friedrich Wieck.

Wieck recognized Schumann's talent: in fact, he allowed him to live with the Wieck family. Unfortunately, a weakness developed in Schumann's fingers which forced him to abandon hopes of a concert pianist's career. He then threw himself into composition, and a stream of piano pieces resulted.

When Schumann first met the family, Wieck's daughter Clara, only nine years old, was already a virtuoso pianist. Trained by her father, she was his best advertisement, and he took her on many European tours. In the late 1830s, Clara and Schumann fell in love, earning not the father's approval of such a musical union, but his violent, near-pathological objections. Wieck resorted to slander and sabotage in his battle with the pair. Since the law required parental permission, it took a lawsuit to enable the couple to marry. The year of their marriage, 1840, is known as Schumann's "song year," as he ecstatically produced a flood of art song. The song cycles for which he is best known come from this time. (Three years later Wieck, by then a grandfather, relented and reconciled with the couple.)

Robert Schumann.

Clara and Robert Schumann are shown at the piano. For both of them, the piano was their first musical love.

For several years, Schumann was an active musical journalist, editing an influential publication, the "New Journal for Music." His first writings hailed a new star on the horizon, the young Chopin, with the words, "Hats off, gentlemen, a genius!" His last published essay paid glowing tribute to another young genius, Brahms. (These two brilliant predictions gave Schumann an inflated reputation as a prophet. He made his share of bad guesses too, because his judgment was very subjective.) Although he also attempted to be a conductor, a municipal director of music, and a music teacher, he failed in these posts. His heart belonged to composition. A long history of mental instability, recently diagnosed as manic-depressive psychosis, perhaps inherited because his father suffered from "nervous disorders," preceded his eventual breakdown, suicide attempt, and early death in 1856.

Throughout their marriage, Clara continued to perform and teach, despite her eight pregnancies (one child died). She had shown creative talent as a child but seemed rather ambivalent about composing. She wrote in her diary, "a woman must not desire to compose—not one has been able to do it, and why should I expect to?" However, Clara's music has been rediscovered lately, performed, and recorded. Her piano trio (in G minor, op. 17) is especially fine. After Robert's death, Clara concertized to support her children—and some of her grandchildren. Her performances and editions of Robert's piano music helped win recognition for it. She died in 1896, active to the end of a long and productive life. (Her effect upon Brahms is discussed in his chapter.)

A

Schumann: A Self-Consciously Split Personality in Music

It is said that the Romantic era was an age of contradictions. Schumann himself demonstrated conflicting tendencies—one minute he was whimsical, the next serious. Though he gave programmatic titles to many of his piano pieces, he admitted that he wrote the music first and then thought up the titles. He told young musicians that they should "make everything in the head," but actually he composed at the keyboard.

Schumann's imagination, literary interests, and split personality can be seen in the pen names he employed. In his early years he assigned himself two imaginary characters: a youthful, contemplative dreamer named Eusebius, and the impulsive, capricious Florestan. (A third character emerged later, Raro, the mature master. His name takes one syllable from Clara and one from Robert.) Schumann attached the names of these personalities to his writings. For instance, this statement from his "Aphorisms" is credited to Eusebius: "It is a sign of the extraordinary that it is not always grasped at once; the majority are inclined to superficial things, such as virtuoso music." But Florestan was quite pithy: "Talent labors, genius creates."

The names of these personalities appear also in his music, as we shall see. All three were "members" of Schumann's imaginary organization, the "Davidsbund" or League of David, the lovers of good music. Their task was to fight the "Philistines," the producers of trivial music and all the smug, middle-class people who applauded their efforts. We might wonder: which personality was the real Schumann? Probably he himself could not say, for he was all of them in turn.

B

Schumann's Music

Schumann wrote many **character pieces** for piano—short works that express a mood or a programmatic idea, identified by their fanciful and evocative titles, such as "Ballade," "Impromptu," "Fantasy," "Album Leaf," and "Novelette." Just as composers linked songs together in song cycles, they placed character pieces in groups, giving the whole collection an overall title. A well-known example is "Träumerei" (Dreaming) (ex. 40.1), from his *Kinderscenen* (Scenes from Childhood), op. 15.

Example 40.1

These pieces were not written *for* children to play; rather they represent an idealized childhood. His *Album for the Young,* op. 68, however, *can* be played by young pianists. Not many Romantic composers were willing to accept such a limitation. His only piano concerto begins with a dramatic outburst for the soloist, an idea imitated by the composer Grieg in *his* well-known piano concerto, which is in the same key of A minor.

Schumann's early *Carnaval,* op. 9, is a set of twenty-one short character pieces with imaginative titles. It illustrates the "split-personality" concept mentioned earlier, because these titles include "Eusebius" (his dreamy self) and "Florestan" (the impulsive self). To cap it off, the work concludes with a "March of the Davidsbund against the Philistines," a most unconventional march in triple meter. His *Symphonic Etudes,* op. 13, a loosely organized set of variations, is a frequently performed masterpiece. In contrast to *Carnaval,* it lacks obvious programmatic content. Except for three string quartets, his chamber music invariably employs the piano. A piano quintet (op. 44) projects an especially rich sound.

Two of Schumann's four symphonies have programmatic nicknames (the first, op. 38, is called "Spring," and the third, op. 97, the "Rhenish," a tribute to the Rhine river). Clara had encouraged him to write larger works, such as symphonies and concertos, but he seems to have been happiest when his imagination had free rein in smaller pieces.

Although Schumann wrote fewer songs than Schubert (for that matter, Schubert wrote more songs than anybody else), at his best he matches Schubert's sensitivity to the texts. Often Schumann's piano accompaniments are especially challenging and imaginative, with extended postludes that intensify the mood of the song after the singer finishes. This is especially true in his **song cycles.** A song cycle is a collection of songs unified in some manner, frequently by being based on the poems of one poet. Some sort of overall story is told, or at least implied. In performance, the musicians go directly from one song to another, with no time lost for applause. One cycle by Schumann, the *Frauenliebe und -leben* (Woman's Love and Life), op. 42, was once very popular with female singers until changing social ideas about women's roles made the male-worshipping text embarrassing. We describe an equally famous song cycle, *Dichterliebe* (Poet's Love), op. 48.

One of the products of Schumann's "song year" is the song cycle *Dichter-liebe* (Poet's Love), drawn from a collection of sixty-five poems by the Romantic German poet Heinrich Heine (1797–1856). Heine's collection does not actually tell a story, but since the first poem describes a happy beginning as love arises in the springtime and the last one calls for twelve giants to carry the coffin in which that love is buried, one can easily imagine a narrative. In his setting, Schumann retained Heine's order and the implied story of a rejected suitor, although his published cycle contained only sixteen songs. Eight of them have extended piano postludes, which play a large part in making a unified whole out of separate songs.

Ich grolle nicht, sometimes translated as "I'll not complain," is the seventh song in the cycle. By now the poet has realized that his love is in vain—but, so he claims, he "bears no grudge." In choosing the cheerful key of C major Schumann seems to take the poet at his word, even repeating "ich grolle nicht" several more times than Heine did. Yet his music contradicts the forgiving message of the poem by strong dissonances (as on the second syllable of "verlor'nes") and a sense of urgency in the piano accompaniment. This allows room for varied interpretations of this song. Of course, a good poem has more than one interpretation, and Heine—Schumann's favorite poet—was famous for his love of irony and double meanings. Schumann followed strophic form less frequently than did Schubert. Here, the two stanzas do begin with similar music, but after that the second differs considerably from the first, in order to reach a suitable climax. The German text shows Schumann's additions and changes to the original text in brackets.

The accompaniment begins with repeated chords, which continue throughout.

 CD3

(0:00)

1   Ich grolle nicht, und wenn das Herz auch bricht. | I bear no grudge, although my heart is broken.

56   Ewig verlor'nes Lieb, [ewig verlor'nes Lieb,] ich grolle nicht, [ich grolle nicht.] | Forever lost love, forever lost love. I bear no grudge, I bear no grudge.

Wie du auch strahlst in Diamantenpracht, es fällt kein Strahl in deines Herzens Nacht. | Although you may shine in diamondlike splendor, there is no ray of light falling in the darkness of your heart.

Das weiss ich längst. | This I have known for a long time.

A brief piano interlude separates the stanzas.

(0:45)

2

[Ich grolle nicht, und wenn das Herz auch bricht.]
Ich sah dich ja im Traum[e],
Und sah die Nacht in deines Herzens Raum[e],
Und sah die Schlang', die dir am Herzen frisst,
Ich sah, mein Lieb, wie sehr du elend bist.
[Ich grolle nicht, ich grolle nicht.]

I bear no grudge, although my heart is broken.
I saw you in a dream,
and saw the night in your empty heart,
and saw the snake that is eating at your heart.
I saw, my love, how miserable you are.
I bear no grudge, I bear no grudge.

The piano ends with more repeated chords and an emphatic cadence.

This song follows immediately after *Ich grolle nicht,* with a nonstop broken chord figure in the piano that outlines the minor key and reinforces the restless quality of the vocal line. The first three stanzas are set to the same music.

Schumann:
Dichterliebe: Song No. 8, *Und wüssten's die Blumen* (1:17)
㊽

CD3

(0:00)

1

Und wüssten's die Blumen, die kleinen,
Wie tief verwundet mein Herz,

Sie würden mit mir weinen,
Zu heilen meinen Schmerz.

Und wüssten's die Nachtigallen,
Wie ich so traurig und krank,
Sie liessen fröhlich erschallen,
Erquickenden Gesang.

Und wüssten sie mein Wehe,
Die goldenen Sternelein,
Sie kämen aus ihrer Höhe,

Und sprächen Trost mir ein.

And if the little flowers knew
how deeply wounded (is) my heart,
they would, with me, weep,
to heal my pain.

And if the nightingales knew,
how I am sad and sick,
they would gladly sound
a comforting song.

And if they knew my woes,
the golden little stars,
they would come from their heights
and speak comfortingly to me.

The music for the last stanza shows subtle changes, storm warnings as the poet's mood darkens.

(0:46)

2

59

Sie alle können's nicht wissen,	They all cannot know
Nur Eine kennt meinen Schmerz;	only one knows my sorrow;
Sie hat ja selbst zerrissen,	she has indeed herself broken,
Zerrissen mir das Herz.	broken my heart.

A brief piano postlude almost explodes, releasing the tension built up in the concluding stanza.

FELIX MENDELSSOHN 41

PREVIEW   The third in our group of short-lived early Romantics is Mendelssohn. Born in Germany to a wealthy and cultivated family which gave its multitalented children rigorous training, he became by today's standards a "workaholic," excelling in performance and in many forms of composition. Scarcely touched by the liberal ideas of Romanticism, Mendelssohn adhered to Classic formal principles and played a vital role in the "Bach Revival."

The most "classic" of the Romantic composers was Felix Mendelssohn [pronounced MEN-dell-son] (1809–47), born in Hamburg, Germany. His grandfather was a distinguished philosopher of the Enlightenment, Moses Mendelssohn (1729–86), who had farsighted visions of a world in which all people would be equal, including the Jews. Both of Felix's parents were amateur musicians; his mother gave him his first music lessons when he was four. The father's financial success as a banker, together with the social equality recently granted Jews as a result of the Enlightenment and political movements in the eighteenth century, made it possible for Felix and his siblings to be reared in a secure, happy environment. The family home in Berlin was large enough to accommodate concerts and theatrical performances for leaders of Berlin society.

A multitalented child, a prodigy second only to Mozart, Mendelssohn also had an older sister who was probably equally talented. Fanny, an excellent pianist, composed six songs in a style similar to her brother's. These were later published under his name. However, Fanny's composing was limited once she became Mrs. Hensel and a mother—she had grown up hearing that a woman's place was in the home. She did leave more than one hundred twenty piano pieces. As with Clara Schumann, her music has also been rediscovered, performed and recorded in recent years, particularly her songs.

Mendelssohn and his siblings received every possible advantage. Their days were full—perhaps too full—of lessons and studies, some of them directed by their ambitious parents. Felix later reported that as a child he longed for Sundays to

Felix Mendelssohn.

Fanny Mendelssohn, sister of Felix, was typical for her time in that her place in society was fixed by her father, her brother, and her husband. Her many compositions are now becoming widely known.

come, so that he did not have to get up at 5 o'clock to begin studying, as the children did the rest of the week. A friend reported that Felix's mother would interrupt her son's conversations by calling out: "Felix, are you doing nothing?" This friend concluded that "his brain from childhood had been taxed excessively." Mendelssohn became a brilliant pianist, organist, and violinist, composing masterpieces at age seventeen.

Mendelssohn's father had the children baptized as Lutherans and later the parents also adopted Christianity, as did many of their relatives. As a symbol of the conversion, "Bartholdy" was added to their last name, or substituted for it entirely. The combined version "Mendelssohn Bartholdy," with or without a hyphen, often appears. Mendelssohn's oratorios *Elijah* and *St. Paul,* written in the style of Handel's *Messiah,* and several works based on Lutheran chorales indicate that his adopted faith played an important part in his life. Martin Luther's famous hymn "A Mighty Fortress" (Ein' feste Burg) forms the basis for variations in *Symphony No. 5,* the "Reformation" Symphony, op. 107. Chorales appear in movements of his organ sonatas.

Mendelssohn was one of the first professional conductors. He imposed a discipline upon the players, demanded high standards—and also saw to it that their salaries were raised. He organized and for a time directed the new Leipzig Conservatory. Throughout his short life he maintained a frenetic pace, composing quantities of music, traveling, writing letters, painting. His early death from a stroke in 1847 was probably due to an inherited heart weakness. (Fanny died of the same cause in the same year.)

Ensuing generations performed Mendelssohn's music with the tempo fluctuations and dynamic extremes characteristic of truly Romantic music. Unfortunately, such practices sentimentalized and trivialized it. Perhaps as a result, though he was immensely popular in his lifetime, a reaction set in and his reputation suffered—he was even damned as a "Victorian." In addition, the anti-Semitic undercurrents that reemerged later in the century inhibited the spread of his music. The Nazis went so far as to destroy a monument to him in Leipzig and erase his name from the history books. Fortunately for us all, sanity eventually returned to Germany. Recently, the understanding of Mendelssohn's Classic roots has resulted in more objective performances of his music and a renewed appreciation of this composer.

A

Mendelssohn: A Classical Romanticist

In many ways, Mendelssohn hardly belonged in the Romantic period. No rebel against society, he seems to have accepted it completely. He worshipped the music of Bach and Mozart, liked polyphony, wrote preludes and fugues, and was perfectly at home with Classic forms. Even in his private life he was old-fashioned: happily married, he fathered five children. Compared with the true radicals of his time, Berlioz, Liszt, and Wagner, the next trio of composers that we study, it might seem as if he were born in the wrong century.

Two examples show how influential Mendelssohn's interest in music of the past was. In 1829, at the age of twenty, he directed a revival performance of Bach's *St. Matthew Passion*. A century earlier, Bach had first produced it for his uncomprehending Leipzig congregation. Almost forgotten, it was considered impossible to perform. Mendelssohn's teacher, Carl Friedrich Zelter (1758–1832), had in fact rehearsed this work himself, but did not think it practical to try to perform it in public—he turned that task over to his student! Bringing it to life was difficult, not only because the work itself is a challenge (two years of rehearsals were needed), but because traditions of performing Baroque music had died out. The tremendous success of this performance is credited with turning the Bach Revival, already underway, into a popular movement.

Besides his participation in the Bach Revival, Mendelssohn organized "historical concerts," in which he conducted older music. "Older," to his generation, meant the work of such composers as Bach, Mozart, and Beethoven. Although today we assume that concerts will include earlier music, in his time they usually consisted of new music. Mendelssohn's experiment in broadening the interests of his own audiences has now become standard programming practice.

The Romantic side to Mendelssohn is seen most clearly when he followed the Romantic trend and wrote programmatic music. For example, he portrayed geographical locations in two symphonies (the "Italian," op. 90, and the "Scotch," op. 56). He published a group of piano pieces with the collective title *Songs Without Words,* some of which bear individual titles, such as "Venetian Boat Song."

B

Mendelssohn's Music

Mendelssohn's most-often played composition has been heard by millions, but in versions that at the very least would surprise the composer. This is the famous *Wedding March* (ex. 41.1).

Example 41.1

Following a tradition established by the British royal family, who were great friends of Mendelssohn (he made ten visits to England), it has been played constantly (as recessional music) in actual wedding ceremonies. Hiring an orchestra to play it is impractical, so a trimmed-down arrangement for organ is what most people have heard.

The *Wedding March,* part of the incidental music for Shakespeare's play, *A Midsummer Night's Dream,* is the concluding movement of a suite made from this score. An *Overture* (written when Mendelssohn was only seventeen) introduces the "once upon a time" mood of the entire play and forecasts some of the action in it. The remainder of the incidental music dates from 1843. A *Nocturne* features a French horn melody which evokes night and the out-of-doors. A nimble *Scherzo* with high-pitched woodwinds matches the airy elfin creatures of this story. Typical for Mendelssohn, each movement is cast in a clear form, such as ABA, rondo, or sonata-form. When Hollywood made a film out of the play, Mendelssohn's music provided the background score, as adapted by composer Erich Wolfgang Korngold (1897–1957). At least two different choreographers have turned the incidental music into a ballet.

Choruses and soloists find Mendelssohn's powerful oratorio *Elijah,* op. 70, grateful for their voices. His chamber music ranks high, with a *Piano Trio in D minor,* op. 49, and an *Octet* (double string quartet), op. 20, the favorites. A virtuoso organist himself, he wrote well for that instrument, which had been neglected by most composers since Bach. Besides his *Preludes and Fugues,* organists frequently play his *Six Sonatas,* op. 65.

Plate 35 Delacroix painted portraits of his friends, showing one of them, Chopin, as if he were "consumed by the fire of his genius."

Plate 36 David Hockney created colorful and imaginative set designs for *Tristan und Isolde*. (Courtesy of Los Angeles Music Center Opera.)

Plate 37 Splendid royal robes add to the setting of *Boris Godunov* and help the lead character dominate the stage. (Courtesy of Video NVC Arts, London.)

Plate 38   The French impressionist artist Pierre Auguste Renoir was famous for his family scenes, as in this 1892 painting, *Young Girls at the Piano*. It shows an expectation of the times: the piano as an item of household furniture.

Plate 39   Pablo Picasso, one of the century's most prominent artists, experimented with a "cut-paper" style in his *Three Musicians,* 1921, picturing the masked players with recognizable instruments. (Philadelphia Museum of Art, The A. E. Gallatin Collection.)

Plate 40 The painting that gave "impressionism" its name is Monet's *Impression, Sunrise.*

Plate 41 This 1894 painting, *Rouen Cathedral, West Facade, Sunlight,* is one of many on this same subject painted by Claude Monet. Changing light patterns altered his impressions each time. (Courtesy of National Gallery of Art, Washington, DC; Chester Dale Collection.)

Plate 42 In 1907, Picasso created quite a stir with his *Les Demoiselles d'Avignon,* a painting with the barbaric qualities of some primitive art. Sculpture from Africa had strongly influenced him. (Oil on canvas, 8′ × 7′8″. Collection, The Museum of Modern Art, New York. Acquired through the Lillie P. Bliss Bequest.)

Plate 43 Years of research made it possible for the Joffrey Ballet to perform a re-creation of Nijinsky's original choreography for the Rite. (Courtesy of The Joffrey Ballet, Herbert Migdoll, photographer.)

The Birmingham (England) Music Festival of 1846 was the subject of this illustration in a London newspaper. The festival featured music by Mendelssohn, who was extremely popular in that country.

Mendelssohn's only violin concerto is probably his most highly regarded work. Written in 1844, its three movements are linked together, an unusual feature in concertos. Its lyrical melodies and ample opportunities for virtuoso display have made the concerto a concert favorite. Unlike the standard concerto of the Classic period, which opens with an orchestral exposition during which the soloist simply rests, Mendelssohn allows the soloist to begin immediately. Also innovative is the placement of the cadenza at the end of the development section, instead of the normal place for it, near the end of the movement.

Mendelssohn: *Violin Concerto in E Minor,* op. 64.

 CD3

(0:00)

1a m1 Broken-chord figures played by strings establish the minor tonality, and sustained woodwind notes provide a background as the soloist enters with Theme I (ex. 41.2).

60

FIRST MOVEMENT: *Allegro molto appassionato (13:20)* (49) **EXPOSITION**

Example 41.2

(0:31)
1b   m24   The soloist, at times unaccompanied, continues to dominate, playing virtuoso passages. There are occasional orchestral interruptions of bold chords.

(1:01)
1c   m47   The soloist is silent as the orchestra plays Theme I, developing it at length.

(1:32)
2   m72   Suddenly soft, the orchestral violins introduce the transition theme, which the soloist then restates (ex. 41.3).

61

Example 41.3

At the end of this section, the soloist leads quietly into Theme II, with a gently descending passage marked "tranquillo" (tranquil).

(2:58)
3a   m131   Theme II (ex. 41.4), in the major mode as is traditional, is played by flutes and clarinets. The soloist now assumes the role of accompaniment and plays a low, long-held note.

62

Example 41.4

(3:15)
3b   m139   Soon the soloist appropriates Theme II, with flute and clarinet playing a soft accompaniment. Things almost come to a halt before the end of this section.

(4:20)

4a m168 The closing theme section begins with a restatement of Theme I by
the soloist; the orchestra then begins a dialogue of Theme I motives
countered by virtuoso passages from the soloist.

63

(5:12)

4b m210 Loud trills and string tremolos signal that the exposition is ending.

(5:35)   *DEVELOPMENT*

5a m226 A soft restatement of the transition theme by the soloist begins the
development; the orchestra loudly restates the transition theme. The
dialogue continues as the orchestra recalls motives from Theme I.

64

(6:19)

5b m262 The soloist recalls Theme I while the orchestra returns to the
accompanying role it had at the beginning of the movement. A soft
timpani roll marks the start of a crescendo that leads into the
cadenza.

(7:20)   *CADENZA*

6a m298 All the notes are written out for this cadenza, but they allow
considerable rhythmic freedom. Arpeggios make up the musical
content at the start.

65

(8:07)

6b m307 Trills begin a section that recalls Theme I motives.

(8:31)

6c m322 The arpeggios, played more rhythmically, return and lead into the
recapitulation.

(8:55)   *RECAPITULATION*

7   m335 The soloist continues with the arpeggios as flute and oboe enter with
Theme I.

66

(9:14)

8a m351 The orchestra plays the transition theme in a fuller, louder version
than that of item 2.

67

(9:28)

8b   m363   Again the soloist restates the transition theme in a brief passage that leads to Theme II.

(9:51)

9a   m377   Theme II returns, played by woodwinds as in item 3, with a long note from the soloist as accompaniment. Here the pitches have been transposed to the tonic key of E, although the major mode of item 3 is kept.

[68]

(10:06)

9b   m385   Now the soloist takes over Theme II, as in item 3b. Again, the music almost comes to a stop near the end of this section.

(11:13)

10a m414   The closing theme section begins with a soft return to the minor mode, as the soloist recalls the motive of Theme II; then comes a dialogue of virtuoso passages from the soloist opposed by Theme I motives in the orchestra, as in 4a.

[69]

(12:12)

10b m459   Again, loud trills and string tremolos signal that a section is ending, as in 4b.

CODA

(12:32)

11a m473   A faster tempo accompanies a return of the transition theme, played by the soloist.

[70]

(12:51)

11b m493   As the orchestra assumes the transition theme, the soloist counters with more virtuoso passages. The duel continues almost to the end, the orchestra concluding with emphatically repeated chords.

(13:20)

11c m527   In performances of the complete concerto, a bassoon plays a sustained tone that begins a transition linking the first two movements.

The middle movement, in C major and in sextuple meter, is an andante in ABA form. Another transition links it to the third and last movement, in E major, and in quadruple meter. A sonata-form design, it bubbles over with high spirits.

HECTOR BERLIOZ 42

PREVIEW   The "radical" wing of Romanticism includes the French-born Berlioz. Like Schumann, he was a gifted writer as well as composer. Though acknowledged for the skillful handling of the orchestra that they displayed, his compositions met with hostility when first performed. Recognition for him came relatively late. He was not attracted to Classic forms, turning instead to programmatic and dramatic music. His life is a demonstration of Romantic ideals, some of them carried to extremes.

Another trio of Romantic composers, Berlioz, Liszt, and Wagner, can be classified as progressive, even radical. They were storytellers at heart, devoted to personal expression at all costs. The earliest of these was (Louis) Hector Berlioz [pronounced BEAR-lee-ohz, with the final consonant sounded, unlike many French words] (1803–69). He was born in a small town in southeast France. His father, a prosperous doctor with a wide range of interests, directed his son's education. Local teachers gave him instruction on flute and guitar, but he never learned to play the piano, a skill almost every other composer has thought necessary.

Sent to Paris to study medicine, Berlioz lived there the rest of his life. After going through the motions of being a medical student for a couple of years, he abandoned his studies, at the price of estrangement from his family and the loss of their financial support. Or as he expressed his choice more colorfully: "Forsake the immortal spirits of poetry and love and their divinely inspired strains for dirty hospital orderlies, the groans and the rattling breath of the dying! No! No!" He studied composition for a time at the Paris Conservatory. There he won the prestigious Prix de Rome despite criticism of his highly individualistic style.

In 1827, he attended a production of *Hamlet* by a visiting English dramatic group. Though Berlioz did not understand the language, both the playwright and the actress who played Ophelia, Harriet Smithson, made a tremendous impression upon him. Thereafter, he read and quoted Shakespeare avidly, basing several works upon his plays. And he fell madly in love with Miss Smithson, claimed he was obsessed with her, and followed her relentlessly, vainly hoping to meet her. When his love soured in 1830, he turned the experience into his *Symphonie fantastique*

Hector Berlioz.

Berlioz's love of the grandiose made him a special target for cartoonists.

A CONCERT OF THE PHILHARMONIC.
Caricature by Gustave Doré, published in "Le Journal pour rire," 1850.

(described later). He eventually met her in person, the obsession returned, and he persuaded her to marry him. Depressing reality then took over. Perhaps he was in love with the characters she played on stage and not with the real Harriet herself. A language barrier and poverty posed serious obstacles to their happiness and they separated after a few years, though he continued to support her.

As a composer, Berlioz earned little. He was forced to make his living as a music critic, a profession he hated in spite of his great talent for it. His witty, sometimes malicious writings are still read today. For instance, he defined music as: "The art of moving intelligent human beings, endowed with special, well-trained organs, by means of combinations of sounds. To define music thus is to admit that we do not consider it, as the saying goes, *fit for everyone.*"

He traveled widely in Europe, conducting his music to great acclaim. Unfortunately, at home in Paris his music was often greeted with hostility—or what was worse, indifference—and he grew increasingly bitter at the contrast. Ill health plagued his last years, and he died in 1869. Only in this century has his music received the recognition it deserves, assisted particularly by recordings.

In many respects, Berlioz's life provides excellent examples of Romantic ideas, some of them carried to extremes. But of course, carrying things to extremes *was* a Romantic idea.

1. He liked to "think big." For example, his *Requiem* (op. 5) calls for an already gigantic chorus and orchestra to be supported by four brass bands and eight pairs of timpani in the Dies irae section, an overwhelming depiction of the Day of Judgment. His *Te Deum* (op. 22) is supposed to be augmented by a chorus of 600 children. Space plays an essential role in both of these works. They require a large hall for performance, not just to fit everyone in but to allow the sound to come from different directions.

2. In his mind, music suggested life and feeling; he was not attracted to absolute music. He paid only lip service to sonata-form and other traditional patterns, relying more on the programmatic content of his music. The resulting forms were loose, but logical.

3. Tone color was a consuming interest. One of the master orchestrators of all time, he was the first to exploit fully the recent improvements in instruments. Colorful new ways of writing for instruments, both alone and in combinations, abound in his scores. Indeed, the orchestra *was* his instrument. He explored its possibilities in the same way that Chopin explored the possibilities of the piano. He authored a treatise on orchestration that still invites study.

4. Berlioz personified the true Romantic. His memoirs, another example of his writing skills, reveal his conviction that the composer is special, set apart from society. A passionate idealist, unwilling to compromise, he believed that music should have no traffic with commercial needs. Subject to violent emotional swings, he composed in a highly individualistic, innovative style.

Besides the titles just mentioned, Berlioz wrote dramatically inspired works, such as *The Damnation of Faust* (op. 24) and *Romeo and Juliet* (op. 17). An opera, *Benvenuto Cellini,* supplied some themes that appear also in his *Roman Carnival Overture* (op. 9), a brilliant concert overture and a good single-movement introduction to his style. His most important opera, *The Trojans,* was set to a libretto he based on Virgil's *Aeneid.* Recently revived with great success, it has become a staple of the operatic repertoire. His symphonies have subtitles indicating their programmatic inspirations. Berlioz submitted the four movements of *Harold in Italy* (op. 16), unified by a prominent viola solo, to the virtuoso Niccòlo Paganini (1782–1840), who was expecting a flashy display piece for his newly purchased viola. (Paganini was disappointed in the results.) Not surprisingly, Berlioz did not write for keyboard or for chamber music groups.

Berlioz, the master orchestrator, filled his score with innovations. For example, he called for an unusually large orchestra: sixty string players—"at least," he said; twenty-three wind players; four players for timpani at one point; four harps. His detailed directions called for such items as a particular type of drumstick and required string players to use the wood of the bow in a brief passage. He also left specific instructions for the seating of the players, with some sections on risers. Carrying on where Beethoven left off in his *Pastoral Symphony,* Berlioz merged the story-telling concepts of program music with the structure of a symphony. Beethoven had claimed that the titles he gave to individual movements of his symphony, such as "Peasants' Merrymaking," were not to be taken literally; rather, they were only expressions of feelings. Berlioz had no such inhibitions. Not content with individual titles for movements, he penned a sensational and detailed program for his symphony, which involved such unsavory associations as drug overdose and visits to witches. He distributed the program for all to read, including the English actress Harriet Smithson who unknowingly had inspired the project.

Berlioz's program begins: "A young musician of morbid sensibility and fiery imagination poisons himself with opium in a fit of love-sick despair. The narcotic dose, too weak to kill him, plunges him into a heavy sleep, accompanied by the strangest visions, during which his sensations, sentiments and memories are transformed in his sick mind into musical thoughts and images. The beloved woman has become a melody to him, an *idée fixe* as it were, that he hears everywhere."

Supplementing the traditional tempo labels for the movements are subtitles that give some hint of the story:

1. Largo—Allegro agitato e appassionato assai. "Reveries, Passions"
2. Valse. Allegro non troppo. "A Ball"
3. Adagio. "Scene in the Country"
4. Allegretto non troppo. "March to the Scaffold"
5. Larghetto-Allegro. "Dream of a Witches' Sabbath"

The melody of the beloved one, the "fixed idea," occurs in all five movements. In the first movement, which has a long slow introduction (the Largo), the melody enters with the Allegro at measure 72. (In a recorded performance lasting 14:18, the melody occurs at 4:42.) Violins and flute play it here, accompanied by a minimal string accompaniment. Its first phrase is shown in example 42.1.

Example 42.1

PART SIX THE ROMANTIC PERIOD

This theme subsequently undergoes constant changes, of meter, tempo, instrumentation, pitches, whatever, in a process called thematic transformation, a Romantic innovation. The very character of the theme is altered. Or in Berlioz's description, it moves from "passionate but at the same time noble and chaste" to "vulgar."

Cyclic form is a term applied to the concept of a multimovement work in which a returning theme provides the unifying element. *Symphonie fantastique* is an early example of cyclic form. In addition, in its first four movements there are some relationships to conventional musical forms, although in the fifth movement Berlioz abandoned conventions and relied on his program to organize the music.

In the fourth movement, the "March," the hero has killed his beloved and must die. A phrase of the *idée fixe* returns at the very end, to be cut off as the fatal blow falls, as if to show that his last thought was of *her*. But this grisly stroke is mild compared to what happens next.

In the fifth movement, "Dream of a Witches' Sabbath," the hero attends his own funeral (the Romanticists found Death and the Satanic fascinating) and the beloved one is there. As if he had not challenged society enough already, Berlioz here dared to quote a sacred Gregorian chant, the "Dies irae" from the Requiem Mass, a chant associated with Death and the Day of Judgment. (We discuss this chant on p. 86.) He continued his blasphemous ways by including church bells. Because of the close relationship of program and music, Berlioz's comments for the fifth movement appear at the appropriate places in the listening guide.

♫ CD4

"He sees himself at the witches' sabbath, in the midst of a frightful group of ghosts, magicians, monsters of all sorts, come together for his funeral. Strange noises, groans, bursts of laughter, shrieks to which other shrieks seem to reply."

FIFTH MOVEMENT: Larghetto—Allegro, "Dream of a Witches' Sabbath" (10:30) ⑤⓪

(0:00)
1a m1 Beginning very softly, cellos and basses play an upward-moving motive which is soon answered by sinister mutterings in the strings and cackles from the woodwinds.

(0:34)
1b m9 The French horn plays alone, but so softly it is inaudible in most recordings. (Berlioz wanted a "stopped" sound here, produced by the insertion of the player's hand.) The dialogue of item 1a continues. One more soft horn call completes this introduction.

"The beloved melody appears again, but it has lost its noble and timid character; it has become a trivial dance tune, mean and grotesque: it is she who comes to the sabbath."

(1:22)

2a   m21   The *idée fixe* (ex. 42.2) appears softly as a clarinet plays a jog-trotting parody version of it, with trills and grace notes adding to its "triviality."

Example 42.2

"Howlings of joy at her arrival. She takes part in the diabolic orgy."

(1:31)

2b   m29   A blast from the full orchestra sets the stage for an extended mangling of the beloved melody. It goes to an E-flat clarinet, which Berlioz chose for its high, piercing quality. He said this made it suitable for "vulgarizing" a melody—his deliberate intention.

(2:11)

2c   m65   A whirling sound in flutes and strings begins a transition, which gets gradually lower in pitch and softer to the point of inaudibility.

"Funeral knell, burlesque parody of the Dies irae."

(2:56)

3a   m102   Bells toll on *dò* and *sol,* continuing until 3e. The viola hints at a tune which will come later, the "Round-Dance of the Witches."

"Dies irae"

(3:24)

3b   m127   As promised, Berlioz quotes the Dies irae, note for note (ex. 42.3). (At this point he called for the ophicleide, a brass instrument invented in France to supply the bass line for military bands. Although revived for authentic performances, the ophicleide is generally obsolete, replaced by the smoother-sounding tubas.)

Example 42.3

(3:47)

3c   m147   Now the Dies irae is harmonized by brass and appears twice as fast. It is answered by an even-more modified and accelerated version in woodwinds and strings.

(4:04)

3d   m163   The original rhythm of the Dies irae returns, followed by an extended section in which the various versions heard in 3c return.

(5:08)

3e   m221   Bass drum rolls and ascending swoops in strings and woodwinds start a transition. Strings forecast (again!) the coming "Round-Dance."

(5:27)

4a   m241   Low strings, alone, begin the Round-Dance (ex. 42.4). Upper strings and soon woodwinds answer in fugal style in an extended section. (Berlioz thought strict polyphony was too mechanical, but he often employed polyphonic sections, like this one.)

"Witches' Round-Dance."

Example 42.4

(6:37)

4b   m305   Repeated brass chords loudly signal the end of the Round-Dance fugue as an extended transition begins. These chords alternate with soft woodwind and string figures, moving downward in pitch, and getting softer.

(7:24)

4c   m348   The Dies irae returns briefly, and fairly softly, in French horn and low strings. A gradual crescendo accompanies hints of the Round-Dance.

(8:26)

4d   m404   Strings return, loudly, to the Round-Dance.

"Dies irae and witches' Round-Dance together."

(8:37)

5a m414 On top of the Round-Dance in the strings, Berlioz superimposes the Dies irae in woodwinds and brass. Berlioz relished this kind of nonimitative contrapuntal technique because, in the words of one authority, it "bore out his faith in the combination of opposites and the juxtaposition of deliberately different materials." Soon the strings return to the whirling motive first heard at 2c.

5

(9:10)

5b m444 Violins and violas are briefly alone as they produce a clattering sound by playing with their bow-sticks contacting the strings. (Berlioz admitted that this effect was "bizarre" but justified by the grotesque subject matter of the movement.) Woodwinds attempt a restatement of the Round-Dance.

(9:55)

5c m486 A last recall of the Dies irae begins in a low range, accompanied by furious drum rolls. Berlioz specifies an even faster tempo for a brilliant end.

FRANZ LISZT 43

PREVIEW A native of Hungary, a touring piano virtuoso with incredible skills, Liszt gave succeeding generations of pianists a model of technique and showmanship that they might envy but could seldom match. Abandoning that career, he dedicated himself to composition, favoring programmatic music. Unusually generous, he promoted the careers of other composers and transcribed their music for solo piano.

Franz (sometimes the name is given as Ferenc) Liszt [pronounced simply LIST] (1811–86) was born in Hungary. His father played cello in the court orchestra and worked as an official for the same Esterházy family that Haydn had served. Recognizing the child's talent, the father began to teach Franz the piano and, when the boy was ten, moved the family to Vienna. There the young Liszt studied with two masters, Carl Czerny (1791–1857), whose piano exercises are still practiced today, and Salieri. (This makes the fourth composer we have met with some connection to Salieri: Mozart, Beethoven, Schubert, and now Liszt.)

A recital at the age of eleven launched Liszt's immensely successful concert career. In 1848, however, he was persuaded by his mistress, the Princess Carolyne Sayn-Wittgenstein, to abandon touring and concentrate on composition. He settled in the German city of Weimar as a court music director. There he wrote most of the works for which he is best known and attracted a loyal band of admiring students. We shall meet one of them, Hans von Bülow, when we read about Wagner and Brahms. Liszt generously encouraged some of the more radical of the Romantic composers, such as Wagner, by conducting their works.

In the 1860s Liszt lived in Rome, where he took minor orders in the church and wrote a good deal of religious music. Though a famous photograph shows him wearing the white collar of a priest, he was never ordained. He was entitled to call himself "Abbé Liszt." Many times earlier he had considered a religious vocation but apparently these leanings had never held him back from his liaisons with high-born ladies. One such relationship had produced a daughter, Cosima, who followed her father's example in scandalizing society by her affair with, and later marriage to, Richard Wagner. During his last years, Liszt resumed teaching and touring,

Franz Liszt.

acknowledged as the grand old man of music until he died in 1886, almost seventy-five. The anniversary of his death in 1986 sparked a renewed interest in his music, especially among pianists.

A

Liszt: A Showman for All Ages

A newspaper review in 1838 described an appearance by Liszt as follows: "We have now heard him. Just look at the pale slender youth; the long, drooping hair, the almost gloomy and yet childlike pleasant face, in this respect reminding one of Paganini, who, indeed, has been his model of hitherto undreamt-of virtuosity and technical brilliance from the very first moment he heard him and was swept away. The thunderous applause knew no bounds." As this review indicates, Liszt was much affected by the violinist-composer Paganini, whom he heard play in 1831. Paganini's technique dazzled listeners—some of them even claimed that in exchange for that technique he had sold his soul to the Devil. He was not above such tricks as cutting three strings of his violin—on stage, while the audience watched—and then proceeding to finish the piece by playing on the one remaining string.

Both in his writing for piano and in his own performance style, Liszt did for his instrument what Paganini had done for the violin. In the process, he wrote music that in its difficulty and exploitation of new effects thrust piano technique far beyond its previous limits. For his public concerts, he also invented a few audience-appealing tricks, arousing his audience to the point of hysteria with his astonishing technique. At some concerts, he had two pianos on the stage and played in turn on each. This way, everyone in the audience had a chance to watch his hands and admire his handsome profile. He wore white gloves, which he removed with great ceremony at the start of a recital and left behind on purpose for the ladies to fight over.

Liszt is generally considered the greatest pianist of his time, perhaps of all time. Despite his on-stage stunts, he was a superlative interpreter of Beethoven and Chopin. Unlike his virtuoso contemporaries, he performed Bach fugues and other Baroque music. He permanently affected concert life. Before Liszt's time, pianists appearing in concert shared the stage with others—in effect they took part in a variety act. Liszt, however, drew audiences to concerts made up solely of piano music and in so doing created the modern solo piano **recital.** His London manager suggested this term as a description of his concerts. A charismatic personality—plus strong and supple hands that could stretch well over an octave with ease—aided his success.

B

Liszt's Music

A work for solo piano, the *Liebestraum in A-flat* (c.1850), is probably Liszt's best-known single piece (ex. 43.1). ("Liesbestraum," which means "love-dream," is a title shared by three piano pieces, also called "nocturnes," which are transcriptions of the composer's songs.)

Paganini's on-stage stunts are the excuse for this caricature-silhouette.

Example 43.1

Equally familiar are his *Hungarian Rhapsodies* (1846 and afterwards) for piano. Some of them he also arranged for piano duet, and for orchestra. Like most Romantics, he did not pretend to conduct any serious research into folk tunes; he simply appropriated melodies that he might have heard played by Gypsies without worrying, as a composer today would, about how "authentic" these tunes really were. Nevertheless, the rhapsodies effectively express the shifting moods and the intense performing style of the Gypsy musician.

Thematic transformation on a grand scale furnishes the basis for Liszt's *Sonata in B Minor* (1852–53), one of the masterpieces of the Romantic piano repertoire. Also favorites are works for piano and orchestra: two *Piano Concertos*, No. 1 in E-flat (1849, 1853–56) and No. 2 in A (1839, 1849–61), and the *Totentanz* (1849), a set of variations on the Gregorian "Dies irae" theme, familiar from Berlioz's *Symphonie fantastique*, fifth movement.

Coming back into fashion are Liszt's piano transcriptions, which are arrangements for piano of other composers' songs and organ and orchestral works. Some of these represent his attempt to call attention to music that was unfairly neglected at the time, such as the songs of Schubert (there is a knuckle-breaking one based on *Erlkönig*) and the organ works of Bach. He even arranged the symphonies of Beethoven, for they were by no means as accepted, at least in the 1830s, as they are today. Other transcriptions, which deal more freely with the original music, are essentially paraphrases, for example, the almost-flippant one he wrote on Mendelssohn's *Wedding March*. (Did he betray in this piece his true feelings toward matrimony, which he quite successfully avoided?) Transcriptions filled a need in an age that had no recordings and no broadcasting. They also show Liszt's uncommon generosity—not many composers have so helped their possible competitors!

Liszt: *Les préludes* (16:41) ⑤¹

Liszt wrote thirteen symphonic poems, most of them between 1848 and 1858, and is credited with inventing the term for them ("sinfonische Dichtung," in German). The best-known is *Les préludes* [pronounced lay pray-LUDE], first performed in 1854. Despite its title, it is not a prelude to anything at all. Rather, the title comes from a long poem by the French poet Alphonse de Lamartine (1790–1869), a typically Romantic brew of Life, Death, Love, Nature, and War. Although Liszt prefaced the work with a paraphrase of the poem, the music was written first and the poem discovered later. Thus the connections between the program that is implied in the preface and details of the music are fairly general. We first quote a condensed version of that preface, then place the appropriate excerpt at the start of each new section.

Although many changes of key, meter, and tempo occur in this work, and the themes seemingly are very contrasting, it is organized by means of one basic motive, C,B,E or *dô-ti-mî*. This motive establishes the key of C major, occurring both as an independent idea and as the beginning notes of longer themes.

"What is our life but a succession of preludes . . . to that unknown song whose first solemn note is sounded by death? Love is the enchanted dawn of every heart . . . But what mortal is there, over whose first joys and happiness does not break some storm . . . What soul . . . does not try to dream away the recollection of such storms in the solitude of country life? And yet . . . when the trumpet sounds the signal of danger, he hastens to join his comrades in arms . . . and amid the uproar of battle regains confidence in himself and in his powers."

"What is our life but a succession of preludes . . ."

 CD4

(0:00)   *ANDANTE*
1a   m1   Two soft pizzicato tones in low strings set the stage: then Theme I
           begins, played by unison strings. The first three notes of the theme
      [6]   are those of the basic motive, C,B,E. Both theme and motive ask
           questions because they ascend.

(0:25)
1b   m6   The flute plays the basic motive; other woodwinds harmonize.

(0:47)
1c   m10 After a pause, item 1a is restated, a step higher.

(1:13)
1d   m15 Woodwinds play their version of the basic motive. After sustained
           chords, the woodwinds sound repeated chords, an accompaniment
           continuing until item 2.

(1:36)
1e   m19 Still in unison, strings play a series of phrases, each a variant of
           Theme I. The harp plays rippling arpeggios; trombones softly intone
           a slow version of the basic motive. Both of these elements continue
           until item 2. A gradual crescendo begins. After it peaks, the tempo
           slows and the strings lead into the next section in a grandly moving
           passage.

(2:36)   *ANDANTE*
2a   m35 No more questions—here is a positive statement, perhaps affirming   *MAESTOSO*
           Life itself, in a staccato transformation of Theme I, played by low-
      [7]   range instruments. A slower theme moves upward, played by higher-
           range instruments, a combination shown here (ex. 43.2). The circled
           notes are the basic motive, C,B,E.

Example 43.2

(3:00)
2b   m40   Brasses add a fanfarelike pattern that is echoed by timpani. Volume
            drops suddenly, exposing a broken-chord string accompaniment that
            continues until item 4.

            ". . . to that unknown song, whose first solemn note is sounded by
            death?"

(3:28)
3a   m47   Strings play an intense transformation of Theme I, restoring the
            questioning mood. Bassoons and basses quote the basic motive at
[8]   ends of phrases, creating an ominous effect suitable to the idea of the
            "unknown song" and of death.

(3:55)
3b   m55   The French horn joins the strings in playing the melody.

(4:21)
3c   m63   A short interlude in the minor mode is played by strings and
            clarinet. The volume drops as strings lead smoothly into the next
            section.

            "Love is the enchanted dawn of every heart."

(4:52)
4a   m70   Theme II (in the new key of E major) is introduced by French horns
            and violas. Though it sounds new, analysis will show its relationship
[9]   to the basic motive (the circled notes, ex. 43.3).

Example 43.3

espressivo ma tranquillo

(5:31)
4b   m80   Theme II continues with oboes playing the melody. Violins and flute
            compete with a soaring countermelody. Soon, tempo and volume
            changes restore the questioning mood of the beginning.

(6:53)

4c m101 French horn returns with the "unknown song" version of Theme I (as in item 3a) but in a new rhythm. The section ends with harp tones and a pause.

"But what mortal is there, over whose first joys and happiness does not break some storm, dispelling his fanciful illusions?"

(7:30)

5a m109 Cellos begin with the basic motive, then rumble up and down the chromatic scale while other strings add to the tension with tremolos.

(7:44)

5b m119 Woodwinds reinforce the string tremolo chords in chromatic, rising lines. Many volume changes make it easy to imagine a gathering storm. Soon French horns interrupt loudly.

ALLEGRO MA NON TROPPO

(8:00)

6a m131 Trombones snap out the basic motive—the storm has indeed arrived. A fairly lengthy section follows.

(8:48)

6b m161 Brasses add a fanfarelike motive in repeated tones; the timpani echoes it.

(9:04)

6c m171 Violins play the fanfare motive. The storm is soon over and a chromatic line played by strings alone leads smoothly into the next section.

ALLEGRO TEMPESTOSO

(9:24)

7a m182 Another statement of the "unknown song" begins in the oboe, using the rhythm of item 4c. The unaccompanied measures of this solo show additions of new notes to the original melody.

UN POCO PIÙ MODERATO

(10:00)
7b m192 Violins play the melody of 7a, as the music grows softer and slower. Again the harp provides a connecting link to the next section.

"What soul thus cruelly wounded does not try to dream away the recollection of such storms in the solitude of country life?"

ALLEGRO PASTORALE

(10:30)
8a m201 A new motive is softly played in turn by French horn, oboe, and clarinet against a static accompaniment of strings, conjuring up pictures of beautiful nature scenes—or a shepherd playing his pipes.

13

(10:53)
8b m214 Woodwinds play together as the shepherd piping sound continues. Strings soon join in the conversation.

(11:51)
8c m252 The flute plays alone, imitated by oboe and clarinet to finish the dialogue. Violins then lead into the next section.

(12:03)
9a m260 Tranquil Theme II—the "love" theme of item 4a—returns, now played by violins, combined with the "shepherd pipe" motive used as a countermelody.

14

(12:34)
9b m280 Flutes join violins in Theme II as the countermelody continues.

(12:57)
9c m296 Theme II is restated in a different key. Tempo increases as a crescendo begins.

(13:25)
9d m316 Another playing of Theme II begins, but a fanfarelike motive in the brass hints that the consolations of nature are no longer needed. A swirling crescendo leads into the final section of the piece.

"And yet when the trumpet sounds the signal of danger, he hastens to join his comrades, no matter what the cause that calls him to arms."

(14:02)

10a m344　Very fast scales in violins alone begin this section, then continue as an accompaniment for a brassy transformation of Theme I, back to the original key of C major. Now it emerges as a march. Lower-range instruments answer with a similarly martial transformation of the basic motive.

ALLEGRO MARZIALE ANIMATO

15

(14:19)

10b m356　A somewhat softer section, in violins and woodwinds, interrupts. After a trumpet call, a crescendo leads into the next item.

(14:38)

10c m370　Theme II returns, also transformed into a march, with a heavy use of the expanded percussion section (snare drum, cymbals, and bass drum).

(14:51)

10d m378　The sounds of 10c continue, but with the martial transformation of Theme I.

(15:07)

10e m386　As in item 10b, a slightly softer moment interrupts. The trumpet call returns; then a long crescendo, using the music first heard in item 1f, paves the way for the grand finale.

"and amid the uproar of battle regains confidence in himself and in his powers."

(15:36)

11　m405　The return of the music of item 2a adds to the sense of culmination. The expanded percussion section and a molto ritardando bring the work to a most emphatic conclusion.

ANDANTE MAESTOSO

16

44 RICHARD WAGNER

PREVIEW The German-born Wagner was linked to the progressive composers by temperament, and, as Liszt's son-in-law, by family ties. Lacking a thorough musical education, he transformed himself into a gifted conductor and a composer whose effect on all music was far-reaching. For various reasons, Wagner is still a controversial figure. Opera was Wagner's field, but opera on his own terms, far removed from the Italian model of recitative and aria. Writing his own libretti, he took his subject matter from Nordic myth and German history.

The third of our "radical" composers, and the one most closely identified with the "music of the future," is Richard Wagner [pronounced VAHG-ner] (1813–83). The youngest of nine children, he was born in the German city of Leipzig. His family was not particularly musical, although his stepfather had several artistic interests, among them acting, writing, and portrait painting. Four of Wagner's sisters became actresses, and as a child he was fascinated by the theater. He began piano lessons but lacked the patience to learn correct technique. As a teenager, overwhelmed by hearing Beethoven's symphonies, he decided that he must devote himself to music.

At first Wagner attempted to teach himself, but he later found a congenial instructor. Biographers disagree concerning the extent of his musical training. Some claim he had only six months of instruction; others suggest as much as four years. Whichever is true, compared to the thorough musical education of most composers, his formal training was minimal. This did not prevent him from becoming the most famous composer of his century and an excellent conductor as well. In his twenties he was a successful opera conductor in a series of European cities. His attempts to produce his works in Paris, however, proved such a failure that he endured a stint in debtors' prison.

Wagner rather foolishly participated in the revolutionary movements that began in 1848. When they failed he was forced to flee Germany and settle in Switzerland. There he doggedly continued to compose operas, though he saw little chance of their being performed. One of the few opera composers to write his own libretti

as well, Wagner often worked on the words for one opera while the music for another was taking shape.

In 1864 Wagner's prospects were especially bleak. It seemed impossible to stage his works. Political situations denied him access to areas where he might have succeeded. Deeply in debt as always, he desperately needed help. Amazingly, the nineteen-year-old king of Bavaria, the largest of the separate German states of the time, came to his rescue. Extravagantly romantic and an ardent lover of Wagner's music, King Ludwig II (1845–86) provided Wagner an allowance, paid his debts, and announced that he would support productions of his operas. Despite growing opposition from his government, Ludwig proved a loyal patron for many years. (Ludwig is often dubbed "Mad King Ludwig," and not without reason. He spent his subjects' money lavishly, building royal castles in a medieval style, castles that are tourist attractions today. Later declared insane, he was deposed. He committed suicide under "mysterious circumstances.")

Ludwig's loyalty was strained to the utmost by the scandal Wagner created in seducing Liszt's daughter, Cosima. Then a mother of two daughters, Cosima was the wife of Hans von Bülow, the distinguished conductor and pianist. That von Bülow was a tireless champion of Wagner's music seems not to have inhibited the pair at all. Cosima bore Wagner three children—named after Wagnerian opera

Locating his "Festspielhaus" on a slight rise in Bayreuth, Wagner designed this functional building specifically for the requirements of his operas.

characters—while still legally married to von Bülow. Von Bülow, amazingly and selflessly, continued to conduct Wagner's music. Eventually, the death of Wagner's first wife and Cosima's divorce enabled the two to marry and the scandal blew over.

Besides supporting Wagner and financing productions of his music, Ludwig also advanced money to build a theater in the small Bavarian town of Bayreuth [pronounced BYE-royt]. Wagner designed this theater especially—and exclusively—for productions of his works. He considered this necessary because the staging of his operas required innovations that existing opera houses could not physically manage. It was difficult to show on stage such things as the Rhine maidens swimming in the river, a giant transforming himself into a dragon, and Valhalla burning. Even today, staging a Wagnerian work is a challenge for stage director and musicians alike. Wagner demanded control of the entire enterprise so that he could select the participants, since the demands his music made upon them were so great. And he personally helped raise money for the project.

Wagner's great "Ring" cycle premiered in Bayreuth in 1876 (we discuss the "Ring" cycle on page 325). An invited, international audience of royalty and musical notables assembled for the occasion, with a host of newspaper correspondents covering the story. Even today, during every summer, Bayreuth festival performances of Wagner's works attract an audience that stoically ignores the lack of air conditioning (too noisy) and other creature comforts (although thin upholstery was added to the seats recently).

The total dedication to his cause that Wagner expected from all he met was matched by his own intense efforts in composing, conducting, producing, and financing his music. Eventually his health suffered and in 1883, while vacationing in Venice with his family, he died of a heart attack. He rests today in the garden of the spacious home he had built in Bayreuth, property which is now an historical monument supported by the German state.

People either loved Wagner or hated him. For example, the Austrian Anton Bruckner (1824–96) dedicated a symphony to Wagner, who rewarded him with these reputed words: "I know of only one composer who measures up to Beethoven, and that is Bruckner." Some disciples ardently imitated his style. The German Englebert Humperdinck (1854–1921), a music copyist and assistant to Wagner, composed *Hansel and Gretel,* a charming accommodation of Wagnerian musical techniques to a German folktale. (Yes, there really was such a person before the twentieth-century pop singer helped himself to the name!) Some admirers later turned against him, such as the great philosopher Friedrich Nietzsche (1844–1900). Others became enemies early and never relented. Wagner's most implacable foe was the enormously influential music critic Eduard Hanslick (1825–1904), whose still widely read book, *On the Beautiful in Music,* is a polemic for the supremacy of absolute music—the opposite of Wagner's theory of music.

Wagner: A Controversial Figure

Even today the dust has not settled around Wagner's image. More has been written about him than about any other composer, because he was active in so many fields, because he was such a singular individual, and because so many unresolved feelings persist about his music and its ultimate place in history. The several reasons that account for this situation can be related either to the man or to his music.

1. Even the most ardent Wagnerites admit that he was not a nice person. At best self-centered, at worst an egomaniac, dangerously close to being a con-man, he pursued his goals ruthlessly. Because he needed a luxurious life-style to stimulate his creative juices, he amassed enormous debts, which he had no intention of repaying. Convinced that his first wife Minna did not understand him, he sought out women who did. Unfortunately, they had husbands who understood Wagner all too well. Principles or conventions of society had no meaning for him unless they could help him in his crusade.

2. Wagner's essays created much ammunition to fuel controversies. Besides music, he discussed such topics as vivisection, which he opposed; the future of Western civilization, which he felt to be in danger; and the influence of Jews in music. His stance on this latter subject caused many to brand him an anti-Semite, a charge that still clings to his name although his Jewish associates at the time defended him. That the Nazis ardently promoted his music for nationalistic purposes makes the charge even more serious.

His opinions on the proper role of art in life differed so strikingly from the prevailing notions of his time that he could hardly avoid criticism. For him, "art for art's sake" was no mere aesthetic principle; it stated his creed, which might be drastically summarized as follows: Music does not exist for the entertainment of an audience; the audience exists for the sake of music and assembles like a congregation to worship at the shrine that Wagner has provided for them. Indeed, the twentieth-century composer Stravinsky in his autobiography asks, "Is not all this comedy of Bayreuth, with its ridiculous formalities, simply an unconscious aping of a religious rite?"

Wagner claimed that he was writing the "music of the future" and, in so doing, following in the footsteps of Beethoven. In Wagner's own words: "The last symphony of Beethoven is the redemption of Music from out her own peculiar element into the realm of *universal art*. It is the human evangel of the art of the future. Beyond it no forward step is possible; for upon it the perfect artwork of the future alone can follow, the *universal drama* to which Beethoven has forged for us the key." The assumption that only Wagner and his friends were the true followers of Beethoven and hence were the "musicians of the future" disturbed a good many people.

Just as he questioned conventional morality, Wagner questioned traditional ideas about opera. In an essay published in 1851, Wagner coined the phrase **music drama** to identify his mature works. By this label, he meant that traditional opera short-changed dramatic values, moving the action forward during the recitative, but allowing it to remain static in the aria. He claimed that opera had become an "arbitrary conglomeration of single, shorter vocal forms." By erasing such distinctions, music and drama would unfold continuously, creating an "endless melody." Not only should music and drama be unified, but all the arts must be brought together in a "universal art work." The ancient Greek tragedy was such a unified art work, or so Wagner believed. Later, separated and isolated, all the arts had suffered. Poetry, song, instrumental music, stage settings—all should be reunited in music drama—Wagnerian music drama, of course. True to his theories, he gave meticulous instructions regarding the sets and acting for his operas. Furthermore, the drama itself should be based upon myth, a repository of universal truths.

3. Wagner's mature music was revolutionary. Extremely chromatic harmony, with frequent key changes and few complete cadences, obscures a tonal center. The distinctive chord at the beginning of his *Prelude to Tristan and Isolde* made such an impact that historians refer to it as the "Tristan chord," saying that in 1857 tonality began to dissolve with this work. (This chord, in Wagner's spelling, F,B,D-sharp,G-sharp, belongs to no one key. However, when notated as F,A-flat, C-flat,E-flat, it is the conventional half-diminished seventh chord.) *Tristan and Isolde* elevates passion to such a commanding position that only death can satisfy it. In Wagner's poetic description of the *Prelude,* the subject matter is "yearning, yearning, unquenchable, ever-regenerated longing—languishing, thirsting; the only redemption— death, extinction, eternal sleep!" Appropriately, the harmony of this work remains unresolved until the end.

Wagner's ideas about musical form were equally extreme. Because most of his music is associated with a text, he had little need for the solutions of the past, such as sonata-form or theme-and-variation. Even if he had written many independent instrumental works, it is doubtful he would have followed these forms. He rejected "transitions" and "bridges" (he described such passages in Mozart symphonies as "mere padding") because he wanted every note to possess dramatic significance. In keeping with his theories, the music is continuous. Seldom is there a pause until the end of an act.

B

Wagner's Music

Everyone has heard at least one Wagner melody because it is his music that traditionally accompanies wedding parties as they process down the aisle. "Here comes the bride" are words that, perhaps unfortunately, fit the rhythmic motive of his "Bridal Chorus," a portion of *Lohengrin,* Act 3. (If brides knew how short-lived the marriage in this opera was, they might be less eager to choose Wagner's music for their processional.) This relatively early (1848) work predates his fully worked-out theories. So does *Tannhäuser* (1843–45), from which comes the stirring *Pilgrim's Chorus* and a hit tune for baritone, the *Song to the Evening Star.*

Tristan and Isolde (1857–59), with its influential "Tristan chord" mentioned earlier, breaks away from older operatic traditions and is arguably the best single example of the mature Wagnerian style. Wagner's monumental "Ring" cycle (*Der Ring des Nibelungen*), based on Nordic myth, is his greatest achievement. It is a set of four operas, each a self-contained work lasting from three to five hours. Wagner planned the four works to be performed on four successive evenings. At the same time, the four operas share many characters and musical motives. He began drafting the text as early as 1848; not until 1876 was the complete cycle performed.

Wagner begins the cycle with *Das Rheingold,* in which Wotan, the ruler of the gods, builds his castle, Valhalla. The exciting *Ride of the Valkyries,* a portion of the second drama in the Ring, *Die Walküre,* is familiar. In the third drama, *Siegfried,* we meet the hero, born of an incestuous mating of the twin children Wotan had fathered by an earthly mother. The cycle ends with *Götterdämmerung* (Twilight of the Gods), in which the gods see their cherished Valhalla destroyed and the world purged by fire as the result of the actions they had taken because of their lust for gold and power. (More than one commentator has seen a parallel between Wagner's "Ring" and modern society!)

To unify his lengthy works on a surface level, Wagner depended upon a technique called (not by him, but by others) **leitmotif** (sometimes spelled "leitmotiv") [pronounced LITE-mo-teef]. Scholars have isolated and labeled anywhere from seventy to one hundred motives in the "Ring" alone. A leitmotif is a short musical motive, a kind of identification tag that represents *something:* a character, event, thing, locality, emotion, or idea. All these "somethings" we shall call "referents." The leitmotif appears in the orchestra when the referent first occurs in the drama. (Although the characters occasionally sing a leitmotif, more often the vocal line is a counterpoint to the web of motives spun by the orchestra.) Thereafter, the motives appear in endless variations or transformations, as their melodic intervals, harmonizations, rhythms, and tone colors change. These are musical indications that the referent itself is changing.

It is true that many composers have treated returning motives in their operas in a similar fashion. Carmen's "Fate" motive undergoes comparable transformation throughout Bizet's *Carmen.* Wagner's leitmotif technique was much like the thematic transformation that Romantic composers such as Liszt found useful in organizing their works. What is striking is how Wagner's motives so well match the essential character of the referent. A simple example is "Siegfried's Horn Call," which begins with a triad-based motive of *do-sol-mi-do* (ex. 44.1).

Example 44.1

When it represents Siegfried as a youthful, free-spirited hero, the motive is played in a fast tempo by a solo French horn. But when he has become the mate of Brünnhilde, Wotan's favorite daughter, now demoted to the status of an ordinary mortal, his motive moves down a fifth, is much slower, and acquires the harmony of three horns. He has, musically speaking, settled down. Significantly, when Brünnhilde sends him off to seek further adventure, the youthful, solo French horn motive returns. Both versions of the motive occur in *Siegfried's Rhine Journey,* a portion of *Götterdämmerung* that is often played as a concert work. (The mature Siegfried motive comes at 2:01, the youthful Siegfried at 5:24 in a recording that lasts 11:44.)

PART SIX THE ROMANTIC PERIOD

An important character in Wagner's *Die Meistersinger,* Hans Sachs was the town shoemaker in Nuremberg. He was also the unofficial leader of the town, which honored his memory by erecting this statue. (Courtesy of the City of Nuremberg.)

While Wagner's ideas were new and controversial, the actual orchestral sounds he called for were typical of other late Romantic composers. Like them, he wrote for a large orchestra with an expanded brass section. He included specially designed "Wagner tubas," which were more like French horns.

Die Meistersinger [pronounced dee MY-ster-zinger] was completed in 1868. The full title of this work is translated as "The Mastersingers of Nuremberg." As was Wagner's custom, he wrote the text as well. The opera contrasts markedly with both *Tristan* and the "Ring" cycle. Here myth gives way to real characters who lived in the town of Nuremberg in the 1500s. The music is more diatonic than chromatic, and earlier operatic traditions still influence this work. For example,

Wagner: *Die Meistersinger von Nürnberg*

As the set designer's sketches show, the concluding scene of *Die Meistersinger* requires a large number of singers on stage. This plan comes from the 1965 production of the San Francisco Opera. (Courtesy of San Francisco Opera. Photograph by Pete Peters.)

Walther's "Prize Song" is suspiciously like an aria. And *Die Meistersinger* is a comedy (Wagner's only one), ending happily with its young lovers united. There is, however, a serious message in the work: how to reconcile traditional values with creative innovation.

The Mastersingers are good, solid, middle-class craftsmen. Musical talent is not needed to join their Guild; passing a test, to show understanding of their pedantic "rules" for writing songs, is. Just as it is easy to suspect that Wagner identified himself with the hero Walther, it is obvious that he equated at least some of the Mastersingers with the carping music critics who had made his life difficult. He turned the chief "marker" or judge of the group, the character Beckmesser, into a thinly disguised caricature of his enemy, the music critic Eduard Hanslick.

Overture (10:07) (52)

The overture establishes the atmosphere of a well-ordered German town while at the same time previewing themes to come. Two of the themes are associated with the Mastersingers themselves, and one of those themes also receives a parody treatment. A third main theme comes from Walther's "Prize Song." In addition, many phrases in the overture can be identified with characters or events in the opera. The overture closes with a combination of the three main themes, creating a complex web that recalls Renaissance polyphony.

CD4

(0:00)

1   m1   The full orchestra announces the pompous "Guild" theme. After its beginning *dô-sol-sol-sol* motive, it moves in even rhythm values up and down the scale (ex. 44.2).

Example 44.2

(1:03)

2   m27 A new theme, more lyrical and with more rhythmic variety, serves as a transition section to the "March" theme to come.

(1:46)

3   m41 A brass fanfare begins the "March" theme (ex. 44.3) and returns many times thereafter. A genuine Mastersinger tune, the theme itself is based on the tonic triad.

Example 44.3

(2:34)

4   m59 Another transition section begins as the "March" theme concludes. The tempo slows as a modulation takes place to a new key (E).

(4:07)

5   m97 Now the violins play a portion of the "Prize Song" in a quadruple meter version (ex. 44.4). (This melody will appear in the song's third stanza.)

Example 44.4

(5:23)

6　m122　Woodwinds alone begin a soft, staccato version of the "Guild"

☐22　theme, making a parody of it with much faster notes. Strings
counter with another theme from the opera and the woodwinds
continue their parody, with the strings finally joining in. (The
Mastersingers have apprentices, who like to make fun of their
masters behind their backs.)

(6:41)

7　m151　At the peak of thematic complexity, the trombones enter solemnly

☐23　with the "Guild" theme, then lead into the polyphonic conclusion.

(7:00)

8　m158　Three themes sound at once: the "Guild" theme (item 1) in basses

☐24　and tuba, the "March" theme (item 3) in mid-range (where it is
harder to hear) but twice as fast as before, and the "Prize Song"
(item 5), soaring in the high range, led by violins.

(8:17)

9　m188　Abandoning the other themes, Wagner recalls the original form of

☐25　the "March" theme, in the brasses, now accompanied by a powerful
running string accompaniment.

(9:14)

10　m211　With a flourish of cymbals and triangle, a phrase of the "Guild"

☐26　theme returns. Wagner ends the overture as it began—perhaps a
bow to convention?

With the resounding cadence of the overture (no pause for latecomers to be
seated!), the curtain rises to reveal the townspeople in church, singing as the service concludes with a chorale worthy of Bach.

Between chorale phrases, the two young lovers-to-be exchange glances.
Walther (tenor) has just arrived in town. He is a knight, a member of the upper
class. He is musically talented, innovative, impatient with tradition, and self-
confident. Eva (soprano) is the daughter of a leading merchant and hence part of
the middle class. Her father, a member of the Guild of Mastersingers, has promised her hand in marriage to the winner of the song contest soon to be held by the
Mastersingers.

If Walther wishes to win Eva, he must somehow enter and win that contest.
This goal forces him to adopt the Mastersingers' traditional ways and compose in
the archaic German song form that they favored. With the aid of the wise, mature
Hans Sachs, the town shoemaker and the most admirable of the Mastersingers,
he pulls it off. Sachs helps him finish a compelling melody that the younger man

Eva and Walther are the center of attention in the conclusion of *Die Meistersinger* in this 1965 production. (Courtesy of San Francisco Opera. Photograph by Pete Peters.)

said came to him in a dream. In the contest, Walther sings this song, a blend of tradition and innovation, and wins Eva, his "prize." That is why his "aria" is called the "Prize Song."

 CD4

When Hans Sachs instructs Walther how to complete his song, he explains the German bar form (AAB, though of course he does not use those letters to describe it). The form resembles a family, Sachs says. The first two stanzas, set to the same music, are like husband and wife. Then there must be a third stanza, not exactly the same

"Prize Song" (4:39)

but similar, like the child in a family. It forms a logical conclusion. Accordingly, in Walther's "Prize Song" there are three stanzas, musically related according to the AAB plan. The third stanza's melody, first heard in the overture at item 5, now occurs in the key of C in triple meter.

(0:00)

1

27

(As Walther prepares to sing, the orchestra plays a simple major triad. Harp arpeggios suggest a plucked string instrument that Walther might play to accompany himself.)

Morgenlich leuchtend im rosigen Schein,	Glowing in morning's rosy light,
Von Blüt und Duft geschwellt die Luft,	the air heavy with scented blossoms,
Voll aller Wonnen nie ersonnen	full of every undreamed-of joy,
Ein Garten lud mich ein,	a garden invited me in.
Dort unter einem Wunderbaum,	There, under a wonderful tree,
Von Früchten reich behangen,	with much fruit hanging,
Zu schau'n in sel'gen Liebestraum,	to see in a blessed dream of love,
Was höchstem Lustverlangen	the highest fulfillment
Erfüllung kühn verhiess,	of joy's desires, the most beautiful
Das schönste Weib, Eva im Paradies.	wife, Eva in Paradise!

(1:48)

2

28

(In performances of the complete opera, between stanzas, Mastersingers and townspeople softly voice their amazement at the unexpected beauty of Walther's song.)

Abendlich dämmernd umschloss mich die Nacht;	In the evening, night enfolded me;
Auf steilem Pfad war ich genaht	on a steep path I approached
Zu einer Quelle reiner Welle,	a spring of pure water,
Die lockend mir gelacht;	which laughingly called to me:
Dort unter einem Lorbeerbaum,	there, under a laurel tree,
Von Sternen hell durchschienen,	with the stars shining brightly,
Ich schaut' im wachen Dichtertraum,	I saw, waking in a poet's dream,
Von heilig holden Mienen,	with a holy and fair face,
Mich netzend mit dem edlen Nass,	sprinkling me with that precious water,
Das hehrste Weib, die Muse des Parnass.	the most wonderful woman, the Muse of Parnassus.

(Once again the listeners should participate, expressing their approval of the song.)

Huldreichster Tag,	Most glorious day,
Dem ich aus Dichters Traum erwacht!	to which I awoke from a poet's dream!
Das ich erträumt, das Paradies	That Paradise which I dreamed of,
In himmlisch neu verklärter Pracht,	lay radiant before me,
Hell vor mir lag,	transformed in the glory of heaven;
Dahin lachend nun der Quell den Pfad	there the laughing spring showed me the
Mir wies; die dort geboren,	path; she who was born there,
Mein Herz erkoren,	chosen by my heart,
Der Erde lieblichstes Bild	on earth the most beautiful image,
Als Muse mir geweiht,	is my Muse,
So heilig ernst als mild,	blessed, sincere, and gentle,
Ward kühn von mir gefreit	boldly have I wooed her,
Am lichten Tag der Sonnen,	in the sun's bright light,
Durch Sanges Sieg gewonnen	and won, through the victory of Song,
Parnass und Paradies!	Parnassus and Paradise!

Walther's song lacks a final cadence, which was Wagner's normal way of operating. The auditors are so moved that they join him on his last syllable and enthusiastically proclaim him to be the contest winner. Then Eva adds her voice, employing the motive that begins the third stanza, ending this section with a long trill in the best Baroque tradition.

Once Walther has won Eva, the opera moves to a conclusion fairly quickly— at least for Wagner. Walther accepts his membership in the Mastersingers after Hans Sachs has persuaded him by singing his tribute to "Holy German art." All ends happily to the accompaniment of the music with which the overture began.

45 GIUSEPPE VERDI

PREVIEW   Wagner's Italian counterpart is Verdi, who was equally dedicated to the transformation of traditional opera. More willing than Wagner to adjust to life's realities, Verdi transformed opera little by little. At the same time, he himself matured musically during an extraordinarily long lifetime. Nationalism affected his career as his name became a symbol of Italian liberation.

Wagner, who composed German opera, is often compared to his Italian counterpart, Verdi, but both probably would say that the differences outweighed the similarities. Giuseppe Verdi [pronounced VAIR-dee] (1813–1901) was born in a village in northern Italy. Apparently mistrusting biographers, he supplied them with misleading information about his youth. For example, he cited his humble origins, calling himself a "peasant," but in fact his ancestors were landowners and tradespeople. His family took much pride in the musical ability he showed as a child, so he was instructed by local musicians. Although he claimed that the instrument he had been given was a "miserable spinet," he kept it all his life.

At the age of eighteen, with the help of a wealthy merchant who later became his father-in-law, he went to Milan to study music. He was denied admission to the Milan Conservatory, a rejection he felt keenly and resented all his life. (In fact, he was four years too old by the institution's standards and his piano technique was "faulty.") So he found a private teacher and learned quickly. He had some early success with his operas, but after the sudden deaths of his wife and two infant children he became so despondent he resolved to give up composing.

At this very time, a friend persuaded him to examine a libretto based upon the Biblical story of the captive Jews in Babylon. His eyes happened to fall on the chorus of Hebrew exiles, "Va, pensiero, sull'ali dorate" (Go, my thought, on golden wings). As he later reported, "I was much moved, because the verses were almost a paraphrase from the Bible, the reading of which had always delighted me." Something in the despair of the Jews at being torn from their native land so touched him that almost against his will he resumed composing.

An American dollar bill shows a picture of George Washington. Similarly, an Italian 1000-lire bill (now obsolete) bears the likeness of Giuseppe Verdi.

The finished opera, *Nabucco* (Nebuchadnezzar), achieved a great success when first performed in 1842, due in part to the political situation. Italy, then divided into many small states, suffered under the ruthless control of Austria. The Italian audiences identified themselves with the exiled Israelites in the story. Verdi's chorus *Va, pensiero,* representing the longing of the Israelites for their home, became enormously popular, almost a hymn of Italian liberation.

This triumph assured Verdi's success. Audiences continued to detect in his operas thinly disguised appeals for liberation from foreign domination. Since many patriots were working for Italian unification and independence under the rule of a king, Verdi's career was further assisted when his name became a political symbol. As luck would have it, the letters of his name coincided with the initials of a slogan: "*V*ittorio *E*mmanuele *R*e *D*'*I*talia" (Victor Emmanuel, King of Italy). While it would have been dangerous to use the slogan in full, shouting "Viva Verdi" might be excused as simply showing approval for the composer. Italy eventually won its independence and unification, and Verdi was honored by being elected to the Italian parliament, although he accepted reluctantly because he had no interest in being a politician.

Other composers might write out of some deep need to create, regardless of demand. Not Verdi. A very practical, down-to-earth man, he wrote on commission, for specific situations. After all, he was also a wealthy farmer who owned a large estate not far from his birthplace and spent much of his time managing it. He extracted a high price for his work, both from publishers and from producers of his operas. Commissions came not just from Italy, but from Russia, France, and even Egypt. He continued to compose and to develop his style throughout a very long life. He was nearly eighty when his last opera appeared. After his death in 1901, Italians closed schools and the world mourned.

Many years before, Verdi had decided to use his wealth to create a home in Milan for retired musicians (Casa di Riposo per Musicisti). With characteristic attention to detail, he helped in its planning and supervised its completion. His will instructed that he and his second wife, Giuseppina Strepponi, be buried there. A former opera singer and a strong, capable woman, she profoundly influenced Verdi. The home is still in service today; in fact, it and the aged singers who live there are the subjects of a warm-hearted documentary video entitled *Tosca's Kiss*. (Tosca is the heroine of an opera by another Italian, Puccini.)

A

Verdi: First Name in Italian Opera

Italians have always loved singing; the language itself is so rich in vowels that even when spoken it sounds almost like music. Italians invented opera, and their operatic style swept Europe. When Verdi began his work, the leading opera composers were Gioacchino Rossini (1792–1868), famous for his sparkling *Barber of Seville* (this is the opera with the oft-parodied cry of "Feeeee-ga-ro); Gaetano Donizetti (1797–1848), whose tragic *Lucia di Lammermoor* contains a superb operatic ensemble, the celebrated sextet; and Vincenzo Bellini (1801–35), best known for *Norma,* a showcase for virtuoso sopranos.

The traditions of Italian opera were firmly established. The typical opera consisted of separate numbers (recitatives, arias, ensembles), the items discussed in Chapter 26. Singers expected their arias to contain abundant opportunities to impress the audience. In fact, if the singers were dissatisfied with the music supplied by the composer, they might substitute something else that suited their voices better. The quality of the drama mattered little, in fact, the more melodramatic the better. Periodically, strong-minded composers attempted to reform opera and impose more discipline upon the singers, but the old traditions stoutly resisted change.

However, Verdi managed to accomplish the near-impossible by an evolutionary process. Never a revolutionary, he worked gradually, accepting the limitations of opera houses and audiences, adapting to the requirements of the ever-present political censor. He invariably provided grateful music for the "prima donna" and for everyone else. And still, he transformed opera. His early operas (before 1850) followed tradition. By the time of his last opera, *Falstaff* (first performed in 1893), he was writing continuous music, not separate numbers. The changes in his style caused some observers to think that he had succumbed to Wagnerian influence. In a letter to his publisher, Verdi marked three exclamation points to express his indignation at this charge: "A fine result, after a career of 35 years, to end up as an *imitator*!!!"

With the passage of time, Verdi developed increasing skill in handling the orchestra, making it an essential element on an equal footing with the singers. Though at first he drew criticism for his "organ-grinder tunes" and "oom-pah" accompaniments, his music became far more subtle, reflecting the complex individual characters in the story. As a source for the libretto, Shakespeare eventually replaced melodrama. And the Italians, who attended opera in search of simple entertainment, much as Americans go to baseball games, followed him all the way.

In many ways, Verdi's success resembled Wagner's. Dissatisfied with opera as they found it, both transformed it. Wagner's influence on the musical world as a whole may have been more profound, but more people whistled Verdi's tunes. However, their basic attitudes differed markedly. Verdi remained true to the Italian genius for vocal melody; Wagner gave most of his themes to the orchestra.

B

Themes from some of Verdi's twenty-eight operas quickly became popular tunes in Italy, ground out by barrel organs, whistled, or hummed as people worked. His early *Il Trovatore* (1853) had its *Anvil Chorus. La Traviata* (1853), with its lilting *Sempre libera,* reached a new audience recently in a filmed version. As Verdi matured, the obvious tunes became fewer, but *Aida* (1871) is remembered for its *Cèleste Aida,* a show-stopping aria for tenors, and its *Triumphal March* (ex. 45.1).

Verdi's Music

Example 45.1

Otello (1887) and *Falstaff* (1893), the products of his vital old age, magically transfer the original dramas of his beloved Shakespeare to the operatic stage. Verdi's expert librettist for these ventures, Arrigo Boito (1842–1918), was himself a distinguished composer of operas.

Verdi also composed a *Requiem Mass* (1874) for chorus, soloists, and full orchestra, which the unsympathetic Germans described as an opera in church clothing. Extremely dramatic—the terrors of the dammed awaiting the fires of hell have never been portrayed more frighteningly than in its "Dies irae"—it commemorated the passing of a great Italian patriot, Alessandro Manzoni. For that reason it is often called the "Manzoni Requiem." There is no point in criticizing it as unsuitable for a regular church service because that was not its purpose. Nor does its composition prove that Verdi was an orthodox church goer; he hated the clergy. It is no accident that the Egyptian priests in *Aida* are portrayed so negatively. His wife remarked in a letter to a friend that he did not seem to need to believe in anything, yet he "observed rigorously every precept of strict morality."

Verdi: *Rigoletto*

Verdi's *Rigoletto,* composed in 1851, is one of his most frequently performed works, broadcast often on public television. It stems from his "middle period," when he was expanding the traditional patterns of Italian opera. Although he still wrote separate numbers, he now began to blend one item into the next. A baritone sings the title role, portraying an embittered, hunchbacked jester. He is both buffoon and henchman at the sixteenth-century court of the licentious Duke of Mantua. Verdi and his librettist Francesco Piave paint an unflattering portrayal of the ruling classes, derived from the original source for the opera, a play by Victor Hugo. Verdi and Piave demoted the King of France in Hugo's play to the Duke of Mantua in order to get around the Austrian censors.

Prelude
(2:38) ⑤④

30

The brief prelude begins with a repeated-note phrase in the brass that is associated with the curse laid upon Rigoletto early in the opera by an aggrieved courtier. The minor mode, chromatic chords from the orchestra, string tremolos, and timpani rumblings create a tense, ominous mood. It is clear from the prelude that the opera will not end happily.

 CD4

Caro nome
(6:38) ⑤⑤

The only bright spot in Rigoletto's life is his beautiful sixteen-year-old daughter, Gilda. He is fiercely protective of her, keeping her secluded, ignorant of her father's true occupation and of her own history. No one at the court knows about her, although the courtiers suspect that Rigoletto keeps a mistress. The Duke (tenor), a notorious libertine whose conquests are usually aided by Rigoletto, has seen Gilda at church (!) and is attracted to her. He follows her home, sneaks into her garden by bribing her guardian, and tells her he is a poor student named Gualtier Maldé. As often happens in opera, they sing a duet and Gilda promptly falls in love. After much pushing from the guardian, the Duke leaves and Gilda, now alone, reflects upon her newly found love in the aria, "Caro nome." It occurs near the end of Act I. (Gilda is sung by a **coloratura** soprano, a descriptive term for a very high, flexible voice.)

Two of opera's best known singers, baritone Lawrence Tibbett and tenor Jan Peerce, created the roles of Rigoletto and the Duke in this 1941 production of *Rigoletto*. (Courtesy of San Francisco Opera.)

Caro nome begins with a section that recalls a recitative in that it lacks word repetition and has little melodic interest. However, it is metrical and fully accompanied. The remaining portion (starting at item 2) displays aria characteristics: it has much word repetition and is out-and-out tuneful, appropriately in major.

(0:00)
1

|31|

(Woodwind chords, both sustained and arpeggiated, furnish the accompaniment.)

| Gualtier Maldé, nome di lui | Walter Maldé, name of my beloved, |
| sì amato, ti scolpisci nel cor innamorato! | you are engraved on my adoring heart! |

(0:42)
2

|32|

(The "Caro nome" melody, ex. 45.2, is forecast in an orchestral passage. It begins with downward motion and continues sequentially.)

| Caro nome che il mio cor festi primo palpitar, | Dear name that first made my heart leap, |
| le delizie dell'amor mi dei sempre rammentar! | You will always remind me of love's delights. |

Example 45.2

(1:35)
3

|33|

Col pensier il mio desir a te sempre volerà,	My longing thoughts will always fly to you,
e fin l'ultimo sospir,	And until my last breath, my thoughts will be,
caro nome, tuo sarà.	dear name, of you.

(2:05)
4

|34|

(The text of item 3 is repeated with new music, ending with a solo moment.)

(3:16)

5

(More text repetition occurs, though the words are obscured by coloratura flights which end with a stratospheric cadenza.)

(4:55)

6

36

(Her song is essentially complete, but Gilda continues to repeat the name of her beloved. She is unaware that some masked and armed courtiers have gathered quietly in the street below. She does not hear them as they admire her beauty—though the ominous sounds of the timpani tell the audience she is in danger.)

Assuming that Gilda is Rigoletto's mistress, the courtiers kidnap her as an act of revenge upon the jester, whose malicious wit has earned him universal hatred. They carry her off to the palace where she discovers that "Gualtier" is really the Duke. He promptly seduces or rapes her—the libretto, of course, cannot be explicit. The next day, when Rigoletto learns what has happened to his beloved daughter, his outrage drives him to hire the professional assassin Sparafucile to kill the Duke.

CD4

The third act takes place on the bank of a river, at a tavern run by Rigoletto's hired killer. It is so tumbledown that characters inside are clearly visible to eavesdroppers outside—who happen to be Rigoletto and Gilda. Her father hopes that seeing the Duke in action will cure Gilda's continued infatuation. When the Duke enters the tavern, he almost immediately sings "La donna è mobile," a hit-tune aria that rather neatly proclaims his opinion of women's fickleness— he was a great one to talk! In spite of its text, the aria is a favorite with tenors.

La donna è mobile
(2:21) 56

(0:00)

1

37

(An orchestral introduction forecasts the Duke's melody (ex. 45.3), an easily remembered tune because of its sequences.)

Example 45.3

	La donna è mobile, qual piuma	Woman is fickle as a feather in the wind,
	al vento, muta d'accento, e di pensiero.	She is changeable in word and in thought.
	Sempre un amabile, leggiadro	Always a sweet, pretty face, weeping
	viso, in pianto o in riso, è menzognero.	or laughing, deceives us.
	La donna è mobil, qual piuma	
	al vento, muta d'accento, e di pensier.	

(1:04)

2

38

(A second stanza begins, with introduction and aria melody the same as in item 1. Some tenors add a cadenza at the aria's conclusion.)

Bella figlia dell' amore (**quartet**)

(4:13) ⑤⑦

The assassin calls for his sister Maddalena (alto) to attend to the Duke, who immediately goes into his well-polished act. He soon sings the melody that introduces the famous quartet (ex. 45.4). Though father and daughter can see and hear the couple inside, and soon join them in singing, the Duke and Maddalena are unaware of their "audience." Each singer projects a completely different emotional and musical message. We hear the Duke's attempts at seduction, Maddalena's coy resistance, Gilda's anguished sobs, and Rigoletto's plotting of vengeance. Each one first sings alone even if very briefly (the texts given below show only their first few words), but soon all four voices blend together contrapuntally.

Example 45.4

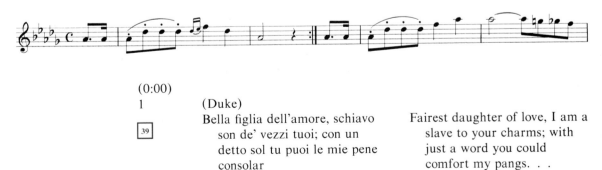

(0:00)

1

39

(Duke)

Bella figlia dell'amore, schiavo son de' vezzi tuoi; con un detto sol tu puoi le mie pene consolar

Fairest daughter of love, I am a slave to your charms; with just a word you could comfort my pangs. . .

(1:10)

2

40

(Maddalena)
Ah! ah! rido ben di core, chè
tai baie costan poco. . .

Ha, ha! I'm laughing, for such
    jokes cost little. . .

(Gilda)
Ah! così parlar d'amore . . .

Ah! to speak like that about
    love . . .

(Rigoletto)
Taci, il piangere non vale . . .

Hush, weeping does no good
    . . .

(2:49)

3

41

(The Duke is briefly alone, singing his original tune. He is soon
joined by the others, as they repeat their individual messages even
more insistently.)

After the quartet, the drama moves swiftly to its tragic conclusion.
Rigoletto sends Gilda home with orders to leave immediately and
meet him in another town. He makes a down payment to the
assassin, promising to return at midnight for the body. Maddalena,
quite taken with the Duke, persuades Sparafucile to spare him,
although he is upset at this breach of his professional ethics.
Reluctantly, the assassin promises to kill the first person who comes
into the tavern and stuff that body into a sack for Rigoletto. They
assume that since Rigoletto plans to throw the body into the nearby
river, they can get away with this deception. But Gilda, disobeying
her father's orders, returns just in time to overhear the plot.
Sacrificing herself, she enters the tavern and is stabbed. Promptly at
midnight Rigoletto returns, pays for the job, and accepts the sack
which he thinks contains the Duke's body. About to throw it into the
river, he hears the Duke singing a phrase of "La donna . . ." Horror-
stricken, the father tears open the sack and finds the dying Gilda,
whose last moments are spent explaining her actions and begging her
father to forgive the Duke. The curse that had been laid on
Rigoletto, and musically forecast in the prelude, has descended
instead upon his innocent daughter.

46 BEDŘICH SMETANA AND BOHEMIAN NATIONALISM

PREVIEW Struggles for national independence occupied many patriots in the Romantic era, and the composer Smetana found his career linked to this cause. He pictured his native land, Bohemia, in tone poems based on folk lore. Another Czech patriot, Dvořák, also wrote music reflecting his native land.

Bedřich Smetana.

Bedřich Smetana [pronounced SMEH-ta-nah] (1824–84), was born in Bohemia, now a part of Czechoslovakia. His father, an amateur musician, gave the composer his first music lessons. Like Schumann, Smetana was in his twenties before he could study music systematically. For a time he lived and worked as a successful pianist and conductor in Sweden, but patriotic feelings for his homeland drew him back in 1861. Tragically, in another parallel to Schumann's life, insanity clouded his later years—after deafness had ended his public appearances. He died in 1884.

A

Smetana as an Evolving Nationalist Composer

When Smetana was a child, Bohemia was under Austrian rule, and thus he grew up speaking German, the official language. His patriotic feelings were kindled by the Prague Revolution, one of the many examples of the political unrest and struggle for independence that swept Europe in 1848. Smetana wrote revolutionary marches and helped defend barricades, but the movement failed in Bohemia and nationalistic hopes had to be put on hold. As the political situation gradually improved, he decided that his duty was to write music in a national style, based on Czech traditions and its language. He set about learning this language, although his diaries show that he only gradually was able to abandon German.

The turning point in his career occurred in 1857, according to an account written by a friend, during a visit Smetana made to Liszt in Weimar. After playing Smetana's twelve character pieces for a group of listeners, Liszt told the audience that the music had been written by "a composer with a genuine Czech heart, an artist by the grace of God." Deeply moved by this encouragement, Smetana "swore in his heart the greatest oath: that he would dedicate his entire life to his nation,

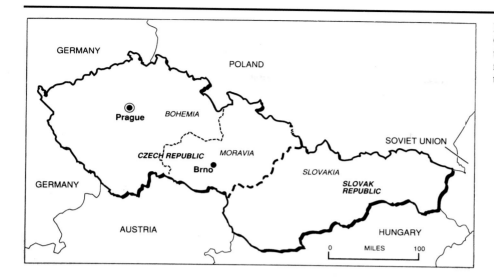

to the tireless service of his country's art." Today he is acknowledged as his country's first major nationalist composer.

B

Smetana's Music

Although he wrote a number of operas, Smetana's best-known opera outside of Czechoslovakia is *The Bartered Bride,* full of Czech musical idioms. Of his many instrumental works, the public knows best his cycle of six symphonic poems, *Má Vlast* (My Country). Written in the late 1870s, each describes a particular place in Bohemia or is built on a national legend.

The work we study, *The Moldau,* is not only a symbol of nationalism of its own time, but also of today's. Following the momentous changes in Czechoslovakia in 1989, it was the composition played during an outdoor concert in Prague televised worldwide to mark the homecoming of the distinguished Czech conductor, Rafael Kubelik. Kubelik had exiled himself for forty-two years, refusing to make music for the Communist leaders, now deposed.

Smetana: *The Moldau* (Vltava) (12:45) 58

A nationalistic symphonic poem that magnificently mirrors the very soul of Smetana's native land, the second work in his "My Country" cycle describes the course of the river Moldau, from its mountain source through central Bohemia and the city of Prague till it joins the Elbe river.

The program for this work, which appears below in quotation marks, is a composite, blending free English translations of the composer's brief explanation of the piece with additions to those comments made by a friend. Before listening, you should read it carefully. At seven places in the score, Smetana indicated by a word or two what specific part of the program was being described. (Asterisks at the measure numbers identify these places in the listening guide.) The listening guide further subdivides the program in order to highlight some possible associations between music and program besides the ones Smetana pointed out. Some evidence in this piece suggests that the role of the storyteller and the musician might conflict on occasion. When that happens, it is clear that the musician wins.

Despite its reliance upon a program, the work is hardly formless. Analysis as a rondo is possible, if one regards item 1 as an introduction and the appearances of the Moldau theme itself as the "A" theme. The story's episodes account for the contrasting themes.

 CD4

"This composition depicts the course of the river Moldau, beginning with its two springs, one cold and tranquil,"

(0:00)
1a   *m1   Soft flutes, over a pizzicato string accompaniment, begin with a rippling theme, in quick upward-moving notes.

42

"the other warm and gushing,"

(0:26)
1b   m16   Clarinets enter with music similar to that of the flutes, but moving down.

"their waves unite and sparkle in the morning sun."

(1:01)
1c   m36   Triangle strokes punctuate a preparation for the Moldau theme entrance.

"Both brooks join into one stream."

(1:07)
2a   m40   Violins (and oboe) play the Moldau theme (ex. 46.1).

43

Example 46.1

Its generally stepwise motion, minor mode, and simple rhythms hint at the theme's folk origins, but one biographer claims that it comes from Sweden, not Bohemia. Its resemblance to the Israeli national anthem, "Hatikvah," is so marked that it might seem as if many folk melodies have a common ancestor. The rippling theme heard at the beginning continues, now in the strings.

(1:51)

2b   m64   Loud repeated notes in the French horns (no, this is not yet the episode of the hunters) briefly interrupt the Moldau theme and mark the start of a crescendo.

(2:05)

2c   m73   When the Moldau theme resumes, it briefly shifts to the major mode.

(2:33)

2d   m64   A repetition of item 2b provides another interruption of the Moldau theme.

(2:48)

2e   m73   A repetition of item 2c allows the Moldau theme to resume.

"The river runs through forests in which are heard the joyous sounds of the hunt; the notes of the hunter's horn sounding ever nearer and nearer,"

(3:00)

3a   *m80   The *real* hunters come on the scene abruptly with loud repeated notes from the French horns, quite similar to the effect in item 2b. The rippling theme of item 1a continues in the strings, but the Moldau theme has disappeared.

44

(3:35)

3b   m103   Now the oboe recalls the beginning notes of the Moldau theme, again briefly in the major mode. Then follows a gradual diminuendo and the effect of a slower tempo.

"and flows through the countryside where peasant weddings are celebrated with song and dancing."

(4:04)

4a   *m122   Strings and woodwinds play in rhythmic unison in a strongly accented, polkalike section, appropriately now in the major mode.

45

(4:32)

4b   m138   French horns, triangle, and timpani add emphasis to the "oom-pah" beat. Soon another diminuendo begins, setting the stage for the moonlight revels to come. Pitch and volume levels fall.

(5:35)

4c   m175   Cellos and basses are left alone to complete the transition. Woodwinds then enter softly in a modulating passage to a new key.

"Water-sprites dance in the moonlight."

(6:00)

5a *m185 In a slow-moving melody, sustained strings picture a tranquil night scene. Flutes recall the rippling theme, and the harp punctuates the ends of phrases with arpeggios.

46

"On nearby rocks there proudly soar ruined castles, witness of the vanished warlike fame of bygone ages."

(7:24)

5b m213 Very softly, the French horns begin to change their previously sustained tones to a rhythmic, slow march, which gradually grows louder and more intense. A dramatic crescendo and a whirlwind of woodwinds would seem to prepare for the next scene, at the St. John Rapids.

(8:40)

6a m239 Rather surprisingly, the Moldau theme returns, played as in item 2a. No hint in the program justifies a restatement of the theme, but the need for musical unity does.

47

(9:07)

6b m255 As in item 2b, a prominent French horn call interrupts the Moldau theme.

(9:21)

6c m264 As in item 2c, there is a brief change to the major mode.

"The Moldau whirls through the St. John Rapids, winding its way through cataracts, and hewing a path for its foaming waters, through the rocky chasm,"

(9:30)

7 *m271 The scene abruptly shifts to the Rapids, with repeated notes in the French horns. Timpani rolls and bass drum strokes add to the sense of turbulence. Soon the piccolo pictures the foaming waters, and cymbals top the torrent of sound. As suddenly as it began, the turbulence subsides.

48

"and flows on in a wide stream towards Prague."

(10:45)

8a *m333 The full orchestra plays the opening phrase of the Moldau theme, now faster and changed to the major mode.

49

"It passes time-honored Vysehrad."

(11:16)

8b *m359 Cymbals mark the appearance of the Vysehrad theme, played by flutes, piccolo, and brass (ex. 46.2).

Example 46.2

Smetana quotes himself here. The first symphonic poem in the "My Country" cycle describes Vysehrad castle, the seat of ancient Bohemian kings. This theme begins that work and is linked with the castle in the same way that the Moldau theme is associated with the river. After this quotation, an extended coda begins.

"Finally the Moldau disappears beyond the poet's gaze into the distance, flowing in a majestic stream into the Elbe."

(12:05)

8c   m407   As the percussion drops out, the "disappearance" of the river begins. While violins continue to sweep up and down, woodwinds, then French horn quit. After the violins have essentially completed the program with a "fade-out" ending, the full orchestra returns for a loud dominant-to-tonic cadence, justified solely by the musical need for a piece to sound "ended."

(* indicates, as explained earlier, that the composer inserted in the score a word or two as a clue to the specific part of the program.)

C

Smetana had an equally famous countryman, Antonin Dvořák [pronounced duh-VOR-zhahk] (1841–1904). Though his nationalism equaled Smetana's, the work most people associate with Dvořák is not Bohemian in origin but American. Written in 1893 during a brief stay in this country, his *Symphony No. 9 in E minor,* "From the New World," overflows with folk-song-like melodies. Some people claim that a beautiful English horn theme in its second movement originated as an African-American spiritual and give it a text, starting with the words "Going Home." However, historians think that the composer was merely reflecting the style of spirituals and native American Indian music, not quoting these sources directly.

Antonin Dvořák

47 MODEST MUSSORGSKY

PREVIEW   Like Smetana, Mussorgsky was an ardently nationalistic composer. Reflecting his Russian heritage, in a short lifetime he composed operas and songs. He was one of a group of five composers with similar ideals, most of them musical amateurs with other professions.

Modest Mussorgsky (1839–81) was born in the Russian district of Pskov. [Pronounced muh-SORG-skee; as with many Russian words, his last name is spelled in a variety of ways.] His father was a well-to-do landowner, although one grandparent had been a serf, and Mussorgsky attributed his interest in Russian folk life to that ancestry. He made good progress in piano studies, with his mother as his first teacher. In his early teens he studied piano seriously and began composing, though his general musical education was, and remained, minimal. Instead, he undertook a military career. The emancipation of Russian serfs in 1861 caused his family to suffer financially, and eventually he found work as a government clerk. In spite of a nervous temperament and alcoholism, which contributed to an early death in 1881 at the age of forty-two, he composed energetically. Operas and songs are considered his greatest achievements.

A

Mussorgsky: A Russian Nationalist Composer

Folk and church music flourished throughout Russian history, but a tradition of art music was relatively young. In the eighteenth century, Italians and other foreigners dominated art music. Russian composers had to go abroad for study. As a result, there was no distinctly national music. Historians consider Mikhail Glinka (1804–57), who combined native folk song elements with Western compositional techniques, to be the "father" of Russian musical nationalism. Not until the reign of Alexander II (1855–81), when sweeping changes altered all aspects of Russian life, were professional music schools established.

"**The Five**" or "The Mighty Handful," a little clique of professed nationalist Russian composers to which Mussorgsky belonged, inherited Glinka's legacy. Others in The Five were Mily Balakirev (1837–1910); Alexander Borodin (1833–87), famous for his tuneful music which found a place in the Broadway musical *Kismet*;

César Cui (1835–1918); and Nikolai Rimsky-Korsakov (1844–1908), whose great skill as an orchestrator can be seen in such works as his programmatic *Scheherazade*. Of this group, only Balakirev had any training as a professional musician; the others were self-taught. Perhaps because they began as amateurs, they were uncompromising in their ardent search for a national musical expression.

A fountainhead for all nationalists is folk song. Russian folk songs tend to be modal, based on scales other than the traditional major or minor. They often move downward in pitch and are confined to a limited range, repeating a motive in an almost obsessive manner. The interval of a descending fourth near the cadence occurs frequently, as do irregular meters. A well-known Russian folk song, the "Volga Boat Song" (described in Chapter 5), illustrates some of these traits. As we shall see, in using Russian folk songs, Mussorgsky left them as they were, with all their characteristic Russian quirks.

Like many nationalists, Mussorgsky sided with the lower classes. He found inspiration in Russian history and language. Describing himself in the third person, he proclaimed his credo: "Art is a means of communication with people, not an end in itself. This guiding principle has determined all his creative activity. Proceeding from the conviction that human speech is governed by strictly musical laws, he looks upon the task of musical art as one of reproducing in musical tones not only qualities of feeling but chiefly qualities of human speech."

Mussorgsky's Music

Because Mussorgsky lacked formal training in harmony and counterpoint, he turned to the other members of The Five for technical help. Rimsky-Korsakov, his chief advisor, prepared most of Mussorgsky's works for publication, correcting the "disconnected harmony and illogical modulations" that he thought he detected in them. To this day, most of Mussorgsky's music is still heard in Rimsky-Korsakov's versions. For example, not until 1975 was an edition available that compared the original score of *Boris Godunov* and the changes made in it. Consequently, it is hard for the average listener to evaluate the unique qualities in Mussorgsky's music.

Mussorgsky's best-known title is his *Pictures at an Exhibition* (1874), recognized by many because the rock group Emerson, Lake, and Palmer made a highly successful arrangement of it. Though *Pictures* is often played in its original piano version, concert-goers know it best in a stunning orchestral arrangement made in 1922 by the French composer Maurice Ravel. The "pictures" in the title refers to an exhibit of paintings, many of them on Russian themes, by the Russian artist Victor Hartmann, a friend of Mussorgsky's. Each picture inspired a section of this programmatic work and provided its specific title. The main theme of the work, often referred to as the "promenade" theme (ex. 47.1), represents the viewer of these paintings (Mussorgsky himself?) as he moves from one to another of the pictures. In its changing meters, prominent fourths, and repeated motives, the promenade theme displays some Russian folk song characteristics.

Example 47.1

Mussorgsky: Prologue to Act I: "Coronation Scene" from *Boris Godunov.* (11:13)
(59)

Mussorgsky himself wrote the libretto for the opera *Boris Godunov* (1868–74), basing it on the tragedy by Aleksandr Pushkin (1799–1837). It delves into Russian history of the early 1600s, built around Tsar Boris, who reigned from 1598 to 1605. Since one of Mussorgsky's goals for music was that it be closely tied to speech, the musical lines reflect the inflections of his native language. Though Tsar Boris is the main character, the "hero" might be said to be the chorus, which represents the Russian people.

Like Wagner, Mussorgsky rejected the traditional Italian ideas about opera. What Boris sings in the prologue approximates Wagner's blend of aria and recitative. This role capitalizes on the deep tones for which Russian basses are famous.

The final scene of Glinka's *A Life for the Tsar* provided a model for Mussorgsky's "Coronation Scene." Set in the courtyard of the Kremlin, which is filled with a mass of common people, the opera shows them eager for the coronation to begin in the cathedral.

♪ CD5

(0:00)

1 *r25 The orchestral introduction is remarkable for its concentration on two different chords (A-flat 7 and D7) (ex. 47.2). Beginning slowly and then in quicker note values, the chords alternate many times, sounding in both solid and broken-chord form, as if to imitate the jangling of bells. While each is a perfectly conventional chord, the juxtaposition of the two is unusual, almost exotic-sounding, because there is no single key into which both chords could fit. The chords do share one written note in common, C. Alternating two unrelated chords with one common tone is another musical feature that has precedent in the music of Glinka.

Example 47.2

(1:05)

2 r26 After a pause, during which the curtain is to be raised, the music of item 1 is restated.

(1:57)

3 r27 A fanfare of trumpets introduces a Prince, who calls out "Long live Tsar Boris." The chorus (the people) answers him, then sings a cheerful, major key hymn of praise, the melody of a Russian folk song (ex. 47.2). (This tune also appears in Beethoven's string quartet, op. 59, no. 2, in the trio section of the minuet. This quartet is one of three that Beethoven dedicated to the Russian count, Andreas Rasumovsky.)

Shouts of the Russian word "slava" (glory) interrupt the hymn. When it resumes, the two-chord accompaniment of the beginning also returns.

(5:14)

4 r32 After a long pause, sustained woodwind tones precede the musical entrance of Boris. At first, he sings a kind of soliloquy, expressing his inner sense of anguish and guilt, appropriately in a minor key. In the original story, Boris gains the throne by having its rightful heir murdered. While this may not be historically true, it is essential to the opera. Boris admits to doubts, fears, and foreboding, and prays that he may be a good ruler of his people.

the opera. Boris admits to doubts, fears, and foreboding, and prays that he may be a good ruler of his people.

(7:25)

5   r33 Another pause and a brief orchestral interlude point to Boris's

5   change of mood. As he shakes off his fears (and his music turns to
the major mode), he now assumes his public role, addresses the
crowd directly, and announces that all should pay homage to the
departed rulers of Russia. Finally he summons everyone, from noble
to beggar, to a feast.

(8:11)

6   r34 The chorus resumes its happy shouts of "slava" and its singing of the

6   hymn. The bells continue to peal tumultuously until the scene ends.
Moscow is full of bells. Sadly, most productions of this opera are
hard-pressed to convey the impact of all its bells tolling at once at
the end of this scene.

*Since measures are not numbered in the edition used for this guide
(the Rimsky-Korsakov version in its piano-vocal score), rehearsal
numbers (r) are given here.

Though Boris's reign has gotten off to an impressive start, the opera ends
with his death after a revolt stirred up by his political enemies.

PETER ILYICH TCHAIKOVSKY 48

PREVIEW Like the members of Mussorgsky's group of nationalistic Russian composers, Tchaikovsky first underwent training in a field other than music. Unlike them, when he finally experienced professional training in the traditions of Western music, he adopted that style most successfully and his Russian roots seem less obvious. With the general public, he is famous for his ballets and the many "hit tunes" found in his concertos and symphonies.

Another nineteenth-century Russian was Peter Ilyich Tchaikovsky [pronounced chi-KOFF-skee] (1840–93). (His name appears in a variety of spellings because the Russian alphabet contains some letters that English lacks. You may find his first name printed as "Pyotr" and his last name indexed in some sources under "C.") An unusually sensitive, emotional child, Peter showed an early interest in music and studied piano with a local teacher. However, nothing in his family background—his father was a successful mining engineer—nor in Russian society, for that matter, encouraged musical ambitions and he was persuaded to study law. (Other Russian composers of his generation encountered similar problems; they too had to undergo various types of professional training.) Completing his legal education, he became a government clerk, though his heart was still set on music. Not until he was twenty-two could he begin serious music study in the recently established St. Petersburg Conservatory.

Tchaikovsky progressed so rapidly that upon graduation he was selected to teach harmony in the new Moscow Conservatory. There he remained for twelve years, writing furiously and creating many of the works for which he is famous. Outwardly successful, he was inwardly a tormented and unhappy man, a situation that has received much attention because many commentators claim that his music is an expression of his emotional life. Indeed, he himself said that his composing was "a musical cleansing of the soul, which boils over with an accumulation that naturally seeks its outlet in tones, just as a lyric poet will express himself in verse. The difference is only that music possesses an infinitely more powerful and more subtle language for expressing the myriad shifts and shades of our spiritual life."

Peter I. Tchaikovsky.

The linkage between Tchaikovsky's music and his private life is perhaps the reason that his homosexuality is openly discussed today, though it certainly was not in his time. What a nightmare this orientation was for him! In his society, public knowledge of his nature would have resulted, at best, in disgrace; at worst, in exile. In 1877 he tried to disguise this situation by impulsively marrying, and soon leaving, an unstable young woman. This disaster drove him to the point of attempting suicide. When he most needed help, a benefactor miraculously appeared and rescued him, much like King Ludwig II rescued Wagner. Nadezhda von Meck, a wealthy widow who adored his music, decided to grant him a generous annuity. Thus supported, Tchaikovsky quit his teaching position in 1878 and devoted all his time to composing.

Madame von Meck's gift carried an unusual requirement: she and Tchaikovsky were never to meet. They did, however, carry on a lengthy, intimate correspondence, subsequently published. The letters are invaluable for the insights they furnish into his methods of work and his philosophy of music. After fourteen years she abruptly cancelled the annuity and severed their communication for reasons that have never been made clear. She claimed to be bankrupt, which Tchaikovsky soon discovered was not true. Although by then he was a world-famous composer, financially successful and in no need of her money, he was shattered by the loss of his confidante. Triumphal foreign tours as a conductor, including appearances in America, failed to raise his spirits. His sixth symphony, a profoundly pessimistic work which ends as gloomily as it begins, was premiered in 1893. Nine days later, at only fifty-three, he was dead. A rumor at the time had it that he committed suicide—and the sixth symphony immediately leapt into popularity. The standard account attributes his death to cholera from drinking unboiled water, at the very least a surprisingly careless, if not fatalistic, act.

A

Tchaikovsky: A Russian Nationalist Composer?

Stravinsky, the most famous Russian twentieth-century composer, called Tchaikovsky "the most Russian of us all," a verdict the average listener today would probably support. Still, Tchaikovsky was not one of The Five, the group of intensely nationalistic but mostly self-taught composers to which Mussorgsky belonged. One of that group, Balakirev, had been very helpful to Tchaikovsky in writing his first orchestral masterpiece, *Romeo and Juliet,* but after 1872 the two had no contact for ten years. The way they treated Russian folk songs provides a clue to the different attitudes of Tchaikovsky and The Five.

Tchaikovsky felt impelled to straighten out the Russian quirks in the folk songs he borrowed, no doubt thinking he improved them. For example, the "Birch Tree" tune that plays such an important role in the fourth movement of the *Symphony No. 4* (see listening guide, below) originally had three-measure phrases. When Balakirev introduced this same melody in his *Overture on Three Russian Themes,* he preserved its rhythm. Tchaikovky simply added a rest at the ends of phrases, thereby turning them into the square, four-bar shapes so characteristic of Western tradition. Because of his conservatory indoctrination in Western-style

harmony, he resisted the modal flavor of Russian folk songs. These songs often contain much repetition of a single motive, and indeed, he subjected some of his tunes to relentless reiteration. But just as often he modified his repetitions by using sequences, a Western musical concept.

In 1882, a Russian champion of nationalism wrote: "The best Russian musicians beginning with [Mikhail] Glinka have never set much store by academic training and have never regarded it with the servility and the superstitious veneration with which it is regarded even now in many parts of Europe." This statement hints that the issue dividing Tchaikovsky from the others was probably not so much nationalism, but his professional training versus their amateur status. In Tchaikovsky's thoroughly professional music, the Russian qualities are still present, but diluted. For the average Western listener, Tchaikovsky's popularity is based on his gorgeous tunes, not his "Russianness."

B

Probably the most famous works by Tchaikovsky are his ballet scores, *Swan Lake,* op. 20; *Sleeping Beauty,* op. 66; and *Nutcracker,* op. 71. From the latter

Tchaikovsky's Music

was extracted the *Nutcracker Suite,* with its colorful dances reflecting various national styles, and the captivating "Waltz of the Flowers." Of his six symphonies, the last three are repertory staples. The sixth was mentioned earlier; the fourth is described below. His Overture-Fantasy *Romeo and Juliet* (1869, revised in 1880) bears witness to the composer's struggles to reconcile the programmatic implications evident from the title with the restrictions of sonata-form. A one-movement work, it falls into the category of concert overture. Similar in many ways is his *1812 Overture,* op. 49, based on an historical event, the French invasion of Russia. Since the French were ultimately defeated, in the music the French national anthem, "La Marseillaise," is torn apart as a Russian hymn emerges triumphant.

His *Piano Concerto No. 1,* op. 23, shares some characteristics in common with the equally celebrated *Violin Concerto,* op. 35. Not only do the soloists engage with the orchestra in exciting duels, but both works have wonderful melodies, factors which have helped make them both extremely popular. The main theme of the piano concerto is shown in example 48.1.

Example 48.1

Tchaikovsky also wrote much solo piano music, some chamber music, operas that are more popular in the USSR than in the West, many songs, and a surprising amount of choral music. Memorable tunes clothed in attractive orchestral dress make his music easily identifiable. A characteristic device is the alternation of orchestral sections in echo or dialogue effects. He also favored great, sweeping scales, especially at climactic moments. Sometimes he is criticized for an excessive amount of repetition, but no one denies that he gets his message across.

Tchaikovsky:
Symphony No. 4 in F Minor.

Madame von Meck, the patroness to whom Tchaikovsky dedicated his fourth symphony, had asked if the symphony had a program. In reply, he wrote: "In our symphony *there is* a program (that is, the possibility of explaining in words what it seeks to express), and to you and you alone I can and wish to indicate the meaning both of the work as a whole, and of its individual parts." The heart of this story is the idea of "Fate, the force of destiny, which ever prevents our pursuit of happiness from reaching its goal, which hangs like the sword of Damocles over our heads. It is invincible." Although Tchaikovsky said that he intended these words for his patroness only, the world does know about his program and it is frequently quoted. Still, before we take it too literally, we should consider a most significant sentence: "But the nature of instrumental music is precisely this, that it resists detailed analysis. *Where words fail, music speaks,* as Heine put it."

Tchaikovsky leaves unanswered the question: Did he want us to consider his symphony to be program music? It is not, if relying on the composer's title is the criterion. But. . .

"Fate" appears at the very beginning of this symphony, portrayed by a dramatic passage for French horns and bassoons in unison. It returns later in the full orchestra at a climactic spot in the fourth movement. However, the third movement is spared any visit from "Fate." Instead, the composer referred to some "intangible" and "disjointed" images, the kind of pictures which might come to mind in the first stages of intoxication. Among these ideas are: "a picture of a drunken peasant, a brief street song, a military procession." It is tempting to match the orchestral sections in this movement to Tchaikovsky's "program." The constant pizzicato of the string section might relate to the "disjointed" images, the woodwinds have the "street song," and as always, the brass section will sound "military." This movement is unique for its sharp separation of orchestral colors.

Besides specifying the tempo, Allegro, Tchaikovsky labeled the third movement "Scherzo." Most pieces so titled are at least light-hearted, and in ternary form: Scherzo, Trio, Scherzo. This was the scheme employed by Beethoven when he substituted a scherzo for a minuet. Romantic composers interpreted "scherzo" more freely, sometimes writing scherzos in duple meter, like this one. Tchaikovsky retains the traditional ternary form and adds to it a substantial coda.

   CD5

(0:00)

1a   m1   The main theme (ex. 48.2) is played softly by pizzicato strings in rhythmic unison, so softly in some recordings that it is barely audible. This simple theme moves down, then up the scale in an even rhythm, in F major.

⎡7⎤

Example 48.2

After a contrasting theme featuring repeated notes, but in the same even rhythm, a conversation of string groups follows.

(0:57)

1b   m77   The original theme (item 1a) returns, followed by more of the conversational music.

(1:39)

1c   m133   A tiny solo for oboe ends the Scherzo and leads into the next section.

TRIO

(1:44)

2a m136 Woodwinds now take the spotlight as oboes and bassoons play a new, quickly moving theme (ex. 48.3). Soon the flute enters, and the clarinets then answer the flute.

8

Example 48.3

(2:12)

2b m162 Sparkling in its high register, the piccolo joins the flute in the new theme.

(2:21)

2c m170 Softly, yet abruptly, the brass enter, playing a marchlike theme (ex. 48.4), which moves down, and then up the scale, as did the original scherzo theme.

Example 48.4

(2:33)

2d m185 While the brass keep on marching, the clarinet resumes the trio theme, item 2a, and the two themes combine effectively. Soon the piccolo returns, as usual dominating the sound.

(2:43)

2e m198 Woodwinds enter, rather unexpectedly quoting the string theme, item 1a. All three orchestral sections then converse in a transition that prepares for the return of the Scherzo.

SCHERZO

(2:59)

3a m1 Item 1a returns, played exactly as before, followed by the contrasting theme and the conversational effects.

9

(3:56)

3b   m77   As in the first playing of the Scherzo, the beginning theme returns and is followed by more of the conversational music.

(4:36)   *CODA*

4a   m349   Woodwinds and strings take turns playing the original string theme.

[10]

(4:48)

4b   m365   The piccolo and the flute attempt to revive the woodwind theme, item 2a, but are challenged by vigorous string chords.

(5:14)

4c   m399   The marchlike theme, item 2c, is briefly recalled. But the last word belongs to the strings.

The fourth movement brings the symphony to a rousing close. Tchaikovsky had this to say about its program: "If you find no joy within yourself, look for it in others. Go to the people. No sooner do you forget yourself in others' joy than merciless Fate reappears to remind you of yourself. Enter into peasant life and life will be bearable." One can easily relate themes to programmatic ideas in this movement. Certainly the opening theme is full of "joy," appropriately in major and in a fast, fiery tempo. The Russian folk song that the composer adapted can be associated with "peasant life." And no one can miss the thunderous recall of "merciless Fate." Though hardly as clearly organized as the third movement, the form of the fourth movement resembles the rondo pattern, with the main theme's returns separated by contrasting elements.

FOURTH MOVEMENT: FINALE (Allegro con fuoco) (9:14)
(61)

♫ CD5

(0:00)

1a   m1   The bold main theme (ex. 48.5) begins with the entire orchestra playing its opening motive of *dô-ti-la-sol,* moving right down the

[11]   major scale. Woodwinds and strings continue the theme with a flurry of fast notes.

Example 48.5

(0:16)
1b   m10   Almost immediately comes a quieter, contrasting moment.
Woodwinds, in minor, play the "Birch Tree" folk song (ex. 48.6).
Like many Russian folk songs, it is repetitious and moves down the
scale.

Example 48.6

mf

This tune has barely begun before the strings attempt to interrupt it.
Soon a down-the-scale dialogue prepares for the return of the
opening theme.

(0:49)
1c   m30   The main theme (item 1a) returns, with a full accompaniment from
the brass.

(1:02)
1d   m38   A marchlike tune (ex. 48.7) enters abruptly.

Example 48.7

ff

After considerable development of this tune, there is an emphatic
cadence.

(1:42)
2a   m60   Now begins a series of variations on the "Birch Tree" theme. Oboe
and bassoon carry the tune first.

12

(1:57)
2b   m68   In Variation II, the theme continues in woodwinds, with upward-
rushing passages in the strings.

(2:12)
2c   m76   Variation III features a bold presentation by French horns, opposed
by ascending tremolo figures from the strings.

(2:27)

2d m84 Trombones proclaim the theme, accompanied by a swirling effect in the strings.

(2:41)

2e m92 Suddenly it is quieter, as the theme goes to the woodwinds. Strings softly answer it.

(2:56)

2f m100 Returning to *forte,* a developmental section begins with a speeded-up version of the "Birch Tree" theme. Soon the down-the-scale dialogue heard in item 1b returns, again preparing for a statement of the main theme.

(3:29)

3a m119 The main theme returns, in the style of item 1c.

13

(3:42)

3b m127 The marchlike tune, item 1d, returns.

(4:22)

4a m149 Another set of variations on the "Birch Tree" theme begins, with the violins finally playing the tune. Here it appears with slight changes of pitch and more complex harmonies.

14

(4:38)

4b m157 Violins continue with the theme; the flute adds an elaborate countermelody.

(5:10)

4c m173 As the flute stops, a crescendo begins. The "Birch Tree" theme appears in fragments as the basis for a developmental section, similar to item 2f. Echo effects help the orchestra build to a tremendous climax.

(5:56)

5 m199 The "Fate" theme, in triple *forte* brasses and woodwinds, thunders its ominous message. Even the silences in this passage are tense. A roll on the timpani, played at first so softly that recordings have difficulty capturing it, serves as a transition to the conclusion.

15

(7:20)

6a m225 Bits of the marchlike tune, item 1d, are played in a dialogue style, paving the way for the main theme's final statement.

16

(7:59)
6b m249 This final statement of the main theme is the most emphatic of all.

(8:30)
7   m269 The "Birch Tree" theme returns to begin a coda, developmental in
          style. It ends in a conclusion that one commentator, Paul Henry
Lang, describes as a demonstration of the "use of the power of the
orchestra for ecstatic-hysterical poundings."

JOHANNES BRAHMS 49

PREVIEW   The German-born Brahms rejected many features of the Romantic era. Unusually interested in the past, he revived some of the forms of absolute music in his chamber music and symphonies. Avoiding opera and program music, he was drafted as a leader by those musical "conservatives" who were uneasy at the directions the "radical" Liszt/ Wagner school was taking. In labeling him as the "third B," they served notice that he must be the heir to Bach and Beethoven.

Standing apart from the Romantic era in which he lived was Johannes Brahms [pronounced BRAHMZ] (1833–97), born in Hamburg, Germany. Recalling many of the earlier composers, his father was a musician, a none-too-successful double bass player, who gave him his first music lessons. Under the instruction of local musicians, he became a proficient pianist and began composing in his teens. The turning point of his life came at age twenty, when he met Robert and Clara Schumann.

The Schumanns were so impressed with the young man's piano playing and with his compositions that they took him into their home. Robert published an article in which he hailed Brahms as a "young eagle." In Schumann's flowery language: "Seated at the piano, he [Brahms] at once discovered to us wondrous regions. We were drawn into a circle whose magic grew on us more and more. We welcome him as a valiant warrior. In every time there reigns a secret league of kindred spirits. Tighten the circle, you who belong to it, in order that the truth in art may shine forth more and more brightly." As we shall see, this article, printed on the first page of the widely read music journal that Schumann had formerly edited, had a great effect upon the young composer's career.

After Schumann's breakdown, Brahms fell in love with Clara, who was fourteen years older than he. Why they did not marry after Robert's death, no one knows. They remained lifelong friends, and Brahms sought her opinion of his works before showing them to the world—although he acted on his own judgments. While his professional life included a few minor appointments as a conductor of orchestras and a women's chorus, he met disappointment in his searches for the established position he always claimed he wanted. No doubt Brahms associated a steady

Willy von Beckerath painted this portrait of a mature Brahms, seated at the piano. (It seems odd that someone as disciplined as Brahms would be smoking his cigar at the same time!)

job with getting married and settling down, something else he claimed he wanted but never achieved. Probably what he really wanted was freedom, both in his career and at home. He spent most of his adult years as a highly successful free-lance composer.

In 1862, Brahms moved to Vienna, still the magnet city for musicians that it had been in the Classic era. A very private person, he led a quiet, reserved life. To his friends and to children, he showed an inner warmth, but the exterior was that of a crotchety bachelor with a caustic wit. He was an internationally acclaimed figure when he died of cancer in 1897, not long after Clara Schumann's death.

Josef Joachim und Clara Schumann konzertierend, 1854. Farbige Kreide.

Two of Brahms's closest friends were Clara Schumann, Robert's widow, and Joseph Joachim, a violinist, for whom Brahms wrote his only violin concerto.

A

Brahms: The Third "B"

Schumann's early, perhaps premature, praise of Brahms achieved mixed results. While it helped Brahms's career, it pushed him in a direction he might not have taken otherwise. About this time, musicians, and especially music critics, were taking sides in a philosophical battle. On one side stood the radicals such as Liszt and Wagner, the leaders of the "new German school" with its "music of the future." Rejecting traditional forms, they favored programmatic music. The conservatives accused the radicals of having abandoned the traditions of the Classic era. Since Schumann was known to be cool to the "new German school," the article in effect cast Brahms as the future leader of the conservatives in this drama.

Brahms participated in the controversy to the extent of signing his name to a manifesto attacking the "new" music as "contrary to the most fundamental essence of music." This declaration was prematurely leaked to the press, making Brahms and the other three signers look a little foolish, and probably convincing him that he should keep his mouth shut in the future. And he did. By the time the conductor Hans von Bülow (you should remember him from the tangled web Wagner wove) coined the phrase "the three B's of music," there could be no turning back. A heavy responsibility was laid on Brahms: to be the successor of Bach and Beethoven, whether or not he wanted that role.

Brahms once told a friend: "You do not know what it is like, hearing his [Beethoven's] footsteps constantly behind one." This expression of awe may help explain why Brahms was so extraordinarily self-critical. Unlike Beethoven, whose messy sketchbooks show the many revisions his musical thoughts underwent, Brahms left no clues to his work habits. As he told his publisher in 1890, he had "thrown a lot of torn-up manuscript paper into the [river] Traun." Not until he was forty did the world hear his first symphony. He knew that it would be compared with Beethoven's symphonies. Predictably, the music critic Hanslick (Wagner's enemy) praised it lavishly: "Brahms recalls Beethoven's symphonic style not only in his individually spiritual and suprasensual expression, the beautiful breadth of his melodies, the daring and originality of his modulations, and his sense of polyphonic structure, but also—and above all—in the manly and noble seriousness of the whole."

As the "third B," Brahms probably felt that people expected him to be ever-serious. A famous story reveals him as possibly regretting this role. Once, in response to a request for his autograph, he sketched out a few measures of the famous *Blue Danube Waltz* by Johann Strauss, Jr., and then added, "Alas, not by Johannes Brahms." Even Hanslick shared this feeling when he observed that "Brahms seems to favor too one-sidedly the great and the serious, the difficult and the complex, and at the expense of sensuous beauty."

Of course, we can never know how Brahms might have developed without that early spotlight. By temperament he was a conservative soul. No other composer we have met was so dedicated a musical scholar; he supported the Bach society, collected original scores—he owned the autograph score of Mozart's *Symphony No. 40*—and edited early harpsichord music. He revealed a veneration of the past in choosing melodies by Baroque and Classic composers as themes for some theme-and-variation works. Indeed, tracking down the relationships of Brahms's compositions to earlier music has occupied many a scholar.

B

Brahms's Music

Example 49.1

Everyone has heard Brahms's "Lullaby" or *Wiegenlied* (Cradle Song), op. 49, no. 4 (ex. 49.1), one of his more than two hundred songs.

Guten A - bend, gut Nacht,   mit Ro - sen be - dacht,   mit Näg - lein be - steckt

The reverence that the music critic Eduard Hanslick displayed for the music of Brahms is ridiculed in this merciless 1890 cartoon, showing him burning incense before Brahms's image.

Almost as well-known are his *Hungarian Dances,* first written for piano and then arranged for orchestra. Growing up in Hamburg, Brahms had heard the lively Gypsy rhythms played by Hungarian refugees as they streamed through this port city on their way to America. They were fleeing oppression in their native lands after the revolutions of 1848. Unusually lighthearted are his *Liebeslieder Waltzer* (Love Song Waltzes), opp. 52 and 65. Although written for vocal quartet and piano four-hands, they are often performed by choirs.

While it may lack Chopin's elegance or Liszt's sparkle, Brahms's piano music has a full, rich Romantic sonority. His first opus was a piano sonata, and he continued writing piano music all his life. His *Eleven Chorale Preludes,* op. 122, for organ, are often compared to those of Bach.

Thoroughly understanding the medium due to his experience in choral conducting, Brahms wrote much choral music, for choirs both accompanied and a cappella. A favorite is the *German Requiem,* op. 45, for chorus, two soloists, and orchestra. The traditional Catholic Mass for the dead is sung in Latin, of course. But for this work, he chose Biblical verses from Martin Luther's German translation, verses which comfort the living more than they mourn the dead, and which look forward to the Resurrection. Not a conventional church-goer, Brahms nonetheless was deeply religious and an avid Bible student.

For the award of an honorary doctorate, he composed the *Academic Festival Overture,* op. 80. Quite untypically for Brahms, this work quotes traditional student songs in a jolly medley. Other orchestral works include the four *Symphonies* (opp. 68, 73, 90, 98), two *Piano Concertos* (opp. 15 and 83), a *Double Concerto* for the unusual combination of violin and cello (op. 102), and a *Violin Concerto* (op. 77). In chamber music for a wide variety of combinations he proved himself to be the successor of Beethoven in this medium as he was in the symphony. One work is a trio for the unusual combination of clarinet, cello, and piano (op. 114.) Not surprisingly, he left no operas and no tone poems.

Brahms respected formal structure. He retained sonata-form, sometimes even calling for the exposition to be repeated, a practice most Romantic composers had abandoned. But he is never obvious. He avoided the standard signals that a Classic composer gave to alert the listener to a new idea—the pauses, the bustling effects, the sudden volume changes. In fact, he seemed to delight in sneaking in a theme's return, or in disguising it almost past recognition. Polyphony, demonstrated in his fugues and many fugal passages, fascinated him.

However much Brahms revered the past, his music exudes a Romantic richness, warmth, and fullness of sonority, with an emphasis upon the lower pitch range. Like most of his colleagues, he wrote continuous, long pieces for a big orchestra. His harmony is often chromatic, and his rhythms are extraordinarily subtle and complex, as in the conflict of duple versus triple meters.

Unlike many Romantic composers, tone color for its own sake did not interest him. What was good enough for Beethoven was good enough for Brahms. The sound of the triangle, in the third movement of his *Symphony No. 4,* is startling: sedate Brahms suddenly steps out of character. Nor was he interested in virtuoso display. Though his music is difficult, it doesn't always sound that way.

Brahms: *Symphony No. 4 in E Minor,* op. 98

***FOURTH MOVEMENT, Allegro energico e passionato** (10:33)*
(62)

Demonstrating his interest in older music, Brahms revived an old form: continuous variations, as in Pachelbel's *Canon in D,* for the basis of the finale of his fourth (and last) symphony, written in 1885. In this movement, the theme is followed by thirty variations and a coda. Tradition says that Brahms borrowed this theme from a Bach cantata, but more recent research suggests that compositions by Buxtehude or Beethoven might have supplied it. These variations are grouped in several ways. Overall, they produce a large ternary form, ABA'. On a smaller level, some variations are linked together in groups of twos or threes.

The theme itself is quite simple, moving up a portion of the E minor scale with one chromatic note added, then falling an octave at the end. In only a few variations is it clearly set forth as a melody. The texture Brahms builds around this theme is complex, with many countermelodies. Typical of the detail he lavished on his compositions is the harmonic variety he achieved. While finding a different set of chords for each of thirty variations might seem to be impossible, Brahms came very close to doing just this.

Placed under the theme (ex. 49.2) are letter-name chord symbols, the kind found in commercial music today. The first set identifies the chords as they occur at the beginning of the movement. The second set is a possible but rather simple harmonization that any student of harmony could devise—significantly, one that does *not* find a place in the movement.

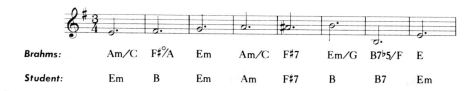

Brahms:	Am/C	F#%/A	Em	Am/C	F#7	Em/G	B7♭5/F	E
Student:	Em	B	Em	Am	F#7	B	B7	Em

CD5

(0:00)

1   m1   Woodwinds and brass play the theme in a bold, forthright style.

SECTION A

18

(0:16)

2   m9   French horns are opposed by pizzicato strings playing the notes of the theme.

(0:31)

3   m17   Flowing countermelodies are played softly by the woodwinds.

(0:46)

4   m25   The theme is elaborated with vigorous staccato chords.

(1:01)

5   m33   Violins play a countermelody as the theme descends to the low strings.

(1:18)

6   m41   Strings move upward to oppose the downward line of the winds.

(1:33)

7   m49   The style of item 6 continues; now the theme is more prominent. A very brief rest, the first silence so far, marks the end of this section.

(1:48)

8   m57   Strings and woodwinds alternate, using the dotted rhythm pattern that was a favored rhythm of the Baroque period.

19

(2:04)

9   m65   Violins play continuous, quick figures. Suddenly the volume level drops.

(2:20)

10   m73   Brahms tries harder, with even faster figuration. Again volume drops.

(2:35)
11   m81   Soft chords are played in an alternating, yet overlapping, style.

☐20☐

(2:54)
12   m89   The sounds of item 11 continue, with quicker notes. A decrescendo
             prepares the way for the big changes to come next.

SECTION B   In the next four variations, the tempo seems much slower because each mea-
                    sure is twice as long as before. The theme itself vanishes, although its individual
                    notes can be found.

(3:15)
13   m97   The flute plays a halting melody that rises, then falls, over a
             throbbing string accompaniment.
☐21☐

(3:55)
14   m105   Woodwinds take turns playing solos, with rising motives enriching
              the accompaniment, as the mode changes to major. Note that
☐22☐   Brahms did not make this change at item 13, where section B starts,
              the obvious place for it.

(4:37)
15   m113   Trombones create a solemn mood in a variation featuring another
              Baroque era rhythm, that of the sarabande. It characteristically has
☐23☐   a stress on beat two, and can be represented graphically
              as: __ ____ _ .

(5:17)
16   m121   Woodwinds are added as the style of item 15 continues. A decided
              pause occurs before the opening music returns.
☐24☐

SECTION A'   Some of the variations in Section A' repeat musical ideas familiar from Sec-
                    tion A, but, as usual with Brahms, with many subtle changes. The minor mode
                    returns.

(6:03)
17   m129   Winds begin a repetition of item 1; soon strings make a dramatic
             entrance.
☐25☐

(6:16)
18 m137 Soft tremolo strings and many volume changes impart a restless
          quality, as cellos play the theme.

(6:28)
19 m145 Cellos and horns are prominent in a bold new melody. In it is a
          speeded-up version of the sarabande rhythm first heard in item 15.

(6:40)
20 m153 Vigorous staccato chords are added to the sounds of item 19.

(6:53)
21 m161 The staccato vigor of item 20 continues, with even faster notes.

(7:06)
22 m169 This variation explodes with fast, ascending scales and timpani rolls.

(7:19)
23 m177 Quiet prevails as strings oppose woodwinds in conflicting rhythms.

26

(7:31)
24 m185 Horns recall the theme, as the rhythms of item 23 continue. A short
          pause marks the end of this section, comparable to that in item 7.

(7:44)
25 m193 Horns and timpani oppose the rest of the orchestra in a variation
          that is similar to item 2.

(7:59)
26 m201 Horns vary the theme, while violins recall the countermelodies of
          item 3.

(8:11)
27 m209 Horns and low strings are prominent in a softer, smoother variation.

27

(8:26)
28 m217 A gently swaying waltz emerges (shades of Johann Strauss!).

(8:40)
29 m225 The waltz continues with more activity in the woodwinds—but it
          soon fades.

(8:54)
30 m233 A duple meter pattern can be felt in woodwinds and pizzicato
          strings.

(9:08)

31 m241 Suddenly louder and more vigorous, this variation is longer, by half, and seems slower at the end, as if to prepare for the coda.

(9:29)

32 m253 With a restatement of the theme, the full orchestra begins a section that has the character of a development. Orchestral forces seem almost combative. An uncompromising spirit continues to the very end—still in the minor.

28

The first movement of this symphony is in the traditional sonata-form, with a gentle, long melody for Theme I. A slow second movement develops extensively the opening melody, played by French horns. The third movement is like a scherzo, although in sonata-form, with a rough kind of humor, accented by the "surprising" triangle.

GUSTAV MAHLER 50

PREVIEW   If we compare the Austrian composer Mahler to our other Romantics, we see that he is the first one whose life extended into the twentieth century. Only recently have Mahler's long and complex works become as well-known as theirs. His brilliant conducting career demanded many sacrifices from him, including that of time taken away from composing. He liked combining voices and orchestra, as well as building instrumental works from vocal themes.

Composers born in the nineteenth century but living into the twentieth are sometimes labeled **Post Romantic.** One of them, the extraordinarily complex Gustav Mahler (1860–1911), is considered an Austrian composer though he was born in a Bohemian town. The son of a successful but abusive businessman, he showed an early interest in music, learning many folk songs and becoming an able pianist. He studied composition at the Vienna Conservatory, where the experience of directing other students in performing his works probably influenced his decision to become a conductor. A series of small-town conducting positions established a pattern he followed most of his life: committing himself to raising the low musical standards he perceived when he began these positions, he succeeded in improving matters by working intensely. A severe taskmaster, he demanded as much of others as of himself. Too often, people preferred the good old mediocre days, and Mahler found that his success was won at the cost of great personal tension and much controversy.

Mahler paid dearly for his distinguished conducting career. One price was the sacrifice of time; only in the summers could he compose. The other obligation was the need to abandon his Jewish heritage. Although Christian mysticism appealed to him, his religious outlook took him well past all conventional belief systems. But to be appointed Kapellmeister in Vienna, he consented to baptism as a Roman Catholic, in 1897. Neither the memorable productions he created at the Vienna Opera nor his baptism seemed to protect him from the notoriously anti-Semitic press in Vienna, which led a campaign against him. He eventually fled to the United States, where he conducted both the Metropolitan Opera and the New

Mahler's conducting style intrigued the artist who produced these silhouettes of him in action.

GUSTAV MAHLER

DR O. BÖHLER'S SILHOUETTEN

York Philharmonic Orchestra for brief periods. A weak heart, a condition diagnosed only in 1907, hastened his premature death in 1911. In recent years, widespread and enthusiastic recognition of his musical legacy confirms, as Mahler himself boldly prophesied, that his time has come.

A

Mahler and the Swan Song of Romanticism

Mahler "sang" a farewell to the era that he sensed was nearing its end. Indeed, Mahler seemed haunted by the idea of saying goodbye. Be it the early *Die zwei blauen Augen* or the late *Das Lied von der Erde* (both of these are discussed later), the German word "ade" (farewell) figures prominently. In his preoccupation with death, he echoed the world-weary bent of his time, as in his *Kindertotenlieder* (Songs on the Death of Children). Mahler had begun these songs before he married. By the time he completed them in 1904—against the wishes of his wife—he was the father of two young daughters, whom he idolized. Tragically, his wife's premonitions came true in 1907, when scarlet fever took their elder daughter. (Mahler's wife, Alma Schindler, was studying composition when he met her, but he insisted she give it up—he made it clear there was room for only one composer in the family! Recently, Alma's music has resurfaced, making her story similar to the experiences of Fanny Mendelssohn and Clara Schumann.)

If Mahler "sang" a swan song, he "sang" continuously, like the early Romantic composer Schubert. Also echoing Schubert, Mahler sometimes transferred his vocal themes to instrumental music. Some themes he wrote himself; others were folk songs. Orchestral song cycles make up an important part of his work.

The Hunter's Funeral Procession is the title of this work by a German Romantic artist, Moritz von Schwind, who had been one of the circle of friends around Schubert. The animals rejoicing in the death of the hunter is the subject of German fairy tales that had inspired Mahler to write a "funeral march" as part of his first symphony. (Courtesy of The Music Division, New York Public Library at Lincoln Center, Astor, Lenox and Tilden Foundations.)

As in the traditional song cycle, Mahler set a group of related poems, but with orchestral instead of piano accompaniment. For example, near the end of his life he wrote a magnificent large-scale collection, *Das Lied von der Erde* (Song of the Earth), for alto (or baritone), tenor, and orchestra. With texts drawn from Chinese poetry, it combines features of song cycle, cantata, and symphony. It has been described as a "requiem for idealism." Four of his nine symphonies include singers in one or more movements, an idea that dates back to Beethoven's *Symphony No. 9.* He left a tenth symphony unfinished, though in this century Deryck Cooke has completed it satisfactorily.

Mahler carried some musical tendencies of his time, the love of the lengthy and the grandiose, for example, to what seems like the ultimate. An hour's duration for a symphony was typical for him. His eighth is nicknamed the "Symphony of a Thousand" because of the gargantuan performing resources it requires. (It can be performed with smaller numbers—a mere 300 to 400!) Yet at the same time, he embodied the contradictions of the Romantic age, for he could use large forces most discreetly, writing chamberlike passages in which only a few instruments play. Autobiographical—even confessional—as were many Romantics, he expressed himself freely in his music and therefore favored programmatic music.

B

Mahler's Music

The slow movement, *Adagietto,* from Mahler's *Symphony No. 5* (first performed in 1904), a wistful, almost glacially slow-moving theme, is probably his best-known melody (ex. 50.1). A 1971 movie, "Death in Venice," appropriated it as background music. The theme's modest orchestration of strings and harp is uncharacteristic of the usually colorful Mahler style.

Example 50.1

An immediately accessible piece is the third movement, *Funeral March,* from the *Symphony No. 1* (first performed in 1889). He unified this movement with a theme that is an altered version of the familiar round, "Are You Sleeping?" Mahler slowed the tune down (ex. 50.2), put it in minor, and gave it an extra note (the second eighth note).

Example 50.2

After about five minutes, Mahler introduces a contrasting section built on a lovely melody—which comes from the third stanza of the song discussed below.

Mahler: *Die zwei blauen Augen,* from *Lieder eines fahrenden Gesellen* (Songs of a Wayfarer) (5:36) ⓺③

Setting his own poetry, Mahler first began this cycle of songs with piano accompaniment in 1883, when he, just like the lonely man described in the poetry, was deeply—and hopelessly—in love. Both in song and in Mahler's real life, "she" loved someone else. Later, Mahler orchestrated the accompaniment. The cycle is sung by both baritones and mezzo-sopranos who revel in the challenge of its two-octave vocal range and its enormous expressive range.

In the fourth and last song, the young lover is resigned to his loss and realizes he must take his leave. The song falls into three distinct sections, each in a different key, unified by the rhythm of the opening four words and their three-note, up-the-scale motive (ex. 50.3). The orchestral accompaniment begins with woodwinds, supported by chords from the harp. A funereal-paced marchlike beat, in E minor, exudes a quiet acceptance.

Example 50.3

(0:00)

1

29

Die zwei blauen Augen von meinem Schatz	The two blue eyes of my sweetheart
Die haben mich in die weite Welt geschickt.	made me wander in the wide world.
Da musst' ich Abschied nehmen	I must bid farewell to the place
Vom allerliebsten Platz!	I love the best.

(0:41)

1b

| O Augen blau, warum habt ihr mich angeblickt? Nun hab' ich ewig Leid und Grämen! | Oh eyes of blue, why did you look at me? Now I have forever grief and sorrow. |

(1:09)

2

30

A brief orchestral interlude continues with the motives of stanza 1. Then it introduces a *dô-sol-dô-sol* motive in the low notes of harp and timpani, as the key shifts to a more cheerful C major.

Ich bin ausgegangen in stiller Nacht	I went out into the quiet night,
In stiller Nacht wohl über die dunkle Heide;	into the quiet night over the dark heath
Hat mir Niemand Ade gesagt.	No one said farewell to me.
Ade! Ade! Ade!	Farewell! Farewell! Farewell!
Mein Gesell' war Lieb' und Leide!	My companions were love and sorrow.

(2:32)

3

31

Another orchestral interlude separates the stanzas, again with harp prominent, again with a change of key, here to F major. The strings will support the folk-song-like melody in the third stanza.

Auf der Strasse steht ein Lindenbaum	By the road stands a linden tree;
Da hab' ich zum ersten Mal im Schlaf geruht!	there I have for the first time in sleep found rest.
Unter dem Lindenbaum!	Under the linden tree.
Der hat seine Blüten über mich geschneit—	There its blossoms snowed on me—
Da wusst' ich nicht, Wie das Leben tut	There I forgot what Life is like.
war Alles, Alles wieder gut!	All, All is good again.
Alles, Lieb' und Leid, und Welt, und Traum!	All: Love, Sorrow, the World, Dreams!

(5:17)

4

32

The flutes have the last word, as they intone, pppp, the minor-key
motive with which they began, leaving the song, and the entire cycle,
"up-in-the-air."

RICHARD STRAUSS 51

PREVIEW   Also living into the twentieth century—even surviving World War II— was the German-born Strauss (not to be confused with the composer of the *Blue Danube Waltz*). Given conservative training by his musician-father, Strauss then adopted the credo of the Liszt/ Wagner school and devoted himself to tone poems and operas. They are constantly performed, due to his skillful treatment of musical forms and singular ability to create exciting orchestral effects and tone colors.

Post-Romanticism's most prominent German composer was Richard [the German pronunciation is REE-card] Strauss (1864–1949), born in Munich. His was a well-to-do musical family, unrelated to the Johann Strauss family, famous for its contributions to the Viennese waltz. Richard Strauss's father, a virtuoso French horn player, saw to it that his talented son had the best possible piano and violin teachers. Of conservative musical tastes, the father made sure that his son heard nothing but the classics. At age seventeen, the young Strauss was a skilled composer in a Mendelssohnlike style and soon was given important conducting positions.

Despite his father's influence, by the turn of the century Strauss was a confirmed follower of Wagner. A series of sensational tone poems had established his worldwide reputation, though his naturalistic musical images attracted controversy. Before the first World War, he produced some operas that further enhanced his reputation and his pocketbook. (Believing that all composers should be well-paid, he championed others' rights as well as his own.) Living long past the era he represented, he died in 1949, shortly after the celebrations of his eighty-fifth birthday.

Richard Strauss.

A

Although Strauss showed in his concertos for French horn that he was no stranger to absolute music, his best-known works are his operas and tone poems. This preference for referential music aligns him with the Liszt/Wagner camp. As we saw earlier, Liszt invented what he called the "symphonic poem," a one-movement programmatic piece. Many other composers followed him in writing

Strauss: The Structured Story-Teller

The confused but courageous Don Quixote was the subject of a tone poem by Strauss and also of the French artist Honoré Daumier (1809–79).

instrumental music based on a literary idea. Strauss preferred the term **tone poem,** although most authorities do not attempt to maintain any particular distinction between the terms. Liszt unified his works by means of thematic transformation; Strauss found this technique useful also. What makes his tone poems unique is the realistic, yet imaginative quality of his musical "pictures," and the way the organization of these works relates to traditional musical forms. Some of these forms Strauss identified in the titles. For instance, the full title of *Till Eulenspiegels lustige Streiche* (1894) is "Till Eulenspiegel's merry pranks, after the old rogue's tale, in rondo form," and indeed, the theme representing Till returns many times. Particularly apt is the transformation of that theme near the end of the piece, when Till is condemned to death for his many misdeeds. His theme squeakily ascends, but soon turns around and descends, as if to hint that Till's destination is not heaven!

Don Quixote (1896–97), with prominent parts for a solo cello, representing the Don, and the viola, portraying his servant Sancho Panza, is almost concerto-like. Its subtitle, "Fantastic variations on a theme of knightly character," suggests that it resembles traditional variation-form. That, however, is not what listeners first noticed. Rather, its programmatic content drew criticism for being too literal. For example, when the demented Don Quixote takes up his sword against sheep, the sounds of their bleating, in woodwinds and brass, were amazingly realistic. Other tone poems have been analyzed in relation to sonata-form: *Don Juan* (1888–89), *Tod und Verklärung* (Death and Transfiguration, 1888–89), and *Ein Heldenleben* (A Hero's Life, 1897–98). The "hero" in this latter work was Strauss himself, introduced by way of the themes of his earlier tone poems.

Strauss's operas were equally well-structured and equally descriptive. His *Salome* (1903–05) was branded as decadent, especially in the scenes where Salome dances her erotic "Dance of the Seven Veils" and kisses the severed head of John the Baptist. Compared to that opera, *Der Rosenkavalier* (1909–10) is a cream puff which revived the artificialities of eighteenth-century opera, and proved that Richard Strauss could write waltzes just as tuneful as those by Johann Strauss—senior or junior.

B

Strauss's Music

While the concert audience is familiar with the works just mentioned, the general public has learned of this composer through association with a brief portion of one of his works, *Also sprach Zarathustra* (described later). *Zarathustra,* for example, demands a mammoth orchestra, with three each of flutes, oboes, clarinets, and bassoons; four trumpets, six French horns, three trombones, and two tubas; six different percussion instruments, two harps, and of course, a large string section. Such a large brass section is responsible for much of the gorgeous, full, rich orchestral sound, which may be the most attractive general feature of Strauss's music for today's stereo-conscious listener.

Of the brass family, Strauss singled out the French horn for very challenging parts—perhaps thinking of his father? Players rise or fall, depending upon how well they negotiate the dangers of the theme (ex. 51.1) that represents the capricious character whose name furnishes the title for Strauss's tone poem *Till Eulenspiegel.*

Example 51.1

cresc.

Strauss labeled this tone poem (1895–96) a "musical commentary on Nietzsche's poem." His musical images unmistakably relate to the various sections of that long philosophical work, with Nietzsche's words supplying the titles. The composition, thirty-five or so minutes in duration, won a new audience when its opening section, lasting barely two minutes, became a part of the background music in Stanley Kubrick's 1968 motion picture "2001: A Space Odyssey." Ironically, the already-famous *Blue Danube Waltz,* by "another" Strauss, also forms a part of this film's music. Nietzsche's words, "We were night-walkers, let us become day-walkers," inspired this opening section. In a few bold strokes, Strauss briefly, yet magically transforms night into day.

Strauss: *Also sprach Zarathustra* (Thus Spoke Zarathustra), opening section, "Prologue: Sunrise." (1:36) (64)

♪♩ CD5

(0:00)

1a   m1   The work begins with a low pitch (C) played so quietly it can
[33]   scarcely be heard. That note continues until the chord change in
               item 1c. Soon trumpets introduce the "nature" theme, *do-sol-dô*,
               and top it off with a short, loud major chord succeeded by the same
               chord turned minor and sustained. In typical Romantic style, the
               dynamic levels constantly change.

(0:27)

1b   m8   Timpani pounds out a *dô-sol* pattern; then the trumpets resume the
               nature theme and the chord series is repeated. Here the first, short
               chord is in the minor mode, the long one in major.

(0:43)

1c   m12   Again the timpani alternates its two notes and the trumpets repeat
               the nature theme. This time, when the chords sound, the long chord
               is a new one (the subdominant) and is extended.

(1:18)

1d   m19   The climax of the passage features the massive sound of the organ
               on a C major chord. A powerful organ may almost drown out the
               rest of the *fortissimo* orchestra.

The remainder of this work follows. A detailed program for it would help greatly in following its major subsections, only outlined below, since each contains several themes.

2.   "Of the inhabitants of the unseen world." Muted low strings suggest shadowy figures.

3.   "Of the great longing" is next, begun by the low strings. Gregorian chant melodies are quoted.

4.   "Of joy and passion" is, appropriately, passionate and intense.

5.   "Dirge" restates the themes of other sections.

6.   "Of Science" treats the original "nature" theme as the subject of a fugue.

7.   "The Convalescent" brightens the mood with a return of themes heard earlier.

8.   "Dance Song" is as long as the previous sections put together and, not surprisingly, includes waltzlike themes.

9.   "Nightwalker's Song" grows ever quieter, leading to an unresolved-sounding cadence.

The Twentieth Century

INTRODUCING THE TWENTIETH CENTURY 52

PREVIEW   Full of conflicting and widely varied tendencies, this century offers few generalities because of the multiplicity of artistic movements. As in similar chapters, we outline the historical background. We alert the student that many composers will appear only marginally and that the few who are given individual chapters are present because each demonstrates an important feature of this century's music. Because of the many individual styles, we can relate twentieth-century music to the characteristics of sound and the elements of music only in very general ways.

There is as yet no satisfactory label for the music written in the 1900s. Indeed, each decade seems to form a mini-period of its own, with the "jazz age" of the 1920s, for example, contrasting as sharply with the depression-era 1930s as any two earlier periods. Calling a 1913 work "modern" or "contemporary" is odd, yet for many people Stravinsky's *The Rite of Spring* still sounds amazingly new. Musical innovations have emerged in great numbers, and because modern communication is so swift and publicity so effective, these innovations have been heard, imitated, and sometimes discarded in a relatively short time span. Certainly the rate of change has vastly accelerated. Lacking the perspective of history, we fail to see any orderly pattern in this century.

The *multiplicity of artistic movements*—cubism and primitivism, to name only two—is a characteristic feature of this century. "Modernism" and "post-modernism" are two more, and no doubt there will be other "isms," a new word, which outgrew its former life as a suffix. Many of the labels given to musical movements are borrowed from the field of visual art, pointing to the increasing ties among all the arts.

Artists in all fields have broken with past traditions. For example, much contemporary poetry is written in free verse, not bound by past ideas of regular meter and rhyme. A German artist, Kurt Schwitters (1887–1948), was asked what art

The work of Frenchman Fernand Léger (1881–1955) is distinctive for the clean, geometric shapes he adopted, as in his *Three Musicians,* 1944. (Oil on canvas, 68 1/2″ × 57 1/4″. Collection, The Museum of Modern Art, New York. Mrs. Simon Guggenheim Fund.)

is. His response was, "What isn't?" Similarly, as we shall see, some twentieth-century composers have stretched the concept of music, perhaps to a breaking point.

In music, the differences among composers are so great that it is hard to see what they might hold in common. Some maintain that the only thing twentieth-century composers agree upon is the need to rebel against Romanticism. Indeed, one composer whom we study, Béla Bartók, clearly articulated this point of view: "At the beginning of the 20th century there was a turning point in the history of

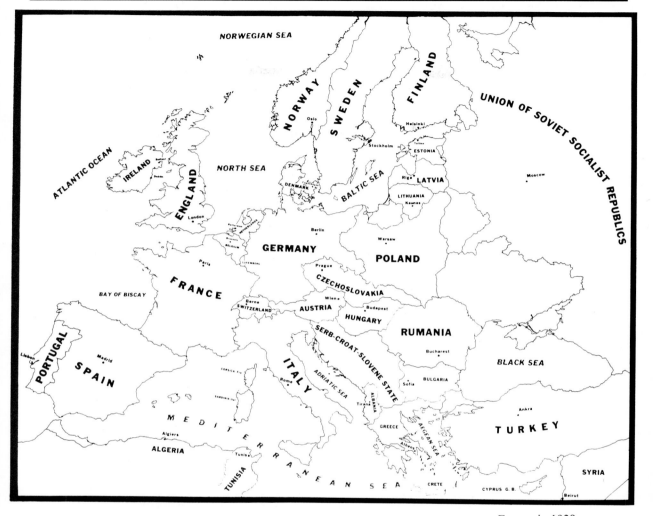

Europe in 1920.

modern music. The excesses of the Romantics began to be unbearable for many. There were composers who felt: 'this road does not lead us anywhere; there is no other solution but a complete break with the 19th century.' "

For many, however, a complete break was impossible. Music, they believed, could not help retaining connections to the past. Consequently, some composers cultivated a Romantic sound well into this century. Regardless of the extent of the "newness" in whatever music we study, we can still look for the quality in it that marks it as a twentieth-century product.

The twentieth century has been so deeply scarred by two world wars that historians divide it into prewar, postwar, and "between-the-wars" phases. Since 1950 especially, this century has witnessed bewildering changes. Industrialization and scientific advancements, far surpassing those of the Industrial Revolution, have transformed the lives of ordinary people. Men walked on the moon. Sigmund Freud (1856–1939) probed the inner world of the subconscious, causing fundamental changes in the ways people think and consequently in their arts. As the historian Barbara Tuchman wrote, "Man in the twentieth century is overtaken by doubt of human purpose and divine purpose. He has lost certainty, and is left with a sense of foot-loose purposelessness and self-disgust, which literature naturally reflects." In 1920, the poet William Butler Yeats (1865–1939) said something similar in his poem *The Second Coming:*

> Things fall apart: the center cannot hold;
> Mere anarchy is loosed upon the world,
> The blood-dimmed tide is loosed, and everywhere
> The ceremony of innocence is drowned.

And of course, music and all the arts reflect social changes. Many historians draw comparisons between the tensions of modern life and the dissonance in much modern music, just as they see parallels between those tensions and the distortions in modern art.

The ways in which people are exposed to music have changed. In this century, a vastly expanded audience has developed as the broadcasting and recording industries have made it possible for all people, not just the elite of society, to hear music whenever they want to—and sometimes when they don't want to. Motion pictures and television employ music consistently as a background to the visual experience. Televised concerts have reached worldwide audiences numbering in the millions. In the United States, as a result of the vast expansion of the potential audience, many more orchestras now exist; professional performing standards have never been higher; and the unionization of musicians has resulted in good wages, at least for the minority of performers who find a place in the system.

In spite of a positive outlook for music in general, problems still exist for performers of "serious music" in this country. Because concerts are so expensive to produce and the audience continues to be a relatively small percentage of the total population—though an extremely influential part of it—they cannot be self-supporting at the box office. Other help must be found. A few wealthy individuals continue to play the role of art patron. Many not-so-wealthy people support arts organizations which advance the cause of music. Large corporations and national foundations often support the arts. A limited amount of help comes from governmental agencies, such as the National Endowment for the Arts and state and local performing arts commissions, though this help is modest in comparison with state support for arts in many European cities and countries.

Some composers have found American colleges and universities to be generous patrons of music, as they offer a haven for performers and composers, engaging them as teachers of music or composers in residence. Indeed, a bountiful source of concerts of contemporary music is the college campus—where the reader of this text is most likely to be found. Almost every music department has its resident composer and its group of dedicated performers and listeners to the new music. Their enthusiasm can be infectious. Among the names of prominent composer-professors are Walter Piston (1894–1976), Roger Sessions (1896–1985), Roy Harris (1898–1979), and William Schuman (born 1910). Elliott Carter (born 1908) has taught composition at several leading American universities.

Twentieth-Century Composers

The closer we get to the present, the more composers we meet and the less consensus we discover about those who should be included in surveys like this one. The relatively few described here in separate chapters were chosen because each illustrates an important feature of this century's music. Many other composers are mentioned in connection with particular topics.

Unique problems face twentieth-century composers. Frequently they are described as alienated from the general audience, which seems to prefer music of the past. Contemporary music is often relegated to a special series or to festivals. If programmed on a concert of otherwise traditional music, it may be boycotted by a conservative audience that manages to arrive late or leave early. Oddly enough, this has happened in an age in which people avidly seek the newest fashions and foods. Until this century, audiences went to concerts primarily to hear the newest music, just as people today attend the theater to see a new play.

If it is possible to say that audiences and composers have collective voices, each of these voices blames the other for the situation. Composers maintain that audiences are stodgy and ignorant. In fact, one prominent composer has claimed that "advanced" contemporary music could be compared to theoretical physics: the layperson should not expect to appreciate either one. Audiences retort that composers, indifferent to listeners' wishes, write "difficult" music. Again, parallels exist in the art world. Taxpayers protest when public funds support sculpture that they fail to understand; people wonder why modern artists refuse to draw "realistically." Artists answer that they must be allowed their creative right to distort reality.

The chasm between composer and audience has become so wide that some composers have turned to electronic music because it offers them a chance to approach the listener directly by way of recordings, bypassing public performance. Historians in the twenty-first century will know how it all turned out, but meanwhile, back in the classroom, the student is advised to explore new worlds of sound, without relying on past expectations. The composer Charles Ives urged listeners to *stretch their ears*. Adopting that spirit of challenge and experiment is the most direct way to approach new music. Nothing is lost by experiencing new art forms, trusting in the dedication of creators and performers.

A 1948 work, *Family Group,* by the English sculptor Henry Moore (1898–1986) is one of the artist's many variations on the theme of the human figure. (Bronze, 59 1/4″ × 46 1/2″ × 29 7/8″, including base. Collection, The Museum of Modern Art, New York. A. Conger Goodyear Fund.)

C

The Characteristics of Sound in Twentieth-Century Music

1. Some twentieth-century composers consider *pitch* a continuum from high to low instead of a series of fixed pitches in half-steps, as on the piano. In this approach, the half-step can be divided into two **quarter-tones,** or into even smaller gradations called **microtones.** For example, Charles Ives wrote *Three Quarter-tone Pieces* for two pianos, one tuned a quarter-tone higher than the other. A self-taught American composer-performer, Harry Partch (1901–74), made a unique contribution by inventing and building instruments to play his forty-three-note scale. The Polish composer Krzysztof Penderecki [pronounced pen-der-RET-skee] (born 1933) won international fame with his *Threnody for the Victims of Hiroshima* (1960). In it, fifty-two string players explore the entire pitch range of quarter-tones and microtones. Other pitch-related effects are the **glissando,** which is the gradually sliding sound from one pitch to the next, and **tone clusters,** which are groups of tones lying close together. A pianist, for example, may play with the forearm or fist on the keyboard in order to depress a number of keys. Specific tones are not important.

2. *Dynamics* cover even greater ranges of volume than in the Romantic period, from ear-splitting *fortissimo* to a near-inaudible whisper. An important new consideration intrudes: if recording or amplification is involved, the sound technician may determine dynamic range as much as the musician.

3. *Tone color* is the element of twentieth-century music that even the most severe critics of "modern music" admit has shown much growth. Nearly-forgotten Renaissance instruments—the recorder, the harpsichord, and the lute—have taken a new lease on life. Non-Western instruments such as the Japanese koto or the Indian sitar have intrigued musicians. Many composers have experimented with the truly new tone color of this century, electronic sounds, a topic discussed in a separate chapter. Other composers remain loyal to conventional sound sources, but develop them in new ways.

a. The extremely high and low *ranges* of instruments, particularly wood-winds, are exploited. New and unexpected sounds result because these ranges are often uncharacteristic of the instrument.

b. Specifying *unusual playing techniques* is common, such as **flutter-tonguing** on some woodwind and brass instruments. (The player rolls the tongue and a distinctive sound results.) Woodwind players can hum while playing, or feature the sounds their fingers make while depressing the keys—and not blow at all. String players might be directed to hit the body of the instrument. Pianists may reach inside their instrument to strike piano strings with a drum stick or pluck them with their fingers. In a **prepared piano,** various objects are inserted in between piano strings, greatly altering the sound. As for acoustic instruments, by means of an attached microphone, sounds can be modified, amplified, and mixed at will.

c. Singers may need to sing higher or lower than their normal ranges, and in addition scream, shout, make popping or clicking sounds, or produce a speech-like quality. In *Ancient Voices of Children* by the American George Crumb (born 1929), the soloist sings *into* the piano, and the accompanying instrumentalists whisper and shout as well as play. Narration may be added to an instrumental accompaniment, as in Copland's *Lincoln Portrait.* Some compositions feature a spoken chorus, such as the *Geographical Fugue* by the Austrian-born American Ernst Toch (1887–1964). While a spoken chorus is not expected to produce specific pitches, the natural span from soprano to bass ensures pitch variety nonetheless.

The *percussion section is expanded* even more than it had been in the Romantic period, be it with wind machines, typewriters, brake drums—anything that can be hit or shaken—or instruments from around the world. Now prominent in many orchestral scores as part of the percussion section, the piano assumes a vital new role. Entire compositions feature percussion ensembles, as in *Toccata for Percussion* by the Mexican conductor-composer Carlos Chávez (1899–1978). In 1931, Edgard Varèse, whose "organized sound" definition of music we encountered in Chapter 2, wrote his *Ionisation* for forty percussion instruments, two sirens, and piano.

In some instances, composers have created *new ways to write music* so that they can specify these new effects. Various chart forms of notation show a graphic, up-and-down representation for pitch, with durations implied by elapsed time in seconds. In such situations, performers find a stopwatch more helpful than a metronome.

New combinations of instruments have been devised, almost as if each composition demanded a new set of sound-makers. Even in writing for the standard symphony orchestra, composers have shifted emphasis. No longer are the "warm" strings automatically the heart of the orchestra; the "cool" woodwinds are often featured. Nor does the full sound of the entire group dominate; individual lines are given prominence, as in chamber music. Indeed, since rehearsal time is prohibitively expensive, writing for the symphony orchestra has become less practical and smaller groups are often favored for economic reasons.

D

The Elements of Music in the Twentieth Century

1. *Rhythm* in general is more complex, more interesting, than in previous centuries, although toe-tappers find themselves frustrated because a steady beat and regular meter are less common. Some composers employ constantly repeated rhythmic patterns, an old effect in music known as ostinato. Unexpected accents add spice to the sound and changes in meter are frequent, a technique labeled **mixed meter.** Composers sometimes write in two simultaneous meters, an effect called **polyrhythm.**

2. Concepts of *melody* have grown constantly through the centuries and will probably continue to do so. Lovers of obvious, singable tunes will be disappointed. Twentieth-century melodies are more apt to be disjunct rather than conjunct. Some melodies are built on new scale patterns; conversely, old modes have been revived. While melodies may still fall into phrases, the lengths of phrases will probably not be equal.

3. Some seemingly new ideas about *harmony* are actually extensions of older developments. Earlier, triads were frequently enlarged with one or two more tones, making the rich sounds of seventh or ninth chords, as in the construction C,E,G,B-flat,D. Expanding that idea further with two more tones, F and A, results in so complex a sonority that it no longer sounds like one chord; instead, it feels like two or three chords sounding simultaneously. Going a bit further down the road, two or more different tonalities sounding at the same time can create **bitonality** or **polytonality.** Conventional harmonic progressions have been avoided, often replaced by successions of chords, related in new ways, and not necessarily driving toward a particular goal. The traditional sound of the cadence, a dominant-seventh chord resolving to the tonic, almost disappears, along with long, drawn-out endings in general.

A revolutionary twentieth-century development in harmony was the emergence of **atonality,** discussed later in connection with the composer Schoenberg. At the same time, many composers have kept their faith in tonality, although vastly stretching the concept of it.

Perhaps no feature of this century's music has perplexed the public more than the generally high levels of dissonance. While some claim that dissonance has been "emancipated," listeners still seem to expect that a dissonance should resolve to a consonance, as it did for centuries. Today, one dissonance may be succeeded by another. If the latter is somewhat less astringent, the traditional effect of relaxing the tension still results.

4. Composers differ greatly in their attitudes toward *texture*. Some reject polyphony as a relic of the past; others rely on it, though in ways that allow greater freedom in the handling of dissonance. Not only is polyphony indispensable to the atonal composers; in the tonal sphere the versatile and prolific German composer Paul Hindemith [pronounced HIN-deh-mit] (1895–1963) habitually wrote contrapuntally, as in his opera *Mathis der Maler.*

5. In similar fashion, all possible approaches to the concept of *form* exist in this century, from the complete absence of any readily perceptible structure to forms as tight as those of the Classic masters.

53 CLAUDE DEBUSSY

PREVIEW Debussy is a transition figure between Romanticism and twentieth-century developments. Living until the close of World War I, his links to his native French culture are demonstrated in his association with the French artistic movement, impressionism. Debussy's work offers a musical parallel to the vague, shifting images of impressionist art.

Debussy's position on the borderline between the Romantic period and the twentieth century has caused many writers to consider him a forerunner of countless modern developments, and one of the greatest musical innovators of all time. Claude Debussy [pronounced DEB-you-see] (1862–1918) was born in a small town near Paris. His was a middle-class family without any particular musical interests. In the last decade of the nineteenth century and the years before World War I, Paris was a center for new ideas in both art and music. Debussy spent ten years at the Paris Conservatory of Music, where he was considered talented but rebellious. When his teacher told him that a certain chord "has to resolve," Debussy's answer was, "I don't see that it should. Why?"

For a brief period he worked in Russia as a pianist and piano teacher at the household of Madame von Meck, who earlier had been Tchaikovsky's patroness. While there, he discovered the music of Mussorgsky and through its folklike melodies based on modal scales became fascinated with the unusual sounds of Russian music. Like many other composers, he made a pilgrimage to Bayreuth, but he eventually reacted strongly against Wagner and German music in general.

A possible antidote to the Wagnerian influence resulted from the Paris Exposition of 1889. There Debussy listened in fascination to a Javanese **gamelan,** an "orchestra" of gongs and metal xylophonelike instruments. (Gamelans vary in size and include social and religious functions that a Western orchestra does not share.) This experience profoundly affected him as he heard the gamelan's gentle, yet percussive sounds, with its variety of scales and intervals not possible in our tuning

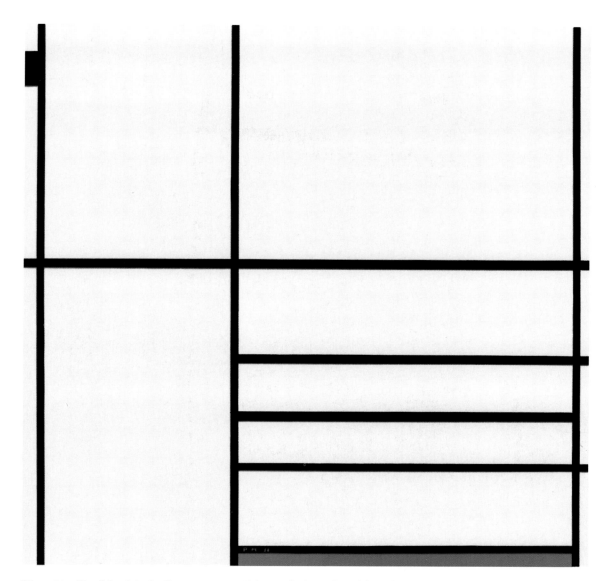

Plate 44 Piet Mondrian's *Composition in White, Black, and Red* (1936) is an example of the twentieth-century movement toward an abstract art without any representational elements. Restricting himself to geometric shapes and the primary colors, the Dutch painter Mondrian (1872–1944) concentrated on the beauty of proportions. (Oil on canvas, 40 1/4″ × 41″. Collection, The Museum of Modern Art, New York. Gift of The Advisory Committee.)

Plate 45 Schoenberg participated in the German expressionist movement in art, painting many self-portraits in that style. (Courtesy Lawrence A. Schoenberg, Los Angeles.)

Plate 46 The Russian painter Vasily Kandinsky (1866–1944) gave his "improvisations" numbers, as in his *Painting No. 198*. Not only did he reject representation in these works, he rejected conscious control and let his subconscious dictate the flow of brilliant colors onto the canvas. (Oil on canvas, 64″ × 36 1/4″. Collection, The Museum of Modern Art, New York. Mrs. Simon Guggenheim Fund.)

Plate 47 This poster was created by Phillip Brazeau, Jr., for a 1990 Seattle Opera production of Prokofiev's *War and Peace.* It recalls the heroic peasant imagery of Socialist Realism, the kind of art that was officially sponsored in Prokofiev's lifetime. (Courtesy of Seattle Opera and Phillip Brazeau, Jr.)

Plate 48 The U.S. Postal Service issued a stamp in 1983 honoring Scott Joplin as part of its Black Heritage series. (Copyright 1983 U.S. Postal Service)

Plate 49 A stamp issued in 1986 as part of the Performing Arts series pictured Duke Ellington against an appropriate background—a piano keyboard. (Copyright 1985 U.S. Postal Service)

Plate 50 The American Jackson Pollock (1912–56) in his *Number 1, 1948,* poured and spattered his colors instead of applying them with a brush. Though in the process he gave up strict control over the materials, art critics feel that his works show a new, lively sense of energy. People frequently compare Pollock's techniques to Cage's chance methods. (Oil and enamel on unprimed canvas, 68″ × 8′8″. Collection, The Museum of Modern Art. Purchase.)

Plate 51   Pictured here is a mandala, a pattern found in Indian religious art as an aid to meditation. All elements of a mandala, the square, circle, and triangle, have cosmic significance. The triangle is a symbolic representation of the female principle, Shakti.

Claude Debussy.

system. Listening to recordings of gamelan music will demonstrate as no description possibly can the unique effect of these instruments and their tunings. (Recordings are available, some made in Java, some made in this country by students of non-Western music.)

One type of gamelan music is based on a five-tone, or **pentatonic,** scale, which can be related only loosely to the Western style of pentatonic scale. To demonstrate the latter, play five black piano keys starting with F-sharp, the lowest of a three-black-key group. The resulting scale, *do-re-mi-sol-la,* is prominent in folk songs, as in the Scotch "Auld Lang Syne" ("Should auld acquaintance be forgot"). The familiar American hymn "Amazing Grace," which has won "amazing" popularity recently, is also based on the pentatonic scale.

As a result of Debussy's introduction to Javanese music, traces of musical exoticism color some of his pieces. *Pagodes,* from a set of three piano pieces (1903) entitled *Estampes* (Prints), reflects this interest. *The Snow is Dancing,* a portion of his *Children's Corner* suite (1908), employs immediate repetition of each melody note, a gamelan feature.

In Paris, Debussy heard a Javanese gamelan, which might have resembled the one pictured here, although these groups vary considerably.

Debussy's reputation developed slowly, until eventually he was recognized as France's leading composer. His work as a music critic won him admiration for his excellent writing style, though he wounded many with his acid-tipped pen. For example, he dismissed an Italian opera in this manner: "The characters fling themselves on one another and tear their melodies from each other's lips." In his last few years, he toured Europe as a pianist and conductor. A dedication to French ideals, as opposed to Germanic musical traditions, became ever stronger throughout his life. (His directions to performers are in French; his last three sonatas show his name as "Claude Debussy, French musician.") Ironically, he died (of cancer) in 1918 during a German bombardment of Paris.

A

Debussy: A Musical Impressionist

Although Debussy's name is customarily associated with the movement in French art of the late 1800s known as impressionism, he disliked the label. He wrote to his publisher: "What I am trying to do is something 'different'—an effect of reality, but what some fools call Impressionism." Still, parallels exist between his music and the paintings of the impressionists, such as Claude Monet (1840–1926), Edgar Degas (1834–1917), and Pierre Auguste Renoir (1841–1919).

A hostile art critic, after seeing a painting by Monet called "Impression: Sunrise," coined the label **impressionism** in 1874. The impressionists hoped to capture on canvas the freshness of their impressions. They were fascinated by the ever-changing patterns of light and shadow, especially in out-of-door scenes, and the effects of color itself, laid on the canvas in patches. The artists wanted to make suggestions, not statements. In impressionist art, the outlines are often somewhat blurred; a painting might be representational but it was not primarily realistic. (Today, the paintings that the critics savaged bring millions of dollars at art auctions, and exhibitions of impressionist art attract vast crowds to museums.)

Debussy's conservative teachers warned him to avoid the dangers of a "vague impressionism." The label moved to music as well, where it has stuck ever since. In musical impressionism, traditional harmonic progressions yield to innovative connections, and a fluid rhythm replaces the obvious repetitive patterns of much Romantic music. The French gift for subtle understatement finds a natural home.

Debussy retained the big orchestra of the late Romantic period but employed its forces discreetly. While the French horn plays an important role, the other brasses and percussion have less to do. Instruments are constantly entering and leaving, with no "hard edges" in these entrances and exits, as one instrumental color blends with the next. Favorite sounds are the harp glissando, quiet solos for woodwind instruments, especially in their low ranges, and the shimmer of muted string tremolos.

Though not all of his music is impressionistic, Debussy was the acknowledged leader in this movement. It strongly influenced many composers, such as the Swiss-American Ernest Bloch (1880–1959) and the American-born Charles Griffes (1884–1920). Fellow Frenchman Maurice Ravel [pronounced rah-VELL] (1875–1937), whose brilliant orchestration of Mussorgsky's *Pictures at an Exhibition* was mentioned in Chapter 47, has been called an impressionist, but only in a few early works does this label seem apt. Ravel himself resented charges that he was an imitator of Debussy. Unfortunately, the general public knows him only for his vastly over-played *Bolero* (1928), which is not at all impressionistic, but which does brilliantly display his orchestration skills. More typical of his style is the colorful music for the ballet *Daphnis and Chloe* (1912).

B

Debussy's Music

Compared to the extensive production of many other great composers, Debussy's output was relatively small, although astonishingly varied. With its soft beginning and fluid rhythm, *Clair de lune* (ex. 53.1), a component of his early (1890) *Suite bergamasque* for piano, is probably the piece most familiar to the general public. The "con sordino" direction instructs the pianist to use the "soft," (left) pedal.

Example 53.1

Although the general public may not realize it, Debussy wrote his share of loud, fast, and metrical music. *Fêtes* (Festivals), the middle movement of his three-movement orchestral work, *Nocturnes* (1897–99), provides a splendid example. (Despite the title, these pieces have nothing to do with night. The first, *Nuages,* evokes in its middle section the sounds of a Javanese gamelan; the third *Nocturne, Sirènes,* features a wordless women's chorus.) Another orchestral work in three movements, *La Mer* (The Sea, 1903–05), is often performed. It, too, has some powerful moments—the sea is not always calm! He labored for years on his opera, *Pelléas et Mélisande* (first performed in 1902), to a libretto he condensed from the drama by Maurice Maeterlinck (1862–1949). It may hold the operatic record for the greatest number of beats of rest and the smallest total decibel level.

French poetry—of course—provides the texts for Debussy's art songs, which show great sensitivity to the subtle nuances of the language. (All syllables in French have more or less the same degree of stress, unlike syllables in English.)

He is considered one of the most important piano composers in music history. Like Chopin, Debussy revealed new possibilities of the instrument, especially in employing the pedal. His two books of *Preludes* (1910 and 1912–13) contain programmatic titles, yet he had these titles printed at the end of each piece, as if to show that they are afterthoughts.

The **whole-tone scale** frequently appears in Debussy's music. (Only two whole-tone scales exist: C,D,E,F-sharp,G-sharp,A-sharp,C; and C-sharp,D-sharp, F,G,A,B,C-sharp.) Since by definition a whole-tone scale lacks half-steps, it has no *ti* to *dô,* and consequently no sense of completion. Not surprisingly, we look in vain for a familiar melody based upon a whole-tone scale. Debussy's *Voiles* (ex. 53.2), from the first book of preludes for piano, consists almost exclusively of whole-tone scales. The title is usually translated as "sails" or "veils." While either word suits the piece's floating, up-in-the-air feeling, "sails" is thought to be more authoritative.

Example 53.2

très doux

Debussy's harmony tended to weaken the sense of tonality as did Wagner's. Many complex chords occur in his music, such as the ninth chord. A series of ninth chords, all moving in the same direction, creates a floating sensation that one can easily relate to the vague shapes of impressionist art. Writers of popular music in the 1930s imitated this effect, as a few chords from Duke Ellington's "Sophisticated Lady" (ex. 53.3) will show.

Example 53.3

The Faun, as a creation of the dancer Nijinsky, is shown in the profile pose Nijinsky adopted in the ballet he based on Debussy's *Prélude à l'après-midi d'un faune.*

Debussy: *Prélude à l'après-midi d'un faune* (Prelude to the Afternoon of a Faun) (9:42) ⑥⑤

This orchestral piece was completed in 1894. A long poem by the French writer Stéphane Mallarmé (1842–98) provided the necessary inspiration. The poem, which defies the best efforts of translators because of its obscure language, unfolds as the soliloquy of a lusty Faun, a mythical creature who is half-man, half-goat. Either in his erotic imagination or in reality, two beautiful nymphs pay him a visit. Or in the Faun's words, "Was it a dream I loved?" As Debussy explained it, his prelude was not a "synthesis" of that poem but rather a "very free illustration" of it. A program note printed with one edition of the score describes the music as "successive scenes through which pass the desires and dreams of the faun in the heat of this afternoon. Then, tired of pursuing the fearful flight of nymphs and the naiads, he succumbs to intoxicating sleep."

With these hints, it seems reasonable to associate the sultry flute melody at the beginning of this piece with the Faun of the story—actually, in one line the Faun refers to his "two pipes." The contrasting middle section of the music then belongs to the nymphs and the return of the Faun's melody in the concluding section suggests that after a (futile?) pursuit he has gone back to relaxing. (It also allows us to notice the relationship to ternary form.) Not only is it tempting to treat this work as program music, but it became a ballet featuring the legendary dancer and choreographer Vaslav Nijinsky (1890–1950). (The ballet is more obvious than the poem; the nymphs are as real as the Faun. But to show its ancient sources, it allows the dancers to appear only in profile, as if painted on a Greek vase.)

This piece shows Debussy's typical attention to detail. Although musical motives are often repeated, he finds a way to change each repetition. For example, the Faun theme enters unaccompanied. With each return, it acquires a different harmony. In typical impressionist style, one section blends into the next. The vagueness of the rhythms and the floating tonality, with its few distinct cadences, are the musical parallels of the poem's ambiguity.

The score calls for an orchestra of strings, woodwinds, four French horns, and two harps. Near the end antique cymbals (in French, Crotales) play. These tiny versions of the more familiar large cymbals are tuned to definite pitches.

 CD5

SECTION A

(0:00)

1a m1 The unaccompanied flute plays the main melody of this piece, assumed to represent the Faun (ex. 53.4). The melody's chromatic
34   motion and fluid rhythm seem appropriate to the dreaming (or intoxicated?) Faun, as does the low range of the flute, with its breathy, almost hazy quality. In the first measure, the top (C-sharp) and the bottom (G) notes of the melody's range outline a **tritone** (three whole tones), an interval notorious for its instability.

Example 53.4

p   *doux et expressif*

(0:19)

1b   m4   Woodwinds and harp glissandos interrupt the Faun melody. A dialogue of French horns follows.

(0:29)

1c   m7   After a pause, the sounds of item 1b return.

(0:44)

2a   m11   Again the Faun melody is played, now with tremolo string harmonies. French horns resume their questioning dialogue.

35

(1:02)

2b   m14   An oboe entrance overlaps the ending of the Faun melody. The oboe continues to lead, as woodwinds build a crescendo. A three-note motive played by the clarinet leads smoothly into the next section.

(1:36)

3a   m21   Harp arpeggios accompany a new version of the Faun theme, still played by the flute, and soon the theme makes a fourth appearance. Both theme occurrences are fancifully embellished.

36

(2:13)

3b   m26   A fifth version of the Faun theme displays new harmonies and melodic embellishments. This section ends with a clearly felt cadence on a simple major triad—a rare event in this work.

(2:48)

4   m30   The clarinet creates a vaguely sinister mood with a much-altered version of the Faun theme. Flute and clarinet echo each other in sweeps up and down the whole-tone scale, a feature of Debussy's style.

37

(3:16)

5a   m37   Now the oboe takes the lead and soon moves to a syncopated motive that is then given to the violins and later to the French horns. Tempo increases as a crescendo builds.

38

(3:59)

5b   m48   French horns introduce a simple six-note motive.

(4:14)

5c   m51   The clarinet returns, playing the syncopated motive of item 5a. The oboe is added as the music moves without pause into Section B.

SECTION B   (4:33)

6a   m55   Woodwinds introduce this new theme (ex. 53.5), accompanied by a pulsating figure in the strings. Metrical, diatonic, and clearly in the

|39| major mode, it contrasts with the elusive Faun melody. (Concealed in the bass line is the same tritone that was outlined in the beginning flute melody.)

Example 53.5

(5:07)

6b   m63   Harp arpeggios accompany the new theme, now given to strings. An insistent two-note motive in the winds builds a crescendo, leading to the only *fortissimo* of the score. (The Romantic world would say, "Finally!")

(6:00)

6c   m75   A solo violin begins a third presentation of the new theme, here almost covered by a woodwind countermelody.

SECTION A'   (6:23)

7a   m79   The harp accompanies an altered version of the Faun theme, played by flute. (There are fewer notes now, but they are much longer.)

|40|

(6:44)

7b   m83   The oboe presents a staccato version of the Faun theme, enlivened with surprising trills.

(6:58)

7c   m86   Again the harp accompanies the slowed-down version of the Faun theme, now given to the oboe.

(7:20)
7d   m90   The English horn is prominent in a passage similar to item 7b.

(7:39)
8a   m94   Antique cymbals add sparkle to the Faun theme, now returned to the flute.

41

(8:18)
8b   m100   As the Faun theme is restated by the flute, a solo cello doubles the tones an octave lower.

(8:46)
8c   m103   The oboe takes the closing notes of the Faun theme.

(9:05)
9   m106   Harps begin a codalike section. Muted French horns and violins quote the beginning of the Faun theme. Antique cymbals punctuate the quiet closing.

42

54 IGOR STRAVINSKY

PREVIEW   We return to Russia to find another composer who had to overcome family reluctance to be a musician. Like Mussorgsky, Stravinsky leaned toward Russian nationalism and, like Tchaikovsky, he won fame with his ballets. Unlike both, he changed styles drastically over a long life span, during which he became an international figure and eventually a U.S. citizen. His 1913 ballet, *The Rite of Spring,* made an enormous impact on all subsequent music of this century.

The third Russian we study, Igor Stravinsky [pronounced strah-VIN-skee] (1882–1971), was born in a small town near St. Petersburg (now known as Leningrad). His family was musical; his father was a leading opera singer. He studied piano as a child, but in spite of the family's musical interests he was persuaded that he should become a lawyer. Encouraged by a fellow Russian composer, Rimsky-Korsakov, Stravinsky eventually abandoned his halfhearted efforts in law school and began to study composition with private tutors.

In the years immediately preceding World War I, the dynamic impresario Sergei Diaghilev (1872–1929) commissioned Stravinsky to write ballet scores for the Paris productions of his Russian Ballet. This company attracted the greatest dancers of the time, such as Anna Pavlova and Nijinsky, who also choreographed Debussy's *Faun.* Leading artists designed the company's sets, and the gorgeous costumes can still be seen in museum collections. While Stravinsky's scores brought him great success, the riotous 1913 premiere (described later) of *The Rite of Spring* was *the* musical event of its time. The French composer/conductor Pierre Boulez calls the *Rite* "the cornerstone of modern music."

World War I and the Russian revolution altered Stravinsky's life drastically. He exiled himself from Russia, delaying a return visit until 1962. World War II persuaded him to settle in the United States. He and his wife became citizens. Living in Los Angeles, he attracted a band of loyal disciples and dominated the musical world for many years. Since he was careful to compose only on commission, including a highly unusual one (the *Circus Polka* was to be danced by the

elephants in the Barnum and Bailey Circus), and kept a sharp eye out for his copyrights, he escaped the poverty-ridden fate of some less-businesslike composers. (Russian copyrights were invalid in the United States, so he frequently revised his earlier works to protect them in this country.) He moved to New York near the end of his life and died there in 1971, acknowledged as one of the most influential composers of the century.

Stravinsky and Twentieth-Century "Isms"

Stravinsky and the Spanish-born artist Pablo Picasso (1881–1973) are often compared. Both lived a long time, with amazingly similar lifespans; both were extraordinarily prolific and financially successful; both dramatically changed styles several times, embracing many of the twentieth century "isms."

Stravinsky began his career strongly influenced by nationalism, as shown by the Russian elements in his first two ballets. *Firebird* (1909–10) is based on an old fairytale; *Petrushka* (1910–11) pictures a street carnival. Both contain relatively mild harmonic innovations. While *The Rite of Spring* contains Russian elements also, it can hardly be called "mild." It is an example of **primitivism,** that is, a sophisticated imitation of primitive music, achieved by means of pounding rhythms, limited melodic ranges, motives repeated at length, and pungent harmonies.

The first performance of the *Rite* in 1913 provoked a riot. Far from hurting the composer's career, the ensuing publicity made Stravinsky world-famous. (As they say in Hollywood, "Just spell my name correctly.") Although some of the blame for the riot could be laid to Nijinsky's choreography, with its earthbound, deliberately awkward stamping movements, or to the story of the ballet itself, which deals with ritual murder and tribal battles, Stravinsky's music is usually considered responsible. An American eye-witness vividly described the event:

> Primitive emotions are both depicted and aroused by a dependency on barbarous rhythm, in which melody and harmony do not enter. A certain part of the audience, thrilled by what it considered a blasphemous attempt to destroy music as an art, and swept away with wrath, began very soon after the rise of the curtain to whistle, to make catcalls, and to offer audible suggestions as to how the performance should proceed. Others of us, who liked the music and felt that the principles of free speech were at stake, bellowed defiance. It was war over art and the orchestra played on unheard.

Stravinsky escaped through a backstage window. Subsequent performances were well received, however, and the *Rite* remains his best-known work in concert performances. Millions of movie-goers heard it when some portions of the score were appropriated—over the composer's objections—to accompany the dinosaur sequence in Walt Disney's "Fantasia." In the 1980s, reconstruction of the original Nijinsky choreography enabled a ballet audience to see it as the 1913 audience did.

Despite the success of the *Rite,* Stravinsky never repeated its style. After World War I, he turned to smaller-scale works, such as *L' Histoire du Soldat* (Story of a Soldier), which could be produced inexpensively. It is a "theater" piece calling for a few instruments to accompany a story narrated and mimed on a small stage. Many of his compositions for the next thirty years belong to a category called **neoclassical,** although he liked that label no better than Debussy liked impressionism. Of course "neo-" refers to a new version of an old idea, but in music, the "classic" part of "neoclassicism" refers not just to the Classic period but to Baroque and earlier music as well. "Back to Bach" was the rallying cry of this movement.

Neoclassicism represented a reaction against the unrestrained emotionalism and subjectivity of late Romanticism. Features of older music returned, such as its dance forms, steady rhythms, tonality, small ensembles, and in some instances actual melodies. Simple generic titles, such as sonata, suite, and concerto, were evidence that absolute music had returned. However, Stravinsky's neoclassical works clearly belong to this century. One example is the ingratiating ballet *Pulcinella* (1919–20), based on themes formerly attributed to the Italian composer Giovanni Battista Pergolesi (1710–36).

Picasso and Stravinsky collaborated on many projects. Picasso's illustration for a piano piece by Stravinsky conveys the wry sense of humor both men appreciated.

Other neoclassical works include his *Octet* (for winds, 1922–23); his opera, *The Rake's Progress* (1948–51), complete with arias and recitatives; and his *Symphony of Psalms* (1930), for chorus and orchestra. Dedicating this masterwork "to the Glory of GOD," Stravinsky, who had returned to the Russian Orthodox church in 1926, set three Psalms in Latin, with moods of prayer, testimony, and praise.

Another startling change occurred when Stravinsky was in his seventies. He turned to serialism, a radical twentieth-century musical innovation, discussed here in Chapter 56. Schoenberg, the "father" of serialism, had lived only a few miles away from Stravinsky in Los Angeles, but the two composers and their respective disciples shunned one another. However, after Schoenberg's death, Stravinsky developed a keen interest in serialism as practiced by Schoenberg's pupil Webern, adapting it for his last works. Received respectfully, these works have not won much popularity. One such work, the *Requiem Canticles* (1965–66), was sung for his funeral services, held in Venice.

B

Stravinsky's Music

Because of Stravinsky's many changes in direction, it is not easy to describe his style. A few generalizations are possible. He liked the ostinato and irregular meters. Conversely, he could maintain a steady beat with almost hypnotic effect, or build on characteristic rhythm patterns such as the tango and American ragtime. Sometimes his dissonance is the result of combining two different consonant chords to make a **polychord,** for example, a C triad (C,E,G) and an F-sharp triad (F-sharp,A-sharp,C-sharp). Employed conspicuously in *Petrushka,* this particular combination is aptly dubbed the "Petrushka chord."

Stravinsky devised unusual combinations of instruments for many of his works, often calling for their extreme ranges. Abhoring emotionalism, he gave more weight to the "objective" woodwinds than to the "romantic" strings. Frequently one or more pianos appear in his orchestral scores, with emphasis on the piano's percussive qualities. He wrote for the entire percussion family with great imagination.

Stravinsky: *The Rite of Spring,* Part I, "Adoration of the Earth"

Stravinsky subtitled this work "Pictures of Pagan Russia" and collaborated in developing the scenario for it. He described the initial impulse that led to the writing of the *Rite* as follows: "One day I had a fleeting vision. I saw in imagination a solemn pagan rite; sage elders, seated in a circle, watched a young girl dance herself to death. They were sacrificing her to propitiate the god of spring." Some of the composer's descriptions of what he "saw" are included below to introduce a few of the separate dances.

Even without knowledge of its origins, one could easily associate this music with scenes of primitive violence. Helping create this atmosphere are the often percussive quality of the instrumental writing, the dissonant harmonies, and the many rhythmic ostinatos. As the composer himself noted, "There is music wherever there is rhythm, as there is life wherever there beats a pulse." Derived from genuine folk music, the melodic style of this work is also primitive: melodies are short, limited in range, repetitive, and often simple in rhythm. However, the instrumentation is anything but primitive. The work demands the largest orchestra (well over one hundred players) for which he ever wrote and employs some unusual percussion instruments. The titles of the individual ballet sections appear in a variety of translations from both Russian and French; those given here are from the composer's arrangement of this work for two pianos (1947). Since the measures are unnumbered in the score, rehearsal numbers (r) are indicated instead in the guide below.

According to Stravinsky, this introduction "should represent the awakening of nature, the scratching, gnawing, wiggling of birds and beasts."

INTRODUCTION
(2:56) (66)

 CD5

(0:00)

1

43

The work's beginning is famous: just as Debussy did with his *Faun,* Stravinsky begins with an unaccompanied melody (ex. 54.1). Here, in its unearthly-sounding high range, the solo bassoon plays a melody, in origin a Lithuanian folk song in A minor.

Example 54.1

As other wind instruments enter, the rhythm remains fluid.

(0:59)

2

44

r4 Repeated notes in the oboe show an increase in activity as instruments enter with independent, contrasting lines. A long trill for violin and a tiny moment for flute alone signal the end of this section.

(1:34)

3

45

r7 Here the rhythm begins to take shape. Woodwinds, and soon trumpet, are prominent with aggressive, rising statements. A long crescendo builds.

(2:26)

4   r12   The solo bassoon returns with the opening melody, as if to silence the torrent of sound created in item 3. Soon pizzicato violin tones introduce a "tick-tock" ostinato figure which continues on into the next dance.

   CD5

AUGURS OF SPRING: DANCES OF THE YOUNG GIRLS

(3:03) (67)

The dancers here represent young half-savages, celebrating their coming of age with a ritual in which they stamp heavily on the ground.

(0:00)

1   r13   With only one interruption, the duple meter created by the "tick-tocks" of item 4 of the Introduction continues throughout this dance. First comes an often-repeated dissonant chord, roughly played by strings and soon challenged by this same chord played at joltingly irregular intervals by eight French horns (yes, eight). Three short sections using this string-plus-horns combination occur, separated by "tick-tocks." Explosive little motives create an increasingly complex texture. The dissonant chord is a **polychord,** the product of two simple chords (E-flat 7 and E combined).

(1:02)

2   r19   Bassoons and later oboes add a simple tune in evenly spaced notes.

(1:14)

3   r22   After a break in the steady rhythm, Stravinsky gets a fresh start. The "tick-tocks" return and strings play with the wooden part of the bow in a soft passage.

(1:36)

4   r25   A new melody (ex. 54.2), somewhat more complicated than that of item 2, is played by French horn and soon repeated by flutes.

Example 54.2

(2:04)
5   r28   Flutes continue to play the new melody of item 4 as a fuller
accompaniment is added. Under this melody, a slower-moving tune is
soon introduced by trumpets. The triangle accents the beat.

51

(2:23)
6   r30   As strings play alone, the volume suddenly drops. Winds almost
immediately reenter, and ostinato patterns build a long, exciting
crescendo. The piccolo is prominent with the melody of item 4. The
music continues without pause.

52

Stravinsky described this section as a "game of chasing a girl." He envisioned   ***RITUAL OF***
a ceremony of young men locking arms in a circle around one girl as a part of   ***ABDUCTION***
country wedding festivities, something he recalled seeing as a child.   *(1:17)* (68)

    CD5

(0:00)
1   r37   This dance begins with sustained brass chords and loud timpani
blows. Explosive swoops add to the violence.

53

(0:13)
2   r40   French horns play a two-note motive. Repeated several times, it
resembles a hunting horn signal. Then follows a wildly exciting
section involving the entire orchestra, with more brass signals and
repeated-note figures.

54

(0:53)
3   r46   Passages in rhythmic unison are played by winds and then strings,
set off by slashing blows from the timpani. Flute trills, which extend
into the next dance (*Spring Rounds*), without pause, suggest that
the game must stop.

55

Spring Rounds is a refreshing change of pace with its slow tempo and steady
quadruple meter. Then comes *Ritual of the Rival Tribes,* a lively tug-of-war between orchestral sections, which leads into the heavy, menacing sound of *Procession of the Sage.* This is followed by a brief but important moment in which the
Sage kisses the ground. The act concludes with the wild excitement of *Dance of
the Earth,* ending most abruptly, without any warning of the approaching cadence.

55 BÉLA BARTÓK

PREVIEW   The fame of Hungarian-born Bartók as a composer came after his career as a pianist had established his name. Protesting the Nazi influence, he left his homeland for the haven of New York, where illness and wartime distractions made his few years in this country unhappy. Only after his premature death did his music become well known in the United States. The folk idiom that Bartók examined as a scholar-researcher of folk music profoundly influenced his own style.

Though the small Hungarian town in which Béla Bartók [pronounced bay-la bar-tock] (1881–1945) was born is now a part of Romania, he is considered a Hungarian. Both of his parents were educators. Interested in music, they encouraged the talent he showed as a child. His mother was his first music teacher. He attended the Budapest Academy and later taught there for more than twenty-five years. He was known as a prominent pianist, piano teacher, and composer.

Recognition as a composer came slowly for Bartók. With the fame of his European tours, his standing with his fellow citizens improved. By the late 1930s he was successful enough to be able to compose only on commission. However, the rise of Nazi Germany threatened him because he opposed fascism. He refused to allow broadcasts of his music in Germany or Italy. In 1940 he left Europe for the promised haven of the United States. Unfortunately, his few years in this country were disheartening. He received little recognition and only a modest appointment to conduct research at a university. Even worse, he suffered from leukemia. A commission from the Boston Symphony Orchestra to write the *Concerto for Orchestra* (1943) revived his spirits; a temporary remission from the disease allowed him to finish this work. Immediately after his death, in 1945 in New York City, his reputation soared. Today he is ranked with Stravinsky and Schoenberg.

Béla Bartók.

A

Bartók: A Twentieth-Century Folk Music Collector

In the early 1900s a wave of nationalism swept over Hungary, at that time a part of the vast Austro-Hungarian empire. Partly as a result of this movement, Bartók became interested in folk music. With another Hungarian composer, Zoltán

Kodály (1882–1967), he accomplished significant research, recording folk songs on the phonographic equipment recently invented by Thomas Edison. Later he widened his interests to include the study of folk music in the Balkans and the Near East. He published thousands of folk tunes and many articles about folk music. He showed greater respect for the unique qualities of folk music than did earlier composers; he did not seek to iron out the rhythmic irregularities and the unusual intervals in folk tunes. Instead, he transcribed them as accurately as possible. Several of his books remain standard texts in **ethnomusicology,** an academic discipline that studies non-Western and folk music in its cultural context.

Bartók's career as a collector of folk songs affected his compositional style in a way that may be unique. Many earlier composers had included folk tunes in their works, Brahms and Liszt among them, but they were not concerned about the authenticity of those tunes. Nor is their personal style much colored by this interest. In contrast, Bartók adopted a reverential attitude toward folk music, and his mature style richly displays many of its characteristics.

In an essay, Bartók explained: "The right type of peasant music is most varied and perfect in its forms. Its expressive power is amazing, and at the same time it is devoid of all sentimentality and superfluous ornaments. It is simple, sometimes primitive, but never silly. It is an ideal starting point for a musical renaissance, and a composer in search of new ways cannot be led by a better master."

Often based on modal scales, Bartók's melodies contain irregular meters and off-beat accents characteristic of the folk music he studied. In fact, he felt more comfortable in any kind of musical innovation if he could justify it as already a part of traditional folk music. His was a unique fusion of folk elements, added onto a foundation of Bach-like polyphony and thematic development in the manner of Beethoven.

Several other composers were equally immersed in the folk music of their own countries. Probably the most familiar of them is the Englishman Ralph Vaughan Williams, whose *Fantasia on Greensleeves* was mentioned earlier as an example of a familiar melody based on a modal scale. His countryman Gustav Holst (1874–1934) had similar interests and also wrote skillfully for military band. Holst's orchestral suite *The Planets* (1917) does for the solar system what Vivaldi did for the seasons. Leos Janácek [pronounced YAN-uh-chek] (1854–1928) was a Czech composer, a worthy successor to Smetana and Dvořák. His *Sinfonietta* (1926) is probably his most frequently played piece, and his original, deeply moving operas have received increasing attention recently. An American with an astonishingly bold personal style, Ruth Crawford Seeger (1901–53), transcribed over one thousand American folk songs and published many of them in songbooks for children.

B

Bartók's Music

Compared with the shattering of musical traditions for which Stravinsky and Schoenberg are credited—or blamed—Bartók's innovations sound rather mild. He continued to compose within the framework of tonality, although stretching its limits. He adopted—and adapted—traditional forms, notably sonata-form and rondo. His early music abounds in abrasive, percussive, dissonant effects, as in *Allegro barbaro* (1911) for piano. Its title alone links it to the primitivism of Stravinsky's *The Rite of Spring,* written two years later. A frequently played masterpiece is the four-movement *Music for String Instruments, Percussion, and Celesta* (1936). Perhaps he mellowed as he grew older, for his last pieces, such as the *Third Piano Concerto* (1945) and the *Concerto for Orchestra* (1942–43), are less aggressive and far easier for a general audience to understand than his earlier works.

The sound of the glissando particularly intrigued Bartók. He employed this effect in his six string quartets, works that are often compared to the chamber music of two other giants, Beethoven and Brahms. An unforgettable trombone glissando occurs in *Concerto for Orchestra,* fourth movement (see item 4b of the guide).

Bartók wrote music for educational purposes, much of it based on folk song, including a set of materials to help students learn to read music. In this way, he fruitfully combined his careers as folk researcher and teacher. For aspiring pianists, he wrote *Mikrokosmos* (1926, 1932–39), a collection that fills six volumes, starting with the very simplest of melodies and leading by gradual stages to virtuoso pieces.

Peasant's Dance, a simple piano piece in his *First Term at the Piano* (ex. 55.1), illustrates in only ten measures several aspects of the folk-influenced Bartók style. Syncopation enlivens almost every measure. A few close intervals (seconds) add a touch of dissonance, the B-naturals identify it as built on the Dorian mode instead of the more conventional minor, and the clipped-off ending is characteristic.

Example 55.1

Peasant's Dance

Bartók
from "First Term at the Piano"

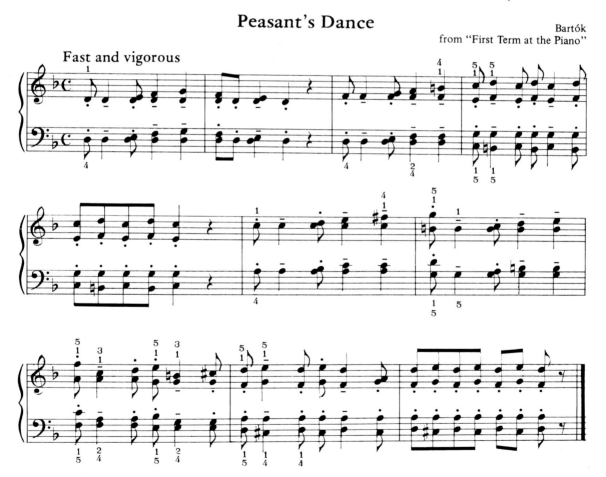

Bartók: *Concerto for Orchestra*

Bartók explained that the unusual title, *Concerto for Orchestra,* was justified by the way he treated single orchestral instruments in a soloistic manner. A showpiece for the virtuoso players of the modern orchestra, the work has become his most widely accepted composition. His own program note suggests a programmatic content: "The general mood of the work represents, apart from the jesting second movement, a gradual transition from the sternness of the first movement and the lugubrious death-song of the third, to the life-assertion of the last one." A Bartók biographer offers a more specific message, that the composer had in mind the fate of Hungary, facing the German invasion. He also found in the fourth movement a description of a young man serenading his beloved, interrupted by drunken rowdies.

 CD5

FOURTH MOVEMENT: "*Intermezzo Interrotto*" (*Interrupted Intermezzo*) (4:15) ⓺⑨

A simple, scalewise tune that occurs in the middle of this movement is obviously "interrupted," but some question exists as to its source. Some see in it "Maxim's" song, from the light opera *Merry Widow* by Franz Lehár (1870–1948). Others, citing the recollection of the composer's son, claim that Bartók was making fun of a melody in the first movement of Shostakovich's *Symphony No. 7.* (The theme in question occurs at rehearsal number 35.) The remainder of the "Intermezzo" features two contrasting themes, the first based on a short motive, the second a broadly flowing melody. Both change meter frequently, an effect sometimes called "mixed meter," a characteristic of much Slavic folk music. The result is a delightfully unsettling feeling of gaining or losing a half-beat. The two themes alternate, making an ABACBA pattern, with C indicating the "interruption." Note that the return of themes has them in reverse order. The resulting pattern was a favorite Bartók design, the equivalent of a palindrone in language, as in "Madam, I'm Adam." ("Arch" form is a musical label for this effect.)

(0:00)
1a   m1   A tiny introduction, played loudly by strings in unison, contains the main notes of Theme A, but in reverse order. Soon the oboe enters
     [56]   with Theme A (ex. 55.2), based on an upward-moving three-note motive of E, F-sharp, A-sharp. Soft strings accompany.

Example 55.2

(0:15)

1b   m13   Clarinet and flute now play Theme A, while the bassoon plays a near-inversion of it. Soon a brief development of Theme A begins in the flute, goes to the clarinet, then to the French horn as the tempo slows.

(0:45)

1c   m33   The oboe returns with the theme, here an octave lower. A flute countermelody almost conceals the theme. Strings accompany.

(1:00)

2a   m43   Theme B begins in the violas, accompanied by harps. Theme B is a more flowing melody, almost a waltz except for the addition and

57

            subtraction of a half-beat now and then.

(1:18)

2b   m51   Theme B is restated, now an octave higher, by violins, as the harp accompaniment continues. The English horn plays the theme in a kind of canon and continues playing after the violins finish.

(1:42)

3a   m62   Theme A returns, again in the oboe, here slightly more extended in range.

58

(1:54)

3b   m69   Strings establish a more regular rhythmic feeling as a transition to the next section, which prepares for the change of mood.

(2:05)

4a   m77   The clarinet begins the quoted tune (ex. 55.3), discussed earlier.

59

Example 55.3

(2:15)

4b   m84   A sudden brass entrance, followed by aggressive woodwind trills, sounds as if Bartók is making fun of the clarinet tune—or of its composer? Trombone glissandi give a musical Bronx cheer.

(2:24)

4c m92 The orchestra begins a loud, "oom-pah" accompaniment, soon joined by the violins with a new version of the clarinet tune (item 4a). Woodwind trills and new percussion outbursts add to the sense of ridicule, but a more tranquil mood soon restores calm.

(2:53)

5a m120 Theme B returns in muted violins and violas, with the harp accompaniment assisted by pizzicato string chords.

60

(3:13)

5b m127 Fragments of Theme A are played by oboe, flute, and clarinet.

(3:28)

5c m136 The English horn begins Theme A, countered by the flute in an inverted version of it. Soon the flute plays an extended cadenzalike passage, supported by strings.

(4:02)

5d m144 A concluding section begins with the oboe, echoed by bassoon, then piccolo.

(4:15)

5e m150 The transition music of item 3b briefly returns and then stops, with the sudden ending that is frequently found in twentieth-century music.

The fifth movement, Finale, is rich in motives and triumphant in character. It begins with a forthright statement played by French horns alone. A kind of "perpetual motion" in the violins provides a second main idea; a prominent trumpet fanfare is the third.

ARNOLD SCHOENBERG 56

PREVIEW   Schoenberg, a native of Vienna, composed at first in the late Romantic style. With his subsequent abandonment of tonality, he began a controversial career that garnered him unprecedented hostility. "Atonality" is the conventional label for this style. As a further development, he worked out a "twelve tone method" of composing, in which he regarded all twelve tones of the chromatic scale as equals. "Serialism" is one label for this method. He too fled the Nazis, settling in Los Angeles, where he lived not far from Stravinsky—geographically, at least.

Like Schubert, Arnold Schoenberg [spelled in German Schön-berg, pronounced approximately SHERN-berg] (1874–1951) was a native of Vienna. When Schoenberg was born, Brahms resided there; the spirits of Haydn, Mozart, and Beethoven hovered over that great city. His parents were not particularly interested in music, but Schoenberg and his siblings showed talent. His chief musical education came from studying scores and playing chamber music with a group of friends. Essentially self-taught, he only valued that knowledge which he had discovered for himself. At first he earned a modest living with various musical jobs and private teaching. He attracted a small, dedicated circle of pupils and supporters. Although composers such as Mahler and Richard Strauss showed interest in his work, his compositions generally met with a hostility unprecedented in music history. Not until age fifty-one did he receive a prestigious academic appointment in Germany.

When the Nazis came to power, Schoenberg's Jewish ancestry provided an excuse for dismissal from his post, even though he had adopted Christianity in his youth. Heeding this warning, he left Germany in 1933 and in a public ceremony returned to Judaism. Religion played a large part in his life from that time on. Indeed, Schoenberg believed that he, like the great composers of the past, had been divinely inspired.

Like many leading musicians, Schoenberg emigrated to the United States. Eventually he settled in Los Angeles, teaching at the University of California at Los Angeles. (Despite his revolutionary style of composing, his harmony teaching

Shown here at the blackboard is Arnold Schoenberg, illustrating a point in harmony for his UCLA students.

was traditional; he even wrote a textbook on the subject.) After his university-imposed retirement, he taught privately and continued to compose. Though known as a logical thinker, he was quite superstitious about the number thirteen. He died on July 13, 1951, at the age of seventy-six. A "friend" had pointed out to him on his birthday that the sum of seven and six is thirteen.

As if to make amends for the neglect Schoenberg suffered in his lifetime, in the 1970s several universities in the Los Angeles area cooperated to build the Arnold Schoenberg Institute on the campus of the University of Southern California. The building houses a replica of his studio, a library for his music, and an auditorium for performances of it and of other twentieth-century music. In 1977 at ceremonies marking the opening of the Institute, the French composer/conductor Pierre Boulez (born 1925) said, "Schoenberg made it impossible to compose at all without taking his discoveries into account."

Schoenberg is a paradoxical figure in music. Although regarded by musicians as one of the most significant forces in twentieth-century music, few of them perform his music. Those who do must resign themselves to public apathy, doubly frustrating considering the enormous difficulty of his works. Indeed, one historian refers to his music as being at the "outer limits of performer and listener capabilities." Popular acceptance of his music never came—nor did he really expect it, trusting that in the distant future his music would be understood.

One of the themes of the German expressionist movement was social protest, as in the poignantly expressed sympathy for the poor that can be seen in prints by Käthe Kollwitz (1867–1945). Her *Death Seizing a Woman* touches upon death, another Expressionist theme. (Lithograph, printed in black, composition: 20 × 14 7/16″. Collection, The Museum of Modern Art, New York.)

A

Schoenberg: The Leader in Serialism

Schoenberg's development of the principles of serialism came after he had worked in a variety of other styles. In his youth he wrote extremely chromatic music that outdid Wagner in that respect. In the years before World War I, he became a part of an Austro-German artistic movement known as **expressionism.** Schoenberg himself was a painter—many of his works are self-portraits—and he contributed to exhibitions of expressionist art. Influenced by Freud's explorations of the subconscious mind, the expressionists plumbed the deepest levels of the subconscious for subject matter. Madness, death, hysteria, and social protest were favorite themes, with distorted forms expressing the artist's inner self. Prettiness was not a concern, nor was accurate representation of the external world.

During these years Schoenberg took a revolutionary step. He claimed that tonality had been so weakened that it must be discarded. He searched for new paths, or as he said later: "Ever since 1906–8, when I had started writing compositions which led to the abandonment of tonality, I had been busy finding methods to replace the structural functions of harmony." The style of these years before 1921 is called **atonal,** although he considered the word to be nonsense. Atonal music has no key center, no sense of *do.* "Atonal" is the opposite of "tonal." Schoenberg, however, preferred the term "pantonal."

Tonality rests upon one all-important tone, a key center or *do.* All other tones relate to it. For atonality to succeed, the sensation of *do* must be eliminated. One way to achieve this is to avoid a series of notes like *do, mi, sol* that outline a triad. Another way is to avoid repeating any one note, since repetitions emphasize it, making it sound like a *do.*

Atonality questions all musical traditions, including formal structure. But Schoenberg soon found that some organizing principles were essential, as he said, to avoid "chaos." In vocal music, the text served as a basis for the piece. However, for instrumental music he needed an organizing tool. He found it in the twelve-tone method. As he explained: "The main advantage of this method of composing with twelve tones is its unifying effect. . . . In music there is no form without logic, there is no logic without unity. I believe that when Richard Wagner introduced his *Leitmotiv*—for the same purpose as that for which I introduced my Basic Set—he may have said: 'Let there be unity'."

Twelve-tone, tone row, dodecaphonic, serial—all these terms appear more or less synonomously as labels for the compositional principles Schoenberg had developed by the early 1920s. ("Dodecaphonic" derives from the Greek word for twelve. Some writers restrict "serial" to a later development in the 1950s, when other elements of music, particularly durational values, were subjected to the same discipline that Schoenberg imposed on pitch.) It is important to remember that atonality is a broad *principle,* while serialism is a *specific* technique. Some atonal music is serial and some is not. Schoenberg's principles were embraced, then extended, by two of his pupils, whom we meet in the next chapter. Gradually, twelve-tone music attracted a group of supporters, particularly in intellectual and academic circles.

Schoenberg's *Variations for Orchestra,* op. 31 (1928), nicely demonstrates the principles of twelve-tone music. First, the composer chose a **basic set,** also called a **tone row,** a series of pitches that governs the entire piece. As Schoenberg explained: "The construction of a basic set of twelve tones derives from the intention to postpone the repetition of every tone as long as possible. . . . The regular application of a set of twelve tones emphasizes all the other tones in the same manner, thus depriving one single tone of the privilege of supremacy."

In the *Variations,* the row is: B-flat, E, F-sharp, E-flat, F, A, D, C-sharp, G, G-sharp, B, C. The octave position of any tone of the series can be changed—in other words, the row just mentioned could start on a low B-flat or a high B-flat. Besides this original form, the row can appear in **retrograde** form, that is, backwards, the last note now first: C, B, G-sharp and so on. A third possibility is **inversion;** the interval that originally went up now goes down and vice versa. The fourth possibility is **retrograde inversion:** the inverted form is played backwards. A fundamental "rule" is that *immediate* repetition of a tone is allowed but no other repetition of a tone is permitted until all twelve tones have appeared—no back-tracking, in other words. The row in any of its four forms can be transposed to any of the twelve tones of the chromatic scale, making forty-eight possibilities in all.

The tones of the series can occur in succession, as melody, and simultaneously, as harmony or counterpoint. The four forms of the row of *Variations* are shown in example 56.1.

Example 56.1

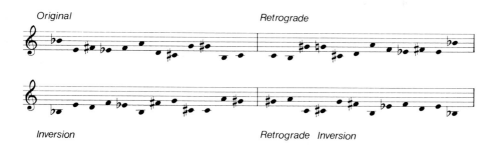

To create the theme for *Variations,* Schoenberg took the four possible forms of the row just described and made four musical phrases by giving the pitches a rhythmic shape. (The complete work begins with a short introduction, about one minute in length, which ends with a pizzicato chord and then an obvious pause before the theme itself is played.) Cellos in their high range play the first three phrases. When violins introduce the fourth phrase, the cellos continue with a new rhythmic version of the first phrase. Derived from the basic row, the accompanying chords to this theme are subject to the same "rules" mentioned earlier concerning repetitions. Armed with the score, a listener can track the row throughout the remainder of the piece, which consists of nine highly contrasting variations and a finale. In fact, the composer marked the tones of the row in the score with a special symbol, as if to facilitate analysis.

Schoenberg did not intend that the listener should be aware of the details of his technique, as just explained. In fact, he discouraged any attempt to follow a tone row by ear. But commentators—including your authors—seem unable to resist such analysis, hoping that a knowledge of the ground rules of serial works can assist in listening to them.

B

Verklärte Nacht (Transfigured Night) (1899) illustrates Schoenberg's quite attractive early style. First written for string sextet and later arranged for string orchestra, it is a tone poem in the late Romantic tradition. At the same time, its extremely chromatic harmony and wandering tonality hint at the more drastic stylistic developments to come. It, and the massive cantata *Gurrelieder* (1901), have the rich, luxuriant sound of the nineteenth century. The clearly atonal *Pierrot Lunaire,* 1912, is described below.

Schoenberg's Music

The twelve-tone method governed the writing of Schoenberg's *Piano Suite* (1923) and most of his other works, including a piano concerto and two of his four string quartets. He left an unfinished opera, *Moses und Aron,* one he had begun long before his death. (He spelled the Biblical character "Aaron" with only one "a" so that the title would not have thirteen letters!) After World War II, he wrote a short, powerful piece called *A Survivor from Warsaw,* op. 46, a work in which his Jewish heritage, his sense of outrage over the Nazi treatment of Jews, and the twelve-tone method all play a part. A narrator recites a text written by Schoenberg himself in English (except for the Nazi commands, which are in German). It tells the grim story of one who escaped the fate of the other Jews in the Warsaw ghetto. At the very end, a male chorus enters with a unison rendition of a tone row melody. The text is that of the ancient Hebrew prayer, *Shema Yisroel* (Hear, O Israel, the Lord is One). (Schoenberg had heard of a situation where Jews, facing the gas chamber, had found the courage to sing this prayer.) Thus, by the end of the piece, the three languages of the composer's life, Hebrew, German, and English, have all appeared. Transcending considerations of its serial organization, the human message of this piece accounts for its overwhelming emotional impact.

Schoenberg: *Pierrot Lunaire,* op. 21 (Moonstruck Pierrot): Songs No. 1 and No. 16

Schoenberg's *Pierrot Lunaire* (1912) is atonal, written before the composer developed his serial technique. In its first performance, the singer was in costume, as if for a cabaret, with the accompanying instruments behind a screen. It took some forty rehearsals to prepare the work for its first performance, which gives an idea of its difficulty. (It also hints at the dedication of the performers!) After a successful premiere, Schoenberg took it on a tour of Germany and Austria.

For this work he chose twenty-one poems from a collection of fifty by the Belgian poet Albert Giraud. Otto Hartleben had translated them into German. In the light of Schoenberg's fear of the number thirteen, it is odd that he picked a source in which each poem consists of thirteen lines, arranged in three stanzas in a fixed pattern of line repetitions. (The first line is repeated to form the seventh and the last lines; the second line returns as the eighth.) These poems are wildly imaginative, describing the stock sad-faced clown character known as Pierrot in French pantomimes. Here he is "moonstruck," or "loony." Pierrot is a symbol for the tormented, rebellious, frenzied modern artist who finally reconciles himself with the traditions of his culture. In both its subject matter and musical style this work is expressionistic.

The text is performed by a soprano in **sprechstimme** (German for "speech-song"), a vocal sound midway between speech and song, which is indicated in the score by an "X" placed through the note stems to show that pitch is only approximate. Performers can glide between these pitches at will, although the notation for rhythm is exact. A small ensemble, including a piano, accompanies the singer. Changing combinations of piccolo, flute, clarinet, bass clarinet, violin, viola, and cello ensure that almost every song has a unique tone color.

CD5

The first song in the cycle pictures the hapless Pierrot looking at the moon. Appropriate to this scene are the high-pitched, evenly spaced piano tones, and the soft flute, and the pizzicato violin. Heavy chords alter the mood dramatically at the beginning of the third stanza and a cello is added. Tranquil moonlight shines again by the end of the song, in which the first line of the poem returns.

No. 1:
Mondestrunken
(Moondrunk)
(1:38) ⑦⓪

(0:00)
1

61

Den Wein, den man mit Augen trinkt,	The wine, that one drinks with the eyes,
Giesst nachts der Mond in Wogen nieder,	pours at night from the moon in waves,
Und eine Springflut überschwemmt	and a springflood overflows
Den stillen Horizont.	the still horizon.

(0:39)
2

62

Gelüste, schauerlich und süss,	Desires, shivering and sweet,
Durchschwimmen ohne Zahl die Fluten!	swim without number through the flood.
Den Wein, den man mit Augen trinkt,	The wine, that one drinks with the eyes,
Giesst nachts der Mond in Wogen nieder.	pours at night from the moon in waves.

(1:03)
3

63

Der Dichter, den die Andacht treibt,	The poet, by ardor driven,
Berauscht sich an dem heilgen Tranke,	enraptured with the holy drink,
Den Himmel wendet er verzückt das Haupt	to Heaven he joyfully lifts his head
Und taumelnd saught und schlürft er	and reeling, sips and slurps
Den Wein, den man mit Augen trinkt.	the wine, that one drinks with the eyes.

In this poem, Pierrot is much less moonstruck: now he is pictured as a sadistic torturer of bald-headed Cassander, another one of the stock dramatic characters in French pantomime. The sixteenth song contrasts greatly to the first, having a strongly rhythmical, aggressive quality.

No. 16: Gemeinheit
(Vulgarity)
(1:19) ⑦①

♫ CD5

(0:00)
1

64

Between the fifteenth and sixteenth songs in the cycle is a short, vigorous interlude in which the cello plays a cadenzalike flourish. The cello continues to dominate the accompanying ensemble: violin, piccolo, clarinet, and piano.

In den blanken Kopf Cassanders,	Into the bald head of Cassander,
Dessen Schrein die Luft durchzetert,	whose screams rend the air,
Bohrt Pierrot mit Heuchlermienen,	Pierrot bores, pretending to be sweet,
Zärtlich - einen Schädelbohrer!	using a skull-drill!

(0:31)
2

65

Darauf stopft er mit dem Daumen	Then he stuffs with his thumb
Seinen echten türkschen Tabak	his own genuine, Turkish tobacco
In den blanken Kopf Cassanders,	into the bald head of Cassander,
Dessen Schrein die Luft durchzetert.	whose screams rend the air.

(0:52)
3

66

Dann dreht er ein Rohr von Weichsel	Then he inserts the stem of his pipe
Hinten in die glatte Glatze	deep into the smooth, bald head
Und behaglich schmaucht und pafft er	and comfortably draws and puffs
Seinen echten türkschen Tabak	his own genuine, Turkish tobacco,
Aus dem blanken Kopf Cassanders!	into the bald head of Cassander!

ANTON WEBERN AND SCHOENBERG'S LEGACY 57

PREVIEW   Vienna-born Webern, as a pupil of Schoenberg, adopted his master's atonality and later the twelve-tone method. He is famous for the brevity and concentration of his few compositions. Not only are they tiny, but they employ only a few instruments and make much use of silence. Alban Berg was another disciple, also with his own atonal style best seen in his expressionist opera *Wozzeck*.

Two other Viennese natives became disciples of Schoenberg. The older, Anton von Webern [pronounced VAY-burn] (1883–1945), was born to a prosperous family. (In 1918, he dropped the "von," which signifies nobility, from his name.) He received an excellent musical education and earned a doctorate in musicology at the University of Vienna. A socialist, he conducted musical groups made up of workers in the 1920s, but the rise of the Nazis brought an end to these organizations. Furthermore, the Nazis condemned his "degenerate" atonal music, so he was forced to spend his time in routine work for his publishers. He survived the war, only to be killed in 1945, near Salzburg. A trigger-happy American soldier, investigating the black-market activities of Webern's son-in-law, shot the composer in the dark, thinking that Webern had attacked him.

A

Like Schoenberg, Webern progressed from a late Romantic style through atonality to twelve-tone methods. He described his musical philosophy in almost-religious terms: "Adherence to the row is strict, often burdensome—but it is *salvation!* The commitment is so powerful that one must consider very carefully before finally entering into it . . . almost as if one took the decision to marry; a difficult moment! Trust your inspiration!"

Webern's influence on younger composers was so great that the eminent music historian Donald Jay Grout gave the label "After Webern" to the years after 1950. Nonetheless, this reputation rests upon a tiny quantity of works. His entire output can be performed in about four hours, and most of his pieces are five minutes or less in duration.

Webern: Serialism after Schoenberg

Anton Webern.

The avant-garde composers chose Webern as an icon rather than Schoenberg because they believed that Webern was less indebted to the older forms of music. While Schoenberg's tone row music may sound revolutionary, Brahms would have recognized the big orchestra and the external forms that Schoenberg employed. Webern's miniature pieces, with their wisps of sound and their expectant silences, seemed more appropriate to a new age. Motives, obvious rhythms, repetitions—all the familiar trappings of music are missing, replaced by an other-worldly sound that is curiously refreshing.

B

Webern's Music

Webern's atonal, but preserial, style is represented by works for string quartet and his *Five Orchestral Pieces,* op. 10, dating from 1911–13. A *Concerto for Nine Instruments,* op. 24, written in the early 1930s, is serial. He wrote several songs and some short cantatas for chorus and orchestra.

Webern: *Five Orchestral Pieces,* op. 10 (4:16) ⑦²

Despite the term "orchestral" in the title, only twenty players are needed at most, and no one plays many notes or creates much volume. Webern parcels out the melodic lines, with each instrument playing only a few notes before giving way to another instrument. The movements are extremely short, as the timings given below in parentheses show. Such brevity is unprecedented in music; in fact, the fourth piece is the shortest of all pieces in the orchestral literature. Looking through a microscope is comparable to listening to Webern. In the guide here, Webern's tempo indications in German are translated into English.

 CD6

(0:00)
1

1

Sehr ruhig und zart (very calm and soft) (0:40)
This movement begins with the sounds of single notes, as within a few seconds the harp, muted trumpet, celesta, viola, flute flutter-tonguing, and glockenspiel appear. Repeated flute notes mark the end.

(0:42)
2

2

Lebhaft und zart bewegt (lively, moving softly) (0:35)
Beginning softly, more instruments participate in this piece. A high trumpet entrance leads to a dramatic, forceful ending.

(1:20)
3

3

Sehr langsam und äusserst ruhig (very slow and extremely calm) (1:28)
Bell-like sounds on repeated pitches begin this almost rhythmical piece, and similar sounds end it. In between these sections, French horn and clarinet appear. A very soft drumroll marks the ending.

(2:49)
4

4

Fliessend, äusserst zart (flowing, extremely soft) (0:25)
The names of instruments appear below in a horizontal arrangement showing the order in which they appear. Their vertical placement is an indication of approximate pitch relationships.

	Viola				Violin
Mandolin	Trumpet				Mandolin
Harp	Clarinet			Harp	
		Trombone			
					Clarinet (trill)
					Celesta
		Drum			

(3:17)
5

5

Sehr fliessend (flowing) (0:57)
This movement calls for twenty players, more than any other in the set. Although it begins with a few wispy sounds, strongly percussive chords mark the middle of the piece. Soon the calmness of the beginning returns.

In another example of
Arnold Schoenberg's
work as a painter, a
portrait he painted of his
student Alban Berg rests
on a wall. Directly above
it, Berg stands at an
open window.

C

The slightly younger Schoenberg disciple was Alban Berg [pronounced bairg] (1885–1935). The three are often linked together in a "second Viennese" group, much as Haydn, Mozart, and Beethoven formed the first. Even more than with that earlier trio, the individual styles of the "second" group varied widely. Berg's most widely performed work is his opera *Wozzeck* (1917–22), a tragic, powerful story of an impoverished soldier, an eventual victim of society's indifference. Most of the opera is atonal, although the climactic orchestral interlude in Act III, after Wozzeck has drowned himself, is centered on D minor. Particularly effective is the ending of the opera: Wozzeck's child, told that his mother is dead, leaves his hobbyhorse and runs off with the other children to see her body.

58 SERGEI PROKOFIEV AND SOCIALIST REALISM

PREVIEW   The career of another Russian composer, Prokofiev, introduces a new dimension: Soviet-style patronage of the arts for mass consumption, known as "Socialist Realism." After making an international reputation, Prokofiev returned home, where his composing was affected—some say hampered—by his forced dealings with the Communist party line. As with some other Russians we studied, he is famous for ballets, but he wrote a wide variety of music. His younger compatriot, Dimitri Shostakovich, also encountered difficulties in adapting to the system, although he outlived Stalin's regime.

The Russian world that Tchaikovsky, Mussorgsky, and Stravinsky knew was torn apart after World War I. How the new Soviet society handled its artists makes a gripping story, with the career of Sergei Prokofiev [pronounced pro-COUGH-fee-yev] (1891–1953) as the focus. He was born in the Ukraine area of Russia to a prosperous family. His mother, a good pianist, began his musical training, and by age nine he had written an opera. He attended the St. Petersburg Conservatory.

In 1918, after the Russian revolution, Prokofiev made his home in Paris, probably thinking that his unsettled country would have no need of his music. Despite his growing success as a composer and pianist in Europe, homesickness drove him back to Russia for good in the early 1930s. He spent the remainder of his life writing music which sometimes, but by no means always, fit the party line. Both he and Josef Stalin died in Moscow in 1953 on the same day and of the same disease (brain hemorrhage), an ironic coincidence considering how the dictator had scarred Prokofiev's life.

A

Prokofiev and the Commissars

While Prokofiev was abroad, the Russian revolutionists settled down to the enormous task of managing their country according to Marxist principles. One expectation was that all the arts should reinforce the ideals of the Soviet government, a doctrine labeled **Socialist Realism.** The party line concerning music had been declared in 1932, with all art expected to be "socially significant." Rejecting

Serge Prokofieff
par Henri Matisse

Artists and musicians seem to be closely connected in this century. For example, Matisse in 1921 made this sketch of Prokofiev to be included in the program for a Ballet Russes production of a ballet by Prokofiev.

the idea of "absolute music," the doctrine claimed that music is always "about" something, whether real objects or ideas. To be acceptable to the state, music must be easily understood by the people and must promote nationalist feelings. As part of the doctrine of Socialist Realism, "modernist" works of Schoenberg and others—including some by the young Prokofiev—were banned.

In return for writing music that the workers and peasants might enjoy, Socialist Realism gave composers support: guaranteed publication and fine performances of their works. Rewarded like great athletes and scientists, the best composers became national heroes. In a sense, this system recalls the days of Haydn and Prince Esterházy. Haydn, who also enjoyed financial security and fine performances of his works, was expected in return to write music that pleased his prince. Few of the commissars, however, could have matched the prince's musical taste.

In spite of the political situation, Prokofiev returned home. Though he must have sensed that his career would be fundamentally changed, perhaps he thought that an exception would be made in his case because of his worldwide reputation. Not until after World War II did the party regulars take direct aim at Prokofiev. In 1948, Stalin's personal representative to the central committee described the work of the most prominent Soviet composers, including Prokofiev, as "alien to the Soviet people" and marked by "formalist perversions." Although according to the Soviet musical dictionary, "formalist" meant "the artificial separation of form from content," it was really a code word for "modern."

While Prokofiev is said to have joked that "formalist" music was music people didn't understand the first time they heard it, the denunciation was no laughing matter. He was obliged to apologize to the Central Committee, confessing that he would renounce any interest in atonality. He tried to explain how difficult it is to write "original melodies" that are also "instantly understandable even to the uninitiated listener." He was forced to thank the Party "for the precise directives of the Resolution, which will help me in my search of a musical language accessible and natural to our people." Some of his non-Russian biographers claim that this experience broke his health and creative spirit and that his music from the last five years of his life was a "sad reflection of his talent." But his chief Soviet biographer found in these years only a "new stage in his creative evolution."

B

Prokofiev's Music

The most familiar Prokofiev works are those written shortly after his return to Russia. They include the *Lieutenant Kijé Suite* (1934), an arrangement of music written for a film. Its satirical story deals with a nonexistent lieutenant. A military bureaucrat's error necessitated his invention. Also from this period is *Peter and the Wolf* (1936), a delightful piece for narrator and orchestra that introduces the instruments of the orchestra. Though tagged as music for children, anyone can enjoy it and, if unsure of these instruments, learn from it as well. Another film score, that for the classic "Alexander Nevsky" (1938), includes an important choral part. As a cantata, it is frequently heard in concert versions, sometimes in conjunction with a screening of the film itself.

Also familiar are some early works. An opera with the odd title of *Love for Three Oranges* (1921) contains a distinctive *March*. His *Classical Symphony* (1916–17) anticipates the "neoclassical" stage of his fellow Russian, Stravinsky. Close to what Haydn might have written, had he lived in this century, it has four short movements. The first and fourth movements are fast, in sonata-form. The second is in ABA form, with the expected slow tempo. Only the third movement departs from Classic era expectations, with a heavy-footed gavotte instead of a minuet. However, the symphony's harmony, with its sleight-of-hand key changes, stamps it as a product of the twentieth century. His third *Piano Concerto* (1917–21) and second *Violin Concerto* (1935) are frequently performed.

Under orders from her father, Juliet prepares to dance with her unwanted suitor, Paris, in this production of the ballet *Romeo and Juliet*. (Courtesy of San Francisco Ballet Collection of the San Francisco Performing Arts Library and Museum.)

In 1935, Prokofiev finished his score for a ballet based upon Shakespeare's tragedy. Not until five years later, after many difficult rehearsals, did it premier. For concert performances, the composer arranged portions of the score into three suites. He also transcribed ten episodes for piano.

The second *Romeo and Juliet* suite begins with a section called "Montagues and Capulets," which is a combination of musical segments found in three different parts of the complete ballet.

Prokofiev: *Romeo and Juliet Suite II,* "Montagues and Capulets" (6:02) ⑦₃

  CD6

(0:00)
1   m1   A brief introduction establishes an ominous mood with a crescendo
          to a strongly dissonant chord, followed by a soft, consonant answer in
[6]   the strings. With changes of pitches, this process is repeated. Early
          in the ballet (Act 1, scene 1), this music accompanies the prince's
          command that the warring families end their feud.

(1:17)

2a m17 A heavy "oom-pah" accompaniment in low strings and brass establishes the quadruple meter of the Nobles theme (ex. 58.1) and its minor mode. In Act I, scene 4, nobles dance to this music in a "Grand Fête at the House of Capulet." The main theme is played by violins in dotted rhythms with chordwise motion as if to reflect the arrogant strutting of the nobles on stage. Drum accents mark the ending of this subsection.

7

Example 58.1

(1:43)

2b m27 The Nobles theme begins a repetition.

(2:02)

3a m35 A new melody in the French horns, moving evenly in quarter and eighth notes, competes with the Nobles theme.

8

(2:26)

3b m45 A second appearance of the new melody, in a new key (F minor), now in low brass and low strings, continues its competition with the Nobles theme.

(2:44)

3c m53 The accompaniment and then the Nobles theme return as in item 2a.

(3:09)

4a m63 A contrasting section begins, based on a pas de deux (dance for two) that occurs later (Act III, scene 1). Obeying her father, Juliet dances with her unwanted suitor (she has already secretly married Romeo). In triple meter, the flute melody here (ex. 58.2) is doubled—almost—by viola, which slides up and down to the high notes that the flute plays in normal style. Harp and pizzicato strings accompany.

9

Example 58.2

(3:41)

4b   m71   A second phrase of the flute melody begins like the first but is changed to fit the slip-sliding turns the harmony takes on its way to the tonic.

(4:14)

4c   m79   A third phrase resembles the first (item 4a), with the addition of a violin countermelody.

(4:46)

4d   m87   In the fourth phrase, the countermelody passes to the celesta.

(5:16)

5a   m94   The accompaniment for the Nobles theme returns, surprisingly soft, and the theme goes to the saxophone, then the clarinet, before

☐10   returning to the violins in a gradual crescendo.

(5:40)

5b   m104 Now the Nobles theme is in full control. A split-second recall of the dissonant sounds of item 1 occurs just before the last, minor, chord.

C

Dmitri Shostakovich

Of course, Prokofiev was but one of the thousands of creative artists who had to come to terms with the Soviet system. Its negative impact on Dmitri Shostakovich [pronounced shos-tah-KOH-vitch] (1906–75) was even more serious and occurred much earlier. An aggressive "modernist," Shostakovich's composition at first reflected the current trends in Europe. In the early 1930s, his opera *Lady Macbeth of Mtsensk* enjoyed great success in Europe and at home. Suddenly, in 1936, an article in the official Soviet newspaper (and therefore assumed to represent the views of Stalin) violently attacked it, branding the opera as "neurotic" and "vulgar." Though the article mentioned only Shostakovich, it was taken more broadly as a warning against all kinds of "modernisms." The composers' union denounced him and his career would have ended right there had he not changed course. His response was the *Symphony No. 5* (1937), which appeared with a subtitle (by someone else): "The creative reply of a Soviet artist to justified criticism." Apparently, the party approved of this work—and so does the public to this day, for it is his most frequently performed work.

Shostakovich also had to make a public apology in 1948, in language all-too-similar to Prokofiev's. Happily, he lived long enough to profit from the relaxation which followed Stalin's death. For the rest of his life, he wrote as he wished. Though he never publicly repudiated Socialist Realism, his memoirs tell a different story. Entitled *Testimony,* and smuggled out of Russia after his death in 1975 in Moscow, the memoirs reveal that he became frustrated with the system because meddling, ignorant bureaucrats interfered in artistic matters. (Soviet authorities dispute the authenticity of the memoirs, however, as does the composer's son.)

Dmitri Shostakovich.

59 CHARLES IVES

PREVIEW   As the United States moves into the foreground of musical development, we can study the careers of some American composers. The earliest is Ives, a New Englander whose roots are clearly a part of his music. Not expecting music to provide a livelihood, he became a leader in the insurance business. Recognition for his complexly textured, unusual music came long years after its composition.

In the next few chapters, we focus on American developments. Our first composer was a rugged New Englander, Charles Ives (1874–1954), born in Connecticut to a musical family. His first music teacher was his father, a well-trained Civil War bandmaster who led the local bands, directed church hymn singing, and involved his son in both of these activities. Ives later described a conversation in which his father defended a local man whose singing at the town camp meeting had been described as "horrible." The father cautioned, in words that Ives must have absorbed: "Don't pay too much attention to the sounds—for if you do, you may miss the music. You won't get a wild, heroic ride to heaven on pretty little sounds."

At Yale, where he was a "big man on campus" but a mediocre student, Ives tolerated indoctrination in the accepted musical conventions. Upon graduation from college, he made a difficult decision. While he could have continued his musical work as a church organist, he realized that a career as a composer might not support a family.

So Ives gave up music as a profession, entered the insurance business, and became a financial success. At one time, his company was the biggest in the country in volume of insurance sold. Composition necessarily became a hobby, and although he piled up score after score, most of them remained stored in his barn. A heart attack in 1918 forced him to abandon composition, or so he claimed, although recent research by Maynard Solomon shows that Ives revised and updated many earlier scores after this experience. In the 1920s, he began to have his music privately published, sending copies to people he hoped would be interested in it.

Charles Ives.

Performances and a slowly growing reputation resulted, even the Pulitzer Prize in 1947—for music he had written almost forty years earlier!

Charles Ives and the Music of the American People

Music in America, at least on a professional level, has always taken a back seat to the more pressing concerns of establishing a nation. While some national leaders found music a rewarding hobby—Benjamin Franklin perfected a "glass harmonica," Thomas Jefferson played the violin—composing music as one's life-work has not seemed feasible. Of course there have been composers in this country, but many were like William Billings (1746–1800), self-taught and an original thinker, but a musician only by avocation.

Probably the best-known names in American music belong to Stephen Foster (1826–64), associated with countless folklike tunes, such as "Old Folks at Home," and John Philip Sousa (1854–1932), whose "Stars and Stripes Forever" alone would justify his title as the "march king." Advanced musical training was available only in Europe, so it was not surprising that talented American composers like Edward MacDowell (1860–1908) found it necessary to study abroad. After the indoctrination they received in Europe, their works naturally adhered to long-established European musical traditions. Even American-trained composers showed this conservative bent. One of them, Amy Cheney Beach (1867–1944), was a trail-blazing woman composer. Her song *Ah, Love, but a Day* won considerable popularity in her lifetime. Her *Gaelic Symphony,* the first published symphony by an American woman, was essentially Romantic in concept.

Ives, however, resisted that European tradition and reflected his birthplace in several ways. New Englanders are known for being rugged individualists, and he certainly was one. The sounds of his childhood experiences directly influenced his music. He liked to imitate the communal effects of fervent, out-of-tune hymn singing, the kind that his father had defended. Many of the familiar American melodies and Sunday-school hymns he had learned as a child found their way into his music. In response to criticism of this practice, he explained that he was trying to communicate the essence of the singing at the camp meetings of his youth: "I remember how the great waves of sound used to come through the trees, when things like *Nearer My God To Thee, In the Sweet Bye and Bye* and the like were sung by thousands of 'let out' souls. Father, who led the singing, would always encourage the people to sing their own way. There was power and exaltation in these great conclaves of sound from humanity." More than one hundred and fifty tunes that he quoted have been identified, and there are probably many more. He was also intrigued by the sounds a bystander hears as two bands march in a parade, one of them drawing closer while the other moves farther away.

Ives displayed an irreverent streak and a taste for musical parody in his youthful *Variations on America* for organ (1891), also arranged for orchestra by William Schuman. Ives takes a solemn, patriotic tune, and then pokes fun not only at its solemnity but also at traditional ideas concerning variation form. One variation is in a Polonaise rhythm; another includes high, flippant, grace notes. This piece includes two short interludes, where two different keys are heard simultaneously, and an optional, improvised cadenza.

The Unanswered Question (1906), a brief work (about eight minutes) for chamber orchestra, has an explanatory foreword. Just as in some Romantic tone poems, a philosophical idea provided a starting point for the composer. The trumpet (Ives said that it was all right to employ some other wind instrument, if desired) is to intone "The Perennial Question of Existence." Flutes hunt for "The Invisible Answer." A string orchestra, seated apart from the winds and playing very softly and slowly, represents the "Silences of the Druids—Who Know, See and Hear Nothing."

Probably his best-known orchestral work is *Three Places in New England*, which, as the title suggests, relates to the musical nationalism demonstrated by many Romantic composers. Composed before 1914 but not performed until 1930, it was the first of his works to be published commercially. The first "place" he described is a statue in the Boston Commons by the sculptor Augustus Saint-Gaudens (1849–1907), a tribute to the Civil War's black soldiers. An example of Ives's use of quotations appears early in this piece, as fragments of "Old Black Joe" ("I'm coming, I'm coming") turn into "Jesus Loves Me." The second piece, *Putnam's Camp,* pictures a Revolutionary War memorial park, the scene of a July 4 picnic. Quoted American tunes are evocative of marches and popular music of the time. The third "place" is described below.

Ives: The Housatonic at Stockbridge (4:14) ⑦④

A programmatic basis exists for the "Housatonic." To the score, Ives attached some lines from a poem by Robert Underwood Johnson which begins: "Contented river! in thy dreamy realm . . ." and ends with this thought: "Wouldst thou away! . . . I also of much resting have a fear; Let me thy companion be/By fall and shallow to the adventurous sea!" As if this poem did not offer enough hints for some story-telling, Ives reported that this music "was suggested by a Sunday morning walk that Mrs. Ives and I took near Stockbridge. We walked in the meadows along the river and heard the distant singing from the church across the river. The mists had not entirely left the river and the colors, the running water, the banks and trees were something that one would always remember."

As is the case with much of Ives's music, snatches of melody emerge and then disappear in this piece. There are few consonant chords—in fact, it is difficult to hear chords as such because of the thick texture. While the meter is a standard 4/4, the slow tempo and lack of a beat give a static effect. Ives calls for a large orchestra, including a piano with two performers to handle the fistfuls of notes.

CD6

(0:00)
1   m1 Beginning very slowly and softly, muted strings create a hazy,
        perhaps watery effect with quickly moving notes that ripple their
[11]   way over a static bass line.

(0:36)
2   m6 A tune emerges (ex. 59.1), played twice, alternating phrases between
        French horn and English horn. Although it is not a church hymn,
[12]   this tune might relate to Ives's description of "distant singing from
        the church." Choosing portions of Johnson's poem, Ives later
        arranged this music as a song for voice and piano.

Example 59.1

(1:40)
3   m17 French horn begins to repeat the tune, but it is soon changed.

[13]

(2:18)
4   m22 Now violins play a version of the tune, somewhat louder this time
        and a couple of tones higher.

[14]

(3:13)
5   m32 In a very subtle change, the bass line begins to move. A crescendo
        and an accelerando, with low brass and a timpani roll, help build the
[15]   music to a quadruple *forte* climax.

(4:11)
6   m43 Quite suddenly the volume drops, and the opening quiet returns,
        perhaps to show that the river disappears into the "adventurous sea."

[16]

AARON COPLAND 60

PREVIEW   Copland made a living as an American composer, something Ives had thought impossible. After study in Paris, Copland returned home with a deliberate intention to write in an accessible, though "modern" style. Living longer than any composer we have met so far, he made an international reputation and received unprecedented media attention.

Coming only a generation later than Charles Ives, Aaron Copland [pronounced COPE-land] (1900–90) found a completely different musical climate. Ives had assumed that it was impossible to make a living as a composer in the United States. Copland proved that it could be done. He was born in New York City in a neighborhood he described in an autobiographical sketch as a "drab" street in Brooklyn. His parents were Jewish immigrants from Russia; his father prospered as a storekeeper. The family had no particular interest in music, although an older sister had taken piano lessons. Aaron learned what he could from her, then sought out professional teachers on his own. They gave him thorough, but very conservative, composition instruction.

At age twenty, Copland financed his own travel to Paris, where he became a pupil of the most influential teacher of this century, Nadia Boulanger (1887–1979). Her first teaching experience came as she taught music to her talented younger sister Lili (1893–1918), who at the age of twenty won the coveted Prix de Rome for a cantata. After Lili's early death, Nadia dedicated her own long life to teaching at the American Conservatory in Fontainebleau. Here she inspired whole generations of composers, Copland being her first American student.

Not only did Copland find Boulanger a powerful teacher, but also he met other composers and musicians in Europe, making contacts for the future. He returned home at just the right time, 1924, when some wealthy patrons hoped to make New York City the "Paris of America," and he attracted their support.

No ivory tower recluse, Copland taught in such influential settings as the Berkshire Music Center, the summer home of the Boston Symphony Orchestra. Equally talented as a writer, his articles and books are widely read. His brief *What*

Aaron Copland frequently conducted his own music.

to Listen for in Music remains in print as a music appreciation course text. His *The New Music* explains contemporary music in clear, nontechnical terms. He also composed background music for films and appeared in many educational television programs both in this country and in England. In his later years he began a career as a conductor, usually of his own works. Active into his eighties, he continued to receive honors from institutions around the world and to be acknowledged as the "dean" of American composers. An unprecedented amount of public attention and media coverage attended his eighty-fifth birthday.

A

Copland: The Successful American Composer

Part of Copland's success stemmed from the emergence of the United States as a musical leader, and part of it resulted from two pivotal decisions he made relatively early in his career. While studying in Paris, Copland noticed that "The relation of French music to the life around me became increasingly manifest. Gradually, the idea that my personal expression in music ought somehow to be related to my own back-home environment took hold of me. The conviction grew inside me that the two things that seemed always to have been so separate in America—music and the life about me—must be made to touch." He decided that he should be recognizably "American" in his writings.

The second turning point came in the 1930s, as he later explained, when the social climate of the Depression years "aroused a wave of sympathy for and identification with the plight of the common man." He became aware of a new public for music that had developed because of the radio and the phonograph. He also realized that the old, traditional concert audiences preferred the sounds of the established classics, and that the audience for "modern music" was limited. It made no sense to him to ignore these facts. As he said, the situation "would naturally induce works in a simpler, more direct style than was customary for concert works of absolute music. But it did not by any means lessen my interest in composing works in an idiom that might be accessible only to cultivated listeners." The latter part of this description applies to his *Piano Variations, 1930.* In fact, late in his career he tried twelve-tone writing, as in the orchestral *Inscape,* 1967. However, the "simpler" pieces (some are mentioned below) built his reputation with a mass audience.

B

Copland's Music

The first of Copland's works to be performed in America was his *Symphony for Organ and Orchestra* (1924), with the solo part written for his teacher, Nadia Boulanger. At the concert, the conductor addressed the audience, saying: "If a young man at the age of twenty-three can write a symphony like that, in five years he will be ready to commit murder." Far from resenting that remark, Copland quoted it frequently with great glee. It says volumes for the attitude toward "modern" music at the time, and also hints that Copland's style was rather aggressive. (Actually, compared to truly murderous music like *The Rite of Spring,* his organ symphony would hardly merit a traffic ticket.)

Copland's works include such staples of the repertoire as *Lincoln Portrait* (1942), in which a narrator reads from President Lincoln's writings. An orchestral prelude and the narrator's accompaniment quote American tunes that Lincoln might have known, although he would probably have been surprised at how those tunes are presented. American influences are also obvious in the scores for the ballets *Billy the Kid* (1938) and *Rodeo* (1942). Both include some folk themes, though often rhythmically changed with syncopations and altered meters. The brief *Fanfare for the Common Man* (1942) makes a fine opener for concerts of American music. *El Salón México* (1933–36), an orchestral work, is a stylistic kin; Mexican rather than American tunes are its inspiration, however.

Syncopation and changes of meter make Copland's rhythmic structures interesting in themselves. Mild dissonance appears in his more accessible works. One effect he especially seems to like is the presentation of a melody in one key with its accompaniment in another key. There is an "open" sound to his music, which people like to compare to the "open" look of an American landscape in the mythical wild West. (The frequent fourths and fifths in his music are responsible.)

Copland subtitled *Appalachian Spring* (1944) as "Ballet for Martha," referring to the influential Martha Graham and the American ballet company she headed. The work's theme is a pioneer wedding celebration, set in rural Pennsylvania in the early years of the last century. Intended for ballet performance, the first version of the music, about thirty-six minutes in duration, was scored for a group of thirteen instruments, including piano. Copland later made a suite from eight scenes of the ballet, deleting about ten minutes of the original score, and

Copland: *Appalachian Spring,* Section VII, "Variations on a Shaker Theme" (3:10) ⑦⑤

arranging the music for large orchestra. The guide below is based on the orchestral version, but both are recorded. Listening to the complete version of the entire ballet will reveal some differences from our guide for Section VII. In the complete ballet, Section VII begins at 21:24; in the suite, at 19:15.

Copland described the seventh section of the suite as "Scenes of daily activity for the bride and her farmer husband." It is a set of variations on an old American folk tune called "Simple Gifts." This tune is associated with the Shakers, a group of nineteenth-century religious zealots who had founded several communities in the northeastern United States. (Though they were hard-working and had marvelous taste in design, their belief in celibacy doomed their sect to eventual extinction.) Although Copland customarily modified the tunes he borrowed, this one he left almost intact. Perhaps the words "true simplicity" in the text influenced him! This song also appears in a group of American folk tunes he arranged for vocal solo with piano accompaniment. Since measures are not numbered in the score, rehearsal numbers (r) are given here.

   CD6

(0:00)
1   r55   The clarinet plays the theme (ex. 60.1) for this ballet section, the
              Shaker tune, appropriately in the major mode, over a simple flute
        17   and harp accompaniment.

Example 60.1

'Tis the gift to be sim-ple,'tis the gift to be free,

'Tis the gift to come down where you ought to be

(Six more phrases continue, as follows:)
And when we find ourselves in the place just right,
'Twill be in the valley of love and delight.
When true simplicity is gained,
To bow and to bend we shan't be ashamed,
To turn, turn will be our delight,
'Till by turning, turning we come round right.

A short transition then modulates and leads to Variation I.

(0:34)

2   r57 Oboe and bassoon harmonize neatly as they play the first variation. A minimal accompaniment in the brass (and later woodwinds) projects Copland's typical empty sound.

`18`

(1:02)

3a   r59 Variation II finds the tune played in augmentation (notes are held twice as long as their original value) by trombone and viola. A busy accompaniment includes a prominent piano.

`19`

(1:17)

3b   r60 Violins enter with the tune, as if starting a canon.

(1:44)

3c   r61 A short, soft transition in woodwinds and strings modulates to a new key.

(1:52)

4   r62 Variation III is a vigorous duet of trumpets and trombones. The tune sounds almost marchlike. Soon it is accompanied by rapid scales in the violins.

`20`

(2:17)

5   r64 Variation IV, a little slower and played by woodwinds, concentrates on the first phrase of the theme, in the bassoons, and the fifth phrase, in the clarinets.

`21`

(2:34)

6   r65 The full orchestra, *fortissimo,* plays Variation V. Here again the theme unfolds in augmentation, producing a hymnlike quality.

`22`

(3:07)

7   r67 A sustained note in the brass functions as a link to the concluding section of the suite, marked in the score "like a prayer."

The ballet suite as a whole shows other aspects of Copland's style. Its eight sections, played without interruption, are as follows:

1. Very slow. Introduction of characters.
2. Fast. A sudden burst of strings begins the scene.
3. Moderate. A duo for the bride and groom.
4. Quite fast. This suggests square dancing with country fiddlers.
5. Still faster. A dance for the bride, who shows "extremes of joy and fear."
6. Very slowly. A transition that resembles the introduction.
7. (Described above.)
8. Moderate. Essentially a coda, muted strings create a prayerlike atmosphere.

61 THE TRADITIONS OF JAZZ

PREVIEW   After defining jazz, we list some of its fundamental principles, then describe examples of blues and rags, two idioms considered to be the "roots" of jazz. An outline of traditional jazz is given in terms of the customary elements—melody, harmony, and so on. A brief sketch of early jazz history concludes with a selection recorded by Louis Armstrong, with further developments of jazz the last topic of this chapter.

Because the United States has imported so much of its culture from Europe, it is noteworthy when a musical development originating in this country is exported to Europe. This is precisely what happened with jazz. American jazz and its leading performers have achieved worldwide acceptance. Justifiably, some of these musicians can claim that they are better known in Paris than in Peoria.

The "respectability" of jazz in today's educational world would probably surprise, if not amuse, its early developers. Paradoxically, while jazz was once considered a type of "popular" or entertainment music, it has evolved into a high art form worthy of study. For example, the two-volume *New Grove Dictionary of Jazz* (1988), edited by Barry Kernfeld, totals 1000 pages. An International Foundation of Jazz is headed by a Ph.D. Jazz can be pursued as an academic major in several conservatories and music schools. The course in jazz history that is increasingly found in American higher education can supplement our admittedly brief coverage of this topic.

What *is* **jazz?** It is not easy to define, which is the point of a story attributed to jazz pianist Fats Waller (1904–43). A naïve listener who asked him this question was told, "Lady, if you have to ask, you'll never know." At one time, the term "jazz" was often loosely applied to any kind of popular music. Even today the line between jazz and the many varieties of popular music is blurred. The *New Grove Dictionary of Jazz* defines jazz as "A music created mainly by black Americans in the early 20th century through an amalgamation of elements drawn from European-American and tribal African musics. A unique type, it cannot safely be categorized as folk, popular or art music, though it shares aspects of all three."

New Orleans jazz musicians march after a funeral for jazz musician Alton Purnell. (Photograph © Claire Rydell.)

Some general principles apply to many examples of jazz, but by no means to all of them because jazz styles differ so greatly.

A

Principles of Jazz

1. Jazz is dependent upon *individual* performers, and a surprisingly small number of people it is. The editor of the *New Grove Dictionary of Jazz* has isolated a group of around four hundred leaders and soloists that forms a central core for the field. Jazz historians and critics focus on outstanding performers and leaders of groups. Examples are: Louis Armstrong (1900–71), Duke Ellington (1899–1974), Benny Goodman (1909–86), Charlie Parker (1920–55), John Coltrane (1926–67), and Miles Davis (born 1926), with some of these almost as important for their compositions as for their performances.

2. The earliest jazz was *improvised*. By tradition, improvisation continues to play an important role in jazz, although the "big bands" depend at least to a certain extent upon a notational framework for those portions of a selection during which the entire group plays. We have seen that improvisation was a common practice in earlier times, certainly in the Baroque period, so there is nothing really new about the idea of improvisation in jazz except, perhaps, the emphasis placed upon it.

3. Since jazz contains a substantial amount of improvisation, no fixed score can be followed in studying a given composition. Instead, most historians and critics depend on *recordings* of jazz musicians and groups. In fact, jazz could not have developed as it did without the invention of recordings. Moreover, modern reissues of old 78 rpm disks on long-playing records, tapes, and compact discs have vastly increased the potential audience for classic jazz. Of the many anthologies that provide a broad coverage of the history of jazz, one of the most helpful is *Smithsonian Jazz,* produced by the Smithsonian Institution in Washington, D.C., in a revised edition, 1987. It contains ninety-five selections on seven records or five compact discs. The recordings in this set were originally made between 1916 and 1981. Supplementing the album is a one-hundred-twenty-six-page booklet, written in a nontechnical style, which offers suggestions to the novice listener. The musical examples mentioned in this chapter (except for *The Entertainer*) are taken from that collection. Anyone wanting more complete coverage of jazz history than we have space for can turn to it.

4. More than most musical genres, jazz is intimately related to *society as a whole.* It is, therefore, of interest to sociologists as well as to musicians. In its origins as entertainment music in New Orleans, it was tied closely to black American culture. It is still considered by many to be primarily an art of black people, who, for example, make up the vast majority of the performers represented in the Smithsonian collection. The racial segregation prevailing in the early days of jazz dictated that there would be "white" jazz and "black" jazz groups. Decades passed before jazz was integrated racially; to this day it is obvious that males still dominate. Women performers make up a decided minority. Japanese-born Toshiko Akiyoshi (born 1929), a leader, composer, and arranger for the Akiyoshi-Tabackin band, is one of the few prominent female jazz musicians today.

The heritage of jazz as entertainment still suggests that it be performed in clubs or restaurants where dancing, eating, and drinking can take place as well. To listen without these distractions, jazz enthusiasts gather at specially planned jazz concerts and festivals, such as those in Monterey, California, and Newport, Rhode Island.

5. Jazz *evolved* out of many earlier idioms. Its musical features are more easily discussed after a brief survey of blues and ragtime, two of the American idioms that are often said to be part of the "roots" of jazz.

B

Blues

After the Civil War black people developed the **blues,** a kind of folk song with the poetic and musical forms we describe in this section, accompanied by the guitar. "Having the blues" means, of course, being in a depressed, melancholy state of mind, and the texts of traditional blues often do reflect feelings of this kind. The blues, however, have evolved to express a much wider variety of moods, especially since blues moved from a strictly vocal style to a type of instrumental music. Incidentally, the word "blues" is not an exact term. Many selections with "blues" in the title are not "blues" as discussed here: conversely, the titles of many selections that *do* follow the blues pattern lack this word.

The lyrics of traditional blues are in strophic form, with three-line stanzas the first line of which is repeated. The standard AAB form of the text is set to an overall musical pattern known as the **twelve-bar blues.** Although the second line of the text is repeated, the music for the second line is sufficiently different that an analysis reads: AA'B. Each phrase fills four measures, with the actual text taking only about half of this time, leaving room at phrase endings for improvised material, either by the singer or by an accompanying instrument. The harmony is based on the three fundamental chords of Western tonal music: tonic (I), dominant (V), and subdominant (IV), in a standardized pattern, each chord symbol representing one measure.

I,I,I,I;   IV,IV,I,I;   V,V (or IV),I,I.

Each new verse, called a **chorus,** is a variation on the original theme. In many ways, the blues form resembles the continuous variation forms of the Baroque period.

Besides the formal pattern, we can isolate melodic characteristics. Prominent are **blue notes,** that is, notes that are slightly flatted or "bent," producing microtones. The pitches usually so affected are the third and seventh of the scale, *mi* and *ti,* and now and then the fifth, *sol.* Singers find it easy to "bend" these pitches at will and players of many instruments can, by various techniques, achieve this effect also. Of course it is impossible to bend notes on the piano, but by playing both versions of the tone, the normal and the half-step lower, the pianist imitates the blue-note quality. An emotional, individual style of singing is expected, with much sliding between pitches. The rhythmic style depends upon a steady beat from accompanying instruments, but with the solo line moving in uneven notes, slightly ahead of or behind that beat.

The legendary Bessie (Elizabeth) Smith (1895–1937) was billed as the "Empress of the Blues." By 1937 more than ten million of her recordings had been sold. One of her famous blues selections (1926) will show how text and chords fit together in the twelve-bar blues pattern. In the guide the chord symbols I,IV,V (do not confuse the "I" chord with "I," first person singular) appear below the words of the first stanza. The remaining stanzas follow the same harmony. In the Smithsonian recording, Bessie Smith is accompanied by piano and cornet, the cornet answering the voice at ends of phrases. These exchanges are derived from the African tradition of "call-and-response," comparable to the preacher-congregation dialogue commonly found in many black churches.

Smith, Bessie: *Lost Your Head Blues* (3:00) (76)

   CD6

1a (Piano and cornet play a four-bar introduction.)
1b I was with you baby when you didn't have a dime,

    I   I   I   I

1c I was with you baby when you didn't have a dime,

    IV   IV   I   I

1d Now since you got plenty money you have sold your good gal down.

          V   V   I   I

Many modern beginning piano method books include a simple "blues" piece, showing how standardized this pattern is. The characteristics of the blues appear in later forms of popular music as well. "Rhythm and Blues," or "R & B" for short, popular in the 1950s, is based upon blues traditions but features a group, rather than a solo singer. R & B in turn spawned rock and roll, as in Bill Haley's 1955 smash hit, "Rock Around the Clock," which is built on the twelve-bar blues pattern.

C

Ragtime

Ragtime is the name given to a style of piano music, at first improvised, later written down, by composers such as Scott Joplin (1868–1917), known in his time as the "King of Ragtime." Not satisfied with the success of his rags, Joplin devoted years to his opera *Treemonisha,* which had to wait until 1972 for its first complete performance. Joplin wanted his rags to be performed exactly as written—and not too fast. Since he made piano rolls of his music, recently transferred to records, one can hear an "authentic" version of Joplin's rags.

Rags usually are in duple meter. The pianist's left hand plays a steady pattern in an "oom-pah" style: bass note, chord, alternate bass note, chord. Frequently found in piano music, the pattern is not unique to ragtime. The right-hand melody is often based on chord skips and features syncopation. Rags consist of separate but similar melodic sections, each usually repeated, a formal pattern found also in waltzes and marches. Many of Joplin's piano rags, recently arranged for small instrumental ensembles, make delightful listening. *Maple Leaf Rag* (1899) is probably his best-known piece, but it has been eclipsed in popularity by *The Entertainer* (1902) after that rag figured prominently in the motion picture "The Sting."

♫ CD6

Joplin: *The Entertainer* (4:15)
(77)

(0:00)
1   m1 The piano plays in octaves to establish a brief introduction.

(0:07)

2   m5   The A section begins with a syncopated melody (ex. 61.1) featuring
            the skip from *mi* to *dô* in its first three phrases, with a contrasting
[25]   phrase to end the section. Then the A section repeats.

Example 61.1

(1:02)

3   m21 The B section features conjunct motion in three phrases, followed by
            a contrasting phrase as in the A section. In the repetition of the B
[26]   section, the right hand plays an octave higher.

(1:55)

4   m37 Now the A section returns.

[27]

(2:23)

5   m53 Joplin goes to a new key (the subdominant) for a C section,
            featuring several rhythmic ideas. It, too, is repeated; then there is a
[28]   modulation back to the original key.

(3:23)

6   m73 A D section, also featuring several rhythmic ideas, ends with the
            same conclusion found in the B section. Like all the sections, the D
[29]   section repeats.

D

1. *Meter* is usually strongly marked. As in blues and ragtime, duple meter is traditional, although triple and other meters are possible. Quintuple meter supplied the title of Paul Desmond's "Take Five," made famous by the Dave Brubeck Quartet. Fundamental to jazz is the long-short effect of dotted rhythms, performed with much flexibility and individual freedom, a quality summed up in the word **swing.** As hard to define as is "jazz," swing "defies analysis," proclaims one music dictionary. But as Duke Ellington observed, "It don't mean a thing if it ain't got that swing." ("Swing" also denotes in a more general way the jazz styles of the 1930s and 1940s.) Syncopation is so standard that the prevailing rhythmic feeling in jazz is: one TWO three FOUR, instead of the more "classical" ONE two THREE four. "Backbeat" is a term for this particular rhythmic effect, one found in many other types of popular music as well.

Musical Characteristics of Traditional Jazz

2. Jazz *melodic line* stresses the "blue notes," the flatted third, fifth, and seventh notes of the scale, as in the blues. A familiar melody may furnish the starting point for a jazz performance. Someone like Benny Goodman may play "Body and Soul" in a simple, direct fashion, while another performer may embellish it past the point of easy recognition.

3. The *harmony* of jazz is derived from traditional tonal sources, with many "substitute" chords expanding upon the basic three chords (I,IV,V). Most triads are enlarged to become seventh or ninth chords. Ending a piece with an extremely complex, dissonant chord has become a cliché in jazz performance.

4. Relatively *small groups* of instruments generate the characteristic *tone color* of jazz. In early jazz, a combination of a cornet or trumpet, a trombone, and a clarinet was supported by bass, piano or guitar, and percussion. Soon the saxophones became so strongly associated with jazz that some listeners have difficulty accepting them in any other type of music. Vibrato, the fluctuation of pitch that is a standard technique of string instrument playing, is a fundamental part of jazz playing, even more widely employed than in "classical" performance.

Drummers play a large assortment of drums and cymbals. Besides moments of solo improvisation, the role of the piano, or guitar, is to provide a harmonic background. The bass player is more apt to pluck the strings than to take up the bow.

5. The "classic" *form* of jazz is related to the concept of *theme-and-variations,* as shown in the blues. A popular song may supply the framework, although the song's harmonic structure is more important than its actual melody. Gershwin's "I Got Rhythm" is a good example of the most commonly found song structure in jazz. The standard length of these songs is thirty-two measures—four phrases of eight measures each, in a pattern of AABA', the same shape we noted earlier for "Deck the Halls." The entire group begins the performance with a collective version of the basic song. Each "variation" or chorus features a soloist or a small group of players. Jazz musicians, responding to the chord progressions of a song, play a fancifully embellished melodic line. For a conclusion, perhaps agreed upon in advance or communicated by signal at the appropriate moment, the entire group again plays the song together.

E

Early Jazz History in Brief

Jazz emerged in the 1890s. Inheriting the steady duple meter and syncopations of ragtime, the continuous variation form and blue notes of the blues, the instruments of the marching band, and the solo and group interaction of African music, a group of performers living in New Orleans blended these elements into something new. Oddly enough, though black musicians developed it, the first group to record New Orleans style jazz was white, the "Original Dixieland Jazz Band" of 1917. Jazz soon moved up the river and spread to many areas of the United States, as the career of Louis Armstrong (1900–71) shows, based as it was in New Orleans, Chicago, and New York.

Louis Armstrong, one of the most influential jazz musicians of all time, was born in New Orleans and recorded with King Oliver's Creole Jazz Band in Chicago. With his own recording group, the "Hot Five," he took as the basis for this selection (1927) a song by Lil Hardin, the pianist for the group and Armstrong's wife. Frequently, her name appears as the "composer" of this selection. Armstrong, primarily a trumpet player who plays cornet on this recording, also sings nonsense syllables in a style called **scat** singing. Clarinet, trombone, and guitar have solos, and at brief moments the piano is prominent.

Armstrong: *Hotter Than That* (3:00)
(78)

 CD6

(0:00)
1
[30] The entire group plays an eight-bar introduction in a fast tempo, with a steady beat.

(0:09)
2a The cornet solos, with piano and guitar accompanying.

(0:25)
2b A **break** occurs, an unaccompanied moment for the soloist; then piano and guitar return. The next soloist, the clarinet, arrives, a bit early for its turn.

(0:45)	
3a	The clarinet solos in its high range in the second chorus as piano and guitar continue to accompany.
(1:01)	
3b	There is another break, now for the clarinet soloist, and again the accompaniment returns. Again, the next soloist (vocalist) enters early.
(1:21)	
4a	The third chorus features Armstrong, singing his nonsense syllables in his typically gruff timbre. Only guitar accompanies.
(1:36)	
4b	After another break, the voice and guitar compete, as if trying to throw each other off the beat.
(1:53)	
4c	With an unexpected slow tempo interlude, voice and guitar echo each other.
(2:13)	
4d	The piano returns to lead into the final chorus.
(2:17)	
5a	Now the trombone (muted) solos, accompanied by piano and guitar.
(2:31)	
5b	After another break, all instruments join in. The final guitar chord at the end is unresolved, leaving the selection "up in the air."

F

Further Developments of Jazz

The pianist and leader Duke Ellington (1899–1974) was a skillful orchestrator who gathered around him a stable core of brilliant players. For half a century, he led a group he called the "Duke Ellington *Orchestra*," as if to show that his was more than a "dance band." He gave concerts at New York's Carnegie Hall. He wrote longer compositions that broke out of the old three-minute limit that the 78 rpm records had dictated. His name is also linked to popular songs such as "Sophisticated Lady," which reflected impressionistic harmony.

The **big bands** of the 1930s and later merged jazz and popular music. They numbered ten to twenty players. Since many of the musicians played more than one instrument, a vast wealth of tone color combinations was possible. Benny Goodman (1909–86) earned the title "King of Swing." With his group, he toured the world as an official representative of the U. S. State Department and forced the issue of integration by employing both black and white musicians. One of the few jazz musicians who moved easily in the "classical" sphere as well, his clarinet

Duke Ellington, at the piano, is surrounded by members of his orchestra.

recordings of the music of Mozart and other composers are still available. While big bands have become commercially unfeasible, they remain very much alive on college campuses.

Jazz has undergone such revolutionary developments in the past few decades, starting with the 1940s, that all of our previous generalizations are called into question. Here we have time to mention only a few of those changes.

Tone color possibilities were enlarged, paralleling the expansions we noted in the "classical" world. Jazz began to employ electronic instruments, for instance, electric pianos and the Hammond organ. As might be expected, the synthesizer has found a place. Less predictably, symphonic woodwinds, such as flutes, have appeared. A variety of mutes enriches the sound possibilities of many instruments. Again paralleling the "classical" sphere, jazz has witnessed the importation of non-Western instruments.

The controversial saxophonist Charlie Parker (1920–55), nicknamed "Bird," reacted against the commercialization of jazz and in the 1940s sought a new freedom. His **bebop** style, calling for quick tempos, complex harmonies, and jagged melodies, became very influential. Ruined by drugs and alcohol, his short-lived career ended before he reached thirty-five.

Miles Davis.

Free jazz was a radical effort in the late 1950s to eliminate predictable stereotypes and discover new procedures. By 1965, another saxophone player, John Coltrane (1926–67), had assumed a leading role in free jazz, enhancing his style with Asian and ancestral African elements. In his long career, Miles Davis (born 1926) has played his trumpet in a variety of jazz styles, including bebop and free jazz. In 1970, he confronted the issue of rock with recordings that demonstrate a blend of jazz with rock's amplified instruments and rhythmic character.

Jazz has continued to change, with some performers strongly affected by avant-garde developments in the "classical" world and others leaning toward the "popular" forms of music. Newer fashions in jazz, however, do not seem to supplant the older styles.

Throughout its history, jazz has influenced "classical" composers as well. For example, the slow movement of Ravel's *Concerto for the Left Hand* (1930) contains "many jazz effects," according to the composer. *The Creation of the World* (1923), by the Frenchman Darius Milhaud (1892–1974), was influenced by jazz the composer heard in Harlem. Stravinsky wrote his *Ebony Concerto* (1945) specifically for Woody Herman's jazz band. Benny Goodman commissioned Aaron Copland to write for him a *Clarinet Concerto* (1948). The concluding moments of its perky rondo contain slapping basses, percussive piano, and a clarinet glissando akin to the one that begins the best merger of "serious" music and jazz idioms: George Gershwin's *Rhapsody in Blue*.

62 GEORGE GERSHWIN

PREVIEW   Brooklyn-born like Copland, Gershwin died before he was forty, enjoying a short but enormously successful career. It represents a unique blend. Not only was he a popular figure in writing Broadway musicals and show tunes, but he also aspired to the "serious" musical world. His concert music incorporates the jazz style.

Like Copland, George Gershwin (1898–1937) was born in Brooklyn to Jewish immigrants without much family interest in music. In response to his precocious talent, his impoverished family managed to provide him with a piano, and soon an excellent teacher introduced him to the standard repertoire of Chopin, Liszt, and Debussy. While he studied music theory briefly, he never became a proficient music reader, though a phenomenal memory and his great skills at improvisation more than compensated for that lack. Leaving high school in 1914, he worked for a music publisher as a "song-plugger," a pianist who went to stores demonstrating the latest in popular songs so that people would buy copies. Soon he began to write his own songs. With his brother Ira Gershwin (1896–1983) as lyricist, he achieved a remarkable success in musical comedy. A brain tumor caused his early death in 1937. Many of his popular songs have become jazz standards, and many others are as familiar as folk songs.

A

Gershwin: Bridging the Gap between Popular and Serious Music

Gershwin enjoyed an astounding commercial success. In 1919, he wrote "Swanee," a song popularized by Al Jolson's smash-hit recording. His musicals and revues in the 1920s added to his fame. In 1931, he won the Pulitzer Prize with *Of Thee I Sing,* the first musical ever to win that award. Such songs as "The Man I Love," "Fascinating Rhythm," and "They Can't Take That Away From Me" are part of the American heritage. Even in the Depression years he made an extremely good living as a composer of "popular" music. At one point he produced a radio show for which he was reported to earn $2000 a week. With this income, he bought masterpieces of modern art for a growing collection. But popular success alone did not satisfy him. George Gershwin wanted to be a part of the "serious"

George Gershwin, like the composer Schoenberg, was an avocational painter. Here the younger man is pictured as he works on a portrait of the older composer. (Photograph © Pictorial Parade, Inc.)

musical world as well. He became a friend of Schoenberg, attended concerts of music by Stravinsky, and was in the audience for the American premiere of Berg's *Wozzeck*. At home as he played for friends, it was the music of Bach and Chopin that he might choose.

Gershwin, who found all kinds of music valuable, was encouraged to compose for the concert world, specifically for Carnegie Hall in New York. Paul Whiteman commissioned him to write the *Rhapsody in Blue* (1924), a piece for jazz band and piano, with Gershwin as piano soloist. This piece is famous for its beginning. An ascending passage for clarinet, an upward glissando wail, sets the jazz mood in a few seconds. Other orchestral works followed in 1925: *Concerto in F* and *An American in Paris*. Though less well known, his three short *Preludes* for piano (1926) also demonstrate Gershwin's cherished hope, to blend jazz elements with the basic requirement of concert music: that it be written down completely. Particularly in the slow, melodic second prelude, the jazz "blue note," the lowered seventh of the scale, is prominent. His extraordinary gift for melody helps compensate for a lack of development that these works show as a whole, as one great tune succeeds another. The standard form for a popular song, AABA, was the basis for most of Gershwin's songs as well.

B

Gershwin's Music

The best-known of Gershwin's works are those just mentioned, but one more is so significant and so unique that it demands attention. *Porgy and Bess* (1934–35) is an opera, some say *the* American opera. Though condensed performances of it have turned Gershwin's recitatives into spoken dialogue, partly to save money and time, and though Hollywood treated it rather casually in a 1959 motion picture version, directed by Otto Preminger, it fits every definition of opera. It is decidedly not a musical comedy.

In composing it, Gershwin had lofty aims: to combine "the drama and romance of *Carmen* and the beauty of *Meistersinger.*" While certainly an ambitious goal for any composer's first opera, there are many parallels among these operas. Both *Carmen* and *Porgy* are full of "hit tunes" that are known to everyone; both contain earthy, realistic characters without false pretenses. Bess, the heroine, is tragically flawed by her inability to imagine life without a man to take care of her; Porgy, the hero, has crippled legs but a spirit that is intact; and the evil Sportin' Life is an unabashed drug pusher. The opera is set in Catfish Row, a waterfront ghetto area in Charleston, South Carolina, whose poor and uneducated residents nonetheless share a strong sense of community and family ties, as did the townspeople of Nuremberg that Wagner pictured in *Meistersinger*. In both works, the chorus, representing their communities, plays an important role.

Porgy and Bess was first a novel, by the Southern writer DuBose Heyward (1885–1940). Heyward is credited with the libretto; Gershwin's brother Ira shares credit with Heyward for the lyrics of the songs. In keeping with the social customs of the time, the residents of Catfish Row are called "Negroes" and their speech is rendered in dialect. Changes in social customs since Gershwin's time have made the libretto a target for charges that it reflects unfortunate stereotypes. Arrangements of this music for instrumental performance allow musicians to bypass the problems posed by the text altogether and concentrate upon its unforgettable music.

Gershwin: *Porgy and Bess*

 CD6

Summertime
(2:27) ⑦⑨

(0:00)
1

[31]

Placed shortly after the opera's beginning and introduced with a brief passage on the clarinet, this beautiful lullaby is sung by Clara, a secondary role, as she rocks her baby. The song's melancholy character is intensified by its minor mode, underscoring such ironic words as "your daddy's rich and your ma is good lookin'."

The lead characters in *Porgy and Bess* are pictured as they conclude their duet, "Bess, You Is My Woman Now." (Courtesy of San Francisco Performing Arts Library and Museum, Kolmar Collection.)

(1:16)

2

[32] A second stanza is melodically similar to the first, although Gershwin's accompaniment is enriched with a choral background. The song demands a soprano who is able to negotiate its high range, yet communicate its poignant text.

CD6

I Got Plenty o' Nuttin' (3:10) ⑧⓪

(0:00)
1

☐33

As he accompanies himself with banjo strumming, the hero, Porgy, expresses his happy, accepting philosophy of life. Appropriately, he sings in a major key and in a solidly marked quadruple meter.

(1:21)
2

☐34

Brief expressions from the chorus in the opera may preface the second stanza (sung to the same music as the first), depending upon the particular performance. Porgy is usually sung by a bass-baritone, a vocal range well calculated to reveal him as the strong, capable person he is.

 CD6

Bess You Is My Woman Now (4:39) ⑧①

(0:00)
1

☐35

As often happens in duets, each singer has a solo opportunity. After a brief lead-in from the cello, Porgy sings the first stanza.

(1:13)
2

☐36

Bess, a soprano, sings the second stanza in a different key, a change dictated by her higher range. Porgy echoes her words as the stanza concludes.

(2:48)
3

☐37

The third stanza is a duet, with Bess carrying the melody while Porgy supplies a truly contrapuntal line that continues until the cadence.

It Ain't Necessarily So (3:07) ⑧②

The role of Sportin' Life is sung by a baritone, although singers improvise many excursions into a high pitch range. Not only does Sportin' Life sell "happy dust," a drug that the Catfish Row residents know is addicting though it apparently is legal, but he is also the local village atheist. He entertains the crowd with this song, in which he calls up before his knowledgeable audience a series of Bible stories. Deftly he points out the flaws in logic shown in the stories—David killing Goliath, Jonah living in the whale, Moses being found in a stream, Methuselah living 900 years—and he casts doubt upon his listeners' chances of getting into Heaven. The insinuations of his words are intensified by the chromatic movement of his melody and its minor mode. He separates stanzas with interludes of nonsense syllables.

JOHN CAGE 63

PREVIEW   As well known for his influential ideas as his own compositions, Cage is something of a guru to the avant-garde. An advocate for the incorporation of chance elements into composing and performing, his notions of music are so different from conventional wisdom that he has attracted much controversy. He experiments with unusual sounds—not to mention silence itself.

Los Angeles, long a hotbed of new ideas, was the birthplace of John Cage (born 1912), though New York City has been his home since the early 1940s. After two years of college and some European travel, he studied composition with Schoenberg and others and worked with dance companies as a rehearsal pianist-composer. He wrote many special works for the Merce Cunningham dance group. Often a center of considerable controversy, he became internationally known as a lecturer, writer (his *Silence* collects writings from 1939 through 1961), and composer. His seventy-fifth birthday was honored with a public open-air celebration in downtown Los Angeles, complete with a giant birthday cake and many performing groups—all sounding simultaneously. For the present-day experimentalist, Cage is not only a leader, he is a kind of father figure.

A

A quiet, gentle, flower-loving, denim-wearing anarchist, Cage challenges the conventional assumptions about music, claiming that all sounds are equally valid. He writes: "Noises are as useful to new music as so-called musical tones, for the simple reason that they are sounds." In this view, he echoes the Italian "futurists," who had advocated an "art of noises" in the years immediately before World War I. Cage has declared that his purpose is "to eliminate purpose" and has taken for a special target the solemn, serious atmosphere of "classical" concerts. His irreverent opinions of the traditional ideas about music find a parallel in art. In 1919, for example, Marcel Duchamp added a moustache and goatee to a reproduction of the "Mona Lisa," producing in the process one of the most frequently copied parodies in all art.

Cage: Guru of Chance and Change

John Cage.

Cage's basic philosophy stems from Zen Buddhism. One's role is not to shape the world but to adapt to it and simply accept what is there. A musical demonstration of this attitude is his 1954 "work" called *4' 33"*. During the specified time of four minutes and thirty-three seconds, the performer sits quietly at a piano, playing nothing. Whatever sounds occur accidentally in the hall or drift in from the outside during this time span provide the "music." Cage's ideas about concerts include calling for audience participation, asking those present to go out into the street and bring back garbage pails for the percussion section—"with or without garbage."

After his study of Eastern philosophy, particularly the Chinese "book of changes," called *I Ching* [pronounced ee king], Cage began to allow some elements of chance into his composing. Music in which random qualities appear that arise from chance is called, not surprisingly, **chance music.** ("Indeterminancy" is perhaps a more academic label.) For example, he made some musical decisions by throwing dice. Because the Latin word for dice is "alea," chance music is also known as **aleatoric.** *Music of Changes* (1951), for piano, was written with the help of charts from the Chinese book and the tossing of coins for deciding pitches, durations, and tone colors. Not content with relying on chance to produce the music in the first place, Cage also suggested that performers might employ this option too. A 1952 piece, *Music for Piano I,* allowed the performer to decide durations,

A mobile by the American sculptor Alexander Calder (1898–1976), *Untitled,* 1976, moves with every passing breeze. The random qualities of nature thus constantly change the "spaces" the mobile defines. (Courtesy of the National Gallery of Art, Washington, DC, Gift of the Collectors Committee.)

the pitches already having been drawn on the page wherever imperfections appeared in the paper itself. *Concert for Piano and Orchestra* (1957–58) consists of parts for each instrument written by chance methods. Any number of players select any number of pages from the parts and play them in any order they choose.

Describing another composer's method, Cage said: "Morton Feldman divided pitches into three areas, high, middle, and low, and established a time unit. Writing on graph paper, he simply inscribed numbers of tones to be played at any time within specified periods of time. There are people who say, 'If music's that easy to write, I could do it.' Of course they could, but they don't."

B

Cage's Music

Two works—or is it just one?—by Cage succinctly demonstrate his methods. *Aria* (1958), for soprano, contains vowels, consonants, and words from five languages, written in a kind of free graphic representation of pitch and duration. The score includes a color code to help the performer decide how to realize these elements, but other aspects of performance "may be freely determined by the singer." *Fontana Mix* (1958) is for electronic tape. The two can be performed together— or separately.

One of Cage's interests was the **prepared piano,** a piano in which the strings themselves have been modified in various ways to produce new tone colors. One way is to insert strips of paper or felt, weather stripping, wood, cloth, metal nuts, and bolts. It is also possible to retune the piano to change pitches. What results is an exotic sound, recalling Asian percussion instruments rather than a Western piano. Two of the four movements of his *Amores* (1943) were conceived for it, and it is the medium employed in the piece described below.

This suite of six short pieces for prepared piano was composed in 1943–44. The score contains detailed instructions concerning the materials (rubber, weather stripping, bamboo slits, wood and cloth, bolts, screws) to be inserted into the piano. These materials affect twenty-five of the notes. Although the notation is perfectly conventional, the preparation changes the pitches drastically and shortens their durations.

 CD6

(0:00)
1   m1   Beginning loudly, with abrupt gestures that seem unpredictable, this
              opening section exposes the lowest and highest sounds that will be
   [39]   heard in most of the piece.

(0:42)
2   m31 This dramatic moment is recognizable because only the highest pitch
              is heard in a short burst of sound. Constantly changing ideas then
   [40]   follow.

(1:41)
3   m71 Softer, with a nearly marchlike beat, this portion then recalls the
              gestures heard earlier.
   [41]

(2:07)
4   m88 A return of the marching bit of item 3 leads to a loud, abrupt-
              sounding ending.
   [42]

ELECTRONIC MUSIC 64

PREVIEW   This chapter begins with a brief history of electronic instruments and electronic music, both in Europe and the United States. We then show how taped compositions can interact with live performers.

Electricity, the force that has altered our world so profoundly in this century, has had a major impact on music as well. Electronic devices can produce, modify, record, and reproduce sounds. Not only are new techniques involved, but also the field is linked to radically new ideas about music, so new that some people question whether electronic music is music at all. Perhaps it is significant that the Schwann catalogue of recordings, while listing all "classical" music under the composer's name, segregates electronic music in a separate section indexed by record label.

A

Early Electronic Instruments

Electronic instruments were developed in practical forms by the 1920s. One was the **theremin,** named for its inventor, Leon Theremin, which generates a single tone, the pitch and loudness being controlled by the proximity of the player's hands. Composers of film music discovered its ability to conjure an eerie atmosphere. Another early example, the **electronic organ,** has continued its development, finding a place in many musical situations. However, the motivation for its invention in the 1930s was to imitate the traditional pipe organ.

Composers began to apply electrical means to create music directly in the 1940s, when a new type of experimental music called **musique concrète** arose in Paris. First, composers recorded on tape a wide range of *real,* or "concrete," sounds. Traffic noises, people talking, church bells—whatever—all furnished raw material for the composer. Utilizing the capabilities of a tape recorder to play a tape backwards, to alter its speed, to repeat sections at will, to add periods of silence, and so on, composers could then assemble collages of sounds. Their next step was to create electronic sounds in the studio, aided by various types of sound generators. Often composers mixed the "concrete" sounds with the purely electronic.

Studies for electronic music production appeared throughout Europe, frequented by composers such as the German Karlheinz Stockhausen (born 1928). His *Gesang der Jünglinge* (Song of the Children) quickly became a classic of electronic composition after its premier in 1956. Only thirteen minutes long, its text consists of syllables from the Old Testament account (Daniel 3) of three Hebrew youths' ordeal in the Babylonian fiery furnace. It combines transformations of a boy's voice, mixed with purely electronic sounds. Other composers with interests in electronic music are the Italian Luciano Berio (born 1925) and the Frenchman Pierre Boulez. Boulez, incidentally, is also a distinguished international conductor, formerly of the New York Philharmonic Orchestra. An electronic piece by the Hungarian György Ligeti (born 1923) formed a part of the sound track for the movie "2001: A Space Odyssey" (the Kyrie section from his *Requiem*).

B

Developments in the
United States

In the United States, the RCA Mark II **synthesizer** installed at the Columbia-Princeton Electronic Music Center in the 1950s made headlines for its size and cost. It occupied an entire room; its cost was said to be a half-million dollars. This instrument consists of thousands of individual electronic circuits that produce simple waveforms and then combine, or synthesize, them to create more complex forms. Advances in technology have made faster, more compact, and cheaper synthesizers available for anyone to purchase. They allow a composer to specify all aspects of sound that can be placed on tape. The only limiting factor is that composer's imagination. The American Milton Babbitt (born 1916), a pioneer experimenter in this field, has continued to be an intellectual leader. As a teacher at Princeton University, he has trained many younger colleagues. His *Ensembles for Synthesizer* (1964) is an example of synthesized sounds on tape, organized serially.

One composer of electronic music, the Frenchman Edgard Varèse (1883–1965), who came to the United States in 1915, explained his interest in this field: "Our new medium has brought to composers almost endless possibilities of expression, and opened up for them the whole mysterious world of sound. For instance, I have always felt the need of a kind of continuous flowing curve that instruments could not give me. That is why I used sirens in several of my works. Today such effects are easily obtainable by electronic means."

In 1958 millions of people heard an electronic piece by Varèse: his *Poème électronique,* a short work (about eight minutes long) created in an electronic tape studio, commissioned to be part of a multimedia experience at the Brussels World Fair. The raw material came from a host of natural and electronic sounds, processed so that they are not easily identifiable. People came and went within a building designed by the famed architect Le Corbusier (1887–1965). Varèse's three-track tape was amplified by more than four hundred loudspeakers, arranged to set the sound spinning around the building's interior. While the tape played, various images and colored lights were projected on all the walls. Although the images were not related to the music, one of them, the mushroom-cloud symbol of the

Edgard Varèse.

atomic age, might have seemed appropriate! The music is still available in recordings but the complete experience cannot be repeated, since the building no longer exists.

Many universities have become centers for electronic music. Often the composers affiliated with these centers have specialized in this field after earlier experimentation with a variety of sound sources. Houston native Pauline Oliveros (born 1932), whose works have included such unusual sound sources as a mynah bird and a cash register, is one example. A composer in residence at several universities, she has been associated with centers for electronic sound in San Francisco and San Diego. Beverly Grigsby (born 1928) is Professor of Music at California State University at Northridge, where she specializes in computer music and directs the Computer Music Studio.

Beverly Grigsby, the composer of the electronic piece we study, is almost surrounded by the equipment in her studio. She is working on the keyboard of a Computer Music Instrument, the Fairlight 2X.

C

How Electronic Music Affects Live Performers

Besides their interest in new sounds, composers have practical motives for wanting synthesizers. Unrestricted by the limitations of a live performer, synthesizers allow them to organize a piece completely, with a serial plan for each element of music should they wish it. By composing for tape, a composer can bypass all the problems of writing a score, rehearsing the music, performing it, and arranging for an audience to hear it. Transferring the composer's tape to commercial recordings establishes a direct link to the listener.

Many composers of electronic music have continued to present their efforts to audiences in concert situations even though the traditional format suits the music badly. (How does the audience know the piece is over? And who, or what, should be applauded?) New listening conditions are called for, which take advantage of stereophonic dimensions and the audience's desire to move about, to come and go. The need for listeners to have someone on stage to look at may have motivated some composers to combine a live performer on a traditional instrument with a tape accompaniment.

Since 1970, most innovations in electronic music have centered on "live" performance, that is, in concert situations, where the manipulation of sound transpires in full view of the audience. For example, *After the Butterfly,* by the California-based Morton Subotnick (born 1933), combines live instrumental performance with modifications of those sounds by a synthesizer.

Just as computers have affected so many other areas of our lives, they have profoundly influenced music. Anything the composer can conceive can be transformed into sound—instantly. Even more amazing is the development of equipment that makes it possible to transform bodily expression into electronic music. One European performer uses a pair of metal gloves that are connected to computers by means of switches. Simply moving his hands creates sounds. Although years of research and technical work go into the programming of the computers, the performer can spontaneously make music at any moment.

In spite of all the twentieth-century wizardry that is now available, the bulk of electronic music that the public encounters is not particularly new, as music. Synthesizers became commercial successes not by creating something truly new, but by building upon the old. In 1968, for instance, Walter (now Wendy) Carlos created "Switched-on Bach," a collection of synthesizer-produced versions of Bach masterpieces. It became the largest-selling "classical" LP album ever made by any one artist. And a thriving market continues for more electronic realizations of "classical" music. By now, synthesizers are able to mimic the sounds of traditional instruments so closely that many people cannot hear the difference. Examples are the background music for motion pictures, as in "Chariots of Fire," and for television features. Indeed, many performing musicians view the synthesizer as a threat to their future. It will be small comfort for these musicians, should their fears be realized, that history offers all-too-many examples of workers displaced by new technology!

Shakti II, first performed in 1987, was commissioned by the soprano Deborah Kavasch, whose voice is heard on the tape. Not only does she sing the text, employing modern extended vocal techniques that call for extraordinarily low and high pitches, but it is her recorded voice that furnishes the raw material for processing through the computer. Those original vocal sounds are then transformed into instrumental and choral voices. Other accompanying sounds, of bells, harp, and sitar, are computer-generated from sampled instrumental sounds.

Grigsby: *Shakti II* (7:15) ⓐ

Compellingly shaped by Grigsby's vision, *Shakti II* exhibits an exciting blend of technology with live performance, of Western and non-Western elements, of structure and emotion. At its Los Angeles premier, the music was part of a multimedia experience, coordinated by detailed instructions in the score concerning vocal production, gestures, and lighting. Samples of each appear in the guide, in brackets. Other visual elements came from slides, projected details from the paintings of the Dutch artist Hieronymus Bosch (c.1450–1516). His imaginative works are crammed with symbolism that art historians are still trying to explain. Any viewer, however, can see that his nightmare visions offer scant hope for humankind.

Half a world away, in the Hindu religious tome *Bhagavad-Gita,* Shakti represents Divine Light and the female principle, the giver of life. In the three sections of the text, written by the composer and to be performed without pauses, moods change from the initial demon-possessed cry of anguish through the prayer to Shakti, to the acceptance of Light at the end. Notice how text repetition enhances expressivity.

 CD6

(0:00)

1

43

I. Demonic Forces
Demons . . . Surround me,
Ensnare me, Eat at my soul,
Devour my being.

Demons . . . With bestial eyes
    burning,
Evil with burning intent.
Lightless, flameless burning,
Searing to destroy.

Insidious, heinous grin,
Screaming mouth roaring,
Flaying claw and fang.
Tear at my soul, Devour my
    being,
My golden being.

The soprano's opening motive, a descending half-step, is an old one in music, associated with grief.

The accompanying vocal sounds are full of glissandos.

The soprano's very low pitches here represent an unusual extension of a normal singing range.
[Use light under face for most ghastly effect.]

(2:35)

2

44

II. The Call to Shakti
Oh Shining One . . .
Summon me from the darkness
Into Your Light, Your Divine
    Light.
Oh Shakti, Shakti . . .
Guide me to the fount of
    wisdom
And eternal blessedness.
From this doom Lift me.

The instrumental background in this section features many echo effects and some ostinatos. [One of the "Summon me" repetitions is to be shouted in terror of losing your soul.]

(6:15)

3

45

III. Rapture of the Divine
    Light
Lift me, Lift me,
Shakti, lift me To the Light.

[Hands in Hindu prayer.]
Crisp, metrical rhythms and sitar tones give the effect of Indian music. The section ends on a major chord, with a clear cadence.

CHAPTER

MINIMALISM 65

PREVIEW   Minimalism, dating from the 1960s, is the most recent "ism" for our study. Compared to the complexities of some music, minimal music seems at first hearing to consist of endless, identical repetitions. In fact, however, minimalist composers do see to it that changes take place, as in the works by the three composers whom we mention.

Minimalism, a style so-called because of its dependence upon repetition of a bare minimum of ideas, appeared in the 1960s and continues to be quite influential in some musical circles, especially in the United States. Not always appreciated, the label of "minimalism" seems to have stuck. For example, Terry Riley, a composer whom we mention a bit later, observed in a 1990 interview that "minimalism is not an apt description of the work I've done, but it's probably going to last for a long time." Some music critics dismiss minimalism as simplistic: others hail it as refreshing, and attractive to young audiences.

Seemingly endless repetition of a motive or a group of motives is the key feature of minimalism, mesmerizing some listeners into a trancelike state. Of course, we did not have to wait until the twentieth century to discover the power of repetition in music. We met it in the twenty-eight repetitions of the same bass line in Pachelbel's *Canon.* Brahms, in the finale of his *Symphony No. 4,* created at least thirty variations on a short melodic idea. And the ostinato is a device Stravinsky cherished, as we saw in the *Rite.*

Some writers relate minimalism to non-Western music, particularly that of Africa and India. It is no accident that the composers mentioned here, all Americans, have been deeply influenced by study of the philosophies and musics of these areas. The hypnotic quality of such music encourages the listeners to shift attention away from themselves and seek instead a total immersion in the music, a process akin to Eastern mysticism. Indian music is built upon a constant drone and continuous repetitions of predetermined rhythmic patterns, features that are echoed in minimalism. Unlike many twentieth-century composers, the minimalists we mention are not connected with the "academic establishment." Moreover, they have returned to tonality, diatonic melody, and diatonic harmony.

"Minimal" sculpture of the 1960s and 1970s employed a minimum of materials, asking the viewer to concentrate on ways they were arranged. For example, in *Untitled (Gameboard and Components #2)* by Judy Chicago (born 1941), pegs of differing lengths rest on a square surface, separated by varying distances. (Courtesy of San Francisco Museum of Modern Art, Gift of Diana Zlotnick.)

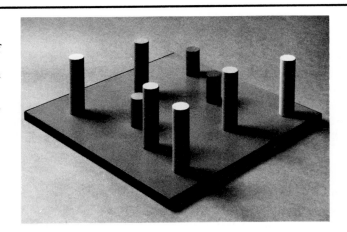

"Op art" is a label given to works such as *Current,* by Bridget Riley (born 1931), 1964. At first glance, it seems to consist solely of lines with a "minimal" amount of change. But after a few moments of concentration, a viewer's eyes begin to swim as if the lines really are moving. (Synthetic polymer paint on composition board, 58 3/8″ × 58 7/8″. Collection, The Museum of Modern Art, New York. Philip Johnson Fund.)

The earliest of our minimalist composers is Terry Riley (born 1935), famous for his *In C* (1965), a work for any number and any type of melodic instruments. Fifty-three fragments of music appear on the one-page score, which instructs the musicians to perform the fragments in their choice of tempo with as many repetitions as desired. In so doing, Riley pays homage to John Cage's chance technique. After composing this work, for a number of years Riley turned to improvisation and the study of North Indian music. His return to composition has produced works for string quartet.

Terry Riley

Another minimalist is Steve Reich (born 1936), whose *Come Out* (1966) was inspired by events of the time. An example of electronic techniques, it is a tape collage built upon a phrase spoken by a young man who had been arrested for his part in the Harlem riots of the early 1960s. Explaining that he had to prove that he was injured before he could receive medical treatment, he said: "I had to, like, open the bruise up and let some of the bruise blood to come out to show them." This recorded phrase begins the selection; then the words "come out to show them" are manipulated in literally thousands of repetitions. A gradually increasing reverberation between two tape channels turns into a multiplying kind of canon during the course of the thirteen-minute composition.

Steve Reich

Reich's "live" music is written for small ensembles in which he plays the keyboards. His *Vermont Counterpoint* (1982), a delightful whirlwind of a piece for three alto flutes, three flutes, and three piccolos, can be performed by one solo flute against a prerecorded tape of nine ensemble parts. This music can also be put on tape by one performer—generously assisted by editing and mixing technology—or live performers can play the whole thing.

Philip Glass (born 1937) builds on a limited number of chords that are repeated with minute changes. Since 1975 most of his work has been for the theater, as in his *Einstein on the Beach* (1976). Hailed by some as the opera of the future after performances in several European cities as well as in New York, it made him famous. According to some listeners, the sheer length of such music is responsible for much of its effect.

Philip Glass

Glass is amply represented in recordings; in fact, CBS signed a contract to record anything he writes. As a convenient way of approaching his work, sample the 1983 film "Koyaanisqatsi," for which Glass composed the score. The title comes from a Hopi Indian word meaning "life out of balance," a theme that is communicated not by narration but by time-lapse photography vividly showing our fragmented, frantic, industrialized life. Abrupt changes of scene in the film are accompanied by equally abrupt changes in musical content. As a follow-up to this

Philip Glass.

film, in 1988 the same producer brought out the film "Powaqqatsi" (sorcerer life), also with a score by Glass. The focus here is on a contrast between land-based cultures of the world and the industrialized societies.

Glass: *Knee Play 1,* from *Einstein on the Beach* (3:52) ⑧⑤

An opera, *Einstein on the Beach* is the fruit of Glass's collaboration with dramatist Robert Wilson. The title refers to Albert Einstein (1879–1955), famous for his theory of relativity, and an amateur violinist. Two electric organs, three winds, a solo soprano, a small choir, and a violinist costumed as Einstein supply the musical forces needed. A performance lasts almost five hours, with no intermissions. The audience, however, is encouraged to take quiet breaks as needed, a practice Glass himself admitted to having followed in the more than fifty performances of his work. What "story" there is must be supplied by the imaginations of those who experience the music. Scenery is changed during the opera's "knee plays," which take place in front of the curtain and which connect the acts of the opera much as a knee connects the upper and lower leg.

♩♩ CD6

(0:00)

1

85

Knee Play 1 begins with the ostinato bass line that underlies the entire piece, a three-note descending pattern of A,G,C, played by the organ, at first very slowly. It picks up steam as the chorus enters, the men singing that same ostinato bass line, the women singing upward-moving pitches of C,D,E. For a text, they count the rhythm, 1–2–3–4, etc., sometimes getting as far as eight, with a skipped count now and then to avoid predictability.

(1:25)

2

As the sounds of item 1 continue, a spoken text begins with the words "Will it get some wind for the sailboat," a text by a handicapped youth with a unique world view. The text, narrated by a female voice, is at first so soft it can hardly be heard and never becomes fully intelligible.

(2:07)

3

Continuing with the same pitches identified in item 1, part of the chorus changes its sung text to the melodic solfège syllables: *la, sol, do,* for the men, and *do, re, mi,* for the women, thus describing the melodies they sing. The counting continues until an abrupt ending.

Glossary

Musical Terms

Note: A minimal definition appears here for terms or topics. Most of them are more fully discussed and defined at the first or second place they appear in the text in a specific context. Some terms are listed even though they do not appear in the text, because they might be encountered in other musical references, such as program notes. Pages with illustrations are indicated by *italic* numbers.

A, 440 A, a letter name in pitch notation; a standardized tuning pitch, 15, 28, 86, 204, 264

A 415, pitch standard adopted by some early music performers, 138

A, a, label for first phrase or section in a ternary form, 59

A', a', indicates a varied restatement of a phrase or section, 59

AAB, (see Bar form)

AABB form, (see Binary form)

ABA form, or AABA, (see Ternary form)

Absolute music, "pure" music free of overt connections to nonmusical ideas, opposite of program music, 11

A cappella, choral music without instrumental accompaniment, 112, 123, 129

Accelerando, becoming faster, to speed up, 37

Accent, Accent mark, stress on one pitch or chord; the notational sign for that stress

Accidentals, symbols in notation to raise or lower pitch by a half-step; sharps, flats, naturals, 18, 113, 121

Accompanied recitative, (see Recitative)

Accordion, hand-held wind instrument with keyboards

Acoustic, not electric, as in an acoustic guitar

Acoustics, the science of sound; how the space characteristics of a place in which music is performed affect the reverberation of sound, 14

Adagio, slow tempo, "at ease," but not as slow as grave, largo, or lento, 36

Aeolian mode, older term for tonality we now call A minor, 132

Aesthetics, branch of philosophy that studies music and the other arts, 13

Affektenlehre, (German term, see Doctrine of affections)

Agnus Dei, "Lamb of God," fifth movement of Mass Ordinary, 96, 97

Air, English term for a melody; see also Aria

Alberti bass, a style of broken-chord accompaniment with tones generally played in order of lowest, highest, middle, highest, 205

Album Leaf, (see Character piece)

Aleatoric, (see Chance)

Alla breve, duple meter with half-note getting the beat

Allegretto, slightly less fast than Allegro, 36

Allegro, fast tempo, literally, cheerful, 36

Allegro giocoso, fast and humorous

Allemande, one of four standard dances in Baroque dance suite, German in origin, 184

Alto, low female voice, 20

"Amen" cadence, ending progression of IV chord, then I chord, 50, 125, 178, 192

Analysis of phrases, (see Musical forms)

Andante, literally, a "walking" or "going" tempo, often said to be moderately slow, 36

Andantino, a "little andante," a little faster, a little more active than andante, 36

Answer, in a fugal exposition, a term often used to identify the second appearance of fugue subject

Antique cymbals, tiny cymbals, with definite pitch, 400

Appassionato, impassioned

Appreciating music, learning to listen attentively to music, as opposed to merely hearing it, 1

Arch form, a mirrored form, such as ABCBA, 416

Aria, solo song in opera, cantata, and oratorio; metrical and fully accompanied, 148, 174

Arioso, a "small aria," combines some features of aria and recitative, 173

Arpeggio, a broken chord, pitches occurring one at a time, 71

Arrangement, (see Transcription)

Art song, art songs, (see Lied, Lieder)

Assai, much, 36

A tempo, resume original tempo after deviating from it, 37

Atonal, no key center; no sense of *do,* opposite of tonal, 292, 421

Augmentation, statement of a theme with its notes made uniformly longer, 190

Aulos, wind instrument with two pipes, played by Dionysus in Greek myths, 72, *74*

Austrian hymn, hymn tune name for Haydn's "Emperor" theme, 220

Authenticity in performance, ideal of recreating performance styles that prevailed when the composition being performed was new, 67, 171, 204, 208, 211, 284

Avant-garde, the most extreme of new styles

B, b, label for second, or middle, phrase or section in a ternary form, 59

B-A-C-H motive, J. S. Bach's name in musical notes: B-flat, A, C, B-natural, 183

Bach Revival, Renewed interest in Romantic period in music of J. S. Bach, 182, 297

Bagpipes, wind instrument with drone sounding a single pitch while melody is played, *46,* 218

Ballad, song in several stanzas, telling a story

Ballade, possible title for a piano piece, see also Character piece

Ballad opera, (see Opera)

Ballate, Italian polyphonic songs, 101

Ballet, term given to the dance element in opera, 153

Ballet, term given to the theatrical dance with especially composed music; also, a possible type of program music, 271

Ballett, term sometimes given to madrigals with fa-la-la refrain

Bar, synonym for Measure

Bar form, archaic German musical and poetic form, AAB, 194, 331

Baritone, mid-range male voice, 20

Baritone horn, mid-range brass instrument used in bands

Bar line, vertical line dividing music into measures, 31

Baroque trumpet, natural brass instrument, for playing in high range

Bars, (see Measure)

Baryton, string instrument, now obsolete, played by Haydn's patron, 214

Basic set, series of twelve pitches that governs an entire twelve-tone piece, 422

Bass, or double bass, or bass viol, the lowest member of the string family, *22, 139*

Bass, lowest male voice, 20

Bass clarinet, clarinet in bass range, an octave lower than standard clarinet, *23*

Bass clef, clef used for left-hand half of piano keyboard, 17

Bass drum, large drum with unchangeable pitch, 25, 204, 266

Basso continuo, Baroque technique allowing keyboard players to improvise chord-based accompaniments while reading from the bass line, 145, 153, 186

Bassoon, low-range, double-reed woodwind instrument, *23, 141*

Basso ostinato, one name given to Baroque Continuous variations

Baton, short stick used by conductors to beat time, 266

Beam, line connecting stems of notes as a substitute for Flags, 28

Beat, a basic pulse that forms a background to everything else in music, 31

Bebop, style of jazz, associated with Charlie Parker, 457

Bel Canto, literally, "beautiful singing," often applied to a lyrical, rather than declamatory, style of singing

Benedictus, "Blessed is he," part of the Sanctus, the fourth movement of Mass Ordinary, 96, 121

Bent notes, (see Blue notes)

Big bands, in jazz of the 1930s and later, 456

Binary form, AABB, 144, 184, 211

Bitonality, (see Polytonality),

Black music in United States, (see Jazz)

Block chords, tones of chord played simultaneously, as opposed to Broken chords

Blue notes, scale tones, usually third and seventh, that are slightly flatted in jazz, 451, 454

Blues, type of black American folk song with stanzas in AAB form, 450

Bourrée, in duple meter; optional dance in Baroque dance suite, French in origin, *185*

Bow, slightly arched stick with horse-hairs, used in playing some string instruments, 22

Boys' voices, boy singers instead of female singers on high parts

Brackets [ ], punctuation to enclose words of a song that show changes from the original poetry, *276*

Brass family, wind instruments made of brass, 23, *24*

Break, brief solo between phrases in jazz, 455

Breeches role, (see Trousers role)

Bridge, (in Sonata-form, see Transition)

Bridge, in string instruments, a wooden device over which the strings pass

Broken chords, chord tones occurring one at a time, 47, 205

Buchla synthesizer, (see Electronic instruments)

Bugle, high brass instrument limited to those tones that the player's lips can produce

BWV numbers, system for identifying works by J. S. Bach, 65, 183

C, another designation for 4/4 meter or Common time, 32

Cadence, melodic and/or harmonic movement that creates a sense of ending, 58

Cadenza, extended solo passage in a concerto, usually near end of movement, 242

Call and response, alternation between a solo singer and a group of singers, 451

Camera, (see Chamber music)

Canon, a more academic term for the imitative polyphony in a round, 54

Cantabile, singable, songlike

Cantata, short, composite work for voices and instruments in several movements, usually to a sacred text for use in a church service, 193

Cantor, director of church music, 180

Cantus firmus (C. F.), Latin term for preexisting melody used as a basis for a new composition, 87, 98, 99

Canzona, Renaissance instrumental piece

Cappella, (see A cappella)

Caret symbol ˆ, used to indicate when a pitch is located in a higher octave, 39

Cassation, Classic period entertainment music, 200

Castanets, hand-held, small percussion instrument widely used in Spanish dance, 266

Castrati, castrated male singers, widely employed in Baroque era, 153

C clefs, clefs that identify middle C on the five-line staff

Celesta, piano-shaped percussion instrument with hammers to strike metal bars, 266

Cello, 'Cello, mid-range string instrument, held between player's legs, *22, 139*

C.F. (see Cantus firmus)

Chaconne, (see Continuous variations)

Chamber music, small instrumental ensembles, with one player on a part, 202

Chamber orchestra, orchestra with reduced number of players, 203

Chance, random qualities that arise from the use of chance elements in composing or performing, 466

Changing meters, changes of meter within a composition

Chant, (see Gregorian chant)

Character piece, short Romantic piano piece; title gives programmatic implications, 290

Chimes, set of tuned bells, 266

Choir, singing group; group of similar instruments, 21

Choral, (See Choir)

Chorale, originally a German hymn-tune, 185

Chorale prelude, organ piece based on a chorale melody, 185

Chord, three or more simultaneous tones, 47

Chordal style, (see Homophony)

Chord progression, (see Harmonic Progression)

Chordwise motion, (see Disjunct)

Chorus, (see Choir)

Chorus, group of unidentified characters in opera, 154

Chorus, in a strophic song, the text and music repeated in a refrain

Chorus, in jazz or blues, each new verse, variation on the original theme, 451

Chromatic chords, chords built on pitches of chromatic scale, 205

Chromatic scale, scale using all twelve pitches in an octave, 40, 268

Church modes, early, white-key scales, 82

Clarinet, mid-range, single-reed woodwind instrument, *23, 204*

"Classical music," familiar use of the term to mean the opposite of "popular music," 198

Clavichord, very soft-sounding Baroque keyboard instrument, 143

Clavier, German term for keyboard or keyboard instruments, 141

Clef, in music notation, a special symbol placed at the beginning of every staff that identifies the specific pitch range covered by that staff, 17

Closely related keys, keys having all but one of their scale pitches in common, 212, 268

Closing theme, last subsection in exposition and recapitulation of sonata-form, 208

Cluster, (see Tone Cluster)

Coda, a possible additional feature in sonata-form and in other forms as well; a concluding section that reinforces the sense of ending, 209

Codetta, (see Closing theme)

Coloratura soprano, virtuoso singer with very high range, 152, 240, 338

Comic opera, (see Opera)

Common time, a name for 4/4 time signature, 32

Complete multimovement work, patterns of tempos, forms, and qualities found in three- and four-movement works with one movement in sonata-form, 210

Con, Italian term for "with"

Con brio, with spirit

Concertato principle, contrasts and combinations of various colors and groupings within a Baroque composition, 146, 148

Concertino, small group of soloists in a concerto grosso, 186

Concertmaster, principal first violinist in orchestra, 204

Concerto, Solo concerto, work for solo instrument and orchestra, 164, 241, 299

Concerto grosso, Baroque multimovement work for a small group of soloists accompanied by a somewhat larger orchestra, usually of strings, 164, 186

Concert overture, one-movement, independent, programmatic orchestral piece, 270

Conductor, leader of musical group, 266

Con espressione, with expression, 36

Con fuoco, with fire, 269

Conjunct, moving along the pitches of a scale, 44

Consonance, restful, stable quality, sense of blending, sense of relaxation of tension, 49

Consort, Renaissance group of similar instruments in varying sizes, 112

Continuo, (see Basso continuo)

Continuous variations, variations on repeated chord progression or repeated melody, 159, 160, 370

Contrabassoon, larger version of bassoon, plays one octave lower, 23, 204, 265

Contralto, (see Alto)

Contrapuntal texture, (see Polyphony)

Contrary motion, musical lines moving in opposite directions, one voice rises, the other falls, 89

Cor, French term for horn, hence French horn

Cornet, brass instrument, similar to trumpet, found in bands, 25, 455

Counterpoint, technique of fitting melodies together in polyphonic writing, 115

Countersubject, distinctive continuation of subject in a fugue, accompanies entries of fugue subject, 190

Countertenor, high, male voice, in alto range, 112

Couple, to link manuals of an organ or harpsichord so that both play at once, 142

Couplet, contrasting sections of a rondo which are placed between refrain statements, 243

Courante, one of four standard dances in Baroque dance suite, of French origin, 184

Credo, "I Believe," third movement in Mass Ordinary, 94

Crescendo, gradually getting louder, 19, 201, 264

Crumhorn, Renaissance double-reed woodwind instrument, 112, *114*

Cyclic form, themes from earlier movements return in later movements of large works, 269, 307

Cyclic Mass, musically unified Mass Ordinary; all movements based on the same C.F., 98

Cymbals, plate-shaped metal percussion instrument of indefinite pitch, 204, 266

Cymbals, antique, (see Antique cymbals)

D. numbers, numbers given for Schubert's music by Otto Erich Deutsch, 65, 274

Da capo, D.C., sign indicating a return to the beginning, 153

Da capo aria, aria in ABA form, especially in the Baroque, 153

Dance suite, (see Suite, Baroque dance)

Decibel, Db, scientific measuring unit for differences in dynamic levels based on the minimum difference in intensity that can be heard, 18

Decrescendo, gradually getting softer, 19, 201, 264

Descriptive music, (see Program music)

Deutsch, (see D. numbers)

Development, general process of modifying any musical element in restatements and extensions

Development section, second, middle section in sonata-form, 208

Diatonic, unaltered, seven-note scale, as in *do-re-mi-fa-sol-la-ti-dò*, 40

Dies irae, "Day of Wrath," Gregorian chant sung in Requiem Mass, 86, 97, 307, 314

Diminuendo, gradually getting softer, 19

Diminution, notes of a theme made uniformly shorter, 190

Discord, sometimes used to mean Dissonance

Disjunct, moving to nonadjacent notes of a scale, 44

Dissonance, sense of a lack of blending, sense of tension, of activity, of needing to resolve, 49

Divertimento, Classic period multimovement entertainment music, 200, 228

Do, first or beginning note of a scale, 39

Doctrine of the Affections, Baroque theory that a musical selection expresses one particular emotion or "affect," 145

Dodecaphonic, (see Twelve-tone music)

Dominant, fifth note of the scale, *sol*, 48

Dominant chord, chord built on fifth note of scale, 48

Dominant preparation, stressing the dominant at end of development section as a preparation for recapitulation, 209

Do-re-mi-fa-sol-la-ti, Italian syllables for scale tones

Dorian mode, a modal, white-key scale, as in: D, E, F, G, A, B, C, D, 82, 415

Dot, symbol in musical notation, makes a note 50 percent longer, 28

Dotted rhythms, unevenly spaced notes in a rhythm pattern with every other note dotted, effect of long-short-long-short, etc., 34, 173, 195

Double bass, (see Bass)

Double-reed, two thin pieces of cane, which players place between their lips in playing oboes and bassoons, *23*, 141

Double stops, playing two strings at once

Downbeat, the first beat of a measure, usually accented

Dramatic, singer with a "heavy" voice quality

Drone, long, sustained note, as on a bagpipe, 46

Duple meter, grouping of ONE two ONE two, 31

Dur, German term meaning Major

Duration, length of time a note or period of silence lasts, 28

Dynamics, loudness or softness in music, also referred to as volume, 18

Early music performance, (see Authenticity)

E-flat clarinet, high version of clarinet, 308

Electronic music, music needing electronic equipment, 469

Electronic organ, twentieth-century imitation of pipe organ, 142, 469

Embellishments, (see Ornamentation)

English horn, alto-range, double-reed woodwind instrument, a fifth lower than oboe, *23*, 265, *266*, 349

Ensemble, characters in opera singing together as a duet, trio, quartet, etc., 154

Ensemble finale, concluding sections of acts in traditional opera, with soloists and chorus singing together, 154

Entry, appearance of subject in fugues, 190

Episodes, passages in a fugue without an entry of complete subject, 190

Equal temperament, tuning system with equally spaced half-steps, 139, 201

Espressione, con, with expression

Ethnic music, (see Non-Western music)

Ethnomusicology, academic discipline that studies non-Western and folk music in its cultural context, 413

-etto, an Italian diminuative suffix taking away from the value of a word, 36

Etude, literally, a "study piece," designed to teach some aspect of playing technique, 285, 287

Evenly spaced rhythm patterns, patterns involving notes of equal durations, 34

Exoticism, music reflecting a national group used by a nonnative composer, 269

Exposition, first main section of sonata-form

Expression, those elements of performance that vary in subtle ways with the performer, 65

Expressionism, Austro-German artistic movement of early 1900s, *421,* plate 45

Expression marks, signs and marks in the musical score that suggest details of expression to the performer, 65

Extramusical reference, (see Program music)

Fa, fourth note of the scale, 39

Fake book, collection of standard songs with harmonies implied in chord letter names, used in jazz and popular music

Fa-la-la refrain, in English madrigals and in "Deck the Halls" 59, 128, 144

Falsetto, technique of male singing to produce female range

Families of instruments, classification systems for instruments, 21

Fantasia, musical work in free, perhaps improvisatory, style

Fantasy, (see Character piece)

Fate motive, name given to a motive in opera *Carmen* and in Tchaikovsky's *Symphony No. 4,* 7, 43, 326, 358

F clef, (see Bass clef)

Fermata, symbol placed over a specific note or chord indicating a possible prolonged duration, 194

Fiddle, medieval string instrument; also a colloquial term for the violin, 104

Fifth, interval covering five letters, as in C to G

Figured bass, (see Basso continuo)

Finale, frequent term for last movement of large works

Five chord, (V chord, see Dominant chord)

"Five, The," group of nineteenth-century Russian nationalist composers, 350, 356

Flags, in musical notation, curving lines attached to note stem, 28

Flat, sign in musical notation indicating a pitch lowered by a half-step, 18

Flute, high woodwind instrument, without a reed, *23,* 141, 204, 265

Flute quartet, violin, viola, cello, flute, 203

Flutter-tonguing, modern effect in wind instrument playing, 391

Folk music, music of the people, communicated by oral tradition, 412

Form in music, designs and patterns created by repetition and contrast, 58

Forte, Fortissimo, loud, very loud, dynamic levels, 18

Fortepiano, older name for early piano, 201, *202,* 242, 256

Four chord, (IV chord, see Subdominant chord)

Fourth, interval covering four letters, as in C to F, 47

Free jazz, radical jazz style of the late 1950s, 458

French horn, mid-range brass instrument, *24,* 141, 265

French overture, Baroque orchestral form, beginning in slow tempo with dotted rhythms, followed by fast, polyphonic section, 173

Frequency, acoustical term for rate of vibrations

Fugato, fuguelike passage in larger work

Fugue, complex composition using imitative polyphony, based on a "subject," 190

Fundamental tone, lowest pitch of a vibrating material, produced as it vibrates as a whole, 20

Fuoco, con, with "fire"

Fusion, combination of jazz and rock elements

Gamba, (see Viola da gamba)

Gamelan, Indonesian "orchestra" of metal xylophonelike instruments and gongs, 394, *396*

Gavotte, optional dance in Baroque dance suite

G clef, (see Treble clef)

Gigue (or jig), one of four standard dances in Baroque suite; in fast tempo, of English origin, 184

Giocoso, humorous, 36, 269

Gioioso, joyful

Giusto, precise, exact

Glissando, continuous sliding from one pitch to the next, 390, 417

Glockenspiel, tuned percussion instrument with little metal bars, 266

Gloria, "Glory to God," second movement in Mass Ordinary, 96

Gong, large, circular, frame-hung metal percussion instrument

Grace note, notes printed in very small type; rhythmic values not counted

Grand opera, (see Opera)

Grand staff, treble and bass clefs linked together as in keyboard music, 17

Grave, slowest of the slow tempos, serious, 36

Gregorian chant, official chant of the Roman Catholic church, 53, 80

Ground bass, one name given to Baroque Continuous variations, 159

Guitar, plucked string instrument with six strings and flat back, 4, 23, 106

H, German letter indicating the pitch B-natural, 183

Half-step, interval between any two immediately adjacent piano keys, as in E-F, 16, 40

Harmonic progression, series of chords, 50

Harmonics, partial tones produced by segments of a vibrating material, 20

Harmony, in general, relationships based on simultaneous sounds, 46

Harp, large plucked string instrument, 23, 266

Harpsichord, keyboard instrument with mechanism to pluck its strings, Plate 21, 142, 186, 204

Hertz, Hz, measure of frequency, number of vibrations per second, 15

Home key, (see Tonic)

Homophony, first type: all voices moving in same rhythm, singing same syllable, 55

Homophony, second type: melody with contrasting type of accompaniment, 56

Homorhythm, (see Homophony, first type)

Horn (see French horn)

Hurdy-gurdy, a folk instrument, *413*

Hymn tune, melodies specifically associated with hymn singing in churches, 43

Hz, (see Hertz)

I chord, ("One" chord, see Tonic chord)

Idée fixe, Berlioz's term for a returning theme, 306

Imitation, Imitative polyphony, statement of melody by two or more parts in succession as in a simple round, 54

Impressionism, movement in French artistic fields in the late 1800s, 396

Impromptu, (see Character piece),

Improvisation, the performer creating music as it is being performed, 145

Incidental music, music for possible inclusion in performance of a drama, 270

Indeterminant, (see Chance)

-ino, an Italian diminutive suffix taking away from the value of a word, 36

Instrumental categories, (see Families of instruments)

Instrumentation, (see Orchestration)

Intensity, quantity of sound energy employed that determines volume

Interval, distance from one pitch to another, measured by counting all the letter names involved from bottom to top, 16, 46

Introduction, possible additional passage, customarily in a slow tempo, that may precede the exposition of a sonata-form movement; found in other forms as well, 209

Inversion, reversal of melodic direction: upward becomes downward, 190, 222

Ionian mode, present-day C major key, 121

Irregular meter, (see Mixed meter)

"isms," labels for (usually) twentieth-century artistic movements, 385

-issimo, superlative Italian suffix, intensifying the value of a word, 19, 36

IV chord, ("Four" chord, see Subdominant chord)

Jazz, Twentieth-century musical style created by black Americans, 448

Jig, English equivalent of Gigue

K., KV. numbers, chronological numbers given to Mozart's works by Ludwig von Koechel, *64,* 65, 227

Kapellmeister, music director for Baroque musical establishment, 137, 180

Kettledrums, (see Timpani)

Key, sense that one particular pitch is *do,* the keynote, the tonal center, 41

Key, the white or black parts of the keyboard action that are pressed by the player's fingers, 42

Keyboard instruments, organ, harpsichord, piano, 25

Keynote, starting and ending pitch of scale: *do,* 41

Key signature, necessary sharps or flats marked at the beginning of each staff, showing the key, 42

Klavier, (see Clavier)

Koto, Japanese plucked string instrument, 23

Krummhorn, (see Crumhorn)

Kyrie, "Lord, have mercy," first movement of the Mass Ordinary, 93, 99, 117

La, sixth note of the scale, 39

Ländler, German waltz

Larghetto, slow tempo, not quite as slow as Largo, 36

Largo, broad, slow tempo, 36

Lead-in, a passage in a concerto that leads into a return of the refrain, 244

Leading motive, (see Leitmotif)

Lead sheet, in popular music, melody-line score with letter name chord symbols

Leaping motion, (see disjunct)

Ledger (sometimes spelled leger) lines, short segments of lines added below or above a staff to show very high or very low notes, 16

Legato, smooth, unbroken connection of notes with no obvious separations, 29, 143

Leitmotif, term for recurring motives in Wagner's operas, 235

Lento, slow tempo, a bit faster than Largo, 36

Letter names, in popular music, a system of using letters instead of Roman numerals to identify chords, 51, 370

Libretto, text of an opera, 150

Lied, (plural Lieder), in Germany, any song; the Romantic period art song, 273

Links, Romantic tendency to write linking passages between movements, 269, 302

Listening, as opposed to merely hearing, 1

Liturgy, organized system of items in worship services, 79

Live music versus recordings, advantages of live performances, 61

Loudness, another term for volume, dynamics, intensity

"Low key," familiar but nonmusical, use of "key," 42

Lute, Medieval and Renaissance plucked-string instrument, *106,* 112

Lutheran chorale, (see Chorale)

Lyre, small, harplike instrument played by Apollo in Greek myths, *72*

Lyric, vocalist with a "light" quality

Lyric, Lyricism, marked melodious, songlike quality

M, in listening guides, "m" and a number indicates that measure in a score, 11

Madrigal, Renaissance secular vocal music, prominent in Italy and England, 126

Major, Major scale, scale with half-steps between *mi-fa* and *ti-dô*, 40

Major key assumption, a work is in a major key unless a minor key is stated in its title, 42

Major/minor tonality, a specific sense of "tonality;" in Baroque period, the tonal system that replaced modality, 144

Manuals, harpsichord and organ keyboards for the hands, 142

Marimba, percussion instrument similar to xylophone, with resonators

Mass, chief service of the Roman Catholic church, 91

Mass, Requiem, (see Requiem Mass)

Mass Ordinary, Mass Proper, (see Ordinary and Proper of the Mass)

Mazurka, Polish dance in triple meter with strong accent on beat 2, 284

Measure, unit of musical time with specified number of beats, 31

Measure numbers, (see M)

Media, (see Performing media)

Medieval, (see Middle Ages)

Melisma, Melismatic, a single sung syllable stretched out over as many as twenty different notes, 80, 175

Melismatic organum, organum employing much melisma in the added lines, with notes of the C.F. stretched out in dronelike tones, 89

Melodic motion, contour, line, or curve of melody, 44

Melody, a series of individual notes that can be perceived as an entity, 39

Meno, less

Menuetto, (see Minuet)

Messe, French word for Mass, 91

Mesto, sad, mournful, 269

Meter, regular, repeated pattern of stressed and unstressed beats, 31

Metronome, mechanical device to indicate a desired tempo, 34, *35,* Plate 5

Mezzo, (see Mezzo-soprano)

Mezzo forte, mezzo piano, medium loud, medium soft, 19

Mezzo-soprano, midrange female voice part, 20

Mi, third note of the scale, 39

Microtones, intervals smaller than half-steps, 390

Middle C, the C closest to the middle of the piano keyboard

Minimalism, dependence upon a bare minimum of musical ideas, 65

Minnesingers, German equivalents of French Troubadours, 100

Minor, Minor scale, at a minimum: scale in which the third tone is lowered by a half-step, compared to major, 40

Minor mode, early name for minor scale, 82

Minuet, dance-related, in triple meter; found as the third movement in many complete multimovement works, 211

Missa, Latin word for Mass, 91

Mixed meter, (see Changing meter)

M.M., number of beats per minute as measured by metronome, 34

Modal, Modality, opposite of Tonal and Tonality; music based on the old church modes, 144

Moderato, moderate tempo, 36

Modes, early, white-key scales, 82

Modulation, change of tonal center within a composition, 144

Moll, German term for minor

Molto, much, very, 36

Monophony, a single musical line, 52

Moog, (see Synthesizer)

Mordent, ornamental figure moving down a step and back up, as in C,B,C, 193

Mosso, moved, agitated

Motet, type of Renaissance polyphonic sacred music, 123

Motive, short melodic idea, a few notes, 43

Moto, movement, motion

Movements, separate, more-or-less independent components of larger works, usually performed with a pause separating them, with a tempo term as a label for each, 35, 62

Music, brief definition: Sounds organized in time, 11

Musical comedy, (see Opera)

Musical forms, shapes or patterns created by repetition and contrast, 58

Music appreciation, (see Appreciating music)

Music drama, Wagner's name for his late operas, 324

Musique concrète, French term; "real" sounds recorded for use in electronic music, 469

Mutes, devices to soften and slightly alter an instrument's tone color, 22, 403

Muzak, trademarked term for "background music," 2

Narration, added to orchestral scores, 391

Nationalism, political movement inspiring composers to write music that pictured favorably their native country, 269, 284, 344, 412, 441

Natural, symbol in musical notation that cancels a previous accidental, 18

Natural instruments, brass instruments limited to tones that the player's lips control, 141

Neoclassicism, Twentieth-century revival of Baroque, Classic, and earlier styles and forms, 406

Neumatic, in Gregorian chant, two or three pitches per syllable, 80

Ninth chords, a five-note chord, as in G,B,D,F,A, 268

Nocturne, "night piece," usually for piano, customarily quiet and reflective, 256

Noise, sounds created by irregular vibrations, 14, 465

Nonimitative polyphony, combination of different melodies, 53

Nonmetrical, stresses created by word accents as in prose, little sense of a regular beat, 33, 82

Non troppo, not too much, 36

Non-Western music, music outside the notated Western art music categories, 16, 475, 477

Novelette, (see Character piece)

Numbers, separate, self-contained items in traditional opera, 336

Number symbolism, (see Symbolism)

Oboe, high range, double-reed woodwind instrument, *23,* 141, *266*

Octave, interval covering eight letter names, as in middle C to the next higher C, 16, 46

"Off-key," in ordinary language, badly mangled pitches, 42

One chord, (I chord, see Tonic chord)

"Oom-pah-pah" accompaniment, bass note, chord, chord, 452

Op., (plural opp., see Opus numbers)

Open string, string played with bow only, no fingers depress strings

Opera, combination of drama, music, and spectacle, 147

Opera buffa, Italian comic opera, 147, 230

Opéra comique, related form of opera with spoken (French) dialogue

Opera seria, Italian serious opera, 147, 230

Operetta, related form of opera with spoken dialogue, 147

Ophicleide, obsolete brass instrument in tuba range, 308

Opus numbers, numbers attached to a work showing its chronological position in a list of the composer's output, 64

Oratorio, a dramatic, but unstaged, extended work for chorus and orchestra, similar to opera in its musical components, 169

Orchestra, instrumental ensemble, often called the "symphony orchestra," combines strings, woodwinds, brass, and percussion, 26, *27,* 203

"Orchestrate," in ordinary language, to manage or stage an event, 267

Orchestration, art of writing for orchestral instruments, 267

Ordinary of the Mass, the five sections of the Mass—Kyrie, Gloria, Credo, Sanctus/Benedictus, Agnus Dei— that are always present, 91

Organ, wind-powered keyboard instrument with pipes, Plate 22, Plate 23, 105, 142, 271

Organized sound, a minimal definition of music, 11

Organum, earliest type of Medieval polyphony, based on preexisting Gregorian chant, 87

Ornaments, little embellishments of melodic lines, sometimes improvised by performer, 143

Ostinato, extensively repeated melodic or rhythmic fragment, 392, 410

Overtones, partial tones, produced by segments of a vibrating material, 20

Overture, orchestral piece played before an opera or some other dramatic work begins, 152

Overture, concert, (see Concert Overture)

Parallel motion, Parallel movement, musical lines moving similarly at a fixed interval, 87

Paraphrase Mass, a Mass based upon preexisting musical motives, 117

Part, any of the lines in a polyphonic composition; a voice part; the written music for one orchestral player

Passacaglia, one type of Continuous variations

Passion, musical setting of one of the Gospel accounts that describe Jesus' last days, 186

Patronage system, support for music from aristocratic patrons, 200, 213

Pause, a period of silence written into the music, 15, 205

Pedal point, long, sustained tone while harmonies change, 191, 220

Pedals, on piano: foot-controlled lever that sustains sounds—the pedal on the right—or mutes the sound, as does the pedal on the left, 264

Pedals, on organ: large keyboard played by the feet, 142

Pentatonic scale, five-tone scale, as on black keys of piano, 395

Percussion family, instruments that are struck or shaken, 25, Plate 4, 105

Performance marks, (see Dynamics, Expression, Tempo terms)

Performance practice, (see Authenticity in performance)

Performance variables, differing qualities in performance of same work, 65

Performing media, frequently used term for various types of soloists and performing groups

Period instruments, (see Authenticity in performance)

"-phony words," (see Texture)

Phrase, basic unit of music, comparable to a short sentence in language, 58

Piano, pianissimo, soft, very soft, dynamic levels, 18

Piano, Pianoforte, the keyboard instrument, Plate 5, 18, 141, 185, 201, 204, 264, 284

Piano quartet, violin, viola, cello, piano, 203

Piano trio, violin, cello, piano, 202

Piccolo, small version of flute; highest of woodwind instruments, *23,* 204, 265

Pipe organ, (see Organ)

Pitch, frequency or speed of vibrations, 15

Pitch, (standardized, see A, 440 A)

Più, more

Pizzicato, plucking strings of normally bowed string instruments, 20

Plainchant, Plainsong, (see Gregorian chant),

Poco, somewhat

Points of imitation, polyphonic entrances, each phrase with its own musical motive, imitated in turn, 115

Polonaise, festive Polish processional dance in triple meter, 284

Polychord, combination of two or more different consonant chords, 408, 410

Polyphony, combination of two or more musical lines, 53

Polyrhythm, simultaneous meters, 392

Polytonality, two or more different tonalities sounding simultaneously, 392

"Popular music," familiar term for mass-disseminated entertainment music

Post-Romanticism, maintaining a Romantic style into the twentieth century, 375

Preclassic, an overlapping span of time between Baroque and Classic, also called Rococo, 199

Prelude, type of keyboard piece, 183

Prelude, (to an opera, see Overture)

Prepared piano, piano with inserted objects between its strings to alter tone color, 311, 457

Presto, very fast tempo, 36

Prestissimo, as fast as possible, 36

Primitivism, sophisticated imitation of primitive music, 405, 414

Programmatic music, descriptive or representational music, inspired by nonmusical ideas, which are authorized by the composer, 11, 270

Program symphony, multimovement symphony with programmatic ideas, 270

Progression, (see Harmonic progression)

Proper of the Mass, variable portions of the Mass that change according to the church calendar, 91

"Pulling out all stops," throwing all available resources into a task, 142

Pulse, (see Beat)

Pythagoras, Greek discoverer of relationships between lengths of sounding strings and their pitches, *73*

Quadruple meter, grouping of ONE two THREE four; see also Duple meter, 32

Quarter-tone, interval that is half of a half-step, 390

Quartet, (see String quartet)

Quintuple meter, grouping of five beats, such as ONE two three FOUR five, 33

R, in a listening guide, the letter r followed by a number identifies a rehearsal number in the score

Ragtime, style of Scott Joplin's piano music, 452

Range, span of pitches from low to high, 44

Rank, a set of organ pipes, one for each key on the manual or pedal keyboard, 142

Re, second note of the scale, 39

Recapitulation, third main section in sonata-form, 209

Recital, concert by a soloist, especially by a pianist, 312

Recitative, solo vocal portions in opera, cantata, and oratorio, in a free, speechlike rhythm, with light accompaniment, 148

Recorder, end-blown, flutelike early woodwind instrument, *103,* 104, 204

Recordings, (see Live music versus recordings)

Reed, vibrating element used in mouthpiece of some woodwind instruments, 23

Refrain, initial section of a rondo, the returning element, 242

Register, a specific segment of the range of pitches available, 218

Related keys, (see Closely related key)

Relative major, key built on third tone of minor scale, 208

Remote keys, keys that are not closely related, 208

Repeat signs, signs specifying portion of music to be repeated, 268

Repetition of exposition, composer's direction for this repeat is not uniformly observed, 208, 268

Requiem Mass, Mass for the Dead, 96

Resolve, Resolution, progression of tones moving from dissonance to consonance, 49

Restatement, (see Recapitulation)

Rests, signs in musical notation calling for specific duration of silence, 15, 28

Retard, (see Ritardando)

Retrograde, notes of a theme played in reverse order, 422

Retrograde inversion, notes of twelve-tone theme played in reverse order and also upside down, 422

Reverberation, time taken for loud sounds to die away, 14

Rhythm, in general, everything in music related to time, 30

Rhythm and Blues, popular music evolving out of the Blues, 452

Rhythm patterns, combinations of longer and shorter tones plus accents and rests, 33

"Ring" Cycle, term for the four music dramas in Wagner's *Der Ring des Nibelungen,* 325

Ripieno, the larger, accompanying group in a concerto grosso

Ritardando, to slow down the tempo, 37

Ritenuto, a sudden slowing down

Ritornello, returning theme in a concerto grosso, 164, 187

Ritornello form, form of Baroque concerto grosso movement containing a ritornello, 145, 195

Rock, type of popular music evolving out of Rhythm and Blues, 452

Rococo, (see Preclassic)

Roman numerals, identification system for chords, reflects position in scale of the chord's lowest note, 48, 51

Rondo, musical form with several returns of main theme in tonic key, as in ABACA or ABACABA, 242, 259

Round, familiar term for a simple canon, as in "Row, Row, Row Your Boat," 54

Rounded Binary, binary form with return of themes from the opening music to conclude section B

Rubato, (see Tempo Rubato)

S. numbers, (see BWV)

Sackbut, early form of trombone, 105

Sanctus/Benedictus, "Holy, holy," fourth movement of Mass Ordinary, 96

Sarabande, one of four standard dances in Baroque dance suite; in slow triple meter with stress on beat 2, of Spanish origin, 184, 372

Saxophone, metal, single-reed "woodwind" instrument, 265, 437

Scales, collection of pitches arranged in consecutive order from low to high, 39

Scalewise, (see Conjunct)

Scat, style of singing nonsense syllables in jazz, 455

Scherzo, originally a replacement in a faster tempo, for the minuet; literally, a "joke," 211, 255, 359

Schmieder, Wolfgang, (see BWV),

Score, in general, the musical notation that musicians read. A conductor's score shows all the players' parts lined up, one under another, 11, *12,* 15

Scotch snap, a dotted rhythm pattern with the short note coming first

Secco recitative, ("dry") recitative with basso continuo the only accompaniment, 153

Second, interval covering two letters, as in C to D, 47

"Second fiddle," myth that second violin parts are less essential than first violin parts, 203

Semitone, (see Half-step)

Sequence, group of notes restated at higher or lower pitch levels, 43, 357

Serenade, Classic period entertainment music, 200, 228

Serial, music built on an established series or "row" of pitches, or on a series of some other musical elements, 408, 422

Seventh, interval covering seven letters, as in C to B, 47

Seventh chord, a triad plus one more note, as in G,B,D,F, 143, 268

Sextuple meter, grouping of ONE two three FOUR five six; see also Triple meter, 33

Sforzando, sfz., suddenly loud, 201

Sharp, sign in musical notation indicating a pitch raised by a half-step, 18

Shawm, medieval double-reed woodwind instrument with a strident, distinctive sound, *104*

Si, equivalent of *Ti,* 84

Silence, (see Rest)

Sinfonia, Baroque term for instrumental piece, often equivalent to Overture, 158

Singspiel, German comic opera with spoken dialogue, 226

Sitar, Indian, long-necked, plucked string instrument, 23

Sixth, interval covering six letters, as in C to A, 46

Skipping motion, (see Disjunct)

Slur, curved line printed over or under notes that are to be performed legato

Snare drum, small drum with wires across one head, 266

Socialist Realism, Soviet doctrine that all art must reinforce the ideals of the Soviet government, 432, Plate 47

Sol, fifth note of the scale, 39

Solmization, singing scale syllables

Solo concerto, (see Concerto)

Solo entry theme, designation for theme in a concerto first given out by soloist alone, 243

Sonata, as the title of an instrumental piece, 210

Sonata-allegro form, (see Sonata-form)

Sonata cycle, (see Complete multimovement work)

Sonata-form, Classic period form including exposition, development, and recapitulation as the three main sections, with Theme I and Theme II as the main feature of exposition and recapitulation, 207

Sonatina, literally, a little sonata; a sonata-form movement without a development section

Song, art, (see Lieder)

Song cycle, collection of Romantic lieder, unified in some manner, 274, 291

Song form, another label for ternary, or ABA, form

Soprano, high female voice, 20

Sostenuto, sustained

Sousaphone, tuba shaped so it can be carried in marching band, 25

Spatial relationships, how positioning of performers affects music, 14, 305

Sprechstimme, vocal sound midway between speech and singing, pitch indicated only approximately, rhythm exactly, 424

Staccato, detached, separated tones, 29

Staff (or stave), set of five horizontal lines for pitch notation, 16, 84

Stage band, (see Big band)

Steps, stepwise motion, (see Conjunct)

Stop, in organs, a mechanism controlling a rank of pipes, 182

Stretto, in a fugue, an entry before previous entry is completed, 190

String family, string instruments normally played with a bow, *22,* 203

String quartet, two violins, viola, cello, 202, 216

String trio, violin, viola, cello, 202

Strophic, song with repeated music for new stanzas, 274, 276

Style periods, historical periods that exhibit certain general characteristics, 70

Subdominant, fourth note in scale, *fa,* 48

Subdominant chord, chord built on fourth note of the scale, 48

Subject, the "tune" of a fugue, 190

Suite, Baroque dance, collection of stylized dances: allemande, courante, sarabande, gigue, 184

Suite, collection of sections from a larger work, such as an opera, ballet, or incidental music, planned for concert use, 184

Supertitles, translation of libretto projected during an opera performance, 151, Plate 26

Swing, dotted rhythms in jazz, performed with flexibility and individual freedom; in general, the big band era style, 453

Syllabic, each text syllable sung to a single note, 80

Symbolism, in Bach's music, the employment of numbers that have religious or other symbolic meanings, 183

Symphonic poem, one-movement orchestral piece with programmatic qualities, 270, 314

Symphony, Classic period innovation, a large-scale multimovement work for orchestra, 216

Syncopation, rhythmic accents occurring on normally weak beats or between beats, 37

Synthesizer, electronic device to produce sounds, 470

Tambourine, hand-held percussion instrument with jangles, 266

Tango rhythm, Argentine characteristic dance rhythm; often associated with Spanish or Latin-American music, 33

Tape studio, (see Electronic music)

Tema, (see Theme-and-variation)

Temperament, (see Equal temperament, Unequal temperament)

Tempo, speed of the beats, 31

Tempo rubato, subtle variations in tempo that are not written into the score, 268

Tempo terms, Italian language terms suggesting tempo and character and used as titles of individual movements, 35

Tenor, high male voice, 20

Ternary form, the beginning music is repeated after a contrasting section, ABA or AABA, 59, 286, 370

Terraced dynamics, Baroque practice of making changes in dynamics in definite stages, 139

Texture, collective term for the "-phony" words: monophony, polyphony, homophony, 52

Thematic transformation, Romantic compositional device featuring extensive transformation of motives, 269, 307

Theme, melody that serves as basis for an extended work, 43

Theme-and-variation, musical form based on varied restatements of a theme, 218, 454

Theme I, Theme II, (see Sonata-form)

Theremin, electronic instrument from the 1920s, 469

Third, interval covering three letter names, as in C to E, 46

Thorough bass, (see Figured bass)

"Three-chord guitar," performer who knows only I, IV, V chords, 48

Three-part form, (see Ternary)

Through-composed form, stanzas of lieder set to ever-changing music; opposite of strophic, 274, 278

Ti, seventh note of the scale

Tie, curved line connecting two notes of same pitch signifying that no break occurs between them, 28

Timbre, French term for Tone color, 20

Time, passing of time as a factor in music, 30

Time signature, two numbers shown at beginning of a score; upper number identifies meter, lower number identifies what kind of note gets one beat, 31

Timpani, large, kettle-shaped drums with variable pitch, 25, 141, 203, 266

Titles, need for complete titles of musical works, 64

Toccata, literally, "to touch;" a keyboard piece in free style, often sectional, 192

Tonality, dependency on tonic note; relationships of all the scale tones to that tonic, 41, 51

Tonal system, (see Major/minor tonality)

Tone, one individual pitch or note

Tone cluster, groups of tones lying close together on a keyboard, played with forearm or fist, 390

Tone color, individual qualities of instruments and voices, 19

Tone poem, (see Symphonic poem)

Tone quality, (see Tone color)

Tone row, (see Twelve-tone music)

Tonic, keynote, *do,* first note in scale, 41

Tonic chord, chord built on *do,* the tonic in the scale, 48

Toreador, character in Bizet's *Carmen,* 7

Tracker organ, organ with a mechanical connection between keyboards and pipes, 142, Plate 22

Transcription, recasting music for a different performance medium, 141, 190, 314

Transformation of themes, (see Thematic transformation)

Transition, link between Theme I and Theme II in sonata-form, 208

Translation, rendering of original language of an opera libretto or of lieder into language spoken by the audience, 151

Transposition, moving music to another key, 274

Transverse flute, (see Flute)

Treble clef, clef used for right-hand half of piano keyboard, 17

Tremolo, rapid up-and-down bow motions in string instrument playing, resulting in very quick repetitions of a pitch, 9

Triad, chord of three tones in an every-other-letter arrangement, as in C,E,G, 47

Triangle, small percussion instrument in the shape of a triangle, 204, 266

Trill, ornament consisting of a rapid alternation of a note and its neighboring note, 143

Trillo, Baroque ornament with many repetitions of the same pitch, 158

Trio, contrasting, middle section of a minuet or scherzo, 211

Trio, piano, (see Piano trio)

Trio sonata, Baroque multimovement work for two melodic instruments and basso continuo

Triple meter, grouping of ONE two three

Triplets, three evenly spaced notes with the duration that two regular notes of that value normally take, 186

"Tristan chord," opening chord in Wagner's *Tristan* prelude: F, B, D-sharp, G-sharp, 324

Tritone, highly unstable interval made up of three whole steps, as in F to B, 400

Trombone, mid-range brass instrument with U-shaped slide allowing complete span of pitches, 24, 105, 204

Troubadour, trouvère, French medieval composer/poet/musician, 100

Trousers role, a female singer portraying a man or boy in an operatic role, 153

Trumpet, high brass instrument, *24,* 141, 204, 265

Tuba, largest and lowest brass instrument, *24, 265*

Tune, another term for melody, usually thought to be singable and easily remembered, 43

Tuning systems, (see Unequal temperament)

Tutti, (see Ripieno)

Twelve-bar blues, overall musical pattern of the Blues, 451

Twelve-tone music, music based on a basic set or tone row, a series of pitches that governs the entire piece, 422

Two-part form, (see Binary)

Tympani, (see Timpani)

Unequal temperament, experimental Baroque tuning systems that made all keys more-or-less in tune, 139

Unevenly-spaced, (see Dotted Rhythms)

Unison, all performers producing pitches with same letter name

Upbeat, notes that are placed before the first accented beat

Ut, Guido's term for *Do,* 84

Variation, (see Theme-and-variation form)

Variations, continuous, (see Continuous variations)

Vernacular language, language spoken by the people instead of Latin, as in the singing of the Mass in the language of the congregation

Vibrato, slight undulation or wavering of pitches in singing or in playing string instruments and in some other types of instruments, 16, 265, 454

Vielle, Medieval bowed string instrument

Viol, Renaissance and Baroque family of bowed, fretted string instruments, 112

Viola, mid-range instrument in string family, slightly larger than violin, *22,* 139

Viola da gamba, largest of viol family, 112

Violin, highest instrument in string family, *22,* 139

Violoncello, (see Cello)

Virtuosity, ability to excel in performing technically difficult music, 261

Vivace, lively tempo, very fast, 36

Vocal categories, voices arranged by pitch levels, 20

Voices, (see Soprano, Mezzo-soprano, Alto, Tenor, Baritone, Bass)

Voices, designation for musical lines in polyphony, 53

Volume, (see Dynamics)

Walking bass, bass line moving steadily in even note values

Waltz, nineteenth-century dance in fast triple meter

Whole-step, interval consisting of two half-steps, as in C to D, 40

Whole-tone scale, scale composed of whole-steps only; without half-steps, 398

Wood block, also called Chinese block; partially hollowed-out wooden percussion instrument

Woodwind family, wind instruments now, or formerly, made of wood, *23,* 203

Woodwind quintet, flute, oboe, clarinet, bassoon, French horn, 24

Word painting, vocal music with musical devices that reflect meanings of specific words in the text, 128, 129, 145, 165

Xylophone, percussion instrument with wooden bars

Credits

Chapter 1
Page 2: Photograph © Claire Rydell;
p. 3: From *Music: A Pictorial Archive of Woodcuts and Engravings,* 1980, edited by Jim Harter, Dover Publications.; **p. 4:** Courtesy, Museum of Fine Arts, Boston. Bequest of John T. Spaulding

Chapter 2
Page 6: Free Library of Philadelphia, Print and Picture Dept.; **p. 8:** Courtesy of San Francisco Opera, Bill Acheson, photographer

Chapter 3
Page 21: UCLA School of the Arts;
p. 24: Photograph © Claire Rydell;
p. 25: Courtesy of Ludwig Industries, Inc.; **p. 27 bottom:** Photograph © Claire Rydell

Chapter 4
Page 35: Collection, The Museum of Modern Art, New York. James Thrall Soby Fund

Chapter 6
Page 46: Courtesy A. R. Clark-Stewart; **p. 47:** Courtesy John E. Rodes, Altadena, CA

Chapter 9
Page 62: Photograph David Weiss, © 1990; **p. 63:** UCLA School of the Arts; **p. 66:** Courtesy of San Francisco Performing Arts Library and Museum, Henri McDowell collection

Chapter 12
Page 74: Courtesy of the J. Paul Getty Museum

Chapter 13
Page 78: Photograph by Sam Adams

Chapter 14
Page 79: Courtesy Father Aquinas, Prince of Peace Abbey; **p. 81:** Bettmann Archives, PG 10481; **p. 84:** Austrian National Library

Chapter 15
Page 88: Historical Pictures, Chicago

Chapter 17
Page 102: Biblioteca Medicea, Laurenziana, Firenze; **p. 105:** Thomas Axworthy, Southern California Early Music Consort.; **p. 106:** Photograph © Claire Rydell

Chapter 18
Page 110: Alinari/Art Resource;
p. 111: From *Music: A Pictorial Archive of Woodcuts and Engravings,* 1980, edited by Jim Harter, Dover Publications.; **p. 113:** The Metropolitan Museum of Art, Gift of William Loring Andrews, 1888 (88.1f.142)

Chapter 19
Page 116: Giraudon Art Resource, NY

Chapter 20
Page 120: Bettmann Archive

Chapter 21
Page 124: British Library, London

Chapter 22
Page 127: British Library, London

Chapter 23
Page 130: British Library, London

Chapter 24
Page 134: Photograph © Claire Rydell

Chapter 25
Page 140: From *Music: A Pictorial Archive of Woodcuts and Engravings,* 1980, edited by Jim Harter, Dover Publications.

Chapter 56

Page 420: Bettmann News Photos; **p. 421:** Plate IV from the series Death (1934.36). Lithograph, printed in black, composition : 20 × 14 × 7/16" collection, the Museum of Modern Art, New York. Purchase Fund.

Chapter 57

Page 428, 430: Bettmann Archive

Chapter 58

Page 433: Paris Opera Library, Bibliotheque Nationale; **p. 435:** Courtesy of San Francisco Ballet. Collection of the San Francisco Performing Arts Library and Museum.; **p. 437:** Historical Pictures Service

Chapter 59

Page 439: Bettmann News Photos; **p. 440:** Courtesy of the National Portrait Gallery, Smithsonian Institution.

Chapter 60

Page 444: American Symphony Orchestra League

Chapter 61

Page 449: Photograph © Claire Rydell; **p. 455:** UPI/Bettmann Newsphotos; **p. 457:** Michael Ochs Archives; **p. 458:** Bettmann Newsphotos; **p. 459:** Photograph David Weiss, © 1990

Chapter 62

Page 461: © Pictorial Parade, Inc.; **p. 463:** Courtesy of San Francisco Performing Arts Library and Museum, Kolmar Collection

Chapter 63

Page 466: © Steve Kagan/Photo Researchers, Inc.; **p. 467:** Courtesy of the National Gallery of Art, Washington, D.C. Gift of the Collectors Committee

Chapter 64

Page 471: Bettmann News Photos; **p. 472:** Beverly Grigsby

Chapter 65

Page 476 top: Courtesy of San Francisco Museum of Modern Art. Gift of Diana Zlotnick; **p. 476 bottom:** Riley, Bridget, Current (1964) Synthetic polymer paint on composition board, 58 3/8 × 58 7/8". Collection, The Museum of Modern Art, NY, Philip Johnson Fund.; **p. 478:** UPI/Bettmann News Photos

Color Plates

1: Courtesy of David Adickes; **2:** Scala/Art Resource, New York; **3, 4:** U.S. Postal Service; **5:** Oil on canvas, 8 1/2" × 6′ 11 3/4", Collection, The Museum of Modern Art, New York. Mrs. Simon Guggenheim Fund.; **6:** U.S. Postal Service; **7:** Reprinted with the authorization of the Abbey Saint-Pierre de Solesmes (France); **8:** Courtesy of Michael Podesta; **9, 10:** Courtesy of J. Paul Getty Museum, Malibu, CA; **11:** Photograph by Val Villa; **12:** Scala/Art Resource; **13:** Cleaveland Museum of Art, Leonard C. Hanna, Jr. Fund, 60.178; **14:** Scala/Art Resource; **15, 16:** U.S. Postal Service; **17:** Art Resource; **18:** Scala/Art Resource; **19:** Photograph by G. Russell Wing;

20: Courtesy of the J. Paul Getty Museum, Malibu, CA; **21:** Courtesy of Jerome Prager, Harpsichord Maker, Los Angeles; **22:** UCLA School of Arts; **23:** Photograph by Sam Adams; **24, 25:** U.S. Postal Service; **26:** Courtesy of Los Angeles Music Center Opera; **27:** Scala/Art Resource; **28:** Photograph by G. Russell Wing; **29:** Courtesy of NASA; **30:** David Lance Coines; **31:** Alinari/Art Resource, New York; **32:** Courtesy of the J. Paul Getty Museum, Malibu, CA; **33:** Photograph by G. Russell Wing; **34:** Alinari/Art Resource; **35:** Scala/Art Resource; **36:** Courtesy of Los Angeles Music Center; **37:** Courtesy of Video NVC Arts, London; **38:** Metropolitan Museum of Art; **39:** Philadelphia Museum of Art, The A.E. Gallatin Collection; **40:** Scala/Art Resource; **41:** National Gallery of Art, Washington, D.C., Chester Dale Collection; **42:** Oil on canvas, 8′ × 7′8". Collection, The Museum of Modern Art, New York. Acquired through the Lillie P. Bliss Bequest; **43:** Courtesy of the Joffrey Ballet, Herbert Migdoll, photographer.; **44:** Oil on canvas, 40 1/4" × 41" Collection, The Museum of Modern Art, New York. Gift of the Advisory Committee.; **45:** Courtesy Lawrence A. Schoenberg, Los Angeles; **46:** Oil on canvas, 64" × 36 1/4" Collection, The Museum of Modern Art, New York. Mrs. Simon Guggenheim Fund.; **47:** Courtesy of Seattle Opera and Phillip Brazeau, Jr.; **48, 49:** © U.S. Postal Service; **50:** Oil and enamel on unprimed canvas, 68" × 88". Collection, The Museum of Modern Art, New York. Purchase

Color Plates

Index

Composers and Titles

Composers who have a chapter devoted to them are identified by the use of all capital letters for their last names. In these chapters can be found the listening guides for the selections named that are identified by a number in parentheses preceding the titles. Also in these chapters are brief descriptions of titles named in this index (marked with an asterisk) that are accompanied by a few measures of musical score. Other compositions by the composer that are mentioned come last.

Page references are given for all titles when they are listed alphabetically. Titles in a foreign language are alphabetized under their initial article for the convenience of students. For example, *Die Forelle* appears under "D," not under "F." Pages with illustrations are indicated by *italic* numbers. Pages where a listening guide or a primary reference in a composer's chapter begins are shown in **bold face.**

General Index

ROMANTIC

Mendelssohn and Bach Revival	**1829**	Typewriter patented
Berlioz, *Symphonie fantastique*	**1830**	First railroad in England
Chopin, *Nocturne,* op. 15, no. 2	**1831**	Poles revolt; crushed
Borodin, b.	**1833**	British abolish slavery
Chopin, *Etude,* op. 25, no. 9	**1834**	Lincoln enters politics
Cui, b.; Saint-Saens, b.	**1835**	P. T. Barnum begins career
Balakirev, b.	**1837**	Queen Victoria crowned
Berlioz, *Requiem*	**1837**	Morse invents telegraph
	1838	Daguerre photography
Schumann, *Dichterliebe*	**1840**	
Grieg, b.	**1843**	Fremont crosses Rockies
Mendelssohn, *Violin Concerto*	**1844**	Emerson, Essays
Rimsky-Korsakov, b.	**1844**	
Fauré, b.	**1845**	Poe, *The Raven*
	1848	European revolutions
	1848	*Communist Manifesto*
Liszt, *Liebestraum*	**1850**	California becomes a state
Verdi, *Rigoletto*	**1851**	Melville, *Moby Dick*
Liszt, *Les préludes*	**1854**	Thoreau, *Walden*
Humperdinck, b.; Janácek, b.	**1854**	Republican party founded
Steinway piano exhibited	**1855**	
Wagner, *Die Walküre*	**1856**	
Elgar, b.	**1857**	
Puccini, b.	**1858**	
	1861	U.S. Civil War begins
	1865	Lincoln assassinated
Wagner, *Die Meistersinger*	**1868**	
Tchaikovsky, *Romeo and Juliet*	**1869**	
Rachmaninoff, b.	**1873**	
Mussorgsky, *Boris Godunov*	**1874**	
Holst, b.	**1874**	Monet and impressionism
Bizet, *Carmen*	**1875**	
Ravel, b.	**1875**	
Tchaikovsky, *Symphony No. 4*	**1877**	Edison invents phonograph
Smetana, *My Country*	**1879**	
Bloch, b.	**1880**	
Kodály, b.	**1882**	
Griffes, b.	**1884**	Pasteur vaccine
Mahler, *Songs of a Wayfarer*	**1885**	
Brahms, *Symphony No. 4*	**1885**	
	1889	Paris Exhibition
Dvorák, *Symphony No. 9*	**1893**	
Debussy, *Afternoon of a Faun*	**1894**	
Piston, b.	**1894**	
Hindemith, b.	**1895**	
Strauss, *Also sprach . . .*	**1896**	
Sibelius, *Finlandia*	**1899**	